CZECHOSLOVAKIA

IN EUROPEAN HISTORY

Czechoslovakia

IN EUROPEAN HISTORY

S. Harrison Thomson, 1895-

PRINCETON NEW JERSEY

PRINCETON UNIVERSITY PRESS

1943

LONDON: HUMPHREY MILFORD: OXFORD UNIVERSITY PRESS

⟨ Foreword ⟩

THE aim of the present work is very modest: to trace the development of several of the more acute problems of Czechoslovak life and history. It is not intended to be a history in the orthodox sense of that term. Though the general treatment follows a chronological order, the subject matter occasions some overlapping between the separate chapters. In view of the complex nature of the story the repetition of a few historical facts may be expected. For example, the Golden Age under the Emperor Charles IV, the Hussite movement, the Hapsburg conquest of Bohemia in the seventeenth century, the work and thought of Palacký and Masaryk, will all be referred to in more than one connection. It is hoped that the repetition will not seem out of proportion to the general scheme.

The reader should be warned that the term "Czechoslovakia" has no political significance in this book. It is used generally to designate the geographical entity lately known by that name. At other times the term "Bohemia" may be used when Slovakia is not included. The Kingdom of Bohemia, for several centuries in the middle period of its history, included as organic parts of the whole, Moravia, Silesia, a part of Lusatia and a larger Egerland than is so denominated at the present time. The continuous fluidity of such designations should always be kept in mind. The maps are designed to make the changes in political boundaries more understandable. The term "Bohemian" is geographical and in no wise an ethnic term. The Slavs of Bohemia are referred to as "Czechs." The Moravian Slavs may usually be understood as included in the term "Czech" unless explicitly or implicitly excluded. The term "Sudeten German," used to designate the Germans resident in Bohemia and Moravia (Sudetenlands, etc.), did not come into general use until the first decade of the twentieth century,

v

and then includes those of both German and Austrian blood. It is used here somewhat anachronistically for the earlier periods as well. It is convenient and sufficiently accurate.

In another matter the reader should be warned: the term "race" is deliberately used in this work in connections which would not be sanctioned by the ethnographer. For purposes of this study it is convenient to speak of a Slavic race and a Germanic race, and to recognize a racial difference between the Magyars and their Slavic and Germanic neighbors.

Chapters Six and Seven have undergone some recasting since they appeared as separate articles in the October 1941 and July 1942 issues of the *Journal of Central European Affairs.*

The author should like here to give tardy expression of gratitude to professors in the Czech and German universities of Prague who bore with patience the importunate questionings of a complete foreigner in the years 1924-1927. In particular, Professors Václav Novotný (d. 1932), Josef Šusta, Jan Jakubec (d. 1936) and Gustav Friedrich of the Charles (Czech) University, and Wilhelm Wostry, Gustav Pirchan, Hans Hirsch and Samuel Steinherz of the German University in Prague were generous with their time and store of scholarly knowledge far beyond what might reasonably be expected of professors in their relationships with a student. May this slender effort not disappoint them.

S. HARRISON THOMSON

Boulder, Colorado

≺ Contents ≻

CONTENTS

⤙ Illustrations ⤚

CZECHOSLOVAKIA
IN EUROPEAN HISTORY

≺ 1 ≻

Introduction

IN TIMES like the present, international events move at such lightning speed that we are prone to lose what little perspective we may have had before this acceleration set in. This bewildering tempo is likely to rob us of the proper realization of the fact that the word "catastrophe" is as old as the Greeks. We too easily forget that peoples and races, ideas and ideals, have for thousands of years survived catastrophes. It is true that they have suffered untold woe and tribulation, but it is no less true that those races and ideas that were fittest to survive usually have managed to live through these periods of grim and menacing trial. Stress and strain, trial and tribulation, are not unmixed evils. But to those who suffer, their good is hard to see. History has the virtue of softening the pain, and bringing the benefit to light. Grandeur in a people as well as in a man is a compound of struggle and rest, tension and release.

> Es bildet ein Talent sich in der Stille,
> Sich ein Charakter in dem Strom der Welt.
> —GOETHE, "TORQUATO TASSO," III, 2

This is pre-eminently the case of the Czech people, their kinsmen the Slovaks, and not less of the Germans who are their neighbors in the Sudetenlands. They have bowed under many catastrophes, and unless history means nothing at all, they are likely to survive this latest hour of adversity.

The pilgrimage of the Czechoslovak people through history has gone on in a land which touches on no seashore, nor has it ever been far from the tumult and the clash of arms. Rather has it been highly sensitive to the disturbances that have shaken the rest of Europe. Lying at the

3

crossroads of the continent, the paths of conquering armies, from north to south, from east to west, have led through the country, and in the great European struggles this land has been the scene of many a conclusive victory. Not alone in the nineteenth century, but throughout all recorded time, the statement of Bismarck has held true: he who is master of Bohemia is master of Europe.

The last twenty years of Czechoslovak history, with which the western world is fairly well acquainted, is a very short period. It was a time of world-wide disturbance and dislocation, and a small country had no real opportunity to follow its own course independent of the rest of the world. The student who interests himself only in this most recent short period is like a reader who chooses only a single chapter late in a book, losing thereby background and continuity. He misses all connection of any given act with its conditioning antecedents. He cannot possibly understand, for example, the deep significance which the early division of the whole land into two parts has had for the historical development of the Czechoslovak people. The western part developed independently as the Czech state, while the eastern half was incorporated into the Hungarian kingdom as early as the eleventh century. Yet, in spite of this political severance, a common destiny guided both halves. Without taking into account the fact of this early separation, it is impossible to realize fully how so many of the trials with which Czechoslovakia was burdened in the years 1918 to 1938 were brought about. During the Middle Ages the Czechs and Slovaks were unable to develop into one nation. Consequently when the opportunity presented itself they had no background of long-standing union upon which to build together a free republic. This last formidable task demanded a longer period of active co-operation than two short decades.

Without a close study of the past of this land the peculiar

importance of the gradual infiltration of foreign influences into the territory occupied by the Czechoslovak people cannot be grasped. Germans came from several directions, Magyars from the south into the living space of the Slovaks. A minority problem was born which in recent times has grown increasingly acute, and has become a determining factor in the fate of Czechoslovakia. If this problem is to be understood, its origins and the course of its development must be carefully studied. If, furthermore, we are to succeed in seeing how vital these matters of past history are to the peoples—both majority and minority—living in these lands, we must appreciate a psychological factor which looms larger to the Central European than it does to us in the English-speaking world, and that is the vital immediacy of the past. The criteria, values and prejudices of the average man and woman in Central Europe are more affected by the events of history than are ours. And as a general rule these peoples are better acquainted with their longer history than we—particularly in the United States—with our much shorter past. The reason for this fundamental psychological difference between Central Europeans and ourselves is outside the province of this short study, but the fact of its presence and its radical importance cannot possibly be overemphasized.

The Czechoslovak question has been brought so vividly to our attention by the events of 1938 and 1939 that it is necessary to explain a few of the most important subjects which are the object of continual interest and discussion. From the many and varied phases of the history of these peoples we have chosen to treat only a few, but to treat them rather thoroughly. It is hoped that the reader will be led toward an understanding of the complexity of the problems, and enabled to distinguish truth from falsehood in the arguments which in recent years have been mustered against Czechoslovak independence. A scientific exposé of the problems of national existence and their projection into the past, which is the proper function of the historian, leads to more reliable conclusions than a journalistic essay, written in the heat of battle. Only through historical analysis and quiet explanation of the facts can we fairly judge, in the light of past events, the ultimate value of a free Czechoslovakia to a free Europe.

$\prec 2 \succ$

The Czech State and the Holy Roman
Empire to 1306

FOR more than a thousand years Czechs and Slovaks have made their home in a land snugly set in the middle of Europe. Since the last World War we have come to know this territory by the name of Czechoslovakia. These Slavic peoples came into this land during the period of the shifting of population in the early Middle Ages commonly designated as the Wanderings of the Nations. The land of their origin, lying between the Volga and the Dnieper rivers, was apparently inadequate for their rapidly growing numbers. Pushed westward and southward by other expanding peoples settled to the eastward of them, they gradually moved, in groups of varying sizes, into the lands which they have since inhabited. These lands had been previously peopled by Celtic tribes (Boii) and, after them, from the first century B.C. to the fifth century of the Christian era, by Germanic tribes (Marcomanni, Quadi and Hermunduri). So far as we can ascertain, until their disappearance from history about the middle of the fifth century these Germanic tribes must be regarded as largely nomadic or at least transient inhabitants. They left no tangible evidences of their stay, or so it seemed to Cosmas of Prague, who, writing in 1125, expressed the belief that the land had been completely uninhabited before the arrival of the Czechs, and that the Creator had reserved this land by an eternal decree for the Slavic people: no other people had any right there at all. The Slavic tribes, filtering into the land toward the end of the fifth century in small groups, gradually came to join into larger tribes soon distinguishable as Czechs, Moravians and Slovaks. Under these

7

larger groupings these peoples have lived in this territory ever since.

The land of Czechoslovakia has a unique conformation. It stretches across Central Europe for about six hundred miles. It consists of three distinct sections, the easternmost and the westernmost parts joined by a slender neck. The western part is Bohemia, called by the native Slavs Czechy (Čechy), forming as it were the head of the body. Almost all the waters of Bohemia drain northwards into the watershed of the Moldau-Elbe, thence through Germany into the North Sea. On three sides Bohemia is cut off from Germany by a wall of well forested mountains at whose height even Cosmas wondered. The line of demarcation on the south, west and north is, for most of its length, drawn so sharply that the Czech-German border may be regarded as one of the oldest and most natural boundaries of the western world. But on the fourth side of Bohemia, that to the east, there are no real mountain barriers. On that side Bohemia merges smoothly into the second component part of the whole, Moravia, which, almost from the earliest period of their recorded contacts, has had a population closely related to the Czechs by blood, language and political organization. Like Bohemia, Moravia's northern boundary is a mountain range, but to the south its boundary lies east and west across the gently rolling hill country north of the Danube. Most of the drainage of Moravia is into the Danube, thence into the Black Sea. Moravia forms a natural nexus between Bohemia and Slovakia, the eastern component of the whole. Slovakia lies between the banks of the middle Danube on the south and the eastern curve of the Carpathian range on the north. Here again these high mountains, majestic and rugged, form an almost insurmountable natural barrier between Slovakia and Poland. The southern slopes of these mountains reach down into the fertile Hungarian plains, inhabited since the ninth century by the Magyars, a race of Turco-Ugrian origin.

In this long and narrow territory, protected in part by the natural fortifications of high mountains, in part by their own racial consciousness, the Czechs and Slovaks have worked out their destinies. The beginnings of their story are lost in the dim dawn of antiquity, but today's tragic chapter lies clear and vivid before our eyes.

In spite of their favorable position, however, these Slavic peoples were not completely free from the danger of invasion. Not long after their arrival they were exposed to such violent attacks that they were unable to stop them before the very center of their land had been reached. At such times the disadvantages of their division into small tribal groups was more evident than in times of peace. We hear of early efforts, on the part of some of the leaders of the better established tribes, to bring about some kind of unification in times of peace. Their motives may in all likelihood have been those of personal ambition and a desire to enhance their own power. But the Slav was an individualist, and it was a long time before there came into being any political organism which remotely resembled the modern state, or which was widely enough accepted to outlive the energy and sagacity of a single conquering founder.

The movement of these Slavic peoples as they expanded over the lands of Czechoslovakia was gradual. Those who came first seem to have been slowly pushed south and west from the mountain passes through the Carpathians. Those that went farther south and west, therefore, would appear to have been the longer in the land, and at the same time, the most venturesome. It is not surprising, then, that we find that life in the southern and less mountainous regions, along the Middle Danube, was more advanced and complicated than in the northern and more mountainous sections, where the primitive cultivation of the soil and the care of

9

their herds was all that concerned the late Slavic arrivals from beyond the Carpathians.

In the gently rolling country along the Middle Danube there began, about A.D. 800, two perceptible movements toward unification of a considerable portion of the population and the creation of a political entity similar to surrounding states. One focal point of this process was Nitra in Slovakia, the seat of the Prince Pribina. The other was at some unidentified place west of Nitra, where the Moravian prince Mojmir had his capital. In the struggles which are but inadequately explained by the scanty contemporary records, Mojmir succeeded in gaining the ascendancy. He was undoubtedly a person of great force and executive ability. His conquest has been given the name of the Great Moravian Empire, but it was a state which had neither clearly defined boundaries nor a sound internal organization. It was more like the vast so-called empires which, during the migration of the peoples, grew up only to collapse, than even the most loosely organized feudal state of Western Europe as we are accustomed to think of them. The territory of the Moravian Empire did not coincide exactly with that of modern Czechoslovakia. Czechy (Bohemia) was connected only very loosely and for a short time with Moravia, which looked rather to the south and east than to the north and west. Under the rule of the successors of Mojmir (d. 846), Rostislav (d. 870) and Svatopluk (d. 894), Greater Moravia strengthened its internal organization and secured its position among the embryonic nations of Europe.

This growth in prestige was due not only to the powerful position of the princes but also to the christianization of Moravia which took place under these princes. Though there had been German missionaries in the land, they had had almost no success, and Latin Christianity was destined to come to these western Slavs from Byzantium. Rostislav

10

requested of the Byzantine emperor that Christian missionaries who knew the Slavic tongue might be sent. Two brothers, Cyril and Methodius, natives of Salonika, were sent in response to this request in 863, and later were to receive the support of the Roman papacy.

In the Moravian Empire tribes related by blood and language had gradually coalesced into some sort of unit, and there is no evidence which would justify us in distinguishing between Czechs and Slovaks at this early date. This empire was a noteworthy effort to create a Slavic state in Central Europe. Its significance is certainly not lessened by the fact that it was built up and maintained for more than a century by native Slavic initiative, unaided by external pressure or guidance. The death of Svatopluk in 894 came at a time when the Magyars had become somewhat settled in their new home, south and east of the Moravian domain. Until that time the Moravian Empire had easily defended itself against the sporadic incursions of the Frankish rulers, and there were periods when the relations between the Germanic Franks and the Moravian princes were amicable.

But a combination of circumstances made the turn of the century fateful for this Slav empire. The Magyars had occupied the fertile valleys of the Theiss and the Middle Danube. Svatopluk's death was followed by a period of dissension in the ruling family, and the Frankish king Arnulf, an energetic and ambitious prince, sought Magyar help against Moravia. The southeastern borders of Moravia were not protected against Magyar invasion by any natural barriers such as the mountains to the north and west, and the task of defending both its southeastern and northwestern borders against superior forces put such strain upon the imperfect organization of the empire that it fell apart into its component parts. The Přemyslid princes of Bohemia profited by the disintegration of the Moravian Empire to regain their independence and, as well, some territory that had been directly under the Moravian princes. To the east of Moravia, those Slavic peoples inhabiting what we have come since to call Slovakia, came under the dominance of the Magyars. The Slavic peoples of the western and southern branch were thus separated by a wedge of an alien non-Slavic, non-Indo-European race.

Those who have regarded Czechoslovakia as an entirely new state which arose unexpectedly out of the chaos into which the last world war threw all of Europe, may not realize that Europe's concern with the destiny of the Czechs and Slovaks was not completely novel in 1918, but that events which befell these two small peoples over one thousand years ago were of immense importance for the political development of all of Europe since that time. No sooner had Greater Moravia collapsed than there was a pressing need for these Slavs to build new foundations for the maintenance and development of their national life. Europe was then just recovering from the chaos into which it had been thrown by the disintegration of the Roman Empire and the inundation of romanized Europe by barbarian peoples. By the end of the first Christian millennium social and political patterns and national boundaries began to have some recognizable character. A new system of boundaries, in course of development for a long time, had by now assumed such fixity that the inhabitants had to adjust themselves to it or face destruction.

Three facts had particular and indeed determinative significance for the future of the Czechs and Slovaks. The first was the severance of their connection with the other Slavic peoples, later called South Slavs, who, after migrating from their northern habitat, gravitated by various routes to the south of the Danube into the mountains and valleys of the Balkan peninsula. Between these South Slavs on the one hand and the Slavic inhabitants of Czechoslovakia on the other, there was a two-fold barrier. In the first place, beginning with the seventh and eighth centuries, there were the German migrants who pushed from southern Germany down the Danube and thence, both north and south, into the mountainous regions, thus creating conditions leading to the establishment of the eastern marches (variously and with some confusion Ostmark, Steiermark and Pannonia), later and more generally known as Austria. The second barrier between the large Slavic groups was the presence of the Magyars in the Hungarian lowlands along the Middle Danube, bordering the German settlements at the point where the easternmost foothills of the Alps run into the Danubian plain. The creation of a Hungarian state in which the Magyars occupied the dominant place barred completely the path of the Central European Slavs from the Carpathians to Byzantium. Before the appearance of this Hungarian state, Greater Moravia maintained continual and close intercourse with its southern neighbors. But after the beginning of the tenth century, such relations are almost entirely unknown.

A second fact of great significance for the future of the Czechs and Slovaks was the Magyar domination of the eastern part of Czechoslovakia. The Slovak territory which for a while formed part of Greater Moravia was cut off from the western lands in the course of struggles which took up most of the tenth and a part of the eleventh centuries. This territory was incorporated into the Hungarian kingdom and remained under Magyar rule until 1918.

A third significant fact, whose effects became evident only gradually, was the repression of the Slavs who settled to the north of the Czechoslovak people from the Elbe westward. This repression and virtual extinction of the Wends and the Sorbs became effective only after sanguinary wars and systematic penetration of the German population into regions that for a long time were purely Slav. If there had been no mountains north and west of the Czechs to serve as bulwarks against this Germanic eastward expansion, the Slavs in Bohemia and Moravia would have met, in the early Middle Ages, a fate similar to that of their relatives north of the mountains. They would certainly have been reduced to such vestigial groups as have persisted up to modern times, of the Lusatian Sorbs in Saxony and Prussia who, though with slight hope of success, stoutly resist any pressure which seeks to denationalize them.

To the Slavic inhabitants of Bohemia and Moravia, protected by mountain ramparts on the north and west from annihilation or absorption, there remained on only one frontier a connection with a neighboring and related people, that toward Poland. But even this connection might be broken if Silesia, reaching out on both sides of the Upper and Middle Oder, should undergo by German colonization a change from a purely Slav into a bilingual region. This door into the Polish region was intermittently open and closed in the earlier centuries. But neither the Poles nor the Czechs profited as much from their contiguity as they might have. There were several reasons for these lost opportunities. Even in the Middle Ages the two countries faced politically in different directions, the Poles eastward, the Czechs westward. In the second place, though the fact is perhaps closely bound up with this opposite orientation, it must be pointed out that the leaders of the Polish state almost without exception failed to understand that the security of Poland depended in large degree upon the security of the Czech state. In the Middle Ages co-operation between the unrelated Czech and Hungarian kingdoms occurs more frequently than between the closely related Czech and Polish kingdoms.

These three political entities, Poland, Bohemia and Hungary, developed along the eastern limits of the broad Germanic territory, which, in the ninth and tenth centuries, was provisionally organized into a vast group of tribal principalities and duchies. These latter were extended eastward, during the period of conquest and colonization, to the limit of the Germanic peoples in the form of marches: The March of Billings, the North March, the March of Lusatia, the March of Meissen. The name which came to be accepted for the loose union of these Germanic principalities, duchies, and marches, the Holy Roman Empire of the German Nation, signified that, so far as its builders were concerned, it was more than simply the creation of a national state. A definite need was felt for a concept of universality such as the Roman *imperium* had represented. A secular universality was aimed at, to parallel the spiritual universality which the papacy, particularly in the late eleventh century, so effectively claimed. The boundaries of this imperial system were flexible, and it would have been difficult to say at any given moment precisely what lands were part of the Holy Roman Empire. Particularly was this true of the southern and eastern borders, where centrifugal forces were incessantly at work. Lands which once formed part of the Empire either broke from it completely, or gained virtual independence and returned to their own hegemony.

The Slavs of Bohemia and Moravia, because of the fact that they had pushed far to the west and were surrounded on three sides by peoples of German race who were already a part of the Empire, were inevitably destined to enter into a closer and more enduring connection with the German Empire than Poland and Hungary, whose contact with German territory was on only one side. The future of Bohemia and Moravia depended upon a satisfactory relationship to the Empire which claimed, in theory at least, a rule over the whole world, particularly at a time when the only alternative was uncertain friendship with two free states, Hungary and Poland, on the remote eastern border. But

15

when Austria, originally closely bound to the Empire, loosened this bond and began to develop as an almost independent state, the possibilities of combination among these four states, Bohemia, Poland, Austria and Hungary, were greatly enlarged. A new focusing, though not a simplification, of political and national forces had taken place.

Historical sources, not even yet completely clear or reliable, allude to the fact that Charlemagne invaded Czech territory with his armies sometime after his coronation on Christmas day, 800. It is also frequently stated that the Czech peoples were obliged to pay him a yearly tribute of 1,200 oxen and 500 talents of silver. This may possibly have been the case, but there is no demonstrable connection between this early tribute and the treaties made by Czech princes with the Emperors later in the Middle Ages. In the Empire and in Bohemia in the ninth and tenth centuries, there was much uncertainty and turmoil, and under these conditions agreements which were not put into writing— and there is no evidence that the conditions of this reported tributary relationship were ever embodied in any document—were soon forgotten. Soon after the extinction of the line of the western Frankish Carolingians, ca. 900, the rulers of the Saxon line took over the remnants of the imperial organization east of the Rhine. It then became necessary that the relations between the rulers of Bohemia and their Germanic neighbor should be reexamined and readjusted. Internal political conditions were different both in Bohemia and in Germany from what they had been a century previously under Charlemagne. The further fact that expansion eastward into Slavic territories became from this time forth one of the cardinal points of imperial policy forced the leaders of the Czech state to think and act in terms of consolidation and defense.

Unification of the Czech tribes, so necessary for the successful development of the land in the ninth and early

NORTH
SEA

BALTIC SEA

Kingdom
of
Poland

Duchy of Brabant
(to Luxemburg 1355)

Margravate of
Brandenburg
1373-1415

Lusatia
1368-1635

1320-1635

Duchy of Luxemburg
1310-1409

RHINE RIVER

MEUSE

Duchy of
Silesia
1327,   1331-
         1742

KINGDOM of
BOHEMIA

1315,
1322,
1353

Margravate of
Moravia

DANUBE RIVER

Duchy of

Austria
1251-1282

ELBE RIVER

ODER R.

County of
Tyrol
1335-1341

Duchy of
Styria
1254-
1282

Carinthia Duchy
1269-1282

Carniola
Duchy
1269-
1282

PO RIVER

ADRIATIC SEA

Territories at various times in the Middle Ages
under the Bohemian Crown

tenth centuries, progressed rapidly. About the year 920, there remained of the numerous tribal chieftains of earlier centuries only two powerful princely rivals. One of these was the ruling house of the tribe of the Czechs who, though originally not numerous, had by energy and a wise choice of their territory in the middle of Bohemia attained great power and given their name not only to the land but also to the whole nation. This princely house stemmed from a certain peasant, Přemysl, who, according to the legend, was called from the plow to be the husband of the Princess Libuše and the prince (*Vévod*) of the people. The rival of the Přemyslids was the family of the Slavnici, whose power in eastern Bohemia, their seat, diminished steadily throughout the tenth century. Their extermination in 995 only hastened the final stage of a natural process. Before the Czechs were unified by the elimination of one rival house, the Přemyslids had spread their power into Moravia and had come to represent both lands, Bohemia and Moravia, to the rest of Europe.

To Prince Václav, whom medieval legends and perennial Christmas carols celebrate as "Good King Wenceslas" (Wenzel), is due credit for realizing that a struggle with so powerful a rival as the first of the Saxon kings, Henry the Fowler, would be vain. He chose, therefore, to enter into a relationship to the Empire similar in many respects to that between Charlemagne and the still ununited Czech tribes. The loose medieval system of feudal orders offered the possibility of an arrangement which would not affect the real independence of the land while it did bind its rulers to certain formal obligations and functions. In this spirit of vague suzerainty there was arranged not only the relation of the Czech duke to the Emperor, but also that of many other rulers over lands bordering on the imperial domain. Such bonds became customary after 962, when the coronation of Otto I in Rome by Pope John XII renewed the imperial idea. Ecclesiastical sanctions gave new vitality and currency to the concept that the head of the Empire was *ipso facto* the head of all Christian rulers. But it is of no little significance that the relationship between the German Emperor and the Czech princes during this feudal period was on a different basis from that of the other imperial vassals. From 800 to 1125 there were twenty-two different reigning Czech princes. Only five of these gave any oaths of vassalage, and then either voluntarily or under extraordinary circumstances. It was customary, on the accession of a new ruler, for the feudal vassals to be summoned to renew their oaths of vassalage. There is no evidence that any of these twenty-two Czech princes were so summoned. But that does not mean that imperial influence was not at times very great in Bohemia. Quite the contrary was the case. The fact that Bohemia was on the German border added to the frequent dissensions among members of the Přemyslid dynasty and made the spread of imperial influence into Bohemia easy and natural.

For generations the Czech state was limited to the territory of Bohemia and Moravia. In accordance with the general medieval concept that the state was the property of the dynasty, the Czech state was regarded as the family domain of the Přemyslids, who could dispose of the land and its population according to the will of the reigning prince. The Czech state therefore constituted a political body distinct, not only from other similar bodies, but also from the Empire. The fact that Bohemia and Moravia had been unified internally by the Přemyslids, and that this unification had taken place outside of, though contiguous to, the lands of the Empire, was expressly recognized by the Emperors. It was a political unit quite different in its original nature from the various lands within the Empire. There was no time when the Emperor felt free to dispose of the land of the Czech state without the consent of whatever ruler or

ruling body might be incumbent. The right of the Přemyslids as individuals or as a house to rule in these lands was
never brought into question. The Emperor never maintained a representative in Bohemia who could in any way
exercise any influence in internal affairs or could legally
bring any pressure upon the ruler in the exercise of his
sovereign rights.

This sovereign independence of the Czech state had been
unmistakably symbolized from the earliest times on royal
seals, coins and insignia. Prince Václav (d. 929), the only
member of the Přemyslid line to attain sainthood, was sub-
sequently honored throughout the land as the protector of
the Czech territory, its special advocate before the throne
of God, and the powerful defender of its security. The persistence of this concept is clearly expressed on the oldest
extant seal of a Czech ruler. The seal of Duke Vladislav of
1146-1147 has this motto: *Pax Sancti Wenceslai in manu
ducis Vladizlai,* which may be freely but accurately rendered: "Duke Vladislav is the custodian of the peace of this
land assured us by Saint Václav." There is no mention of
the Emperor. A span of over two centuries and the guardianship of the peace still in the hand of a Přemyslid can
hardly mean anything else than that this guardianship had
not been successfully challenged. The further fact that Václav was a national saint, had, in the eyes of the medieval
man, a special significance, documenting, as it were, the national self-sufficiency of the Czech state. We must not overlook the spiritual and psychological potency of such sym-
bolisms in the early history of the growth of national
consciousness.

According to the fundamental assumptions of feudal law,
the person who accepted a pledge of fidelity was bound as
strictly as the one who gave it. The relationship was a bilateral contract. There was no lack of cases in the medieval
world where the oaths so solemnly given were either broken

20

by one or both of the parties involved, or so interpreted as to negate completely the original intentions of those parties. The German emperors made numerous efforts to extend their influence over the Czech state in a way not warranted by feudal legality. The growth of Czech power was not welcomed by imperial policy, and we can trace a consistency in the actions of successive German rulers as they endeavored to bind the lands of the Czech state more tightly to the Empire. But the Czech rulers, as consistently, insisted on maintaining the original intent of the bonds and obligations which had become in the course of time an integral part of Czech traditional policy, though there were several successful efforts by Czech rulers to weaken these bonds. The dependence or independence of the Czech state with regard to the Empire at any given period was directly contingent upon the relative need or strength of the two parties. If the Emperor needed the help of the Czech prince, or, on the other hand, if a candidate for the Czech throne had to appeal to the Emperor for support against his relatives or other claimants, the bargaining position of each party was directly affected. Two whole centuries, the eleventh and twelfth, are replete with incidents of this sort. To recount them, even in outline, would lead the reader into a labyrinth of negotiations and wars in which even Czech historians easily lose their sense of proportion.

At the end of this period, that is at the beginning of the thirteenth century, the see-saw jockeying for position seems to have come to a stop. The Czech dukes definitively repulsed the efforts of the Emperors to extend their influence over Bohemia both by alert diplomacy in a time of general European disturbance, and by a number of clear military victories in the field against imperial attacks, which had as their object the incorporation of the Czech state into the Empire. This period is one of the decisive epochs in Czech history. The Czech rulers gained greatly in power and prestige, and the title of king, which had been held rather precariously for short periods earlier, was now finally universally recognized. The Czech king now held a position to which the other powerful princes of the Empire did not attain until many centuries later. The first Czech ruler who properly bore the title of king was Vratislav, who was crowned by Emperor Henry IV in 1085. His neighbor, the Duke of Bavaria, did not bear the royal title until the Napoleonic era, in 1805. If, in addition to the mere chronological discrepancy, we note that the Czech rulers were granted the royal title by Frederick Barbarossa in 1158 to be held also by their successors, and that the Czech kingdom was powerful at a time when the Empire was led by strong rulers, we may realize even better the contrast between Bohemia and the other lands of the Empire.

But the path of medieval Bohemia was not an even one. There were times when the preponderant power of the Empire assumed threatening proportions, and it appeared that the Emperor would succeed in breaking the union hitherto existing between Bohemia and Moravia. The next step would have been simple: to reduce the separate parts of the Czech state to the level of other imperial lands. These critical periods usually came when the succession to the princely power was in doubt, largely because of the lack of a definite law of heredity. Dissension in the princely family would eventuate in one or the other claimant asking for the help of the powerful German neighbor. This situation arose several times in the course of the eleventh and twelfth centuries. Once, in 1182, the same Emperor who had raised the Czech prince to the hereditary honor of a king, Frederick Barbarossa, drove a wedge between Bohemia and Moravia by making Moravia a margravate, a direct fief of the Emperor. The chronicler tells us that Barbarossa ordered brought into the hall where the negotiations concerning the new feudal arrangments were proceeding, axes such as executioners commonly used. The Czech legates seem to have been impressed. But only four years later, the newly constituted Margrave of Moravia admitted the suzerainty of the Duke of Bohemia, and thus the effort of the German Emperor to weaken the Czech state was frustrated. But he tried again. In 1187, he raised the Bishop of Prague to the rank of a Prince of the Empire, thus freeing him from the control *in temporalibus* of the Czech duke. But a subsequent bishop, in 1197, took the feudal oath of allegiance to the Czech duke directly, and another effort of imperial politics to weaken the Czech state by dividing it had failed.

This decade and a half was a period of acute crisis for the Czech state. But at the end of this period of trial, it was clear that the foundations of the state were sound, and that, having survived such moments of danger it not only could maintain its place among European powers, but might hope to exercise an even greater political influence.

The Holy Roman Empire had by now reached and passed its period of greatest power. The years that followed the death of Barbarossa (1190) were marked by dissension and disintegration. Those who were integral parts of the Empire were unable to profit from the chaos of the Guelph-Hohenstaufen struggles. But the Czech ruler, Přemysl I, by clever maneuvering as devoid of high ethics as the opportunism of his contemporaries, was able to eliminate completely the danger which had threatened the Czech state from its connection with the Empire. He sought for and achieved a workable relationship with the Empire, and this survived him many years, and assured his realm an independent and untrammeled development.

This new relationship between Bohemia and the Empire was clearly delineated in a letter, one of the most important in Czech history, preserved since its issuance in the archives of the crown, and known as the "oldest charter of the liberties of the Czech crown." The Hohenstaufen Emperor

Frederick II sent this letter to Přemysl I in 1212, and, because he affirmed it with the seal which he used as King of Sicily, it was called the Golden Sicilian Bull. The relation of the Czech king to the Emperor was established by this letter on a solid basis, and a guarantee was given that the rights of the kingdom of Bohemia should be honored in perpetuity.[1] According to this charter, freely given by the Emperor, such attempts as had been made by Barbarossa to break up the Czech state would be forever impossible.

The Czech king made no effort to sever his connection with the Empire. He realized, perhaps better than anyone else, the great benefits that would accrue to him from the new arrangement by which he and his kingdom would be protected from any attempt to interfere in the internal affairs of Bohemia. It is also fairly clear that he was alive to the possibility that his new position would enable him to participate in the affairs of the Empire, while at the same time he was safe from imperial interference. The more disturbed the Empire might be, the greater would be his opportunity to play the role of an arbiter in intra-imperial disputes. Arbiters have a way of becoming rulers. The part played by Czech rulers in subsequent centuries in imperial affairs fully justified the discernment and anticipation of Přemysl I.

The Golden Sicilian Bull raised Bohemia—for the third time[2]—to a kingdom, but this time in perpetuity, and its place among the national states of Europe was thus established. Previously, in 1204, Pope Innocent III had recog-

---

[1] The Latin text is quite explicit: "ipsum regem [Přemysl I] constituimus et confirmamus et tam sanctam et dignam constitutionem approbamus, regnumque Boemie liberaliter et absque omni pecunie exactione et consueta curie nostre iusticia sibi suisque successoribus in perpetuum concedimus, volentes ut quicumque ab ipsis in regem electus fuerit ad nos vel successores nostros accedat, regalia debito modo recepturus. Omnes etiam terminos, qui predicto regno attinere videntur, quocunque modo alienati sint, ei et successoribus suis possidendos indulgemus."

[2] See above, p. 22.

nized Přemysl as king. He now had *de jure* recognition from the two leading powers of the world. One article of the Golden Bull decreed that whoever was *electus* king in Bohemia and offered the Emperor the usual *regalia*, should be accepted as king. This provision assured the internal independence of the kingdom. In another article, the boundaries of the kingdom are decreed to be inviolable. The obligations of the Czech king to the Emperor were reduced to a minimum necessary to the maintenance of the connection. The Czech king was obliged to obey the Emperor's summons to only three cities, near the Czech borders, Babenberg, Nürnberg and Merseburg. He was finally obligated to accompany the Emperor to Rome for his coronation with three hundred men, but this obligation might be commuted into a nominal money payment of three hundred marks.

Thus after several centuries of uncertainty, the relations between Bohemia and the Empire were settled on an essentially permanent basis. In the past much of the confusion in Bohemian-imperial relations had been traceable to the existence of rival claimants of the Přemyslid family who did not hesitate to call upon the German emperor for help. But now that the legal foundation of Bohemian-imperial relations was securely laid, fortune smiled more warmly upon the Czech state by allowing all but one direct line of the Přemyslid family to die out (1241), so that the possibilities of capricious attacks on the part of the Empire on at least one score diminished. Early in the thirteenth century the mining of silver in the mountains in north Bohemia began to bring considerable wealth into the coffers of the Czech kings, and their political prestige was enhanced by this increase in their economic resources. Throughout the thirteenth century and into the early fourteenth century, the Přemyslids were able to influence Central European politics in a comprehensive and almost dominant fashion. The grandson of Přemysl Otakar I, Přemysl Otakar II (d. 1278), conquered gradually Austria, Styria, Carinthia and Carniola. At the height of his power he ruled from the mountains of the Czech-German boundary on the north to the shore of the Adriatic on the south. Much of this expansion toward the south was wrested from Přemysl Otakar II by Rudolf of Hapsburg, yet the Czech kingdom was destined to see its king rule over an even more extended territory in the next century.

The son of Přemysl Otakar II, Václav II, was asked by the Polish nobles to rule over them and was crowned King of Poland in 1300 at Gnesen. Petitioned by the Hungarian nobles to accept the crown of Hungary, he refused on the ground that he already had a very onerous task to rule two kingdoms, but at his suggestion, his son, Václav III, was crowned King of Hungary (1301). The latter died in 1306, the last male member of the Přemyslids who had ruled over Bohemia for almost four centuries.

≺ 3 ≻

The Czech State, the Holy Roman and the Austrian Empires: From the Luxemburgers to 1867

AFTER more than four centuries of rule by the princes of a native dynasty, a long rule in the Middle Ages, the Bohe- mian Estates[1] called in a foreign dynasty to rule over them. The house of Luxemburg was predominantly German, but had many French connections and at this period leaned strongly toward the French ruling house. There had been no direct relations existing between Bohemia and Luxem- burg, and the great distance between the two countries was, to the suspicious Czech nobles, a favorable circumstance. Under the Luxemburgers, Bohemia had her Golden Age but she also suffered devastating war with foreign powers and exhausting dissension within.

Under King John, the first of the Luxemburg dynasty which, after four years of dissension, succeeded the Přemy- slids in 1310, the territory ruled by the King of Bohemia did not reach the same extent to which it had spread under the last Přemyslids. But the gains made under King John were much more enduring, because of their lesser extent and their geographical location. In 1322 the Egerland (Chebsko) was permanently added to the territory of the Bohemian crown. This small district, lying on the western border of Bohemia, had once been inhabited by Slavs, whence they had been driven by Germanic immigrants.

---

[1] The Bohemian Estates were a gradual expansion of the early group of nobles whom the Přemyslid dukes and kings had chosen as advisers and lieutenants. The right of this small group of *comites* or *castellani* to elect a ruler in the event of a vacancy had been accepted as early as the tenth century. By the beginning of the fourteenth century it had come to include the greater (magnates) and lesser (knights) nobility, the upper clergy and representatives of the patriciate of the towns. The manner of selection, par- ticularly of the last group, seems to have followed no clear pattern.

The Czech name "Cheb" used from time immemorial concurrently with the German "Eger," is, to the student of place names, proof of the fact that Slavic peoples had given it a name before it became almost exclusively Germanic in population. From the tenth century it had been counted a part of the German Empire, and for some time it had belonged to the Hohenstaufen family, as the ruins of a castle built by Frederick Barbarossa witness to this day. During the thirteenth century it alternated between the rule of the Empire and the power of the Czech kings, so that the final cession to King John by the Emperor Louis of Bavaria was gradually being prepared for. The union between the Egerland and the Bohemian crown was for centuries a loose one, and it was not until the later Hapsburgs, in the eighteenth and nineteenth centuries, that this separatism completely disappeared. The acquisition of King John, it should be remarked, was considerably larger than the present Egerland.

The growth and consolidation of Hapsburg power to the south made expansion in that direction hardly possible. King John therefore turned his attention to the north and northwest, where several Přemyslids had in times past made short-lived conquests. Without great difficulty he conquered territories north of the Czech mountains, around the towns of Bautzen and Görlitz, known together as Upper Lusatia. This territory, originally inhabited by Slavic tribes known as Lusatian Sorbs, was still at this time more Slav than German, though the population of the towns was predominantly German by the end of the twelfth century. John campaigned victoriously also in Silesia, which, like Lusatia, was bilingual—Slav and German. The majority of the Silesian nobles were forced to acknowledge John's suzerainty. The way was thus paved for the incorporation of Silesia into the lands of the Bohemian crown. John's expansion in both directions—the Egerland to the west and Lusatia and Silesia to the north—was consolidated and even increased by his son Charles. During the reign of Charles IV (1346-1378) Lower Lusatia and Lower Silesia were added to the territory of the Bohemian crown, and were to remain such for two and a half centuries, in spite of differences in population and antecedent development. By 1368 the term "Lands of the Bohemian Crown" included Bohemia, Moravia, Silesia, Upper and Lower Lusatia and the Egerland. Brandenburg, bought by Charles in 1373, and Luxemburg were legally in the same category, but before the middle of the fifteenth century they go their separate ways, and no Bohemian regarded this separation as anything but logical.

This great and steady growth in the territory and prestige of the Bohemian crown was made possible, not only by the virtual independence granted the Czech king by the Golden Sicilian Bull, but also by the increasing decline of the central power of the Empire. The principle that the Emperor, as temporal head of all mankind, should be chosen by a formal election, similar to the procedure for the choice of the Pope, and not by hereditary right, had gained universal acceptance. As a result, the power of those who claimed the right to elect the Emperor grew immeasurably. In earlier times, when there was no formulated law according to which the election should be governed, it was only natural that special and local interests should prevail over the interests of the Empire as a whole.

The origins of the electoral college of the Empire are shrouded in the mist of scholarly dispute, but it is certain that during the thirteenth century it came to be commonly accepted that the holders of the seven highest positions in the Empire—three spiritual and four temporal lords—were entitled to elect the Emperor. The Czech king, though not a German, was one of these seven, by virtue of his title of imperial cupbearer, which he had held from the twelfth century. The six imperial princes were quite aware of the fact that there was a difference between them and the Czech king with regard to their relations to the Emperor. Quite naturally, therefore, they objected to his participation in imperial affairs. The grounds for this objection are clearly expressed in the well-known *Sachsenspiegel,* a collection of German laws and customs to be dated about 1230, which says: *Die schenke des rikes die koning von behemen, die ne heuet nenen kore, umme dat he nicht düdesch nis,*[2] and about ten years later repeated by the chronicler Albert of Stade: *Rex Bohemiae, qui pincerna est, non eligit, quia non est Teutonicus.* But their position was so strong that the Czech kings gained and exercised the right to participate in all imperial elections. The advantages of this position can hardly be exaggerated. The Czech king held the deciding vote in case of a tie in the electoral college, and could thus determine the direction of imperial political development, and at the same time, by the provisions of the Golden Sicilian Bull, was secure against interference from the Empire in the internal affairs of the crown lands of the Bohemian kingdom. The balance tipped so far in favor of Bohemia that a Czech king (Přemysl Otakar II) was almost elected Emperor in 1257. What nearly came to pass so early actually happened less than a century later when, in 1346, Charles of Bohemia, on his father's side a Luxemburger, on his mother's a Přemyslid, was elected Emperor Charles IV of the Holy Roman Empire.

The possibilities inherent in this union of the Czech crown with the crown of the Empire were made use of by Charles in a manner which calls for some explanation. At this time the Czech state was so powerful that it could perfectly well have existed as a completely independent kingdom on the southern border of the Empire. It was quite equal, indeed in some ways superior, to Poland and Hun-

---

[2] "The cupbearer of the Empire, the King of Bohemia, cannot elect, because he is not German."

gary. As Emperor, Charles had every right, had he so desired, to issue a new bull which would have freed the Czech king from even the loose bonds which bound him to the Empire under the provisions of the Golden Sicilian Bull. All the conditions for a radical separation were therefore present. But Charles made no such move. He followed the lines of his father's policy, and bent his energies toward the construction and strengthening of the kingdom of Bohemia as a great dynastic state. As the head of an extensive and well-organized kingdom, he could deal with other princes of the Empire and with the college of electors on advantageous terms. There is no lack of evidence that Charles wanted to establish his dynasty in the imperial office partly from reasons of pride, but certainly largely because he felt that so large an organization needed dynastic stability if it was to continue to exist. Thus if he, the head of the Czech kingdom, was to achieve the transformation of the free electoral Empire into a dynastic-hereditary monarchy, his own kingdom must remain a part of that Empire, though internally independent, in order to support the Luxemburg family in imperial politics. This reasoning lay behind Charles's determination not to sever the connection between the Czech kingdom and the Empire, but rather to give it a more articulate legal basis, at the same time assuring the Czech king all possible benefits from his position.

By the Golden Bull, which was promulgated and accepted at the imperial diets of Nürnberg and Metz in 1356 at Charles's instance, the position of the Czech king in imperial elections was definitively provided for. He was given first place among the lay electors, without having his sovereign rights within the kingdom of Bohemia in any way affected. The seventh article of the Golden Bull provides that the king of Bohemia has the privilege of determining, in case of the extinction of an electoral family on the paternal side, who shall possess the electoral dignity. To

31

all intents and purposes he occupies the position of a feudal lord over the other temporal electors. In the case of the elector of Bohemia, that is the king, the right belonged by law and custom to the Estates. They alone, as representatives of the people, elected their king. The clear implication of this distinction is that Bohemia had never been a fief of the Empire in any real feudal sense. In addition to this crucial stipulation, there were other provisions that explicitly recognized the distinction between the imperial princes and the king of Bohemia.

A close reading of this bull, confirmed by the imperial German diet, can lead only to the conclusion that it is a clear recognition of the fact that the Czech state had developed quite independently of the Empire, that its organization and consolidation had been the work of a non-imperial dynasty outside the boundaries of the Empire, and that its association with the Empire in recent centuries had been absolutely voluntary. In the words of Josef Kalousek, the historian of Czech constitutional law,

The Roman Emperors exercised no sovereign rights over the Czech state, judicial or legal. They never held imperial diets in the land, they never set foot on its soil unless in war, they had no imperial cities, estates or other holdings which they could give away or turn into fiefs, nor did they have any regalian rights, rights of investiture to ecclesiastical prebends. The Emperors never exacted any military levies, nor were any imperial taxes ever levied upon Bohemia or Moravia. Imperial laws, aside from this Golden Bull of Charles IV, had no validity here, nor did any international treaty which the Empire concluded with any foreign rule ever affect the Czech crown. The state of the Czech nation was sovereign and independent. Whatever may have been lacking or still *in lite* was supplied or strengthened by Charles.

Charles endeavored not only to secure the leadership of the Empire for his family, but also to emphasize its international character. Only by this emphasis could the dissatisfaction felt by the German princes that the head of the German Empire was the half-Luxemburger, half-Czech king of a non-German state be allayed. This must have been the reason that lay behind the provision in the Golden Bull that the sons of the secular electors should learn not only German, but also Italian and Czech.

The desire of Charles to secure for his own dynasty the imperial honor was not realized for a variety of reasons, not the least of which was the lamentable lack of administrative capacity shown by his two sons, Václav and Sigismund. In addition to this personal factor, we may discern a clearly defined current away from nationalization of the Empire coincident with the increasing independence of the imperial principalities. The Czech king was unable to strengthen his position in the Empire, but on the contrary materially weakened it, and finally broke completely, in the fifteenth century, the slender bond which Charles had so carefully forged in the Golden Bull.

But there were powerful forces, at first far removed from matters of national policy, which were destined to affect crucially the development of the state. Most important among these contributory factors was the Hussite movement and the wars resulting from it. John Hus, reformer and national leader, had been burned by the Council of Constance in 1415, and Emperor Sigismund had sanctioned the sentence. The issues, both religious and national, which Hus had raised in his lifetime were but made more acute by his death. Under the inspiring leadership of men like Jan Žižka and Jan of Rokycany, military genius and eloquent ecclesiastic, the Czech people were engaged in a sixteen-year struggle for the legacy of John Hus (1420-1436). This struggle soon assumed the proportions of a war between the Bohemian state and the Empire. Sigismund, a younger son of Charles IV, had been unable to gain acceptance as king by the Bohemian Estates. But he had become Emperor in

1411 and was, in the opinion of the Bohemians, their principal enemy. At all events, they were aware of the fact that the numerous crusading expeditions sent to crush them were organized on imperial soil and with the encouragement and active participation of the Emperor. In these wars the Czech armies won brilliant victories over their imperial enemies, often against great odds. The national consciousness of the Czechs was thus greatly fortified, and another step had been taken on the road toward the creation of a national state which should finally break completely with the ancient union with the Empire.

At the end of these wars, the old order of a royal Czech state was essentially re-established. But such efforts to rationalize the relation of the Bohemian kingdom to the Empire as had previously been made were no longer timely. Conditions on both sides had changed too much. The feeling was gaining that there was no other relationship between the Empire and Bohemia than that symbolized by the fact that the King of Bohemia retained the office of head cupbearer of the Empire with its attendant formal obligations and privileges: he had still to renew his oath of fealty, but he had at the same time a principal place in the college of electors. The prestige of the Empire was waning, and there was little talk of its superiority over other states, particularly in view of the fact that all around it national states were growing, both in power and in their consciousness of that power, and explicitly or implicitly rejected any claims to world supremacy on the part of the Empire. The imperial princes themselves were abandoning any idea of universality and had begun to accept the concept of an empire of the German nation. But even with this deterioration of the imperial concept, it is important to observe that there was not yet any thought of an hereditary monarchy, but only of a group of states with an elective ruler at the head. In such an organism there could be no place for a state predominantly Slav, particularly when its rulers were also of Slavic origin, lacking the neutral background that the Luxemburgers had.

By the middle of the fifteenth century a good deal of water had gone under the bridge of political thinking in Central Europe. Nobody in the Empire insisted that the end of the Hussite wars meant a return to former conditions. The Czechs were perhaps themselves more desirous of retaining some of the ancient forms than were the Germans. There was good reason for this desire for the sanctions of long-established custom. In 1458 a member of the Czech nobility, George of Poděbrady, was elevated to the Czech throne by a free election of the Estates. He could be called, with perfect justice, a national and Hussite king. Largely because he was a national Czech king, the German capital city of Silesia, Breslau, offered him determined resistance. A year after his election by the Estates of Bohemia, he gave a formal oath of fealty to the Emperor Frederick III, and claimed the title of cupbearer of the Empire, and the prerogatives of an imperial elector. His motives for this step are not hard to understand. His position among the rulers of Europe was sorely in need of legal and formal support. He was not of royal blood, and, what was equally serious, he was an openly avowed Hussite—and Hussitism was rejected as heresy by the Roman curia. If, therefore, he could secure the Emperor's recognition of his claims to these honors, traditionally the property of the Czech king, he could look forward to a participation in the affairs of the Empire all the more influential because of the fact that the Emperor at that time was himself in need of prestige and material support.

In 1462 Frederick III recognized these claims of the Czech king, and once again, for reasons not unlike those which prompted Charles IV to bind Bohemia to the Empire, the Czech ruler was bound to the Emperor in a loose feudal way, none the less legal. But George must have sensed that though the words were very nearly the same, the substance and facts of the relationship had changed greatly. He took care that the bonds uniting the Czech kingdom to the Empire were less close than those provided for in the Golden Bull of 1356. The Czech king was obliged to give the oath of fealty to the Emperor only if the latter were to visit Czech territory, or were to be in some place within ten to fifteen miles of the Czech border. As it turned out, the oath of fealty was given but a few times in all the years this stipulation remained in force. It was not formally revoked from the time of its declaration in 1462 until the dissolution of the Holy Roman Empire in 1806. By the Letter of Majesty of Frederick (1462), Bohemia regained its ancient position as a kingdom, and, by the looseness of the stipulations of the Letter, gained virtual freedom to develop in its own way.

The Czech kingdom in the fifteenth and throughout the following century developed in every respect as an independent state. Maps in textbooks of European history or in historical atlases, which put the lands of the Bohemian crown within the bounds of the Empire as if they were on the same plane with other imperial principalities, disregard fundamental distinctions that were very real, and distort clearly ascertainable facts. This distortion becomes more serious as we leave the Middle Ages and move down into modern times. On the other hand, to introduce a different shade in coloring to indicate a separation from the rest of the Empire might go farther than the facts would warrant. To show the true situation accurately there might be a heavy line delineating the border of the lands of the Czech crown, and the color for Bohemia and the Empire should be the same. In this way, the internal independence of the land would be indicated and yet its connection, however tenuous, with the Empire would also be made clear.

In early modern times Bohemia was excepted from the manifold reforms to which the Empire was subjected. In 1512, when the Empire was divided into ten "circles" in an effort to simplify administration of matters which concerned the Empire as a whole, the Czech kingdom was completely unaffected, though there were voices which called for the incorporation into this new imperial administrative system of those parts of Bohemia which had at one time or another been integral parts of the Empire. But the Czech state maintained its administrative independence without difficulty, and the Czech kings gradually withdrew from any participation in the affairs of the Empire.

Under these conditions of independence, the Czech rulers and the Estates began to look elsewhere for political support. The kingdom, because of its strategic position, its growing population and its economic strength, was an important factor in central and southeastern Europe, particularly at a time when the danger of Turkish expansion into central Europe was looming on the southeastern horizon. Those states which were threatened directly, because of their geographical proximity to Turkish territory, had, unless the rather vague plans for an international expedition against the Turks should materialize, to organize immediately and independently in order to preserve their own existence. From 1471 to 1526 kings from a junior line of the Polish-Lithuanian Jagellons ruled in Bohemia. This dynastic connection gave some promise of co-operation with Poland, but, in spite of the fact that this co-operation would have been to the interest of both states, it did not eventuate.

But other groupings did take place. In 1490, on the death of the vigorous king of Hungary, Matthew Corvinus, the Hungarian Estates elected the Jagellonian king of Bohemia, Vladislav II, to the throne. There now appeared the possibility of close co-operation between the two states in their foreign policies. If we think only of the years 1918 to 1938 we are likely to emphasize the tension between these two countries. But we should not forget that from 1490 to 1918 they had common rulers.

By various treaties of marriage and arrangements for mutual heirs in case of extinction of one or the other line, entered into between the Polish-Czech-Magyar Jagellons on the one hand and the Hapsburgs on the other, the lands over which the Hapsburgs had ruled since 1273 (i.e. Austria) were in 1526 added to the territories of the dual Czech and Hungarian kingdom. Early in its history Austria had leaned toward complete incorporation into the Empire, but the direction of its development soon changed, and it became gradually even more independent than the other principalities. Under Hapsburg rule it achieved the position of a virtually independent state, yet even so its connection with the Empire was closer than that of Bohemia. With the extinction of the male line of the Czech-Hungarian branch of the Jagellon dynasty on the death of the young king Louis I at the battle of Moháč in 1526 the stage was set for the union of Bohemia, Hungary and Austria under one ruler. All the previous interlocking treaties providing for mutual heirs worked to the advantage of the Hapsburgs. In that year a member of this family, the Archduke Ferdinand, younger brother of the Emperor Charles V and brother-in-law of the late King Louis I, became the ruler of all three countries as Ferdinand I and, in 1556, on the abdication of Charles, Emperor. From his rule we may date the building of the Danubian empire known before 1918 as Austria-Hungary. The imminence of the Turkish threat from the southeast was such as to call for the unification of the separatist aims of the interests of the whole central European region. In this case the Czech kingdom made the greatest relative sacrifice, as it was farthest removed from the Turkish frontier and thus the least threatened, and yet, because it was by far the richest of the three kingdoms, it bore the greatest burden of the long wars against the Turks.

These three quasi-united states were together quite formidable and their territory very extensive. But the Hapsburgs were apparently not yet satisfied. In the sixteenth century this dynasty was at the zenith of its development, and easily assumed the primacy among all the European ruling houses. Under Charles V the Hapsburgs were more Spanish than Austrian, but after his death (1558) the scales began to tilt to the other side. The idea of a universal Empire had long since lost much of its appeal, and the territory legally embraced within the empire was now largely reduced to German lands. It is not, however, difficult to understand the desire of the Hapsburgs to combine their vast Danubian territory, recently acquired, with its accompanying political potentialities, with the ancient imperial title.

So long as Charles V was Emperor the question of the relation of Bohemia to the Empire was of relatively little significance. Charles was so engaged in his struggle with Francis I on the one hand, and with the German Protestants on the other, that there was no occasion for an issue to rise. There is documentary evidence that the Hapsburgs accepted the independent position of Bohemia at this date, from a letter written to Ferdinand by Charles in 1526, in which Charles draws Ferdinand's attention to the prevalent concept *que le dict royaulme est exempt de l'empire*. In pursuance of this reminder Ferdinand, some time after his coronation as Czech king, refused to include the lands of the Czech crown in plans for public taxation to raise funds for the Empire. He went so far as to forbid the levying of any imperial taxes on those regions of the Bohemian crown lands with a German-speaking population which had at one time or another been a part of the Empire. A protocol of the imperial diet at Augsburg in 1548, published by Ferdinand in his crown lands, makes these conditions clear:

Although his Royal Majesty as King of Bohemia recognizes certain lands and estates of German speech as imperial fiefs, yet these lands and estates receive neither protection nor aid, neither peace nor law from the Empire, but have been separated from it from antiquity, and not incorporated into it; they are therefore not subjected to burdens, taxes or contributions to the German Empire.

Upon the abdication of Charles V the situation changed. The imperial title came to Ferdinand I and to his heirs of the Austrian branch of the Hapsburg family. Expansion of the family power to the east and southeast was blocked by the aggressive might of the Turks. To the west, in the Italian peninsula, the Austrian Hapsburgs could make little headway, as the French and the Spanish entertained plans of conquest that would have made a third party unwelcome. If the Hapsburg family was to extend its power, there was only one path open: the congeries of greater or lesser principalities, bishoprics, imperial cities to the north and west which we may call, somewhat loosely, Germany. The Hapsburg rulers had two entering wedges into German affairs. Austria, as a land of German speech, could count on participation in imperial councils. Of itself this wedge was not sufficient. As King of Bohemia, the Hapsburg ruler was still imperial cupbearer and entitled to a place in the college of electors. In the interests of the dynasty, therefore, without regard to the future of the Czech people or to the direction their history had been following up to that time, the ancient connection between the Empire and Bohemia was brought back from the dead. In order to effect this resuscitation, historians and legists connected with the Hapsburg court set to work to counteract the lack of interest in the matter on the part of the Czech Estates. Another important and equally difficult aim of the Hapsburg propaganda was to overcome the growing distaste evidenced by the imperial princes for the expansionist ambitions of the southern dynasty. Above all, the Hapsburgs had to make sure that no member of any other imperial house should be chosen Emperor. It is worth remarking that the Hapsburgs were following the same policy Charles IV had held to two centuries before: to use their strong legal position as kings of Bohemia in order to extend their influence into the Empire.

In order to perpetuate their position as rulers of the Empire, the Hapsburgs gradually brought about a dualism between their family domains and the Empire that was to be almost indissoluble. From the point of view of political logic it is safe to say that this eventuation was implicit in the election of a Hapsburg to the Czech crown in 1526. The Bohemian Estates naturally expected at that time that Ferdinand I and his successors would respect the ancient rights and liberties of the kingdom. Their expectation was rudely deceived. After Ferdinand I, a struggle broke out over the question of political and religious liberties which was not to cease even in our times. By 1618 the Protestant Estates of Bohemia had given up all hope that the differences between them and the Catholic Hapsburgs could ever be peaceably settled, and declared themselves completely independent of Hapsburg rule. Unfortunately for them, their military and political leadership was sadly inadequate, and after two years of war they were exhausted and were decisively defeated at the Battle of the White Mountain, not far from Prague (November 8, 1620). Taking full advantage of this military victory, the Hapsburgs restricted the freedom of the people of Bohemia to a minimum. The established foreign relations of the kingdom were entirely subordinated to dynastic interests and reorganized to serve those interests most effectively. In imperial affairs the policies of the Hapsburgs were dictated by the firm desire to

41

assure to the family its ancient primacy, without taking account of the changes that Germany was undergoing in the seventeenth and eighteenth centuries.

At this late date the imperial title was hardly more than a shadow. The Empire was a federation of states and territories of varying sizes. The imperial diet maintained some sort of loose union, but after 1663 it met but rarely and then only for some specific purpose. As an active institution it had ceased to function. But even in this moribund body the Hapsburgs determined to surround themselves with every conceivable legal show of power. As Austrian dukes they could vote in the diet, but as such they had less influence than the imperial electors. It was therefore more useful to emphasize the fact that in Bohemia the Hapsburg ruler was not only a king, but also an elector of the Empire, and as such was entitled to a place in the College of Electors. In order to gain current acceptance for this technicality, Joseph I, in 1708, succeeded without any difficulty in getting the imperial diet to accept his representatives to all elections and councils of the diet (of which the college of electors was a part) as the representatives of the Elector, the King of Bohemia. This move is known as the *readmission*. The convention was a purely dynastic move, for the Bohemian Estates were not asked beforehand for their consent, as would have been indicated if the convention were to bind the whole kingdom. After the action of the imperial diet the Emperor obtained from the Bohemian Estates their approval of the convention and persuaded them to set aside a specified sum each year to defray the expenses incurred in carrying out the provisions of the readmission.

But the situation brought about by Joseph in 1708 lasted less than a century. The Hapsburgs kept the imperial title in the family, yet, aside from some slight satisfaction of the family's vanity, the honor was meaningless. During the Napoleonic wars, the props under all political structures were subjected to shocks that threatened to be devastating. Emperor Francis I came to the conclusion that it would be expedient to surrender his claim to first place among European rulers in exchange for something less grandiose but more real. In 1804 the family domains of the Hapsburgs were declared to constitute the Austrian Empire. In 1806 Francis gave up the title of Emperor of the Holy Roman Empire. By a few simple acts and without any fanfare, the dissolution of the Holy Roman Empire of the German Nation was proclaimed. In the court decree of August 21, 1806, we read:

... that the imperial feudal property of the electoral dignity and the office of Cupbearer, associated with the crown of Bohemia, and their every connection with the Empire stemming from the Privileges of 1212 and 1459 [should be 1462], then of the act of Readmission of 1708 for sitting and voting in the electoral college, is hereby dissolved.

Thus all previous arrangements which the Hapsburgs had assumed from time to time, for their own benefit, were legally cancelled, though it should be pointed out, in retrospect, that the Hapsburgs seem to have followed consistently a certain anachronistic pattern in that most of the engagements they entered into with the kingdom of Bohemia were based upon legal or political concepts which were a century or two or even more behind the actual conditions.

In place of the now dissolved Holy Roman Empire there grew up a free confederation of German states which had a definitive organization after the Congress of Vienna in 1815. The Hapsburgs, undismayed by their own failures in the past, set about to exercise a dominant influence in this new body. Against strong opposition Prince Metternich succeeded in arranging that Austria should have a perpetual delegate in the congress of the newly established *Bund* (Confederation) which was to meet at Frankfort-on-

Main, just as they had had at the now defunct imperial diet. As might have been expected of reactionary absolutism, of which Metternich, the Hapsburg Emperor's adviser, was the leading exponent, the Estates of the kingdom of Bohemia were not consulted as to whether they wished to join the German Confederation or not. The Estates, because of the pressure which had rendered independence of thought unfashionable, might have been complacent toward this violation of constitutional rights, but there can be no doubt that there was no sentiment among the people of Bohemia and Moravia favorable to entrance into the German Confederation.

Unfortunately for the peaceful success of the absolutistic Hapsburg reaction, the rule of Metternich coincided with the growth of Czech nationalism. It may be that reaction and suppression of national freedom were partly responsible for precipitating the demand for that freedom. In 1848, after the fall of the Metternich régime, it became possible for the first time to discuss freely the relation between Bohemia and the Austrian Empire, and one clear voice spoke in no uncertain terms in the name of the Czech people. The suggestion was made by the Frankfort Congress that elections should be held in the Czech lands to choose representatives for a constitutional convention. The great historian and leader of the liberal Czech bourgeoisie, Francis Palacký, replied to this invitation in a letter from which we may well quote a few passages:

I am unable, gentlemen, to accept your invitation for my own person, nor can I send any other "trustworthy patriot" in my stead. Permit me to give you, as briefly as possible, my reasons.

The object of your assembly is to establish a federation of the German nation in place of the existing federation of princes, to guide the nation to real unity, to strengthen the sentiment of German national consciousness and in this manner expand the power and strength of the German Reich. . . . I am not a German. . . . I am a Czech of Slavonic blood. . . . That nation is a small one, it is true, but from time immemorial it has been a nation by itself and depends upon its own strength. Its rulers were from ancient times members of the federation of German princes, but the nation never regarded itself as belonging to the German nation, nor, throughout all these centuries has it been regarded by others as so belonging. The whole union of the Czech lands, first with the Holy Roman (German) Empire, and then with the German Confederation, was always a mere dynastic tie of which the Czech nation and the Czech Estates took no real cognizance, and which had little effect upon them. This is a fact as well known to German historians as to myself. Even if it were to be fully accepted as true that the Bohemian crown had at one time been in feudal relationship to the German Empire—a contention which Czech publicists have always denied—it could not occur to any well informed historian to doubt that, so far as internal affairs are concerned, the government and land of Bohemia were originally completely sovereign and independent. The whole world is quite aware of the fact that the German Emperors never had, by right of their imperial title, anything to do with the Czech nation, that they possessed neither legislative, judicial nor executive power either in Bohemia or over the Czechs, that they never had the right to raise troops or levy taxes in that country, that Bohemia together with its crown lands was never considered as belonging to any of the former ten German states, that the jurisdiction of the Reich Supreme Court of Justice never applied to it, and that therefore the entire connection of the Czech lands with the German Reich was regarded, and must be regarded, not as a bond between nation and nation, but as one between ruler and ruler. If, moreover, anyone asks that, over and above this heretofore existing bond between princes, the Czech nation should now unite with the German nation, that is at the very least a novel demand, devoid of any historical or juridical basis, a demand to which I, so far as I personally am concerned, would not feel justified in acceding until I receive an express and authentic mandate to do so. . . .

In conclusion . . . I must briefly express my conviction that those who ask that Austria, and with her Bohemia should unite on national lines with Germany, are demanding that she should commit suicide—a step lacking either moral or political sense. . . .

Along this line, in succeeding years, Czech scholars investigated the history of the relations of the Czech state to the Empire, and even after the dissolution of the Bund in 1866, Czech scholars like Josef Kalousek, author of a classical study of Czech constitutional history, Jaroslav Čelakovský, and others emphasized those facts that showed the internal independence of the Czech state; and German scholars, studying the same data, emphasized its dependence upon the Empire. From this intensive investigation into Czech history, new areas of significant interest were brought to light: on the one hand, the early medieval period, before the growth of Czech power and the Golden Bull of 1212; on the other hand, important documents and decrees put into effect during the period of the systematic suppression of Czech liberties by the Hapsburgs, such as the readmission of 1708, were thoroughly studied.

A careful examination of the whole development made it clear that the Czech state grew up in the early Middle Ages independently of the Empire, and received its particular organization from the rulers of its native Přemyslid dynasty. But because of its geographical situation on the edge of the Holy Roman (German) Empire, even protruding westward into the imperial territory, it could not resist completely the expansion of the Empire eastward. Czech rulers, in order to secure some protection against imperial aggression, took upon themselves certain feudal bonds according to the practices of the time. But it cannot be too strongly emphasized that these feudal bonds in no way extended to matters of internal jurisdiction. Quite naturally, efforts were made by the German Emperors from time to time to interfere in the internal affairs of the Bohemian state, but the Czech rulers appealed to treaties and letters in which the independence of the state was explicitly confirmed. Throughout its history, the Czech people have held to the tradition, founded upon these treaties, that their state was legally and constitutionally independent, though willing at all times to enter into agreements with neighboring states, large or small, by which portions of that independence might be, for reasons of general European welfare, abridged or delegated. As a small nation it has of course been unable to resist overwhelming military superiority, but so far as the constitutional history of the Czech state represents its own will and traditions, it has been, in all essential aspects of political existence, a history of unrestricted freedom. These scholarly conclusions, built upon patient and detailed study of the ancient documents, were readily appropriated by the mass of the people in the latter part of the nineteenth century. To a remarkable degree, the Czech peasant and laborer understood the history of his own land. The ultimate failure of Hapsburg rule is not difficult to understand in the light of that fact.

⊰ 4 ⊱

The Czechoslovaks and the Hapsburgs
to the White Mountain

THERE are few chapters in European history more interesting and dramatic than that of the relations between the
Czechs and Slovaks and the Hapsburg dynasty. There are
those in our day who entertain the idea of a Hapsburg
restoration and the revival of the pre-war Austro-Hungarian monarchy. They would do well to study thoughtfully this chapter of European history, lest they should not
realize how, even after the events of the last months and
years, the conditions favorable to the restoration of the
ancient régime are completely absent in Czechoslovakia
and indeed in the whole Danubian region. Certainly to the
average person living in that region it is abundantly clear
that to bring about such a restoration would be to turn the
clock back. It could in no wise be regarded as a positive or
constructive solution of the very problems which this Hapsburg régime in the past has only made more acute.

The Hapsburgs are a very old dynasty. There have been,
in their periods of grandeur and éclat, serious efforts made
to show the descent of their family from Old Testament
kings, or from heroes of Greek mythology, or from Roman
emperors. Historical criticism has never given these far-
fetched genealogies anything more than amused tolerance.
But the fact remains that their verifiable history is a very
old one, among the oldest of the established families of
Europe. They originated in the mountainous part of southern Germany, in a region watered by the upper Rhine and
its tributaries. Some member of this vigorous family built,
on the river Aar, in what is now the canton of Aargau in
northern Switzerland, about the year 1020, a castle which

was called the castle of Habicht, i.e. Habichtsburg, which became shortened, in common use, to Habsburg or Hapsburg.

Several centuries passed rather uneventfully. The family gradually increased its holdings and improved its political position, either by loyal service to needy Emperors or by advantageous connections with the rich ecclesiastical landlords in the region. Even at this early date the family showed a remarkable tendency toward numerous offspring, and by the end of the twelfth century we begin to notice the frequent recurrence of the name in documents and charters. But in spite of some substantial increase in both land and prestige, the Hapsburgs, until the seventies of the thirteenth century, could not be compared to the powerful dukes and princes of the Empire, and were content with their title of counts. In 1273 a very significant turn in their fortunes takes place. One of the members of their family, Rudolf of Hapsburg, elected to the imperial throne, transferred the scene of his activities from the headwaters of the Rhine to the Middle Danube. With that move there began a new chapter in the history of the family. As chance would have it, the rise of the Hapsburg family was made possible by the humiliation of the Czech king and the break-up of the state which he had but recently built. The outcome of this first skirmish between the Hapsburgs and the Czech state did not augur well for the future.

Taking full advantage of the privileges granted the Czech king by the Golden Sicilian Bull of 1212, and profiting by the impotence of the imperial government, Přemysl Otakar II built up a state which soon reached far beyond the boundaries left him by his father in 1253. His expansion was mostly to the south of Bohemia and Moravia. By marriage, by treaties of friendship and by conquest, he extended his rule over the eastern Alps, and even to the coast of the Adriatic. The population in this newly conquered region was partly Germanic and partly Slav, though it must be remarked that at this early date the distinction between the two races had less political significance than in more recent times. Certainly the forebodings of the princes of the Empire at this growth of Přemysl's power did not stem from the fact that his state was predominantly Slav, but rather that this single state, virtually independent within its own borders, was coming to have a leading voice in imperial affairs. It was an open secret that Přemysl was hoping for the imperial crown. The princes did not contemplate with pleasure the changes that would take place in the administration of the Empire if he were to gain that honor. In order, therefore, to have at the head of the Empire someone whose power would not overshadow that of the great principalities, Rudolf of Hapsburg was elected Emperor in 1273, after the death of the ineffectual Robert of Cornwall. Recommended by the Archbishop of Mainz, Rudolf was already well known for his personal courage and ruthlessness. But the principal fact that recommended him was his relatively modest domain, from which the other princes felt they had nothing to fear in the way of aggression.

Rudolf was well aware of the reasoning behind his election, and, as soon as he was firmly established in his new position, set about to increase the wealth and power of his family. He knew also that it would be suicidal for him to try to increase his own domain at the expense of any of the imperial princes, since he would only solidify their opposition to him by any such procedure. He determined to attack in a direction where he could count on support, rather than opposition, from the imperial princes. The Alpine lands which Přemysl had gradually added to the Czech crown were the most vulnerable territories, both because of their geographical position and because they had been won by conquest, that Rudolf could attack. In the war which ended in 1278 with the defeat and death of the Czech king,

Rudolf was supported by some imperial princes, and also by the King of Hungary, who was jealous of the growth of Czech power. Certain misunderstandings which Přemysl had had with the papal curia bore fruit in that the imperial forces had the active encouragement of the papacy. In his conduct of the war Přemysl must be adjudged guilty of overconfidence until it was too late to correct the mistake. Before he knew it he was faced with an enemy superior in numbers to his own army. He then bethought himself of the possibility of help from Silesia and Poland. A document is still extant, composed in Přemysl's chancellery, which tells of his effort to enlist help from the north. It is not certain whether this letter was ever sent to the rulers to whom it was addressed, but several sentences in this letter present an amazing parallel to the situation in 1938 and 1939, when Poland and the Czech state might well have been drawn together by a common danger, if circumstances and mutual confidence had been more propitious.

Remarking that among all the nations of the world no closer relationship is to be found anywhere than between Poles and Czechs, not only because of their common boundary, but because of a common language, a common origin and a common blood, Přemysl expresses the hope that the mutual love the two peoples have always borne and should now bear one another may bring the Polish king to join him in combatting the common danger, the aggression of the German ruler. "There are," he goes on, "other good reasons. If we should be defeated in the present conflict, which God forbid, the greed of the Germans would reach even farther, and they would be after your lands too. We are for you, as it were, a protective outpost [*praeurbium*], and, if we are unable to hold out, you must then face the danger that threatens you, for their omnivorous greed would not be satisfied with conquering us, but your domains would be subjected to unbearable hardships. O with what afflictions would your whole nation be oppressed by the Germans! O how fearful would be the servitude to which a free Poland would then be reduced, and how dire the calamity under which all your people would groan!"[1]

Whether the letter was ever sent or not, we know that there was no aid forthcoming from this quarter, and the power of the Czech state in central Europe was greatly reduced after this conflict. Bohemia and Moravia were for a time in the hands of Rudolf and his allies, and the failure of the Czech king was paid for in lives and estates of Czech leaders. If anyone is looking for concrete evidence that history repeats itself, the events of 1278 may suggest some similarity to those of 1938: the German Empire and its head supported by the Hungarian king on one side, the Czech king calling in vain for help from his Silesian and Polish blood-relations on the other.

The Czech state soon recovered from the disaster and appeared as a united country with its original boundaries, but the Hapsburgs had won a great victory, and were not to be denied its fruits. Their power was firmly planted on the middle Danube. Vienna remained from that time until 1918 the eastern spearhead of Hapsburg influence. But the relations of the Hapsburgs to the Czech kingdom fluctuated with circumstances, and until 1526 the dynasty had no preponderant influence in Central Europe. Between 1278 and 1526 two members of the family were kings of Bohemia, but in each case for only a short period, and their participation in Czech political life left no visible effects. The first Hapsburg occupant of the Czech throne was also named Rudolf, a grandson of the Emperor Rudolf who defeated Přemysl Otakar II. He came to the Czech throne in the troubled times after the extinction of the male line of the Přemyslids in 1306, who had ruled the land from the earli-

[1] Letter in Emler, *Regesta Imperii*, vol. II, No. 1106; extracts in Palacký, *Dějiny českého národu* (ed. 1908), pp. 285 f. and notes.

est recorded times. A great deal of pressure was brought to bear upon the Czech nobility by his father, Albrecht, before Rudolf was accepted at all. His rule was hardly more than an episode in Czech history. He died in less than a year, on an expedition against some rebellious Czech nobles in southwestern Bohemia. This first Hapsburg made an unfavorable impression on the Czech people. The contemporary chronicler, known under the name Dalimil, recounts a story, without doubt current in the whole land, which must have raised suspicions concerning the new king. During the preliminary negotiations the Emperor, Albrecht, recommended to his son Rudolf that he should disregard his promises to the Czech nobles. The advice of the father to the son was "Give the Czechs parchment and ink, all they want, then take it away again, and shave off their heads, if they resist, with the sword." It could hardly be expected that, dying after a short rule, Rudolf would be deeply mourned by the Czech people. Dalimil adds this advice to his notice of Rudolf's death:

> Shed no tears for him, my children,
> But know, I pray you, only this:
> Had this your prince ruled o'er you longer
> Then had our land more evil wars.

The leading writer of the time thus expressed the feeling of the whole Czech people concerning the first king of the Hapsburg family to rule over them. And Dalimil, all unconsciously, in these four lines, set the tone for Czech opinion of the Hapsburgs of later centuries.

The rule of the second Hapsburg in the Czech kingdom was hardly longer or more successful than that of Rudolf. The Emperor Albrecht ascended the Czech throne by virtue of having married the only daughter of Sigismund, the last of the Luxemburg dynasty which had ruled in Bohemia from 1310 to 1437. Albrecht had the support of only a part of the Czech nobility, because of the general expectation that he would try to uproot Hussite heresy. The severity of his rule in Moravia, where he had ruled in Sigismund's name since 1423, was well known. Just because Albrecht was favored by some of the Catholic nobility, he was unacceptable to the other party. During the Hussite wars (1419-1436) nationalistic feeling, both among the lower and the higher nobility, of those who supported Hussite doctrines and waged a successful war for their defense, had been crystallizing. To this group Albrecht was a representative not only of Catholicism, but also of a foreign dynasty, from the very nation and land whence crusading expeditions against Bohemia had come. There circulated in Prague and the surrounding towns a pamphlet under the title "Short Selection of Czech Chronicles to Warn Faithful Czechs." It began with the significant statement: "Czechs must be on their guard and alert against every effort to draw them into the use of a foreign tongue, particularly German, for the history of the Czech people shows that that tongue is most likely to destroy the Czech and the Slovak languages and works toward that end unceasingly, and with manifold ruse and malice tries to stifle our language."

Dislike and distrust of the Hapsburg king strengthened national sentiment for an alliance with Poland. Bohemia was weak from two decades of war and dissension, and perhaps this alliance seemed particularly desirable at this moment, though there has never been a time in Czech history when widespread sentiment for closer relations with Poland was absent. But at this time, when Poland's foreign policy was greatly influenced by the powerful Catholic hierarchy, distaste for the heretical Hussites was stronger than mere abstract political logic. There was in Poland, therefore, little sympathy for the projected union of the Polish and Czech crowns and even less willingness to support actively the party in Bohemia which was desirous of such a union.

And so Albrecht became Czech king, though only for a short reign, as he succumbed to an illness in October 1439 during a campaign against the Turks. His short rule left no impression upon Czech history. Neither his appearance nor his personality won popular favor.

It used to be accepted, in books written before the dissolution of the Austro-Hungarian Empire, that it was under Albrecht that the three states which were the principal lands of the monarchy were for the first time united. In a certain sense this is true, because as the son-in-law of the Emperor Sigismund, Albrecht ruled not only in Bohemia, but also in Hungary. But there was no real union of the separate lands, and after his death it was to be more than eighty years before these three central European states were to be again under a single ruler. Two weighty factors helped to bring the three states together. In the first place, the Empire, from which Bohemia had by now become almost completely free and from which the Austrian lands had gained a virtual independence, had broken up into quasi-independent principalities within itself. In the second place, the threat of Turkish expansion from the southeast was becoming more serious each year, and only by mutual aid and common action could the states of central Europe hope to defend themselves. The fate of the Balkan states showed only too eloquently that any lack of co-operation between states could open to the Turks the path into central Europe, and that no land in the way of Turkish aggression could withstand this attack unsupported.

In treating the history of Central Europe in the early sixteenth century the very important fact is often lost sight of that the Hapsburgs did not win the Czech throne by conquest. Rather, they became rulers of Bohemia by an accident over which they exercised, in the nature of the case, no direct or indirect control. It is well known, at least in Czech literature, that in many parts of the land, Ferdinand was accepted as nothing more than the husband of the late king's sister. But in other sections, and these might be regarded as more indicative of the national opinion, the powerful nobility opposed him. The desire of the upper nobility to use a change in dynasty in such a way as to weaken the central power apparently never dies. At this juncture the nobles insisted that Ferdinand recognize the fact that the Czech throne was vacant and that the Estates had the right, by free election, to choose the successor to Louis regardless of the claims of Ferdinand and his wife based on dynastic treaties. Ferdinand was very reluctant to accept this view of the throne, but finally was induced, partly by the strength of the candidacy of the Duke of Bavaria, and partly by the firmness of the Czech Estates, to compete with the other candidates on an ostensibly equal basis of bribery and promises. But, if we may judge by his subsequent actions, he was proceeding according to the lucid injunction of his ancestor, Albrecht, to Rudolf I: "Give the Czechs parchment and ink, all they want, . . ."

Czech historians, such as Antonín Rezek and others of more recent date who have studied this period closely, make no effort to justify the very questionable circumstances attending the election of Ferdinand in 1526. The unwillingness of the nobility, in whose hands lay the control of election to the Bohemian crown, to recognize the force of the hereditary claims of Ferdinand did not arise solely from elevated motives of tradition and legality, but certainly in large part from a desire to oblige him to increase his bribes after they negotiated with other candidates. Yet selfishness was not their only motivation. The leaders of the Czech nobles were not unaware of general European conditions or of those nearer home. They realized perfectly well that the Hapsburg family was now the first power in Europe, with Spain, Burgundy, the Lowlands and the German crown in its possession. Bohemia, after the misgovernment of two Jagellon kings, was badly in need of a financially solvent ruler, who would at least not further involve the land in oppressive indebtedness. And after the disaster of Moháč in 1526 it was painfully clear that Central Europe must unite to protect itself against the Turks, lest the rest of Europe share the fate of the Balkans. A united rule over the three Central European lands—Bohemia, Hungary, and Austria—seemed the best arrangement, particularly when it was possible to anticipate that the new ruler of this union of states would receive more substantial support from his brother, Emperor Charles V, than the recent Jagellons, ruling over Bohemia and Hungary, had been able to win from any source.

It would be an anachronism to speak of national oppression at this time. To attempt to explain the obstructionist tactics of the Czech nobility in their dealings with Ferdinand by nationalistic feeling would be to ascribe to the sixteenth century characteristics which do not actually apply until much later, when in the eighteenth century the relations between the Czech nation and the dynasty were in bitter turmoil. Ferdinand, before his election to the Czech throne, ruled in his Austrian lands over a people whose native tongue was German. But he was in no sense a typical German. Even when he decreed that German was to be spoken in the governmental offices as the language of general use, he had no intention of denationalizing his subjects in the newly acquired territories. By the very fact that they ruled in lands with such diverse populations the Hapsburgs took on the aspect of a supra-national dynasty. The distrust of them felt by the Czech leaders and people arose from two quite different sources. From the time of the Hussite movement, in the first half of the fifteenth century, the religious problem was pre-eminently the national problem. The Hussites, though not completely united among themselves, were in a large majority, and openly antipathetic toward the Catholic minority among the Czechs. In general the German minority in the kingdom was allied with the Catholics. Just a few years before Ferdinand became king of Bohemia, the situation was greatly complicated by the spread of Lutheranism. Among the Germans who had formerly been counted as Catholics, the doctrines of Luther began to gain adherents, and among the Czech Hussites Lutheranism also had its converts, because Luther had openly avowed that his doctrines were fundamentally the same as those of Hus.

Thus, because of the injection into the Czech religious question of a new German but anti-Catholic element, the unity of Catholicism in Bohemia was greatly weakened. But Ferdinand was a Catholic, and apprehension was widely felt that he would interfere in ecclesiastical affairs in active support of the Catholic party. Yet it must be said to his credit that he was a moderate by nature—he was a great admirer and frequent correspondent of Erasmus by whom he would certainly have been influenced in the direction of toleration, rather than of fanaticism. A second source of distrust of Ferdinand might well have been the fear that, utilizing the power of his position and his family, he would oppose the nobility with determination and even strip them of much of their power. Later developments were to show that these fears were well grounded, but in 1526 the Czech nobility thought itself well established in its position and was convinced that if there were any benefits from the change in dynasty they would accrue to the Czech nobles rather than to the new ruling family.

Whatever else Ferdinand I may have been, he was not colorless. Contemporary sources bear ample witness to his air of distinction, his individuality and his abilities. The Venetian ambassador Contarini wrote of him in a dispatch of April 11, 1527:

The person of his Most Serene Highness: Beginning first with the physical traits: he is a person rather on the stocky side than slim, sallow, not too well built, but very active, a fine horseman, an accomplished jouster, a keen huntsman, particularly interested in all kinds of firearms, and is continually at some kind of exercise or other. He is a person of high intelligence, and for his age, which is twenty-four, he gives evidence of being experienced in the ways of the world more than one would expect. He speaks French, English, Spanish, High and Low German, Italian and Latin, all excellently. He has dignity and ambition, and evidently hopes for a fine career.[2]

From Czech writers of his time as well we gain an impression very similar to that of the Venetian ambassador. In the memoirs of Mikuláš Dačický of Heslov there is a description very closely corroborating that of Contarini:

He was not of large stature, spare, his mouth usually open, slightly stooped, rather large eyes, slightly aquiline nose, sallow complexion, unruly hair, slender limbs, his speech exceedingly rapid, his thought profound, but along with that easily angered and vindictive, withal of a sharp wit.

The chronicler Bartoš Písař writing about 1530 praised his concern for justice and order.

But very soon after the coronation it became obvious that the rule of Ferdinand in the Czech kingdom would be no fair idyll. The accession of the Hapsburgs to the throne of Bohemia had introduced a factor into Czech political life which was destined to create and maintain disturbing tensions. For a time Ferdinand was occupied in his Hungarian kingdom where a national candidate, John Zapolya, Prince of Transylvania, was widely supported. Ferdinand had also to take into consideration the presence of the restless Turks who, in 1529, drove as far north as Vienna and even after retiring from the walls of the city, maintained themselves on the plains of Hungary. The disturbances in imperial

---

[2] Fiedler, *Relationen Venetianischer Botschafter über Deutschland und Oesterreich*, in *Fontes rerum austriacarum*, Abt. II, vol. 30, p. 2-3.

Germany, where the Catholic church was losing ground with incredible rapidity before the wildfire spread of Protestantism, were also of deep concern to him. Yet with all these uncertainties he still had time and peace enough to keep a strong hand on the trend of affairs in Bohemia, and he was able to direct that trend in a way favorable to his interests. The fond hopes that the king would generously reward his partisans and would, from his own purse, pay off the public debts, were quickly dissipated. Gradually, and indeed before the Estates were aware of the new situation, he so increased the burden of expenditures for public works that he appeared more and more frequently before the Bohemian Diet with requests for taxes. Later on requests became almost annual affairs. Ferdinand continued for long to hope that the schism in the church would be healed, that the popes would be content with reasonable concessions and that the leaders of the reform movement would moderate their demands. He worked toward some such compromise in Bohemia where, because the religious conflict had a more embittered past than elsewhere in Europe, there was even greater need not only of a firm hand but also of clairvoyant tact.

It was Ferdinand's policy to repress radical tendencies, and he supported the conservative wing of the Hussites which favored peace with the Catholic church on a basis of minor concessions. But he encountered opposition and had to endure sharp criticism from the Czech nobility. He found it expedient to relax his rigorous aims for a time, but he never completely gave up the hope of bringing the wayward Hussites back into the fold of the Roman church.

The first serious conflict between the Hapsburgs and the leaders of the Czech people did not, however, arise out of the growing weight of taxes for general public expenditures, nor because of religious differences, but rather over fundamental constitutional questions. Ferdinand had become king of Bohemia by election of the Estates, but he was determined that his hereditary rights to the throne should receive unqualified recognition. He realized, further, how the great power of the Czech nobility was detrimental to his plans for centralization of the government. There is no evidence that he would have gone so far as to deny to the nobility some participation in the administration of the state, but he was resolved to whittle their privileges to the extent guaranteed by the written charters. They soon understood that this policy would mean the loss of all the gains made under the weak monarchs of the preceding generation.

In 1541 there was a devastating fire in Prague, which began on the Malá Strana and swept up to the Hradčany, where the ancient royal palace stood. Among other irreparable losses, the volumes in which were bound the important public records—charters, privileges, and treaties—were destroyed. The volume in which the electoral proceedings of 1526 were recorded was also burned, and the belief spread that the king had himself set the fire, in order to be rid of the embarrassing document. Whether this suspicion was correct or not, or whether someone else was guilty, the fact remains that when these privileges were rewritten after long negotiations with the nobility, the wording was not that of the originals but in its new form favored the king's openly avowed wishes. This embarrassing "parchment" granted to the nobility under some pressure, was now, according to the Hapsburg principle first voiced by Emperor Albrecht to his son Rudolf in 1306, taken away from them. The promised shaving of the heads of the opposition was to come somewhat later.

The intermittent war between the German Protestant princes and the Emperor Charles V flared up again in 1546. This episode, known as the War of the Schmalkaldic League, from the town of Schmalkald in which the Protestants had formed their union, was to have its repercussions in Bohemia. Ferdinand wanted to help his brother and the cause of Catholicism, while the German Protestant princes counted on help from the Hussite and pro-Protestant Czech nobility. An armed conflict between Ferdinand and the Czech Estates inevitably followed in 1547. But there was a lack of unanimity both of thought and action among the Czechs. The Estates were only half-hearted in their opposition to their Hapsburg ruler at this juncture, particularly when it appeared that the Emperor was going to be victorious in his war with the German Protestant princes. Ferdinand was careful, in planning reprisals after the rebellion died out, not to provoke more determined opposition. The towns were punished severely, for he saw in them the focal points of discontent and radicalism. He also began a persecution of the *Unitas Fratrum*, the organization which represented the Hussite evangelical tradition. He regarded the *Unitas* as Protestant, and because of its excellent discipline and organization he saw it as the greatest obstacle in the way of his plans to bring Catholics and Protestants together. A part of the Czech nobility was punished for its temerity in appealing to arms by confiscation of property and abrogation of numerous privileges. As an example to the rest of the nobility and bourgeoisie, four "rebels" were executed on the square before the royal palace on the Hradčany—two members of the lesser nobility and two burghers. It was anticipated that reprisals would be more severe, but Ferdinand had no desire to widen the rift between him and the people, and he particularly desired to win the upper nobility over to his side by moderation.

For some years, during the early part of the reign of Ferdinand's son and successor, Maximilian II (1564-1576), a lively hope persisted that he would heal the breach between the Czech people and the dynasty. It was bruited about that he was really sympathetic with Lutheranism and that fundamentally there was little difference between him and his moderate Lutheran subjects. His obligation, as a member of a Catholic dynasty, to remain in the church was readily forgiven. But the basis for these hopes was much less real than was commonly believed. The best that could be said of him in retrospect is that he did make an effort to minimize the religious and political tension that existed between the court and the people, or at least not to aggravate it. This temporizing policy succeeded only in postponing the inevitable outbreak. The roots of the differences were left untouched.

In the last quarter of the sixteenth century the Czech kingdom was drawn more definitely than ever in its history into the swift current of events moving over the face of Europe. Bohemia was, by reason of its position, its relatively dense population, and its natural resources, the most important unit of the Hapsburg lands. The eyes of Europe had been on the religious struggles that convulsed the country. And in an age when constitutional questions disturbed all of Europe, the growth of the power of the Estates at the expense of the monarchy was of no little interest. At a time when the absolutistic régimes of the next century seemed to be presaged, and when the Catholic church, led by the aggressive and disciplined Jesuit order, was carrying the war into Protestant territory, a good deal depended upon the outcome of the struggle in Bohemia. There was little doubt that any rearrangement of political and ecclesiastical conditions elsewhere in Europe would follow the lines of the Czech settlement. Once again the geographical situation of the land, and its exposure to pressure and influences from all sides, were productive of both benefit and harm to Bohemia, and the kingdom was to become the testing ground for conflicting political, social and religious forces.

At the beginning of the seventeenth century the Czech

Estates could be proud of some very significant gains. In 1609 they won from Rudolf II, Maximilian's successor, the Letter of Majesty which assured more extensive religious liberties than were in effect anywhere else on the Continent. Then an understanding with the ambitious younger brother of Rudolf, Mathias, led to an enlargement of the influence of the nobility in affairs of state, and the restrictions under which the Estates had fretted during the rule of Ferdinand I were done away with. But these gains served only to excite the party of the Czech nobility who had been won by Jesuit action for the Catholic cause. This party was weak in numbers, and unable of itself to take the offensive; but it enthusiastically supported the Hapsburg court, and was an important factor in the action against the Estates, by now predominantly Protestant. Ferdinand II, a nephew of Mathias, who had been elected Emperor in 1612, was elected King of Bohemia with the short-sighted consent of the Protestant Estates (1617). While his uncle Mathias was still alive, he set on foot an active, Jesuit-guided Counter-Reformation. He received the hearty commendation and hopeful support of all who thought the hour for a decisive attack on the Protestant Estates had come.

The open conflict was precipitated by a series of isolated acts of violence in 1618, though the issues were far-reaching ones of religious and political liberty. It is customary to date the beginning of the war from the famous Defenestration of the imperial lieutenants, Slavata and Martinic, from the high windows of the royal palace on the Hradčany, May 23, 1618. They were Czechs, but belonged to the Catholic minority and had been denounced by the Protestant majority as public enemies. So long as Emperor Mathias was alive the Czech Estates maintained the position that they were not opposing him but rather his evil advisers. But Mathias died in March 1619, and both sides, Ferdinand II and the Czech Estates, dropped all pretense. A bitter war was inevitable. It is impossible to resist the conclusion that, though much of the deliberations of the Prague Diet in the years 1619 and 1620 was taken up with local and even petty intrigues, the leaders of the Estates were well aware of the significance of their struggle for the whole of Europe. The Czech Estates avowed that they were fighting to defend the principles of the Letter of Majesty granted by Rudolf. The leaders of the Protestant party had been largely instrumental in the composition of the Letter, but its basic principle was toleration, and its adoption and observance would have assured internal peace to any land with a population consisting of divergent faiths. It was not only a recognition of existing confessions, but, by emphasizing the principle of toleration, pointed the way to the appeasement of strife between religious bodies.

But the Estates were not fighting for their religious rights alone. They were perhaps even more zealous in their defense of the privileges they had won in the preceding century against the growing will of the Hapsburg rulers to gather all power into the central offices of the court. The Hapsburgs on the other hand, loyally supported by their Spanish cousins, the papal curia and a number of imperial princes, resolutely championed the Catholic cause, determined to recapture positions lost to Protestantism since the beginning of the Lutheran revolt. And, what was of great significance to the Czech nobility, the Hapsburgs made no secret of their deep-seated dislike for the state of affairs hitherto obtaining in which the Estates shared the powers of government with the monarch.

In spite of the fact that the far-reaching implications of the struggle in Bohemia should have been obvious to anyone, not even all those who could expect to be adversely affected by the expansionist ambitions of the Hapsburgs rallied to the defense of the Czech Estates. The Union of Protestant Princes in Germany remained neutral and took no active steps even when their leading member, Frederick of the Palatinate, was elected by the rebellious Estates to the throne of Bohemia. Under normal conditions of dynastic rivalry, France would have been expected to lend assistance to anyone who was opposed to the Hapsburgs, but the Regency before the advent to power of Richelieu could hardly be accused either of firmness or vision.

The English king, James I, was a bitter disappointment to those who had hoped that he would come to the aid of his daughter's husband, who was in addition a fellow Protestant and desperately resisting the aggression of the Catholic Hapsburgs. While the Czech Estates, mustering what defenses they could, were being enveloped by the superior forces of the Catholic imperialists, James I was earnestly studying the Czech constitution, and refused any assistance until he could decide whether the crown was really elective, as the advocates of Frederick's election claimed. When at last he recognized that the need for help was desperate, he offered to act as mediator in the dispute, failing completely to see that his envoys in Vienna could speak convincingly only if they could point out to the Hapsburgs that troops were on the march from England, and would be followed by more if the first hint were disregarded. The naïveté of the King of England was not lost on the Jesuit advisers of the Emperor. The story went the rounds in Vienna after the Battle of the White Mountain (November 8, 1620) that a messenger was telling the courtiers that King Frederick would be able to muster a great army even after this defeat: the King of Denmark, his uncle, would send him a hundred thousand, the Hollanders a hundred thousand, and James I also a hundred thousand. Someone asked, a hundred thousand of what? The messenger replied "The King of Denmark will send a hundred thousand red herrings, the Hollanders a hundred thousand cheeses, and the King of England a hundred thousand ambassadors."

The Duke of Transylvania, Bethlen Gabor, whose interests would have been served best by a check to the Hapsburg power, vacillated, and changed his policies as the needs of the moment seemed to dictate. The Estates of the United Netherlands were the only ones to come to the aid of the Czechs. Their support was in money, as their armed forces were still busy defending their land against the Spanish Hapsburgs. But their help, welcome as it was, could not balance the lack of support from other quarters. As a consequence of the failure of the Czechs to gain substantial aid, though they did win minor engagements in the early stages of the war, the final outcome could hardly be in doubt. In the fall of 1620 the most powerful ally of the Hapsburgs, Maximilian, Duke of Bavaria, joined the campaign against the Czechs. From that moment, the result was only a matter of weeks. The armies met not far from Prague on a hill known as White Mountain (Bilá hora) on November 8, 1620. The battle was short and decisive, and the imperial and Bavarian forces easily routed the poorly organized and almost mutinous troops of the Czech Estates. The Hungarian troops of Bethlen Gabor, sent to the assistance of the Estates, fled at the first encounter. This defection only hastened the final result. Defeat would have been certain in any event. The outcome of this battle determined not only the fate of Frederick, but the fate of Bohemia for three centuries.

As a statesman Ferdinand II was not the equal of his ancestor Ferdinand I. He was lacking both in constructive vision and in moderation. The situation in 1620 was much different from that of 1547. In 1547 the dissension between the ruler and the people did not lead to war. Then Ferdinand I had been sure of his power, even if there were no crushing victory over the Estates, such as Ferdinand II insisted upon in meting out humiliating punishment to the Czech leaders. In 1547 Ferdinand I acted moderately on his own initiative with regard to the Estates. But Ferdinand II had a number of active advisers who supported his position and urged him on to a complete eradication of all revolutionary sentiment. This group of advisers consisted of a small number of Czech Catholic noblemen, Jesuits and a whole troupe of zealous helpers from the far corners of Europe, quite willing to sacrifice themselves in imperial service, if they were rewarded for their labors with parts of the confiscated lands and wealth of the Protestant Czech nobles. Once more a situation had arisen which the advice of Albrecht to Rudolf fitted exactly. Again the Hapsburg ruler could take away the privileges of the Czechs and shave off the heads of those who resisted. There were, in Ferdinand's entourage, a few who counselled moderate and even mild measures, but he disregarded their advice in favor of the more violent action urged upon him in a sermon preached by the court preacher, the Capuchin friar Sabinus, who took as his text the words of the Psalmist (II, 9): "Thou shalt break them with a rod of iron; thou shalt dash them in pieces like a potter's vessel." This policy, thus enounced only a week after the battle of the White Mountain, with all the sanction of holy religion, was to bring death and disaster in its wake: death to some Czechs and disaster to the Hapsburgs and their Empire.

⤙ 5 ⤚

The Czechoslovaks and the Hapsburgs
after the White Mountain

As soon as the rebellious land was substantially pacified, a wave of reprisals broke upon the native population. A contemporary chronicler recounts how faithfully the Emperor Ferdinand II labored at the revision of the privileges which the Czech Estates had won from previous Hapsburg kings of Bohemia: after carefully examining each document, he would cut the signatures and the seals off and throw the rest of the charter into the fire. Ancient grants and privileges, if they did not fit in with imperial interests as interpreted by Ferdinand and his advisers, were summarily revoked. In the archives of the Czech crown the original of Rudolf's Letter of Majesty is still extant. The face of the Letter has been slashed crosswise. This defacement by Ferdinand was his way of showing that it was no longer valid. It would be difficult for a defender of the Hapsburgs to point to their faithfulness to engagements solemnly entered into by themselves or their predecessors as one of their nobler characteristics.

Ferdinand was relentless in his demands for formal and judicial condemnation of individuals and societies. Twenty-seven leaders of the Czech cause, both noblemen and burghers, were executed on June 21, 1621, in front of the Town Hall on the Old Town Square in Prague. A great number of nobles and free burghers were forced to flee beyond the borders of their native land. The confiscation of the property of persons more or less involved in the rebellion far exceeded anything that had ever occurred in the country before. The great majority of the Czech nobility was punished in one way or another, some by execution, some by

69

exile, others by partial or total confiscation of their estates.

In 1627 the Emperor felt that his position was so strong that he decreed a new administrative code for Bohemia to be known as the Revised Ordinance of the Land (*Erneuerte Landesordnung*). It was a collection of laws and ordinances by which the constitutional life of the land was to be regulated. In the past there had been certain constitutional limitations on the power of the Hapsburgs in Bohemia. These limitations were now done away with, or so altered as to be devoid of force. The assumption that the Czech throne was elective, which had been a jealously guarded foundation stone of the Czech state from earliest times, was eliminated completely from the new code, and in its stead, at the beginning of the revised constitution it was declared that the Czech lands were the hereditary property of the Hapsburg family. The constitutional and legislative balance between the crown and the Estates was radically modified to the advantage of the crown. The diets of the several lands of the crown, Bohemia, Moravia and Silesia, in which members of the Estates had previously initiated, fully debated and passed upon measures of public interest, were deprived of virtually all their power. They were permitted now to discuss only those matters which the king or his representatives might bring before them. The Diet henceforth lost all power of initiative and actually did nothing more than approve from year to year royal demands for additional taxes. The highest officials of the kingdom were chosen mostly from the local nobility, but the king was under no obligation to consider the desires of the Estates in making his choice. These officials had as their principal function the protection and furtherance of the interests of the king. The people's interests were entirely secondary.

Before the battle of White Mountain the decision as to who could purchase land in the kingdom, and thereby have the rights of a free subject, lay in the hands of the nobility.

After the Hapsburg victory the king arrogated this right to himself, thereby being enabled to portion out the confiscated estates to foreign officers who had served in his forces or to any whose services called for some such suitable reward. He reasoned that anyone who received confiscated land as a reward for loyal service would be anxious to support the régime that had given it to him. Such retainers would certainly be more loyal than even the members of old Czech families who, though they might be perfectly good Catholics, yet had lost some of the ancient political rights to which they had grown accustomed through the centuries. Foreigners were henceforth to find entrance into the Bohemian aristocracy very easy. Soon the Bohemian nobility was so diluted with foreign blood as to give an impression of an international society which had little connection with the land or the people which supported it in such luxury.

It would be almost impossible to overestimate the significance of the battle of the White Mountain in the history of the relations between the Hapsburgs and the Czech kingdom. Up until that fateful date there was always the possibility that a workable *modus vivendi* might be found under which the ruler and the people, although of different nationality and, it might be truly said, of different religious faith, might work together in peace and contentment. The shadow of the two years of struggle, 1618-1620, and the crushing humiliation the Czechs suffered at the end of that time hovered over the whole course of Czech history until 1918. *Bílá hora* (White Mountain) lived in the minds and memories of the Czech emigrants as a symbol of Hapsburg oppression while they wandered over Europe, exiles from their own land. Mikuláš Drabík, a contemporary of Comenius, spoke for many of these emigrants when he called the whole Hapsburg house "the Austrian viper" (*vipera austriaca*). But even among the Catholic population in

Bohemia we find no evidence of affection or trust for the ruling dynasty and its imported satellites.

The exhausting burden of the devastating Thirty Years War bore more heavily upon Bohemia than upon the other Hapsburg lands, both because armies marched, pillaged and fought on her soil, and because heavy taxes were heaped upon a dwindling population. The impoverishment and depopulation seemed only to irritate the government into increasing its demands. What money was collected was sent to Vienna, where the court usually functioned, and was either spent there or sent out of the country to support the Hapsburg cause in faraway Spain or the Lowlands. No profit came to Bohemia, directly or indirectly, from these investments. It was long before the nobility of Bohemia was able to absorb its foreign admixture and become once again a group with any sentiment of loyalty to the country—that *Landespatriotismus* of which the Sudeten Germans have long been justly proud.

This recovery of a sense of attachment to the land came about when, in the second and third generation from the White Mountain, members of the old Czech families began to intermarry with the children of the new arrivals, who were originally of bourgeois families and had come into Bohemia as officials in the service of the Hapsburgs. This interpenetration of foreigners and native nobility had a result somewhat different from that planned by the Hapsburgs. The resultant nobility, although it was germanized to the extent of using German as its common tongue, began to look upon the centralization of power and administration in Vienna with something of the same repugnance felt by the native Czechs of all classes. For several decades after the White Mountain this repugnance had been necessarily unexpressed, but, with a certain revival of normal conditions after the return of peace, it began to make itself felt again.

72

Sometime around 1670 the Jesuit Bohuslav Balbín wrote a tract entitled: *Dissertatio Apologetica pro lingua Slavonica praecipue Bohemica.* The whole book breathes his plaint that the Czech tongue is dying out and the ancient Czech kingdom is on the decline. This moving lament was meant for the eyes of the Hapsburg rulers, but was not published until almost a century after Balbín's death, when Joseph II relaxed materially the rigid censorship. He apostrophizes the Hapsburg family:

You have utterly destroyed our home, our ancient kingdom, and have built us no new one in its place. Woe to you! Some day you will have to render an account for the heritage you have received. How rich it was when first you had it all men know, and you have brought it but ruin and disgrace. The nobles you have oppressed, great cities made small. Of smiling towns you have made straggling villages, of pleasant towns rows of wretched hovels. Where before happy craftsmen labored, now hungry starving wrecks of men stalk the weeded paths. You are indeed the father of your country. No true statesman would ever treat his court as you have treated the Czech kingdom, once so prosperous, all of whose beauties and sources of revenue have been pillaged. I can call all the extortion and violence which I see going on every day nothing else than pillage. The court at Vienna, its appetite whetted by the sweet savor of Czech money, cries out daily: "Give us more, Give us more."

Balbín was closely connected with many of the old Catholic Czech families, and as a Jesuit and a Czech he spoke not only for himself, but for the leading spirits of the Czech nation.

The latter half of the seventeenth and the first half of the eighteenth century witnessed an increasing bitterness among the Czech nobility over the growth of the power of the court at Vienna at the expense of the ancient rights of the kingdom of Bohemia. But this feeling never quite flared into open revolt. By contrast, the Hapsburgs found it necessary to crush by arms several outbreaks in Hungary. A substantial reason for this difference between the course of events in Bohemia and Hungary was the fact that the Czech nobility had been so weakened by emigration and the punitive measures of the Hapsburgs after the White Mountain that the native Catholic remnant was outnumbered by the newly imported German, Italian and Spanish nobility who made up the court party. Under these unfavorable conditions it is hardly surprising that their patriotism never reached the point of armed revolt. But their feelings were known, and even those whose allegiance to the Roman church was unquestioned, and whose conversion to things German was well established, were never completely trusted. Balbín remarks upon this suspicious attitude in another passage in his "Apology":

If they see a castle being repaired, or any sort of a group of retainers, if they see any prosperity among the nobles, they immediately conclude that it is all part of preparations for a new revolt. They think that the forests, the woods and the valleys, yes, even the leaves and the branches of the trees cry out: Rebellion, rebellion. . . .

There was no lack of counsel at the court at Vienna that the whole Czech nobility, Catholic or not, should be further humbled, but the government finally decided to be satisfied with keeping the Czech nobles in a subordinate position by the simple means of increasing their taxes and duties almost to the breaking point. These taxes could be collected, but they could not be made popular by legislation, particularly when those who paid the taxes had no voice in determining how they should be spent. The friction thus established was to become very acute during the eighteenth century. The Hapsburg possessions were a heterogeneous conglomerate of kingdoms and principalities with widely divergent traditions and institutional backgrounds. In times of peace and quiet, these divergences caused very little inconvenience, but the disadvantages of this heterogeneity became only too obvious when aggression from the outside necessitated some common measures for defense, or when, for dynastic reasons, it was necessary to legislate for the whole Empire. At such crucial moments almost everyone would have agreed that centralization and constitutional uniformity had its advantages. The model of the unified state of France under Louis XIV was before the eyes of Europe, and the Hapsburgs were not above learning from a brother monarch.

From 1711 to 1740 Charles VI ruled over the Hapsburg lands. After the extinction of the Spanish branch of the family with the death of the pitiful Carlos II in 1700, he was the last male representative of the dynasty. When the last hope of his having a male heir died, he was faced with the necessity of assuring the succession to his daughter, Maria Theresa. His early negotiations to gain the assent of the various lands of the Empire to his daughter's succession showed him the inconvenience of the separate jurisdictions of these lands. Charles was reluctant to win over the nobility of the several lands to his viewpoint by granting wide concessions, and was wise enough to realize that promises to support his daughter gained by such means would very quickly be repudiated. He then followed another course. He negotiated definitive treaties, and it looked as if he had succeeded in his aim. One after another (1720-1725) the Estates of the various Hapsburg lands recognized the Emperor's claim that all the lands which had become part of the Hapsburg possessions, regardless of the manner of that acquisition, now constituted an indivisible whole, and, after the death of one ruler, were bound to recognize unconditionally his successor. They also recognized the principle that, in case there was no male heir to the throne, the Hapsburg lands were obliged to accept a female heir, particularly the daughter of the deceased Emperor. This was a great diplomatic victory for the Hapsburgs. These agreements

75

absolutely excluded the possibility of calling in a non-Hapsburg ruler. The principle of heredity within the Hapsburg family had won out over the earlier principle of an elective monarchy which, in the case of Bohemia, had been one of the cornerstones of the national existence.

In 1740, on the death of the Emperor Charles VI, his daughter Maria Theresa succeeded to the Hapsburg throne. From the moment of her accession she had to face foreign enemies who regarded their promises given to her father lightly, as well as opposition to her in parts of the Empire. The Czech kingdom became the seat of war, as the leading enemies of Maria Theresa, the Duke Elector of Bavaria, the Duke Elector of Saxony, and, most dangerous of all, the King of Prussia, Frederick II, ruled over lands touching on the borders of Bohemian crown lands. These three princes attacked from three directions, as if they had agreed to divide the booty among them: the Duke of Bavaria, Charles Albert, occupied most of western Bohemia, the Duke of Saxony occupied Moravia and part of Silesia, and Frederick overran the rest of Silesia.

Frederick's invasion differed from the others in being completely successful. Maria Theresa fought three wars to gain Silesia back from the Prussian king, but had finally to admit the loss of almost all of Upper and Lower Silesia, excepting only a small section around Troppau (Opava) and the duchy of Teschen (Těšín). It will be remembered that the partition of this part of Silesia between Poland and Czechoslovakia by plebescite in 1920 caused some bitterness. As a matter of historical fact the territory so partitioned in 1920 had been a part of the lands of the Bohemian crown since the times of King John in the fourteenth century. Maria Theresa was also obliged to surrender to Frederick the county of Glatz (Kladsko) in Upper Silesia which had previously been regarded as a semi-independent unit of the Bohemian crown lands.

Charles Albert, Duke of Bavaria, was able to take over the government of Bohemia, and maintained himself in the country for some time with the aid of the French who had for centuries been rivals of the Hapsburgs. A considerable part of the Czech nobility, whose grievances against Hapsburg rule had become traditional by now, rallied to the Bavarian prince, who cleverly appealed to the ancient traditions of friendship between Bavaria and Bohemia. In November 1741 more than 400 members of the upper Czech nobility, with the Archbishop of Prague, Manduscheid, at their head, gave the oath of loyalty to Charles Albert as King of Bohemia. The single fact that the crown jewels of the kingdom were in safe keeping in Vienna prevented the coronation of a rival of Maria Theresa as king of Bohemia.

This is the third revolt against the Hapsburgs in Bohemia (1547, 1618). It was different from the first two in that there were wanting the earlier motives of religious zeal and nationalism. The rebellious nobility were just as Catholic as the Hapsburgs, and Charles Albert was certainly just as German as Maria Theresa—perhaps more so, as Maria Theresa was a member of a family which was fully as Spanish as it was Austrian. The reason behind this rebellion is not completely clear, but the best explanation would seem to be that Czech resentment at the course taken by the court toward the kingdom had reached the point where it was irrepressible. To add fuel to the flames, the demands made on the kingdom became daily more oppressive and there was no evidence that anyone in Vienna had any desire to lighten the already intolerable burden Bohemia was bearing. The Czech nobility, in supporting the Bavarian duke, obviously calculated that by joining Bohemia to Bavaria they would not have to support the grandiose political ambitions of the Hapsburgs, and their land would have a chance to recover from the devastation and impoverishment of the Thirty Years War.

By surrendering Silesia to Frederick II, Maria Theresa eliminated her most powerful enemy from the field, and was able to act more effectively against the Bavarian duke and his French allies. By 1743 she was again mistress of Bohemia, and signalized her victory by having herself crowned Queen of Bohemia in Prague. Naturally the matter of punishing the rebellious nobles came up. She was even more conciliatory toward the leaders of the revolt than Ferdinand I had been in 1547. A special commission examined, with a good deal of legal technicality, the guilt of leaders in the Bavarian incident and set the punishments. But the general political situation was still so delicate that such drastic measures as executions or even large-scale confiscations were not deemed wise. Some of the more active of the Czech leaders were deprived of their offices, and many were punished by banishment from the court at Vienna. The deep-rooted hatred Maria Theresa felt for the Czech nobility was no secret, in spite of the fact that from the beginning of her reign some of her most loyal counsellors and adherents were of Czech origin. The kingdom of Bohemia, greatly weakened by the loss of Silesia, continued to lose prestige during the rule of Maria Theresa, and still more of its ancient liberties. The queen scorned Prague as a capital city, and there is no doubt that her gesture of having herself crowned in the ancient capital of the kingdom was made simply to show Europe that she was the ruler in the land. The crown of Bohemia as the symbol of the greatness of an ancient kingdom with glorious traditions meant little or nothing to her, if we may judge by her persistent efforts to reduce it to an unimportant province during the next forty years.

The first Silesian war and the Bavarian incident only hastened her decision to do away with the old order of things and to effect a centralization of all the Hapsburg lands. A far-flung and loosely organized state was helpless against an aggressor like Frederick II who had behind him a perfectly responsive and obedient military machine organized for instant action. Maria had surrendered Silesia, but in her own mind she was determined to win it back again as soon as she had effected reforms in internal administration. Maria Theresa has been given credit for breaking down feudal barriers in the Empire, though her reasons were not any basic opposition to the principles of feudalism, but rather her desire for an efficient state which would enable her to avenge her humiliation at the hands of Frederick and repossess Silesia. After a second war against Frederick, at the end of which he retained Silesia on the same terms as before, she extended her plans for administrative reform still further than before, and whittled away even those vestiges of Czech independence which had remained during the years of revolutions and wars and under the absolutistic régime of the preceding century. However, like her father before her, Maria planned her procedure so as not to prejudice the chances of a successful retaliatory war against Frederick by precipitating disturbances and unrest at home. Consequently she carefully avoided the appearance of attacking the structure of the kingdom, and limited herself to the introduction of corrections and simplifications at points where ancient usages and institutions obstructed the even tempo of the political development of the state. The end result was the same. The Czech kingdom had lost all substance of independent action.

Maria Theresa ruled in the lands of the Czech crown as Queen of Bohemia. Decrees and ordinances were sent to Bohemia, after being prepared by a Czech chancery and published by offices subordinate to this chancery. A similar practice obtained in the other lands of the Hapsburg realm: decrees substantially identical were published and carried out in the name of the ruler by a number of offices. It was a tedious and ordinarily somewhat ineffective administrative method. Maria Theresa was realistic enough to want to effect simplification and centralization where she would be likely to succeed. She knew the temper of her Hungarian subjects well enough to foresee that the Magyar nobility would strenuously object to the loss of their political power. And as Maria could ill afford to have serious trouble in the eastern part of her realm, she refrained from raising the issue in any definite form, and contented herself with introducing what reforms she could control in Bohemia and Austria.

These two lands, throughout the Middle Ages and early modern times, had been completely independent of each other. Economically, however, the relations between them had been complementary, and trade across the borders had been constant and flourishing. The differences between the two lands were very important in two respects: political history and organization; and the language of the people. Austria was predominantly Germanic in blood, culture and speech; in Bohemia the Czechs were in the great majority among the lesser nobility, the bourgeoisie and the peasants. There had been times when common interests or common fears minimized these differences so that common action resulted. At the beginning of the seventeenth century, for instance, Protestants among the nobility of both countries fought side by side against the Catholic imperial forces. But Austria looked upon the Hapsburgs as the Austrian dynasty, and no one would have thought of doubting the legality or the propriety of Hapsburg rule. From the time of the White Mountain the Hapsburgs were desirous that the Czechs should look to Vienna and the Hapsburg court with the same steadfast devotion and loyalty as the Austrians had shown for centuries.

The changes that had taken place in the make-up of the population in Bohemia were favorable to this Hapsburg hope. The Czech nobility, that is, what was left of it in

Bohemia, had been so interbred with the foreigners who had settled in Bohemia in the seventeenth century, and had come into such close relations with the Austrian nobility, that there was no noticeable difference between the germanized Czech nobility and the Austrian. New townspeople, from districts where the Thirty Years War had wrought less devastation than in Bohemia, both from Austria and from southern Germany, had poured into the depopulated Czech towns. There was thus a certain equalization in population between the Alpine Austrian provinces and the Czech kingdom. The peasants clung to their Czech speech, but they were completely dependent upon the nobility who owned the land, and of course they had no voice in public affairs. In the days of the Enlightened Despots, the masses of the people existed to be benefited by the reforms their rulers planned for them, particularly if these reforms would allow the masses to contribute more generously to the support of the ruler and his court.

Superficially there seemed to be so much similarity between Bohemia and Austria that an administrative union appeared to be not only advantageous from the point of view of dynastic interests, but even beneficial to the two countries involved. Some of Maria Theresa's advisers urged such a union. It is true they were of the nobility, but the ideas of the Enlightenment had penetrated even to the Austrian upper classes, and they were not unwilling to discuss the good of the state as a whole even when the immediate aims of individuals or privileged classes might have to be sacrificed. Their patriotism was not limited to the ancient lands of the dynasty, but envisioned the whole region now ruled over by the Hapsburgs which they planned to build into a great and unified state.

The first step in this new and formidable program was the administrative union of the Czech and Austrian lands. The mere fact that the Czech kingdom had a long history as an independent state and still retained much of the framework of that independent existence was not thought to be any real obstacle to the unification. It would be difficult to find in the progressive and enthusiastic atmosphere of the Enlightenment any profound respect for historical facts and ancient tradition such as had marked even so recent a régime as that of Maria Theresa's father, Charles VI. On the other hand, the complete iconoclasm of Joseph II had not yet made its meteoric appearance. As a matter of fact Maria Theresa, motivated by a determination to regain Silesia from Frederick II, was anxious to effect centralization in governmental operation as a means toward the end of a successful war against Prussia. She was thus a transition between her father Charles VI, who left traditions much as he found them, and her son, Joseph II, who left nothing as he found it. The readiness of the Czech nobility to accept the Bavarian duke as king in 1740-1742 only confirmed her in her decision to leave untouched the *forms* of the ancient Czech kingdom.

But in 1749, after preparations extending over several years, she made a very significant move. At that time she abolished the Czech chancery (*Hofkanzlei*) which until then had symbolized the unity of the Czech lands and, functioning at Prague under, for the most part, Czech officials, served as a constant reminder to those who were aware of the importance of such symbols that the Czech kingdom continued to exist as a juridical unit and that the Hapsburgs ruled over those lands only by virtue of their position as kings of Bohemia. At the same time the Austrian chancery in Vienna was also abolished. In place of the two chanceries that were thus summarily abolished, new offices (*Directorium in publicis et in cameralibus*) were created whose jurisdiction covered both Bohemia and Austria. There were obvious advantages for the central administration in these changes, as unity in policy for a larger governmental area could be achieved. But it is hardly necessary to remark that there was no place for any official use of the Czech language in the new arrangement. In the lower ranks of Czech society there would hardly have been any audible protest against the new administrative order, even if they had taken time to consider the implications. But the upper nobility, traditionally more jealous of their ancient privileges, immediately expressed their vigorous opposition to the centralizing measures of the court party. Yet even among the upper nobility there were a few who joined forces with the individuals and groups who had identified themselves with the court, had helped in preparing the reforms and were over-eager to assist in putting them into effect.

The transitional nature of the government of Maria Theresa, mentioned above, was evident in the fact that she did not persevere in the course she began, but, when the opposition was strong, gave in to it. During the Seven Years War the call for a return to the earlier régime became insistent. The new supreme office, governing Bohemia and Austria from 1749, was not, however, completely abolished, nor were the previous conditions restored. The name was revised so that there might be some visible trace of the former political entities. It was given the title, late in 1761, of the Austro-Bohemian Chancery. In other minor matters Maria Theresa made some concessions to those who opposed her efforts at centralization, but there can be no doubt that it was now the fixed policy of the Hapsburg dynasty to create a great Central European power by the consolidation and integration of all the various lands under the family rule. The jealously guarded rights and privileges of the Czech kingdom could not be allowed to stand in the way of the accomplishment of this policy. In minor and unimportant details concessions to the rich Bohemian nobility might have to be made, but the substance of centralized power could not be yielded in any important particular.

The son and successor of Maria Theresa, Joseph II (1780-1790), was not embarrassed by the qualms which restrained his mother. He abandoned all thoughts of vengeance against Prussia and great military campaigns, and thus did not have to consider the effect of radical and precipitate internal reforms on his success in foreign affairs. Joseph was a Hapsburg only on his mother's side—his father was Francis, Duke of Lorraine. The dynasty to which Joseph properly belongs must be called the Hapsburg-Lorraine family. There has been much speculation as to which of his parents he resembles the more, but the speculation is perhaps pointless. Neither of the families takes much pride in his record—both would regard him as an *enfant terrible* rather than as typical of either dynasty. He was not particularly fond of the church, and even issued decrees for it in which the interests of the church were subordinated to those of the state. He had little to do with the feudal nobility, and disregarded deliberately their political and economic interests. Among the common people he was very popular for the reforms which so improved the position of the peasant class. They looked upon him as their protector and thought that the reports of his death in 1790 had been falsely spread by their overlords so that these latter would not have to obey Joseph's patents and could again lay heavy burdens on the backs of the people. He openly avowed the principles of the Enlightenment; he proclaimed toleration for the Protestant confessions, relaxed the censorship and encouraged his subjects to travel abroad and profit by contact with the outside world. He wrote his own epitaph: "Here lies Joseph II who was unfortunate in all his enterprises," and from many points of view it is perfectly correct. Yet it must not be overlooked that he did more in his short reign to make Austria, and indeed the whole Hapsburg monarchy, modern than any of his line, before or after him. The little ventilation he was able to bring to the Empire, painful both to Joseph and his people, was such a tonic that its effects could not be forgotten.

On two fronts Joseph's program of reform met opposition in Bohemia. In the first place, the powerful nobility could not complacently endure the increased tempo of centralization which Joseph demanded. Maria Theresa's efforts in that direction had been bad enough, but Joseph was both more determined and more radical. Their repeated efforts to stop the progress of "reform" were vain, and they took refuge in hope of better days to come when they would be in a stronger position to wage a successful campaign against an aggressive central government. In the second place, Joseph's reforms were not well received among the lower classes, because of the emphasis put upon the exclusive validity of German in all government posts, in the lower schools, and in the army. Their native Czech tongue was about the last sign of their nationality, and the common people clung to it with all the deeper devotion for that reason. Even the most unlettered could understand this kind of denationalization. In these two directions Joseph, misled by his reforming enthusiasms, had overstepped the bounds of the possible. His program for reform, in the judgment both of his contemporaries and of later students of his time, was dangerously overloaded. Even those who were the gainers from his social reforms could not deny that this ruler, so much of a philanthropist in the abstract, was yet a passionate and confirmed germanizer, rigid and arbitrary, and much less tractable than any of his predecessors had been. His insistence upon an immediate systematization where, in other countries, there had been only a gradual development—that is, in the political maturity of a whole group of peoples—obscured whatever good the practicable points in his program held, and postponed the day when even the first steps to liberalism could be taken.

The death of Joseph in 1790 was the signal for a spontaneous attack on his whole political structure. The conservatives, now the majority among the Czech nobility, took the lead. They had bemoaned the loss of their former position of privilege, and the present circumstances were exactly the opportunity they had been hoping for. Joseph's brother and successor, Leopold II, ruled but a short two years, but the direction of Hapsburg policy reversed itself in that time, and the Czech Estates again found their voice. Their actual gains were not so considerable, but the seeds of their later victory were very clearly germinating in this last decade of the eighteenth century. The nobility in the closing years of Joseph's reign had come in contact with the beginnings of the Czech revival of interest in native history and literature. They had thus come to an astonished awareness of the former independence of the Czech lands from any control from Vienna. It is not without interest that the researches into the past glories of Bohemia had been made by scholars of the middle classes, and in some cases by men of peasant origin. They wrote either in Latin or in German, but these disguises could ill conceal the spirit of patriotism that gave their writing its fire. The ideas of the French Revolution were contagious, and the Czech people were fertile soil for the spread and growth of ideas of liberty and equality.

We can trace a very interesting situation at the end of the eighteenth and the beginning of the nineteenth century. On the one hand there is the court of the Hapsburg monarch, which in some measure is moved by the plaints of the nobility and revokes an unpopular set of measures without at the same time giving up any of its dynastic claims. Although concessions are granted, there is no evidence that the plan for an organic union of all the separate lands of the Hapsburg territory has been discarded at all: quite the contrary.

Early in the nineteenth century Francis II, another Hapsburg-Lorrainer, took a step for which much of the work of Maria Theresa and Joseph II was but the prelude. In 1804 he proclaimed himself Emperor of Austria, and his lands in Central Europe began to be called the Austrian Empire. The older titles of the separate lands were still in formal use, but a new supergovernment was now a fact. In view of the difficulties experienced in earlier centuries in achieving a popular basis for a centralized state, the court made an especial effort to encourage the people to think of themselves in terms of the larger unit. A Hungarian should cease to think of himself as a Hungarian or a Czech as a Czech, but all should regard themselves pridefully as Austrians. Centralization in political administration which had already been effected to a considerable degree should logically be paralleled by unity and uniformity of the object of patriotic impulses, that is a single and unified Austrian Empire, transcending national loyalties. On the other hand, and in direct opposition to this Hapsburg program of denationalization, there comes to vigorous life a national consciousness among the rank and file of the Czech people. In its beginnings this new movement was relatively weak, and quite incoherent as to its eventual aims and the details of its program, but after a few years of uncertainty it acquired power and decision and waged a long drawn out conflict with the might of the Hapsburg Empire on an entirely new battlefield.

‹ 6 ›

Czech and German: Action, Reaction
and Interaction

A GREAT PART of European history is concerned with the impact of one people upon another, whether by war, conquest, commerce or political and social rapprochement. As we read this history, our interest and curiosity are aroused, and we could often wish that the impact did not so soon soften to the point where it produces an amalgam. For if individuality is lost in union we can never find out whether the one or the other people has inherent superiority. The Roman, the Goth, the Lombard, the western Greek and the Moslem became a composite in medieval Italy. The Arab, the Iberian and the Visigoth in Spain; the Germanic Frank, the Vandal, the Norman and the Gallo-Roman in France; the Celt, the Anglo-Saxon and the Norman in England—these all furnish us with abundant material for an analysis of the process of racial amalgamation. But we have fewer cases of inter-racial impact where the two peoples involved have not joined. We have studied amalgamation, but hardly at all racial and national persistence by one people in the face of pressure from another vigorous people. It is an example of just such ethnical integrity over a period of centuries which we have an excellent opportunity of studying in the case of the Czechs and the Germans in Bohemia.

Recent events in the field of international politics have made us more conscious of some of the facts and forces that lie behind the thinking of the peoples in Central Europe. We recognize readily that present turmoil is hardly more than a continuation of past struggles. Precisely for that reason we must discover whether this turmoil has been inevitable, and, because it arises from apparently ineradicable traits in the two peoples concerned, whether it is going to continue to be so.

Two large ethnic groups are immediately concerned: the German and the Slav. The Germanic group has been throughout history increasingly homogeneous, and the Slavic group in some measure increasingly heterogeneous. The tendency of German history has been toward consolidation—the concept of *Grossdeutschtum* has dominated directly or indirectly almost all Germanic political thought. The tendency of Slavic history on the other hand, in spite of sporadic efforts toward Pan-Slavism, has been in the direction of the formation of distinct branches of the larger group. It may be that geography—mountain ranges and rivers—have been responsible for this centrifugal tendency in Slavic history, but the importance of the invasion and settlement of the Magyars in the ninth and tenth centuries so as to form a wedge in the middle of Slav territory has been pointed out in a previous chapter.

The Czechs and the Slovaks, western branches of the Slavic race, suffer and have always suffered from a twofold isolation. This isolation has both advantages and disadvantages. In the first place, geography and distance separate them from their fellow-Slavs, Poles, Lithuanians, Russians and South Slavs. This separation would appear to be mostly disadvantageous. In the second place, they are, also by geographical factors, isolated and insulated from the Germanic peoples who are on their northern, western and southern borders. Normally we should regard this as an advantage, from the point of view of ethnic survival. But the pressure from the Germans has been none the less persistent and severe through the centuries. The land of Bohemia has been the scene of fifteen centuries of struggle between these Western Slavs, whom we shall call for convenience sake the Czechs, and the Germans. Throughout this period the intensity of this struggle has varied greatly, but it has apparently always been there, latent or active. The ultimate causes of this struggle are now and have been debatable, but the fact and importance of its presence have been admitted by all students of this history, Reich German, Sudeten German, Austrian and Czech.

Francis Palacký, the historian of the Czech people who was partly responsible for the direction taken by the Czech revival of the nineteenth century, wrote:

"Czech history is the ground on which, from time immemorial, the antagonisms of Germanism and Slavism have broken out in their sharpest form and have come to their clearest focus. The essential content of Czech history is a perpetual struggle between the German and Slav elements." Adolf Bachmann, writing in 1904, representing the point of view of German historiography, concluded: "Bohemia, or rather the Sudetenlands considered as a unit, have been for centuries the classic land of national battles between German and Slav."

But it must be added that this has not been a struggle at all times equally tense and bitter, and a study of its course shows us that success has never crowned the effort of one or the other of the antagonists for long at a time. In politics, culture and economic status, there has been a pendulum-like swing between dominance by the Czechs and dominance by the Bohemian Germans, or those Austrian Germans who spoke for and ruled through the Sudeten Germans.

The earliest contacts of the Western Slavic tribes and the Germanic peoples, and the coming of Christianity from Byzantium to the Moravian Empire in the ninth century have been briefly described in an earlier chapter. This Byzantine Christianity was unable to maintain its favored position, and by the end of the ninth century Bavarian and Saxon priests flowed into the land, introducing a Latin liturgy with the open support of the Czech rulers. Their influence was spread by the foundation of monasteries throughout the lands of Bohemia and Moravia. But with the establishment of a separate bishopric at Prague in 973 the growth of German influence in matters ecclesiastical was stayed. It would be hard to emphasize too strongly the importance of the establishment of this bishopric in the history of Christianity and Latin culture among the Czechs. The second bishop of Prague was a Czech, St. Adalbert (Vojtěch), and of his seventeen successors to the year 1200, ten were Czech. These Western Slavs apparently found Latin Christianity congenial. But as was to be expected, the influence of the German monastic foundations upon monasticism in Bohemia in general, and upon agriculture in particular, was determinative. We must also note that these establishments were gradually czechized as the members of the foundations came to be, in the majority, Czech.

Czech society does not begin to show distinct germanization until the Czech princes and kings of the Přemyslid line —and, imitating their example, the leading Czech nobles— began to take wives from princely German houses. From 1034 to 1280 a round dozen Přemyslid ruling princes married German wives, and Czech nobles by the score followed suit. All these wives brought German retainers, nobles and ladies, chaplains, courtiers and servants. German communities grew up around the castles which in turn attracted German traders and craftsmen. German princesses endowed chapels, canonries and monastic foundations. Inevitably many of these educated Germans rose to positions of importance in the royal service, and some became royal councillors; others, bishops and abbots of important monasteries. Troubadours, minnesingers and artists came to these germanized courts in great numbers. The social and cultural influence of these marriages upon the patterns of life among the Czechs was, in the very nature of the case, tremendous. Of antagonism to this germanization of their aristocracy we find few traces in documents dating from the eleventh century. But Cosmas of Prague, writing in 1125, records that Prince Spytihněv, on the day of his enthronement in 1055, performed a great and memorable deed, ordering all of German blood, rich or poor, native or transient, to be driven from the land of Bohemia within three days. Spytihněv's mother and wife were German. Having noted this fact, Cosmas does not remark further upon the prince's motivation. But the bitter resentment of Cosmas and other Czechs was of no avail.

The end of a period was at hand. The first three centuries of this period were almost completely Czech, with little or no trace of lasting German influence. The last three centuries witness an increase in German infiltration, mostly among the nobility, until by the middle of the twelfth century rising Czech feeling measures the acuteness of the situation. We shall call this first period of approximately six centuries a period of Czech action, and put its end approximately at the middle of the twelfth century.

Throughout the twelfth century the Germans continued to come into Bohemia and Moravia. But it may be noticed that the nature of the newcomers had changed somewhat from that of their predecessors. The first arrivals had been of the feudal nobility and its hangers-on, traveling merchants and the clergy. In small numbers they could be absorbed, and the Czechs would be the first to admit that they brought salutary cultural benefits with them. But by the middle of the twelfth century the records tell us that those who came—merchants, artisans of all sorts, farmers—were desirous of settling and identifying themselves with their new homeland. A new problem had to be faced. The first documentary evidence of any attempted solution of this problem is the so-called *Sobieslavum*, a royal patent granted about 1170. According to the form in which this grant is preserved, the reigning prince, Soběslav, gave to German townsmen the right to have their own town, with German town-law, their own priest and judge, in the outskirts of Prague. The provisions of this grant are so interesting that a translation of significant parts of the document are here given:

I, Soběslav, duke of the Bohemians, herewith advise all men, present and future, that I take under my grace and protection the Germans (Theutunicos) who are living in the suburb of Prague, and it is my pleasure that, just as the said Germans are distinct from the Bohemians as to race, so they shall be separated from the Bohemians as to their law and customs. I therefore grant to the said Germans that they shall live according to the German law and justice which they have enjoyed from the time of my grandfather, king Vladislav. I grant them a priest, whom they shall freely choose for their church, and likewise a judge, and the bishop (of Prague) shall under no conditions deny this request of theirs. . . . They are bound to take part in no expedition save in defense of the land. If the duke is out of Bohemia on an expedition, then the Germans are to guard Prague with twelve men-at-arms at each gate. . . . If a Bohemian has an accusation to bring against a German which must be tried with witnesses, the Bohemian should have as his witnesses two Germans and one Bohemian, all known to be men of good repute. In the same way, if a German has a case against a Bohemian, he should bring two Bohemians and one German as witnesses, but they must be reliable persons. . . . If a Bohemian or a Roman or anyone else should accuse a German, then the high chamberlain shall send a messenger to the judge of the Germans and this judge shall have jurisdiction in the case, and the chamberlain shall have nothing more to do with it. Also I grant to the Germans that they are free men, free from demands of hospitality, from pilgrims and from foreigners. Know ye all that the Germans are free men. Any foreigner or guest from any land at all, desiring to stay in the town with the Germans, must obey German law and custom. If a thief is a German, the prince will judge him. If a thief is taken at nighttime, he is to be hung, if in daytime etc. . . .

This grant was reissued by three succeeding Bohemian rulers. The explicit protection of German extraterritoriality is typical of a long series of privileges granted to groups of German merchants and artisans. The Přemyslid kings followed a consistent policy of open encouragement of German colonists. City after city gained its privileges from one or other of the later Přemyslids, and many others from the local nobility. The chancellor of Přemysl Otakar II, Bishop Bruno of Olomouc, a Schleswig noble in the middle of the thirteenth century, was responsible for the foundation of approximately two hundred towns and villages in Moravia and eastern Bohemia. In all these new settlements German law was recognized. Guilds of various trades grew up. The townsmen were soon divided into a patriciate and a craftsman class, and class struggles in the fourteenth century were as common in Bohemia as in the rest of Europe. The encouragement to Germans to immigrate into Bohemia was so general that a not inconsiderable number of German farmers joined Czech farmers on the soil.

For reasons it would not be easy to analyze, the German urge to colonize soon reached its peak. By laws of population which would seem to have been natural in the Middle Ages, the Czechs, largely a rural population, soon increased so as to make inroads on the superiority of the German population already well entrenched in the towns. By the middle of the fourteenth century many towns originally completely German became czechized to an alarming degree, e.g. Pilsen and Mies. German merchant families who had made substantial fortunes in the preceding century had bought or built castles and identified themselves with the land of Bohemia as fervently as the native Czechs. These German colonists came from all over Germany, Saxony, Thuringia, Bavaria and even farther away. Because Germany was not in any sense at this time a political or cultural unit, they had no common political or social tradition, and did not form, at this date, any kind of ethnical or national unit within Bohemia. When Czech resurgence came, these Germans were to be unable to offer a unified resistance.

Czech opposition to this German immigration grew passionately bitter during the fourteenth century. An anonymous pamphlet written about 1325 recites the grievances of a Czech against the Germans of all classes, but he is particularly bitter against the German cleric and merchant:

> Let the wise man note and the prudent man consider how this astute and fraudulent people insinuates itself into the richest prebends, the leading benefices and the most fruitful possessions, even into the councils of the princes. . . . In the German cities their artisans of every kind have conspired so that anyone must sell his product at a price set by them. If he sells for less he will be punished corporally or fined heavily, and sometimes a man may be forced to give up his trade for good.

Then, after blaming the Czech princes for encouraging these German "vultures" he breaks out:

> Oh, my God, the foreigner [*alienigena*] is favored; the native is trampled upon. The normal and proper thing is for the bear to stay in his forest, the wolf in his cave, the fish in the sea and the German in Germany. In that way the world would have some peace.

This may seem exaggerated, and if it were only an isolated expression of resentment we should have to dismiss it as jealousy or peevish disgruntlement. But the patriotic Czech chronicle of Dalimil, written in the second quarter of the same fourteenth century, gives something of the same picture. Dalimil praises the words of Prince Ulrich when he explained why he chose a Czech peasant girl for his wife and not a German princess:

> The German woman will favor my people less.
> She will have German servants
> And teach my children German,

And thence will come
Dissension among my people and ruin to the land.

He criticized Přemysl Otakar II bitterly for inviting the Germans wholesale into the land and added: "It were better the land be a desert than that, by the king's order, the Germans should hold it."

But in this vituperation of the Germans we would do well to remember that the real resentment was against newcomers—*alienigenae*. The German families who had for generations been established in the country and had given evidence of having a genuine *Landespatriotismus* were generally not aimed at in these recriminations. The fact that the chronicle of Dalimil was twice translated into German and circulated among the Bohemian Germans with approbation is sufficient testimony to the fact that, even at this early date, many Germans were accepted as having a definite right to regard themselves as Bohemians. The native Germans resented the influx of foreign-born as keenly as the native Czechs. Yet these outbursts are the distant voices of a growing resentment which as it gains volume is to turn the tide of this German period of action, which may be estimated roughly to have lasted a little more than two centuries. It should be made perfectly clear that this period, from the middle of the twelfth century to about the middle of the fourteenth century, is in no wise a German reaction. Reaction would connote a previous action, which, in this case, was not present. The German action was a widespread outgoing movement from a growing Germany, a part of the greater *Ostbewegung*. The Czechs were only incidentally in the way of this eastward push.

From the vantage point of the twentieth century we can be very sure that in many ways this large German immigration was beneficial to the land and people of Bohemia. Western Latin culture and society in its manifold forms was mediated to the Czechs by these Germans. Czech literature, both in form and content, was vastly influenced by the literature which the Germans brought with them into the land. The disturbing and healthy democratic movements, both in and outside of the cities, moved into Bohemia along with German merchants and artisans whose dearest belief was the slogan: *Stadtluft macht frei,* which we may freely translate: "The very air of the city inspires freedom." This characteristic of the urban mind of the Middle Ages was congenial to the freedom-loving Czechs, and they acquired rapidly from their German teachers a mastery of the complexities of the function and organization of the town. Biologically, as pioneer and adventuresome stock, these immigrants may have been superior to those who stayed behind in Saxony, Bavaria or Thuringia. The end-result, because they never succeeded in outnumbering or absorbing the Czechs, may have been to strengthen Czech love of freedom and national consciousness and thus to fortify Czech resistance to Germanism.

This period of German aggressive colonization, most clearly characterized by its effects in commerce, mining, bourgeois pursuits and a rapid urbanization, and by its influence in high political circles, we have called a period of German action, following a long period of Czech dominance which we have called a period of Czech action. From this time on, that is from the middle of the fourteenth century to early in the sixteenth century, less than two hundred years, our pendulum swings back. It is a period generally known as the pre-Hussite and Hussite period, the Golden Age of Czech nationalism. It is a tempestuous time, coinciding with the growth of nationalistic feeling elsewhere in Europe. A strong case might be made for regarding Czech history in these centuries as part and parcel of the general movement toward national cultural and political unity. Or again, in view of the extremely democratic basis of the Hussite movement, we might either draw parallels or make some sociological connection between the democratic and popular movements in Florence, the Ciompi; in France, the Jacquerie; in England, the Peasants' Revolt; and similar uprisings in Hungary and in the Lowlands.

But we must not, we dare not, disregard weighty factors which distinguish this nationalistic movement from its contemporaries. Nowhere else in Europe was the symbiosis of two peoples so painfully evident. Norman and Englishman had long since accepted their amalgamation. The problem of the too powerful feudatory which disturbed France and postponed its unification was relatively unimportant in Bohemia. The Czech Estates might under some circumstances be troublesome, but this source of disturbance was of relatively little moment. Indeed during most of their history, the Czech people could look to the Estates to protect their national interests. The Czech nobility were never so consistently disruptive as, for instance, the Polish nobility. Nowhere else in Europe in the Middle Ages did religion combine with nationalism and social privilege to make the cauldron boil.

One other powerful factor enters into consideration: language. The early history of the Czech language is one of long-retarded maturity. For the most part the courts—of king and noble—used German, which was the honored tongue of a whole world surrounding Bohemia. Czech was the language of the farmer and the servant. When German ascendancy became irksome, the native Slavs quite naturally clung to their tongue which the German scorned and was, furthermore, unable to pronounce. Yet German as a language was destined to live on in Bohemia, largely because it was supported by commercial interests and political connections with greater Germany beyond the mountains. An impasse was thus created. The very inevitability of the German language spurred the Czechs on to regard their own language as the sign and symbol of their nation. There may have been little consciousness of the problem of the language at that time, but we can see that it was a fundamental factor in all national problems. The psychological effects of the language differences have been too little emphasized in a study of the relations of the two peoples.

The Hussite movement, reforming, evangelical, anti-ecclesiastical, anti-feudal in intent, grew upon soil that had been in active preparation for almost a century. It is difficult to see how, in view of the deep-rooted social and ethnic cleavage which the rapid ingress of German stock had accentuated, an eventual conflict could have been avoided. To consider only the matter of feudalism, it is certain that the native Czechs could never take kindly to the social aspects of a system of landholding by which their superior was always a foreigner who scorned them. As any spirited people might be expected to do, they reciprocated his scorn with interest. The Hussite movement gave them an opportunity to identify their dislike for their feudal and German ruling class with religious idealisms. The international struggle in its beginning centered around the representation of the "nations" at the University of Prague. Of the four "nations" of students and masters—Bavarian, Saxon, Polish and Czech—the first three were predominantly German in membership. After the death of the founder of the university, Charles IV, and the establishment of several other German universities in the Empire for German students, the Czech students and masters felt that they had a right to have the controlling voice in their own university. A dispute over academic administrative procedure reflected long-smoldering issues that were of much broader import, and furnished war-cries for noble, townsman and peasant. The Kutná Hora (Kuttenberg) decree which King Václav was induced to issue in 1409, giving the Czech "nation" three votes to one for all the other three "nations" together, only precipitated the conflict. Once the issue had been joined there were theological and philosophical doctrines upon which the Czechs and the Germans took sides. These doctrines were important in themselves, yet in this connection they should rather be regarded as additional occasions for the extension of the conflict along a wider front, incidental to the deeper issue at stake which was, we may take it, whether or not the Czech people, longer in the land and more numerous than the Germans, should continue to be ruled within their own boundaries by an alien privileged minority, entrenched in church, court and society along feudal lines. On this issue the Czechs may be said to have won a qualified victory.

The almost incredible impulsive force of the Hussite hosts may be explained if we realize that the Czechs were able to identify and combine the two most powerful national motivations—race and religion—against their opponents, the Germans, who, in addition to being Germans, were, in the eyes of the Czechs, enemies of the law of God as it had been preached by Hus and the evangelical preachers who preceded him. The victory was a partial victory. But it was a victory in the sense that German immigrant stock began a wholesale emigration from Bohemia, beginning even before the departure of the German students and professors from Prague after the Kutná Hora decree of 1409. In other lands of the Bohemian crown, Moravia, Silesia and Lusatia, the German population was less affected, but the tempo of this exodus from Bohemia increased until the battle of Lipany in 1434,[1] when the mod-

---

[1] As early as 1417 two currents of conviction within the Hussite movement may be discerned: the conservatives and the radicals. The former, known variously as Calixtines, Utraquists or Praguers, drew their strength, for the most part, from the nobility and the upper bourgeoisie. The radical group, known generally as the Taborites, represented the lower bourgeoisie and the peasantry. Even during the last years of Jan Žižka's life the differences between the two groups led to armed conflict on several occasions, and, intermittently after his death, to further bitter civil strife.

erate Hussite party won a decisive military victory over the radical Taborite element of the Czechs. Because the Czechs were both exhausted from their long struggle against superior forces, and at its end divided among themselves, the lot of the remaining Germans was less hard. Within a few decades we find definite indications that the tide of immigration is again flowing from Germany into Bohemia, though it is almost a century before it assumes the proportions of a German flood.

The victory of the Czechs in this Hussite period was a qualified or even dubious victory in that Bohemia lost, through the exodus of the Germans, much of its most energetic and cultured population. Cultural life in the course of the century deteriorated seriously, and toward the end of the rule of George of Poděbrady, in the 1470's, the University of Prague almost ceased to function. Socially and politically the land was virtually isolated from the rest of Europe for decades during the fifteenth century, with tragic consequences for native culture. The guilds and trade associations lost many members, though it is now fairly clear that no essential craft or business disappeared. In the latter half of the fifteenth century the international-mindedness of the moderate Hussite King George brought many Germans back into Bohemia, and particularly into towns which had lost in population from years of war. German artists found employment at the courts of Czech nobles and had no inconsiderable influence on the art and architecture of the land. Currents of communication and cultural and social flow were re-established. The rise of capitalism throughout Europe stimulated the demand for the gold and silver that lay in the mountains of Bohemia, and from the end of the fifteenth and throughout the sixteenth centuries, there was no lack of employment for experienced miners. German miners were so superior to the Czechs that Joachimstal, Kutná Hora (Kuttenberg) and Iglau, centers of the mining industry, became almost exclusively German in population. Some of these Germans became czechized in time, but for the most part they retained their German town law, local customs, culture and connection with Germany beyond the mountains. By all of these means the way for the interflow of German Lutheranism and Czech Hussitism in the sixteenth century was being prepared. The period which we can properly call a period of interaction was at hand.

Hussitism was in essence anti-ecclesiastical and individualistic. Lutheranism began by emphasizing these same basic attitudes. A common enemy, the established Roman Catholic church, naturally brought Hussites and Lutherans together. After the bitterness of the preceding century and a half, both Germans and Czechs were doubtless a little surprised to find themselves in the same camp. But surprise quickly gave way to enthusiasm. Luther himself remarked in 1520: "We have all been Hussites without knowing it. Even Paul and Augustine were Hussites. . . . It is high time we join with the Bohemians and abolish this hatred and jealousy on both sides." The implication of the existence of hatred and jealousy on both sides, coming from a Saxon who may never have met a Czech in his life, is very significant of a general feeling that must have been a part of the social background of the average German. Bartoš Písař, the Czech chronicler, remarked in 1530 on the fact that Luther had changed German hatred for the Czechs into love—a greater miracle than was ever performed by any of the saints.

We have spoken of this period as one of interaction. It was at least that—confusion might perhaps be more accurate. It is indicative of the great change that had supervened that the Czech Brethren,[2] who remained the most

---

[2] The spiritual heritage of John Hus was gradually incorporated into a formal ecclesiastical organization by the second half of the fifteenth century

nationalistic and anti-German of the various Czech groups, were persecuted by both Catholic and Utraquist Czechs. Apparently as a proof of their complete impartiality and detachment from nationalistic prejudices, the authorities of the city of Prague burned two Czech Brethren and two German Lutherans in 1526 and 1528. The German-speaking world was divided into two large camps: Protestant and Roman Catholic. Germans in Bohemia were divided among themselves along the same lines. Among the Czechs there were a few who still clung to their Roman Catholic allegiance, but the Czechs were in the great majority either moderate or radical Hussites. In the whole of Bohemia there were by the late 1530's two large camps each harboring unaccustomed allies. In one, Czech Hussites or Utraquists aligned with German Protestants; in the other, Roman Catholic Germans with what Czech Catholics there were. National lines were for the time being minimized. The isolation of fifteenth century Bohemia was now a thing of the past. The rest of Europe was squabbling with gay determination and welcomed as one of their own another country which was so advanced as to be able to have civil dispute on doctrinal and confessional questions. The Czechs had already proved beyond peradventure that they belonged to the society of nations. The Czech Protestants now formed part of an international movement.

To complicate the pattern of alignment, the Czech nobility began to ally itself with the German nobility, because of a growing fear that the old concept of an elective kingdom resting upon the Estates was, with the advent of the Hapsburg dynasty in 1526, in danger of being superseded by an hereditary kingship. Their fears, as it turned out, were only too well grounded. This class allegiance often

and took the name Unity of Czech Brethren (*Unitas fratrum bohemorum* or *Jednota českých bratří*). The Moravian Brethren of the time of John Wesley and since claim the same heritage.

conflicted with national and confessional allegiances. A Czech Catholic noble might find himself acting in common with a German Protestant noble, and both would feel some embarrassment in justifying their stand when their respective co-religionists were at swordspoints. The Hapsburg king was, for dynastic reasons, above national commitments in politics, and supra-national in his ecclesiastical policies, particularly after the Jesuit influence became dominant. It is obvious that this four-cornered balance—Czech Hussites and German Lutherans, Czech Catholics and German Catholics, Czech nobles and German nobles, and a supranational king—was both delicate and temporary.

The extension of the front along which conflict raged was so great that the University, which had been the seat of the nationalistic controversy at its beginning, early in the fifteenth century, declined almost to extinction only a century and a half later. In 1409 the Czechs had rejoiced to see the German students and masters leave. But late in the sixteenth century students were so few that the arrival of a single German student was the occasion for a celebration.

The situation as it developed abounds in anomalies. The Czechs had just won a long struggle in the name of nationalism, but in the sixteenth century they showed a disposition to give up their national unity willingly. Yet this disposition seems to have changed at the end of the century when some among them realized the results of their close connection with German Lutherans. They again desired to distinguish themselves from the newcomers who, either because of a certain community of faith with the Hussites or because they felt that economically Bohemia had more of a future for them than their own lands, had come across the mountains in great numbers, and had maintained their national solidarity. The Czechs awoke to the danger of an aggressive and united German population, and their dormant nationalism in turn came to life. The Bohemian Confession of 1575[3] showed a firm desire to prove that their faith was different from Lutheranism, perhaps most carefully formulated where doctrinal similarity between Hussitism and Lutheranism was greatest. This nationalistic spirit becomes more determined in the following years until in 1615 the Estates issue a decree providing that all children in Bohemia, of native or of foreign-born parentage, should learn Czech, and that only those children who spoke Czech could inherit the land or immovables of a deceased landholder. Thereafter no foreigner who did not know Czech could become a citizen of any town in the kingdom. This revival of the spirit of the Kutná Hora decree of 1409 was completely impracticable. Many contemporaries realized that the decree came too late. Dačický of Heslov (d. 1626), himself no friend of the Germans, remarked of the decree: "It had no validity. The whole issue is a thing of the past, and the damage cannot now be repaired."

Then in a few years, 1618, the Estates tried to defeat germanization at the hands of a cosmopolitan Hapsburg by the self-contradictory expedient of electing a German Protestant, Frederick of the Palatinate, King of Bohemia. The futility of this illogical move was made terribly manifest at the battle of the White Mountain in 1620. However the Spanish Hapsburg victory on that day was not, strictly speaking, a German victory, but fully as much a Spanish and Roman Catholic victory over Protestantism, both German and Czech, though the Germans were to reap such grim benefits as there were to be gained. By this humiliat-

[3] The king (Emperor Maximilian) had called a meeting of the Diet of the Czech Estates to vote money for the war against the Turks. The Diet countered with a demand for royal assent to a creed which was in effect a compromise between the Augsburg Confession, supported by the German and Czech pro-Lutherans, and the older Hussite doctrines. Some Calvinistic points are to be found in the definitive text of the Confession. Maximilian's verbal assent was violated a few days after it was given.

ing defeat, the summary execution of twenty-seven Czech leaders in the Old Town Square in Prague in 1621, and subsequent determined persecution, the pride and spirit of resistance of the Czech people were crushed. Ferdinand II took all real power from the Estates, decreed the Catholic faith to be the only licit faith in the land, and raised German to legal parity with Czech as an official language in Bohemia. In practice this last provision soon relegated Czech, the language of three-fourths or more of the population, to second place. The imperial ordinance of 1627[4] sealed the fate of Protestantism in Bohemia, signalized the victory of an absolutist monarchy over the Estates, and ended for centuries the rule of the Czech language in Czech lands.

The next two centuries are a period of German dominance, not only dynastic and political, but literary, economic and social. Yet there was little glory for anybody in this dominance. During the devastation and persecutions of the Thirty Years War, the best blood of the Czech nobility and bourgeoisie emigrated. Only twenty-seven families of the old Czech nobility remained in the land. Between 1624 and 1637, around 30,000 (almost a quarter of the total) of the more important established families of the bourgeoisie emigrated, to Germany, Hungary, Poland, the Lowlands and even to England. Along with them went much of the best of the German Protestants. But German Catholics came into the land in great numbers, took over commerce, industry, the control of agriculture and political position. Three-fourths of the land was confiscated from its Czech owners and given to court favorites, mostly German Catholics, though a few non-German names like Bucquoy, Marradas, Verdugo, appear prominently in the lists of those who received confiscated lands. It was a second period of German colonization, more effective, more determined,

4 See above, p. 70.

better organized and more comprehensive than that of the thirteenth century. The agricultural class, by now almost exclusively Czech, was enserfed by royal patents. The Bohemian Diet ceased to be Czech and lost, furthermore, almost all its power of initiation. The tax burden increased, and of course fell most heavily on the Czech peasantry, now reduced to a feudalism such as had not obtained in the Middle Ages. The Czech people became a nation of helots. In 1622 the Czech University was merged with the Academy conducted by the Jesuits and put completely under Jesuit control. As the Jesuits had already been given control over the rest of the educational system in the land, the last vestige of Czech cultural independence disappears with this merger. Czech spiritual resistance was effectively worn down by the able preaching and missionary work of the Jesuits. Czech books were proscribed, and all works, whether in Latin, Czech or German, in which the past greatness of Bohemia was discussed in a favorable light were prohibited. The great humanist pope, Pius II (Aeneas Sylvius Piccolomini) had written a *Historia Bohemica*. It also was prohibited.

The public victory of the German government over Czech nationalism was not so complete as the Hapsburgs would have wished, nor so far-reaching as the virtual extinction of the evidences of Czech national distinctiveness would have indicated. It is suggestive of a difference between appearance and reality that a considerable number of the German immigrants who had come into Bohemia in the late fifteenth and sixteenth centuries became czechized during the seventeenth century. Many of them openly shared the desire of the Czech peasants and lower bourgeoisie for independence from the rule of what they now considered a foreign court—the court of Vienna. Another significant proof of the national feeling surviving from earlier centuries is the ardent patriotism of men like the

Jesuit Bohuslav Balbín (1621-1688). He rejected Hussitism and all its manifestations, but looked upon the age of Charles IV as the Golden Age of Bohemian glory. A fervent Catholic, he was, if possible, a more fervent Slav patriot, and by his researches in Bohemian history furnished the Czech people the material and formal basis for their pride in a glorious past which they might possibly sometime reclaim. In their judgment of the Germans and their instinctive passion for the independence of Bohemia, there is little difference between Balbín in the seventeenth century and Dalimil in the fourteenth.

It is often pointed out that the Age of the Baroque was another evidence of the germanization of the Czechs, in that they took over a whole set of artistic concepts and criteria from their German conquerors without demur. But this is hardly exact. In the first place the artists and architects brought to Prague during the Thirty Years War by Valdštejn (usually misspelled Wallenstein) were mostly Italian and Spanish. And developed Czech Baroque, on examination, is quite different from either Dresden or Vienna Baroque. The Prague Baroque, instead of showing how far the Czechs were germanized, reveals how czechized Baroque became in their hands. To the extent pointed out here the germanization of Bohemia in the seventeenth and early eighteenth centuries may be said to have failed, though in many other ways it was very successful.

The Roman Catholic Counter-Reformation proceeded rapidly. By 1735 Protestantism had virtually become a crime, and in 1752 a declaration of Protestantism subjected the declarant to a death sentence. Yet the Hapsburgs cannot be accused of a specific and intentional German nationalism. There was a certain cosmopolitanism or supra-nationalism which was more successful in denationalizing the Czechs than pure German nationalism would have been, since it was more difficult to combat or resist. An avowed program of germanization would certainly have aroused all the latent patriotism of the Czechs and would have given them a rallying cry equal in its emotional content to the hymns of the Hussite hosts under the great general, Žižka.

From the point of view of a vigorous culture, these two centuries, the seventeenth and the eighteenth, offer us very little from either the Germans or the Czechs in Bohemia. Apparently the sole purpose of the German literature in Bohemia in these centuries was to support the Catholic church and promote piety. The drama was under the direct influence of the Jesuits. Of secular drama, aside from traveling players, there is almost no trace during the whole seventeenth century. Under Maria Theresa and even more under Joseph II non-Jesuits were given some influence in the University of Prague, and literary standards in Bohemia began to be faintly comparable to those in lands where the Enlightenment was in full course. But Czech literature was as yet hardly alive and native art had no outlet in the higher ranges of society. Spirit and élan were lacking even for the German.

In the eighteenth century the German language was the language of business and society. Czech had been almost totally driven underground. The Czechs had indeed been so denationalized as to their Slavic language that the more charitable and liberal of the German leaders felt called upon to encourage the Czechs to use their own tongue. When the censorship was lightened somewhat in the seventies and eighties of the eighteenth century Czechs and Germans worked side by side in the newspapers and in the pamphleteering campaigns that marked the revival of the press. This was all in German. In 1787 a German writer said: "The German tongue is now universal, and will soon drive out the Czech unless earnest patriotic measures against that eventuality are taken." Czechs and Germans, speaking a common language—German, were associated in many enterprises. The native German was proud of his Böhmen, but the Czech, where expression was possible, and *a fortiori* where it was not, remained unreconciled, if compliant.

The suppression of the Jesuit order in 1773 gave the Czechs hope that they might recapture their own educational system and the direction of their own cultural life. It was a short-lived hope. The reforming Emperor, Joseph II, of whose desperate passion for uniformity and centralization we have spoken in an earlier chapter, drove the Czech language from the schools of Bohemia, from all offices of government, from the church and the courts of law. The year 1790 was the nadir of Czech national fortunes. In 1792 the great Czech scholar Dobrovský published his *History of the Bohemian Language and Literature* in German, as if Czech were as dead as Latin.

But once again for the Czech people, it was darkest before the dawn. Forces were at work which were to further the Czech revival. Joseph himself, had he but known it, was largely responsible for the reversal of Czech fortunes, because of his very efforts at centralization, which would have destroyed Czech as a language and with it Czech national consciousness. The repressive effort shocked into new life the very thing it aimed to kill. The liberal thinkers of northern and western Germany furnished added impetus and encouragement to the renaissance of Czech national feeling. Perhaps the most significant single German contribution to the Czech rebirth, aside from the unintentional help from Joseph II, was the impassioned apostrophe of Herder to the Slavic peoples, written in the late 1780's:

The wheel of changing time turns on and on. . . . and when a law-abiding spirit, instead of a lust for war, promotes quiet industry and peaceful concourse between peoples, then will also you—now sunk so low—once a busy and happy people, be freed from the shackles of slavery and rule over your own fair lands, from the Adriatic to the Carpathians, from the Don to the Moldau, and you will there celebrate the ancient festivals of your peaceful labor and commerce.

Goethe was also appreciative of Slav and particularly Czech aspirations to rise to the fulness of their native greatness. He is reported to have begun the study of Czech in order to understand the spirit of their literature.

A number of scholars in Bohemia of German ancestry, e.g. Dobner, Voigt and Pubička, aroused Czech pride by their publications in Bohemian history. Dobner learned Czech after reaching manhood, but became so imbued with admiration for the glorious past of the Czech kingdom and her people that he spoke of "our mother tongue" (*patria nostra lingua*) and referred to the Slavs as "my people" (*gens mea*). Voigt, too, born a Sudeten German, learned Czech at about twenty. He inveighed bitterly against the "well-known hatred of the Germans for the Czechs" and praised the Czechs for their intelligence, sense of justice and love of freedom. He defends and justifies the ardent patriotism of Dalimil as directed against the German immigrant of the fourteenth century and expresses high regard for the beauty and flexibility of the Czech language. These German scholars, and others like them in the eighteenth century, were not advocates of a German-oriented *Landespatriotismus*, a vague geographical concept, but were anxious to revive the love of the Slavs for their traditions, now almost buried. They urged the German government to respect this glorious past and potentially glorious present and future and to promote its early realization. In the early stages of this renaissance, the services of these German scholars and publicists to the cause of the Czech revival cannot be exaggerated. Without their impetus, we can well doubt whether the nineteenth century would have seen the spiritual rebirth of a whole people take place so decisively.

Our study of the relations of Germans to Czechs will be continued in later chapters, but it may be well to review those relationships as we have tried to trace them until the end of the eighteenth century.

We are now presented with a total picture of two clear periods of German dominance, the first from about the middle of the twelfth century until the middle of the fourteenth century; the second from early in the seventeenth century until 1918; and two periods of Czech dominance: the first from the arrival of the first Slavic tribes at the end of the fifth century until the twelfth century, the second from the middle of the fourteenth century until the beginning of the sixteenth. We have called these respectively periods of German action and Czech action. One century unaccounted for in this rough and inadequate scheme, from the beginning of the sixteenth to the early part of the seventeenth century, we have called a period of interaction. Without oversimplifying a very complicated symbiosis, it is safe to say that this 1,500-year phenomenon is unparalleled in Western European history with respect to the persistence of the constituent elements. We would be oversimplifying in our analysis if we did not recognize the fact that our dates of demarcation, even qualified as approximate, are arbitrary and that a general picture of the whole land or of all classes of society at any given time would be almost impossible to present in clear colors. But in spite of these well-founded doubts and qualifications, it is submitted that, so far as such an analysis is possible, the divisions and terms we have used are sufficiently true to warrant us in seeing in Czech-German relationships through the centuries the unique story here presented. This very uniqueness has occasioned much speculation as to cause and ultimate tendencies.

Palacký, writing in the middle of the last century, saw the whole course of Czech history as a racio-religious struggle. But his great *Geschichte von Böhmen* stopped with the battle of Moháč in 1526. He could not have maintained his theory throughout the period of the Lutheran Reformation, which was, as we have seen, a time when most Czechs allied themselves gladly with the German Lutherans, and we are compelled to speak of German and Czech interaction.

Rudolf Wolkan, a Sudeten German literary historian, writing in 1925, held that when North German culture is high, that of the Sudeten Germans is also high, and Czech culture follows the Sudeten German. A parallel situation obtains, he found, when North German culture is low. This condition may be true at certain points of history, but it disregards Czech original contributions, of which there have been many—in religion, art, military science and in political consciousness.

Emanuel Rádl, a Czech social philosopher, writing in 1928, held that when German culture has been high, Czech culture has also been high, and conversely—a parallelism of development which was simultaneous, but not necessarily causally related. It must be remarked, in all justice to Professor Rádl, that history was not his forte, and Czech historians have been rather sharply critical of some of his historical arguments.

Konrad Bittner, a Sudeten German literary historian, writing in 1936, held that when German cultural vigor in Bohemia has been dominant, Czech has been proportionately low, and conversely. There are two objections to this explanation. In the first place it is too simple, particularly as he diagrams this course of cultural variation in his book, *Deutsche und Tschechen*. It is based solely on literary standards and literary expression among a very limited group—the patriciate. In the second place, his assumption of an oppositeness of cultural achievement is contrary to the findings of all the other historians. The mere fact that he is in a minority is no objection to his theory: it only emphasizes the fact that he has selected data more deliberately than sound historical science will allow. In other words, we must object to Bittner's assumptions on the ground that Czech cultural achievement is uniformly high when the German is high. Bittner's study has not thus far gone beyond the Hussite period. It is difficult to see how he can treat the Reformation period of interaction on this theory, or the seventeenth century, which all German historians recognize as a period of insignificant literary or cultural achievement. The Czechs then had nothing to offer, either. Both cultures were about as inactive and insipid as they could be.

None of these theories of the cultural relations of the Czechs and Germans can be said to be satisfactory. To be at all acceptable, each of them must choose a limited period or sphere of treatment within which the facts may fit the theory, and outside that narrow period or category exclude so much indisputable data as to be invalidated.

No substitute theory is here offered. It may well be doubted if there can ever be any simple solution or rationalization of this age-old problem which will satisfy all the conditions which history and human nature present. Both the German and the Slav have undergone change and development, and, because of conditions which they could not even partially control, the tempo of that development has varied from age to age. We would be treading very dangerous ground if we tried to find a parallelism where it may not exist. Yet there are some observations which may be made on a basis of our study, which leave to one side the question of right or wrong, of permanent ethnical or national characteristics, and attempt only to analyze the nature of their conflicts.

1. Whenever the Czech-German question has become acute, the precipitant has come from outside—either geographically, as Germany or Austria, or politically, as the Roman Catholic church, the Holy Roman Empire or the Hapsburg dynasty.

2. The early division into opposing camps was: the Czechs against the German newcomers—*alienigenae*, foreign born—and there have always been native-born Germans on the side of the Czechs, opposing the foreign-born newcomers. A later division, in the seventeenth and eighteenth centuries, was between the Czech liberals on the one hand, and, on the other, the reactionaries or the patriciate, who were, as it happened, both Czech and German. We cannot therefore find a division on purely national grounds that will hold for our whole period.

3. The Czechs have always recognized, implicitly or explicitly, that they were indebted to German civilization for mediating the culture of the West to them, and have not objected to this mediation as such, but they have insisted that they have a right to accept or reject this civilization in part or as a whole in their own way, and, if they do accept it, they have their own contributions to make.

4. There has been repeatedly a fundamental divergence between the two peoples in their respective concepts of the state. The Germans, perhaps because of their greater numbers, more mixed origins and their traditional lack of organic cohesion, have been moved to insist on an inclusive state, which would be a sort of super-state including variant peoples. The Czechs, fewer in number but more cohesive, have tended to demand that their separateness from the Germans be recognized. When this separateness has as a matter of fact been recognized, the Czechs have had no hesitation in co-operating as closely as the situations indicated with their more powerful neighbor.

5. The battlefield upon which the two peoples have contended would appear to have changed somewhat in the course of the centuries. At first the two peoples fought for commercial supremacy. The Germans who came into Bohemia in the twelfth and thirteenth centuries took over urban commerce with hardly any competition from the Czechs, to

115

whom town organization was as yet *terra incognita*. Later it became a religious and spiritual war, carried on by arms, yet in the name of religious freedom. On this battlefield, victory lay with the Hussite Czechs. Latterly the struggle shifted to the field of political theory: should the smaller people be ruled in a dynastic German state, or should they be their own rulers in a federation of autonomous states? This phase of the long struggle began toward the end of the eighteenth century and did not reach its conclusion until 1918. The winning weapons on this battlefield were pamphlet, poetry, and patience, wielded by their scholar-patriot leaders. In 1918 at least this engagement was won by the Czechs.

≺ 7 ≻

The Germans in Bohemia from
Maria Theresa to 1918

THE history of the Germans in the lands of the Bohemian crown for a century and a half preceding the end of the last World War is a curious mixture of confusion as to aims, indecision as to loyalty, and uncertainty as to their own position in the Hapsburg Empire.

The determination of both Maria Theresa and Joseph II to centralize the Empire had, at first sight, favored the Germans. Linguistically and culturally they were no longer in the minority, but could point with pride to the fact that the German language had replaced Latin in the universities as the language of lecture and dissertation and that no language but German was to be taught in the elementary schools. All public acts were published in German, all imperial and local officials were to conduct their official business in German. Careers in business and political life were open only to those whose German was beyond reproach. Czech had been relegated to the position of the despised speech of the peasant and the servant. One would have thought—and many Germans did think—that the superior political organization and culture of the Germanic people had finally and with complete justification won out over the West Slavic Czechs. The apparent acceptance by those who could expect to be regarded as the leaders of Czech nationalism—the nobility—of German customs, and the fact that they intermarried with north German and Austrian German noble families, seemed to indicate that the militant Czech nationalism of the period before the White Mountain was dead. The Czech bourgeoisie, by virtually abandoning Czech as their mother tongue, appeared to sanction the germanization of the nobility and indicate their own acceptance of the inevitable. The Germans in Bohemia and Moravia could afford to be almost benevolent in their attitude toward their fellow Bohemians whose names indicated that they were of Slavic extraction. Aside from the lower classes—and who paid any attention to them? —Bohemia was by now, to all intents and purposes, just another German province, and the Slavs of Bohemia could be, and almost were, regarded as adopted members of the great Germanic family with equal rights to its culture, its language and its civilizing mission in Europe.

This is a picture that is almost true. But the Germans in Bohemia of the last half of the eighteenth century who accepted this mirage of German cultural and racial conquest failed to evaluate properly certain complicating factors that made their apparent victory illusory. They were confused as to the vitality of the passion of the Czech populace for their own national life. This national Czech revival we shall discuss at length in subsequent chapters. The Bohemian Germans were furthermore confused by the circumstance that a large number of them were not of Austrian origin. No satisfactory statistical study of the place of origin of the German population in western and northern Bohemia seems to have been made. It is possible that the common feeling that the vast majority of those Germans who live, for example, in Bohemia just south of the Saxon border, originated in Saxony is an exaggeration. There persists among many of these people the tradition that their forebears came from Austria. No exact or even approximate proportion could be given, but any traveler in Sudeten areas of Bohemia in the post-war period would, from conversations with peasants and townsfolk, have to register the impression of this feeling. On the other hand, there is no doubt at all that a majority of the Germans who migrated into northern and western Bohemia in the seventeenth and eighteenth centuries came from contiguous or nearly contiguous provinces of northern Germany, Bavaria, Thuringia, Hanover, Saxony and German Silesia. But the great majority of the total German population of Bohemia and Moravia and Austrian Silesia were, by ca. 1750, of stock long settled in the land. The line of language demarcation between Czech and German had markedly encroached upon territory formerly purely or mostly Czech, as a comparison between two linguistic maps representing the conditions in 1600 and 1775 would immediately show.

By reason, on the one hand, of a great increase in their numbers stemming mostly from immigration from northern and western Germany, and, on the other, of the political and social position they enjoyed as members of the ruling people, the Germans in Bohemia were strongly entrenched in business, education, the church and official life. Yet in spite of this predominance, their position was vulnerable from several points of view. The fact that the regions which were exclusively or almost exclusively German in population did not then, any more than in our own times, constitute a solid geographical unit contiguous to German Austria upon which it was politically dependent, was an element of weakness. A German living in Gablonz, Leitmeritz or Reichenberg would have to pass through several hundred miles of purely Czech territory to get to Vienna. Even to travel no farther than to Budweis or Eger, his most convenient route would take him through a hundred miles or more of Czech Bohemia. Almost the whole German population of Bohemia lived in a narrow tangential, hook-shaped strip of mountain and foothill country attached to German Austria at the southwestern end. Their social and cultural connection with Austria was therefore tenuous.

A second weakness in the position of the Bohemian Germans, obviously related to the first, was the fact that the flow of immigration into Bohemia from Germany was from so many different parts of a Germany which was still strongly separatist that no community of feeling between a family emigrated from Hanover and a neighboring family emigrated from Bavaria could spring naturally into being. When we add to this diversity of origin the geographical fact that there might be hundreds of miles between two Bohemian-German centers in one direction, and only a few miles in another direction between a Bohemian-German center and Saxony on the north and Czech Bohemia on the south, the trying situation of the Bohemian Germans becomes more evident. The unfortunate consequences of these weaknesses are to become more manifest in the early years of the nineteenth century, when there comes a certain awakening of Bohemian-German feeling paralleling the rise of Czech nationalism. The Germans found it almost impossible to develop a common Bohemian-German nationalism in the face of the adverse factors of geography and origin. The two conditioning factors of cultural and racial connection with Germany on one side and proximity to and political and economic association with the Slav Czechs on the other have had a uniquely determinative effect upon the political and spiritual development of the Sudeten Germans.[1]

It would be natural for us to assume, other things being equal and favorable, that such a situation would have tended to enrich the culture of the Sudeten Germans, so placed as to be able to choose the best from both German and Slav. Yet we find, for the most part, that the opposite was the case. The Sudeten Germans were unable to discover any real cultural or social thesis to which their whole group

[1] The term "Sudeten" is of course somewhat anachronistic here. It does not come into common use until about 1910, though the historian Bachmann uses it as early as 1904. It is, however, a useful designation for the Germans living in Bohemia, Moravia and Austrian Silesia and is used here purely for convenience.

could subscribe, for the very reasons of diversity of origin and geographical position already mentioned.

It will be illuminating to see how these adverse factors influenced the cultural and political development of the Sudeten Germans in the period before 1848. We shall find that the progress of the Sudeten Germans toward a consciousness of their unique place in an Austria-dominated Germany and Pan-Germany will exercise a controlling influence upon their relationship to the Czechs in Bohemia. In proportion as they are unable to agree among themselves as to their future they will be unable to offer effective resistance to the advance of Czech nationalism. We will be able to decide whether, while the Czechs were growing in national consciousness, in concreteness and coherence in aims, in social prestige and in economic and political power, the Sudeten Germans were making corresponding gains, or losing in these same respects.

The Age of the Enlightenment was in many ways an international movement. As this brilliant age came to its close, the Romantic spirit took possession of the hearts and imaginations of men. Developing Romanticism made a powerful appeal to feelings of national pride and tradition. Herder's (d. 1786) exhortations to the various peoples to revert to their traditional nationalisms evoked an avid response. While he encouraged the Slavs to claim their glorious past, he also fed the flickering flames of German nationalism. Klopstock, Lessing and Gottsched produced literary masterpieces that revived German pride. Kant was a name to conjure with in all Europe. The hegemony that French language, French manners, and French culture had won during the seventeenth and early eighteenth centuries could now be successfully challenged. Toward the end of the eighteenth century Germans everywhere began to feel that the German language, German philosophy, and German culture should now command the respect of the whole civilized world.

The Sudeten Germans felt this glorious enthusiasm to the full. The sons of the bourgeois of means traveled and studied at the universities of Erlangen, Jena, Halle, Tübingen, Leipzig, and Bonn. This thirst for learning was real, but if we examine the cultural situation among the Sudeten Germans around the turn of the century, before the advent of the Metternich régime, we will be disappointed at the low quality of literary production. It was imitative and stilted and in no way manifested the existence of a vigorous native culture at all worthy of the name. The literary and scientific leaders among them recognized that there was a serious lack of background and common cultural tradition. They felt that the remedy was more and better education on a broader base in the Sudetenlands. After Rousseau, an aristocratic philosophy of education would have been difficult to maintain. Their very eagerness to take advantage of the superior education in the famous universities of Germany deprived them of the opportunity to foster whatever native culture there was. Romanticism fostered the preservation and cultivation of local customs and traditions. It was then only consonant with the ruling thought of the time that the Sudeten Germans should come to regard the culture of their own region as eminently worth emphasizing. This was the tendency at the beginning of the century, but it was not destined to weather the storms of the Napoleonic era.

In the early years of the nineteenth century the armies of Napoleon won victory after victory over German arms. Defeat and humiliation formed a common bond, uniting all Germans in hatred of a non-German conqueror. War against Napoleon became a common German effort. The Sudeten Germans shared the passionate nationalism, an enthusiasm for everything German, of Fichte, Jahn, and

Arndt. In their thought Austria became more German than ever before, and they were persuaded that it was only right and proper that the Germans in the Austrian Empire should undertake as a heaven-decreed mission the task of evangelizing the non-Germans in the Empire, and convincing them of the superiority of German culture. The importance of the Austrian Emperor as the leader in realizing this scheme of a Greater Germany was only too obvious. The Sudeten Germans were active in the Wars of Liberation. Whole regiments of Sudeten Germans fought enthusiastically and courageously at Austerlitz, Jena, Wagram and Leipzig, and after the victory of the Allies at Waterloo, many of the younger leaders of German Bohemia looked forward hopefully to the fulfilment of their dreams of a Greater Germany, united in tongue, in blood and in spirit.

But the Congress of Vienna sanctified the victory of extreme conservatism, and the *status quo* became throughout Europe an article of faith for all rulers and peoples. Metternich wanted no disturbing liberal movements which would reach beyond the boundaries of the Empire to gain support in northern Germany. It was therefore both reasonable and consistent, though it may have seemed irritating and annoying to the Sudeten Germans, that Metternich was more severe upon nationalistic movements among Germans in the Empire than upon similar movements among non-Germans. The non-Germans were so divided and heterogeneous that they could find no substantial support outside the Empire, whereas the Germans could look north and west to an area of their own language and blood more populous than the Austrian Empire itself. Strict German nationalism could only mean the formation of a German state so large that Austria would be a minority member and could not hope to control it, indeed might even lose what autonomy she had. On the other hand, national aspirations of the various Slav groups could, because they were relatively small and inimical to each other, be accommodated within the larger framework of the Hapsburg monarchy. The Czechs could quite well and consistently work for autonomy for themselves within the Austrian Empire, since they all lived within its borders; but the Sudeten Germans, in working for a Greater Germany, could not avoid seeing that the great majority of Germans lived outside Austria and Bohemia and would, in any combination of states or peoples making up a Greater Germany, dominate the Austrian and Sudeten Germans. Metternich could not permit such disruptive ideas to circulate freely.

Then, his absolutist régime had raised up against itself a second enemy. The political connotation of the ideas of liberty, equality and fraternity, spread over Europe by the French Revolution, was, at the very least, a vital liberalism. The political connotation of literary and philosophical Romanticism was individualism. The two can easily merge into one under the oppressive rule of an intransigent and reactionary government. By his very determination to keep things as they were Metternich solidified the opposition to him, particularly among the Sudeten Germans who had been exposed to the nationalistic, Romantic and liberal thought of a Germany just beginning to be aware of its potential unity through the ordeal of wars of liberation against a foreign aggressor. There grew up throughout the Sudeten lands, in the high schools and at the universities in Prague and Olomouc, student associations—*Burschenschaften*—which harbored national and liberal ideals. Though encouraged by a few of the professors, some concealment of the real nature of the *Burschenschaften* was necessary in the face of the avowed intention of the Metternich régime to suppress all such dangerous societies agitating against the established Austrian absolutism. The actual suppression, carried out by the military and the efficient bureaucracy, was indeed so effective that great numbers of young Sudeten

nationalists fled across the border to Leipzig in Saxony—
or, strange as it may seem, to Vienna—for safety. These two
cities became in reality centers of Sudeten German action.

In the early stages of this growth of national Sudeten
consciousness there was no little co-operation between nationalist Czechs and nationalist Sudeten Germans. They
had a common grievance in that the ancient kingdom of
Bohemia had lost its autonomy. Repeatedly during the
'forties the Bohemian Diet, consisting of both German and
Czech nobility and bourgeoisie, claimed the right to refuse
the demands for taxation made by the Vienna court. A loyalty to the land of Bohemia—*Landespatriotismus*—was
shared by Czech and Sudeten German alike. But, though
they owed much to the liberals among the Sudeten Germans, the Czechs realized, sooner perhaps than the Sudetens, that the logic of their history did not lead them into a
union with an all-German Germany, but that they might
logically hope for a large measure of autonomy within a
polyglot empire in the Danube basin in which they would
not be so grossly outnumbered. The Sudeten Germans, on
the other hand, were alarmed at the nationalistic claims
which the Czech leaders, Palacký and others, were making,
and feared the loss of the position of cultural and political
superiority which they had gained through the centralizing
work of the previous century. Thus the Czechs and the
Sudeten Germans parted company in the 'twenties and
'thirties of the nineteenth century, and later efforts from
both sides to bring them together in a common cause against
the Hapsburg absolutism were doomed to failure.

This separation of Czech and German was apparent in
the field of historical writing. Palacký, the historiographer
of the Kingdom of Bohemia, began to publish his *Geschichte von Böhmen* in 1836. It was immediately clear that
this great work was to be a history of the Czechs in Bohemia.
J. L. Knoll, a Sudeten German professor of history at the

University of Olomouc, feeling keenly that Palacký had been unjust to the contributions of Germans to the glorious history of the kingdom, entered into a polemic with him that showed how far apart scholars could be in interpretation and proportion while treating the same historical facts. Knoll made the Sudeten Germans more conscious of their own history, and to that extent was an important factor in consolidating Sudeten nationalism.

It cannot be said, however, that the cause of the Sudeten Germans was blessed with inspired leadership from its men of letters. Karl Egon Ebert (d. 1882), perhaps the ablest Bohemian German lyric poet, was strongly influenced in his youth by Goethe, but he had no real understanding of the significance of the struggles of 1848. His lively interest in the past glories of Bohemian history was romantic and nostalgic, but in no sense nationalistic or strictly German. The close friends, Moritz Hartmann (d. 1885) and Alfred Meissner (d. 1885), began their careers by celebrating Bohemia's glorious past in poetry of better than average competence, but they both became active and vocal Sudeten nationalists in 1848. At that time Hartmann wrote to Meissner: "My dear friend, the time has come for us to take our stand in Bohemia as Germans. That will be our position henceforth. It is our duty and at the same time our glory." Meissner's real forte was the drama, and, profiting by wide travel and familiarity with English and French literature, he brought new ideas of social change and a more realistic approach to civic morality to the rather provincial Germans of Bohemia. Bernhard Bolzano (d. 1848), professor of the philosophy of religion in Prague, and at the same time a mathematician of note, was the only one of the professors who had any influence among the younger German intellectuals. He advocated openly a revived independent Bohemia, in which Czechs and Germans would work together in friendship and understanding for the common good of the whole kingdom. But his voice was stilled by charges of heresy brought by the Jesuits. He was removed from his chair at the university and his influence ceased to be felt.

Most of the leading German intellectuals left Bohemia for many years at a time, and the Sudeten Germans were deprived of any consolation or pride which they might have had in their accomplishments by the realization that much of their excellence was due to their travel and acquaintance with literary lights in Germany. Taken by and large, it must be said that the Germans in Bohemia could not boast, at least in the critical period before 1848, of any high political or intellectual leadership.

In political matters they were handicapped by a threefold confusion as to aims. Should they support the Pan-German nationalism of north German liberals? Should they cast in their lot with the Czechs, build anew a closely knit Kingdom of Bohemia and recapture a proud past? Should they give their loyalty to an inclusive Hapsburg Empire in which they would be in a numerical minority but yet part of the ruling group? The Sudeten Germans were unable to come to any decision which would have represented a majority will in the years before 1848. Their indecision can be said to have cost them the social and political advantages they had gained in the preceding century.

Their intellectual leadership was affected by their indecision in the realm of political allegiance, but it was further weakened by the censorship which stifled all originality of thought and forced the liberal youth to leave the land and go to Saxony, Bavaria or Vienna. Those that remained were either already without initiative and therefore of little consequence, or were soon obliged to be contented with the dullness of a pleasant if stuffy and fatuous Victorianism, for which the Austrian term is *das Biedermeier*. The performance of Goethe's *Faust* and of Kleist's *Zerbrochener Krug* was forbidden in 1831, and that of Schiller's *Räuber* in 1833. Lessing's *Nathan der Weise* was drastically censored before permission to show it was granted. The censor took the liberty of improving many lines in Shakespeare's *Romeo and Juliet* which he found to be wanting in dramatic excellence. It was not only the theater which was so carefully protected from its own shortcomings. Books, newspapers and all scientific production had to be submitted to the judgment and correction of the omniscient censor. The government seemed determined, even at tremendous cost to itself, to shield the Austrian and Bohemian mind from the vicious onslaught of liberal ideas. In some ways the censorship was more severe upon the Germans in Bohemia than upon the Czechs. At the same time it should be remarked that the Germans had more cultural outlets—education, the press and the theater—than the Czechs, and the censorship seemed and indeed was, for that reason, more irritating. The Czechs had fewer means of expression to be censored.

But it was not only in political and cultural matters that the Germans as well as the Czechs suffered under the Metternich régime. The economy of the Empire labored under a twofold handicap. On the one hand the protracted effects of the exhaustion of the Napoleonic wars made recovery slow. On the other, the government took a completely paternalistic attitude. No independence was left to any official, and men of ability were unwilling to enter such a stultifying service. As far as the government was concerned, anything new was anathema, not only in official techniques, but also in industry and commerce. As a consequence, Austria was one of the most backward states in the economic structure of Europe. It was not until 1848 that there were any visible signs in Austria that the world had gone through an economic revolution two generations before. On the land the antiquated system of feudalism was still in vigor, largely because the governing authorities were incapable of understanding how any society could function if the farmers were to be allowed to own their own land and the government could not use the feudal lords as cogs in the administrative scheme.

But the greatest tension grew out of the increasing ethnical consciousness of the national groups in the Empire. The hope that it might be possible to create a united state with at least some show of being German—a hope which had been general at the end of the Napoleonic period—had gone with the wind. In the revolutionary era, and during the long wars with France, political boundaries between European states had undergone radical changes, and much of their sacrosanct character was gone, never to be brought back again. At the Congress of Vienna, Europe had been subjected to some expert carving, and the peoples concerned were neither urged nor permitted to express their preferences. Reaction ruled the councils of Europe, and reaction has never been sensitive to underlying currents of popular feeling. It never occurred to Metternich that changes in the boundary lines between states or provinces within states might interest anyone save the ruler of the state and the small circle of his advisers. But in 1848 his régime collapsed at the first determined impact of the popular movement. All his patient efforts to unite the divergent national groups around the Hapsburg dynasty and to foster among them Austrian patriotism and a sense of loyalty to a single unified state were completely in vain. In 1848 the great problem still remained, how the separate nationalities might be satisfied and at the same time how their national aspirations might be reconciled with the inevitable needs of the whole Austrian state. If we add the positive annoyances in their cultural, political, and economic life, to the failures of the Metternich régime to deal satisfactorily with the broader problems of nationalism inherent in the makeup of the

Empire it is not difficult to understand the enthusiasm with which all shades of Sudeten German opinion greeted the events of the early months of 1848. This seemed to be the chance they had long been waiting and praying for.

The significance of the revolutionary movements of 1848 is, as a general rule, inadequately appreciated in western Europe. It was a veritable epidemic which, after the outbreak of disorders in Paris in February, spread immediately to Central Europe and within a very short time effected far-reaching changes in political and social life. The liberals among the German bourgeoisie were convinced that the time had come for consultations concerning the union of the almost numberless petty states of Germany into one great national Reich. Events seemed to confirm the hopes aroused by the nationalistic movement in Hungary, led since 1840 by the eloquent Louis Kossuth. The February revolution in Paris appeared to signal the downfall of repressive reaction everywhere in Europe, and it was inevitable that the long pent-up storm in the Hapsburg lands should soon break. On March 13, 1848, Metternich's rule came to an end. Two days later, public notices were posted bearing the signature of the young Emperor Francis Joseph I, promising a liberal constitution for the Empire. There was universal if uncritical rejoicing. Blasts of oratory, fervid and long, proclaimed the dawn of a new day for all—Germans, Czechs, Magyars, Poles, Ruthenes, South Slavs and Italians. Demands for separate and independent national states deluged the imperial councillors. But, particularly for the Germans, disillusionment was hastened by over-expectancy. The uncomfortable realities of readjustment, with loss of long-enjoyed prestige for the Germans, and ebullient enthusiasm, eagerness to exercise a newly won power, on the side of the Czechs, showed that the two peoples in Bohemia entertained conflicting aspirations. The next sixty-five years were not destined to find any compromise formula whereby these aspirations might be reconciled. Therein lies, for this land, much of the tragedy of the pre-war period.

For the Sudeten Germans complications multiplied. Political liberalism implied government by representation—heads would henceforth be counted, not weighed. The Sudeten Germans can be forgiven for fearing that the reorganization of the Hapsburg monarchy along federal and democratic lines would mean their subjection to the rule of a Slavic majority. The Vienna government made no secret of its opposition to the aspirations of the Sudeten Germans to join in the formation of a *Grossdeutschland* which would mean the end of the Hapsburg monarchy. Successive ministers, therefore, as the lesser of two evils, encouraged the Czechs in their plans for the virtual reconstitution of the lands of the Bohemian crown in a reorganized Danubian Hapsburg state along federal lines. We are thus confronted with the anomaly of a German government opposed to the wishes of the majority of its German population, and favoring the hopes of its several Slavic minorities.

The Germans—hitherto socially, politically and economically dominant in the Bohemian crown lands—could not be expected to welcome complacently relegation to a subordinate position, and when the invitation came to participate in the Pan-German Parliament at Frankfort, they eagerly accepted. Amidst feverish Pan-Slavic agitation, when a great Slavic federation was being seriously suggested, the Sudeten Germans felt that they could be safe only if there were a great and united Germany to defend their interests. When time came for the elections to the Frankfort Parliament, it was significant that, whereas 25 out of 28 electoral districts in Moravia chose delegates, only 18 out of the 68 districts in Bohemia held any election. The Czech districts simply ignored the call for an election. This proportion, 18 out of 68, nearly represents the proportion of German electoral districts in the whole of Bohemia.

The high hopes raised by the Frankfort Parliament for the formation of a Greater Germany on a foundation of social and political liberalism were completely disappointed. Indeed liberalism as a political and social gospel suffered much among the Sudeten Germans from the ill-conceived and premature assemblage that finally met at Frankfort. As might have been expected, the pendulum of reaction went even to the other extreme, and the complete restoration of political absolutism in the Empire by the Hapsburg ministers Schwarzenberg (d. 1851) and Bach (to 1859) was amazingly easy.

The period of the Bach reaction was as great a blow to Sudeten hopes for a national state as it was to the Czechs. The latter were sufficiently numerous and by now strong enough to be able to wait for the pendulum to swing back. The Germans, in the position of a minority people, felt that time was against them. But, against the shattered hopes and the bitter sense of frustration which they felt from 1849 on, two considerable gains should be counted. Hans Kudlich, a Sudeten German from near Jägerndorf in Silesia, pushed through the Reichstag of 1848-1849 in Vienna a law giving the peasant in the Empire political rights. This was an indubitably tangible victory for liberalism, and remained, after the smoke of battle had cleared away, the most important single act of the whole revolutionary movement of 1848 in the Hapsburg monarchy. At about the same time there was formed in Vienna a league of Germans in Bohemia, Moravia and Silesia for the protection of their nationality (*Verein der Deutschen in Böhmen, Mähren und Schlesien zum Schutze ihrer Nationalität*). This was the first real evidence that there was any common national consciousness among the people of German blood living in the three lands of the Bohemian crown. The ancient boundaries between these three lands now for the first time began to lose their separative and insulating aspects. This *Verein* had great influence in the Reichstag of 1848-1849 for the simple reason that it offered a consistent and coherent program. Germans from the crown lands had heretofore presented no united front, and had consequently been dismissed as politically inconsequential. Now the project of a radical redivision of the three crown lands as well as of Austria according to nationalities, disregarding the ancient boundaries of the Bohemian crown, was bruited about. It remained only a project, but the fact that it was seriously considered was of great significance.

Sudeten nationalism can thus be said to have been born at about the same time that Pan-Germanism in the Sudetenland passed to its reward. The Frankfort fiasco was the cause of its death. Nor is it inaccurate to suggest that these two facts should be juxtaposed as contributing to a general and more comprehensive consolidation of the national spirit of Sudeten Germans of all classes. Under modern conditions certainly no national movement can hope to achieve ultimate success without the support of the less favored and more numerous economic groups. A free peasantry, fortified in its patriotism by political privileges, is a powerful ally to any national movement. A small book appeared in 1851 which signified further the maturing of the Sudeten national consciousness. Anton Schmalfuss, a minor participant in the events of 1848-1849, published the first serious general study of the Sudeten Germans under the title: *Die Deutschen in Böhmen: Geschildert in geographischer-statistischer, staatswirtschaftlicher, volkstümlicher und geschichtlicher Beziehung*. It was far from being a rival of Palacký's great work for the Czechs, but it was significant as a pioneer effort, destined, during and after the Hapsburg reaction, to remain the only essay of its kind for almost two decades. In 1862 a further sign of the fact that the Sudeten

Germans recognized their national character was the foundation of the *Verein für Geschichte der Deutschen in Böhmen*. The journal of this society first appeared in 1862 and has continued to appear in various forms until the present. It is a mine of information concerning the history, archeology, society and literature of the Germans living in Bohemia. There was a certain amount of defensive reaction in the increased tempo of Sudeten German cultural activity. Czech social, economic and cultural growth during the first part of the century had been so great as to create a demand among the Germans for measures calculated to match the development of their fellow Bohemians. They had only to consider the far-reaching effect upon Czech national consciousness of Palacký's historical work to realize how much a similar scientific enterprise might mean for their own German nationalism.

The Hapsburg reaction, ably supported by the military, bore almost as severely upon the Germans as upon the Czechs. It was, if possible, more odious and irritating to them by reason of its complete surrender to Roman Catholic direction. Along the borders of Saxony, Protestant connections had been maintained more effectively than elsewhere in Bohemia. Bach is reported as having said to an intimate: "The only sound internal policy for Austria is one which is favorable to Catholicism. The monarchy has really only two solid bases for its unity: the dynasty and religion." The public educational system was once again placed in the hands of the Catholic hierarchy. Public opinion throughout Austria and particularly in the regions bordering on Germany was soon exasperated by an aggressive clericalism. Many of the Sudeten leaders fled to Saxony and neighboring centers where the air was freer. From some points of view it is fair to say that the Sudeten Germans were treated with less consideration by the Vienna reactionaries than were the Czechs. At least most of them felt that their future, as a German minority in a polyglot empire, was one of despair. A Concordat was negotiated in 1855 between the Empire and the Vatican. It freed the upper clergy from any control by the state, increased the powers of ecclesiastical courts, and put education in the hands of the clergy, which meant the Jesuits. The opposition to this reactionary measure was as sharp and determined among the Sudeten Germans as among the Czechs.

From appearances the absolutist ministers of Francis Joseph had every reason to congratulate themselves on complete success. But they were too confident. Within a short time Lombardy was lost (1859), Austria suffered a diplomatic defeat in the Danish War (1864) and was completely humiliated in the short war with Prussia in 1866. The reactionaries at court were consequently discredited, and liberalism was again in the saddle. Hopes revived throughout the Empire that the work begun in 1848 and so quickly and disappointingly halted might now be taken up again and carried to a successful conclusion. The feeling of relief and hope was especially lively in the Sudeten regions. The Prussian troops, passing through these lands in 1866 on their way to fight Austrian troops, had been welcomed with unfeigned joy by the Sudeten Germans, who cast longing looks toward a Germany which promised union for their whole race. But the treaty of peace concluded by the Hapsburgs on Bismarck's terms had excluded Austria from the northern Germany (*der deutsche Bund*) which the apostle of Blood and Iron was welding into an empire to be ruled by Prussia. Henceforth the only political outlet for Sudeten Germans was participation in the Vienna government. As liberals, this was possible for them, and important members of the Auersperg ministry of 1867 were Germans from Bohemia and Moravia. Yet even under these more favorable circumstances one may distinguish two well-defined groups among the Germans of Bohemia. In one group were those who still thought in terms of *Grossdeutschtum*, that is an organic union of German Austria and particularly the Sudeten lands with the growing empire to the north. The other group was made up of those who would have preferred to preserve a Danubian Hapsburg polyglot state in which the Germanic groups would continue to maintain their political and social hegemony. This second group was commonly referred to as *kleindeutsch*.

One very important consequence of the series of defeats suffered by the reactionary ministries of the 'fifties and early 'sixties was the granting of autonomy to the Magyars in 1867 by the so-called *Ausgleich* or Compromise. This was a victory for the Magyars, but other national groups in the Empire were dismayed by the implications of the agreement, for, by the terms of this arrangement, Slavs (Slovaks in this case) in considerable numbers were given over to the not very tender mercies of the Magyars. The Slovaks could no longer count on the protection of the Vienna government against Magyar oppression. This concern on the part of other small national groups gave rise to demands for guarantees against further surrenders of a similar nature which might subject a smaller national group to a larger. The Sudeten Germans were particularly fearful lest they be forced to submit to the rule of the Czechs in Bohemia and Moravia. The new law of the Empire, the December (1867) Constitution, made many concessions to liberal demands, providing for freedom of religion and the press and increasing the power of the several Diets. Though at this time the Germans had representation in the Bohemian and Moravian Diets which was larger than their population warranted, they had reason to fear that the Czechs would demand and perhaps gain an even more predominant place in the crown lands than they already occupied. All kinds of proposals for compromise and settlement of the imminent dispute were made, in the press and through legislative channels, from about 1870 until early in the next century. In 1871 the Fundamental Articles were proclaimed by the Hohenwart ministry. The Czech language was given parity with German in courts and public administration of Bohemia and Moravia. To the Germans this seemed an unbearable indignity to their tongue, and a riot of Germans at Teplice convinced the ministry that it had made a serious mistake. The Articles were withdrawn, and the Germans breathed easier for some years.

But there were those among the Sudeten leaders who realized that their position was intrinsically weak and becoming weaker. Their own lower classes, the fourth estate of farmer and laborer, were clamoring for more political and economic representation. Marxism was spreading among them, and a spirit of international class consciousness would certainly run counter to the clear-cut and aggressive nationalism which the Sudeten German leaders felt would be their only salvation. These leaders redoubled their efforts in the 'seventies and 'eighties to foster in these classes a united Sudeten national consciousness by the formation of national labor unions (*Deutschnationale Arbeitervereine*). Aided by encouragement from the German leaders in Austria, this homoeopathic treatment of Sudeten labor was partially successful, and in 1904 labor became a political factor under the name of the German National Labor Party (*Deutsche Nationalarbeiterpartei*).[2] To a people who had for several generations been accustomed to confusion as to aims and split loyalties of all sorts, it was reassuring to see visible evidence that it was possible for socialism and nationalism not only to co-exist but even to work together effectively.

[2] In 1918 the name was changed to German National Socialistic Labor Party—*Deutsche Nazionalsocialistische Arbeiterpartei*—later to be known briefly as Nazis. A considerable change in tenets and program has taken place in more recent years.

In 1882, after years of agitation by Czech leaders, the ancient University of Prague, the oldest in Central Europe, was divided into two autonomous corporations, a German and a Czech. Because of the fact that before this division a considerable number of the professors had been Czechs who lectured in German, from some points of view the change was a gain for the Germans to have their own university whose professorate and student body were now more homogeneous than before. Yet some felt that the Czechs gained more than the Germans by the new arrangement, as they now had an organ by which they could challenge German social and intellectual dominance.

Throughout this whole period the ancient divisions in loyalty persisted among the German bourgeoisie and intellectuals. Some saw in Bismarck the essence of German destiny and, though not openly, looked to the Reich for inspiration and guidance. Their sons went to the universities of Jena, Halle, Leipzig, Dresden or Berlin, and made commercial connections with Reich industry and business. Others went into professional pursuits and identified themselves completely with their new fatherland. The professorate and the students were in general sympathetic to this program. On the other hand there were others who, openly and sincerely, proclaimed their belief in the future of the Austrian monarchy, sent their sons to Vienna and offered unquestioning allegiance to the Hapsburg court. Inevitably there were still others who wanted to effect some sort of compromise formula before it was too late; before the Czechs who, by contrast with the Sudeten Germans, were united, aggressive and growing in numbers and power, should push the Germans out of all positions of power and influence in economic and political life. But the voices of these prophets pleading for rapprochement and understanding seemed to cry in the wilderness.

It has just been suggested that the Germans were facing

the possibility that the Czechs were growing in power and numbers so rapidly as to threaten what qualitative predominance the Germans felt they rightfully enjoyed. A few typical statistics may make more clear the problem of population late in the nineteenth and early in the twentieth century. In Budějovice (Budweis) in southern Bohemia the German population increased between 1880 and 1910 only from 17,774 to 23,584, while the Czech population more than doubled in the same period, from 24,810 to 50,909. In Prague itself the German population decreased between 1900 and 1910 from 20,272 to 18,753, whereas the Czech population increased from 178,123 to 202,067 in the same period. Prague was fast becoming the capital of western Slavdom. As to the language of ordinary use, the *Umgangssprache*, the statistics show that the use of German decreased from 1880 to 1910. In 1880 37.17 per cent of the population used German, in 1910 only 36.76 per cent. In the same period the use of Czech increased from 62.79 per cent of the population to 63.19 per cent. The seriousness of this loss is made more manifest if it is remarked that the German districts lost less by emigration than the Czech. A Czech laborer moving into a German district would have to use German; more Czechs moved, and obviously more Czechs would be forced to use German than Germans obliged to use Czech. Yet in spite of this the Czech language gained on German. During the thirty years for which figures have been given, Czech laborers took over almost completely some industrial regions like Tschausch (Souš), and greatly increased the population in other industrial centers like Brüx (Most). Sudeten leaders fostered the formation of *Schulvereine,* which founded and maintained German schools in districts where the German population would not justify the expense. But in spite of the devoted and generally effective activity of these organizations the figures for the pupils in the German public schools show a steady proportional diminution in the late nineteenth and early twentieth centuries. In a few districts however, like Reichenberg, the Germans more than held their own in the thirty years we have used, but this was the exception and not the rule. In Moravia the gains of the Slav population were more considerable than in Bohemia, particularly in the larger towns like Iglau (Jihlava), Kroměříž (Kremsier) and Olomouc. There was a certain gallant desperation in the efforts of the German leaders to fortify and maintain their cultural and economic hegemony.

A multiplicity of political parties was the fashion in the late nineteenth century. It was a predictable product of political liberalism. This tendency to division became almost an epidemic among the Germans of Bohemia and Moravia in the 1890's and the early years of the twentieth century. But it was a particularly unfortunate tendency for the Sudeten Germans, as it accentuated the already deep-rooted division between *Kleindeutschtum* or Austro-Germanism and *Grossdeutschtum* or Reich Germanism, and multiplied this division many times over by the introduction of new social, economic and—regrettably—personal issues. Party loyalty assumed more importance than national consciousness, and the Sudeten cause as a whole was thus immeasurably weakened.

Yet in spite of all discouragements, efforts to bring the Germans in the Sudetenlands together on some workable basis persisted. Some of their leaders blessed with vision pointed out that unless they united they would be completely submerged by the growing and vigorous Czech nationalism which was threatening German dominance in commerce, industry and society, realms in which the Germans, in spite of their lesser numbers, had remained supreme throughout the nineteenth century. In 1903 Dr. Titta, who had been an active German nationalist at Trebnitz, northwest of Prague, since 1889, formed the German

People's Council in Bohemia (*Deutsche Volksrat in Böhmen*). It was intended to be above parties and classes, to embody the cultural, economic and political aims of all Germans in Bohemia. Titta hoped to minimize local, party and personal differences which had hitherto vitiated all efforts to elaborate a common Sudeten German program. But his hopes were far beyond his accomplishments. Misunderstandings, personal animosities and rivalries lay too deep to be composed by the proclamation of a formula, however finely conceived. Yet his project did have some definite and favorable results. It focused the attention of Germans throughout the Empire upon the need for a clear and unified program and common action. The wide geographical distribution of Germans in the lands of the Bohemian crown had always made union of any sort impracticable. Almost immediately after Titta's initiative similar centralizing organizations were founded in Moravia and Silesia. But it was not until some years after Titta's Council had begun to gain general support among the Germans that the broader denomination *Sudetendeutsch*, comprising all the Germans in Bohemia, Moravia and Silesia, displaced the more restrictive terms *Deutschböhmer, Deutschmährer* and *Deutschschlesier*. A common and inclusive name indicated the recognition of common problems and a common destiny, and was inseparable from common aims and cooperative action.

Around the turn of the century extremists among the Czechs as well as among the Germans made any compromise arrangement as to political representation almost impossible. The radical Czechs demanded proportional representation in the Reichsrat and in local and provincial government. The Germans, noticing that they were falling behind in the race for population, wanted guarantees of their political position which would fix permanently their representation at a point indicative of what they regarded as their proper importance in Bohemia and Moravia. Efforts toward a compromise solution in Bohemia almost achieved success in 1890, only to fail on matters of detail. But in 1905 a workable compromise was achieved in Moravia. The Czechs made up about 72 per cent of the population of Moravia, the Germans a little over 27 per cent. By the terms of the compromise the Germans were to have the same number of representatives as the Czechs (20) in the *curia* of the towns; in the rural *curia*, where the Czechs had 39 representatives, the Germans were to have 14; and in the general *curia* the Germans were to have 6 to the Czech 14 votes. These arrangements were incorporated into the electoral law of 1907, which gave the franchise to every man in the Austrian monarchy of twenty-four years of age and over. The liberal von Beck endeavored to introduce into Bohemia a compromise similar to that accepted in Moravia, and might have succeeded had not general opposition to the annexation of Bosnia-Herzegovina in 1908 on the part of Slavs throughout the Empire driven his ministry from office.

By 1909, as a result of the decades of disastrous tension and uncertainty concerning the relative position of Germans and Czechs in Bohemia, the conviction was accepted in all quarters—Czech, Sudeten German and Austrian—that the monarchy could have no consistent foreign policy unless its most pressing internal question was solved. The Sudeten German deputies presented to the new minister, von Bienerth, in November 1908, a memorandum in which they said: "Any ministry must make the solution of the national question in Bohemia its first task." Many efforts followed. Count Thun worked almost all of 1911 to reach some acceptable compromise, but in vain. Both sides broke off negotiations. In 1913 the government dissolved the Bohemian Diet on the ground that it was doing nothing but squabble. In January 1914 negotiations were initiated again only to be broken off late in February because the German delegates could not agree among themselves. But there was still agreement among all parties that some solution was absolutely imperative, and a committee consisting of representatives of both the Czechs and the Sudeten Germans was appointed in June 1914. It was to hold its sessions in Vienna with the government acting as mediator when necessary. This was the plan, and great expectations for its success were held.

But this committee, which to many seemed the most hopeful development yet envisaged, never met. The Archduke Francis Ferdinand was assassinated in Serajevo on June 28, and the war came in the wake of a single act of violence. By irresolution, procrastination and inept political action, the Hapsburg monarchy entered a four-year war which was to spell its extinction with its most important internal question not only unsolved, but still actively irritating. The Sudeten Germans were loyal to the monarchy, and paid for their loyalty with a greater proportionate loss on the field of battle than other parts of the Empire, and indeed than the German Empire itself. The figures of war losses tell an eloquent story. In the German sections of Bohemia the losses were: 34.5 per thousand of population; in Austria 27.7 per thousand; in the whole German Empire, 27.8 per thousand. Naturally the respective roles of Czech and German during most of the war from 1914 to 1918 were a reversal of the situation in the years immediately preceding the outbreak of hostilities. Previous to the war the Germans had been on the defensive, outvoted in their own lands by aggressive Czechs. But during the war the Czechs, unwilling to support the war, were on the defensive and suspect, while the Sudeten Germans supported the avowed aims of the imperial and ruling party.

When it finally became evident, in 1918, that the Empire

could not hold together after the war was over, the Sudeten Germans were attracted by Wilson's doctrines of "self-determination." They saw in this doctrine the final and satisfactory solution of their long-standing difficulties, hitherto insoluble within the framework of a polyglot empire. On this program, at least, there was complete unanimity among them. Where there had been partisanship and class enmities before, there was now unity and harmony. Sudeten nationalism seemed on the verge of attaining its goal. Their hopes may have been too rosy and their plans for the future may have lacked the quality so necessary to political success—realism—but their fervor was none the less warm for all that.

The end of the war brought them disappointment. According to the decisions of the makers of the treaties they had to be content to be a national minority within the boundaries of a Slav state. Bitter as this position seemed to them, it had one salutary effect. It brought harmony and union out of the chaos of the bitter partisanship that had made any satisfactory settlement before the war impossible. In the years to come, when they found that they could continue to live their German lives as freely as they had before, and even more abundantly than their German neighbors and cousins in Germany and Austria, parties began again to spring up with all their pristine vigor. But for a while, in 1918 and 1919, the Sudeten Germans were one large and harmonious family. Their history from that time to September 1938 must be merged in the history of the Republic.

⤙ 8 ⤚

The Renaissance of the Czech
People: to 1867

THE second half of the eighteenth century was one of the most critical in the history of the Czech people. Would Bohemia become once more an active member of the family of European nations, or would the lingering weakness which the nation had suffered since the White Mountain lead to certain extinction? Either eventuality was possible, but external indications pointed to the second and more malign end rather than to the hope of any revival of national vitality and consciousness. But before the end of the century, the lowering clouds on the horizon had begun to clear and one of the most interesting movements of modern times, a national renaissance, was on the way. There begins thus, at the end of the eighteenth century, a new era of Czech history which is to culminate only in the year 1918, the year of the renewal of political independence and the joining of Czechs and Slovaks in one state. It is not easy to describe this phenomenal movement in one short chapter, for it is necessary to bring into the story the pattern of movements in the other lands of the Hapsburg monarchy as well as dominant currents of political development in the rest of Europe. For the history of the Czech lands in modern times is only a part of a great whole. Events in Bohemia would lose both clarity and interest if they were not properly placed on a background of political events in Europe, and, toward the end of our period, of events all over the world.

The long and persistent oppression of the Czech nation which began after the White Mountain and increased in intensity after the Thirty Years War, bore fruit. It was not necessary to look beneath the surface to be convinced that the advantages gained by the dynasty which won at the White Mountain were lasting, and that, to all intents and purposes, the Czech question was no longer a pressing one. The nation which, after fifty years of unremitting Jesuit missionary activity, was still ninety per cent Protestant at the beginning of the seventeenth century, was at the end of the eighteenth century almost completely Roman Catholic. In the mountain districts in distant parts of the country, and in some remote valleys, there were still a few "stubborn goats" as the Jesuit missionaries called these crypto-evangelicals, but their influence among the rest of the people was hardly noticeable. The Catholic hierarchy had labored hard and effectively to make the Czechs forget their national hero, John Hus, by raising up another native hero and saint, John of Nepomuk, general vicar of the archdiocese of Prague at the end of the fourteenth century. The Jesuits as well as the secular clergy worked with exemplary zeal to make Nepomuk the national hero, and not only Bohemia but distant lands were filled with pictures and images of the orthodox Czech Catholic saint. A life of Nepomuk was written in Chinese, and distributed by Jesuit missionaries among their oriental converts. The hold of Hus on the Czech people must have been deep for the Jesuits to have thought necessary such an energetic campaign in favor of his successor.

The traditional opposition of the Czech Estates to the Hapsburgs and their Viennese court seemed also to have quieted to compliance. After 1763 the unpleasant interlude at the beginning of the reign of Maria Theresa when the Duke of Bavaria had been elected King of Bohemia was forgotten. A part of the Czech and Moravian nobility could be relied on to support the court and serve the interests of the Hapsburgs as wholeheartedly as if they were a native dynasty. A striking example of this participation of the

Czech nobility in the service of Maria Theresa is Václav Kounice, her minister of foreign affairs. Even in its Germanized form, Wenzel Kaunitz, the name betrays his Czech origin, and connection with an old family of Moravia.

Of a middle class which, in other countries, was already enjoying the fruits of the capitalistic system, or at least was on the threshold of its new day, there was almost no trace in Bohemia. After the virtual depopulation of Bohemia and Moravia following the Thirty Years War, the internal resources of the country were insufficient for the needs of recuperation, and a flood of Germans either from the Alpine districts of Austria or from those parts of Germany which had been spared the ravages of war poured into the Czech lands. In the towns the German invasion was most obvious. If there remained any Czech population at all, or if any Czechs moved into the towns from the surrounding country, they were almost lost. The towns gave every appearance of being German. In the nature of administration they were in closer contact with the central government, and because they were German, they were disposed to support a German administration, particularly when they would be likely to gain in tangible ways in return for that support.

Only the rural population resisted the germanization, although even the country was affected by it, particularly in those regions which bordered on the belt of German population in the north and west. But what could be expected of simple folk from whom the Jesuits had taken what Czech books they had, on the ground that they contained heretical doctrines? Could a farmer have any cultural initiative who was bound to the soil, who had to work both the overlord's land and his own, and who was burdened with payments to that lord and ever-increasing taxes in addition? How could a peasant make any contribution to a national life who could not leave his land, or indeed marry without permission from his lord, and could not even make any disposition concerning the future of his children without making sure that he had the approval and consent of his lord?

But the reign of Maria Theresa was from many points of view a transition period. As might be expected in an empire both polyglot and heterogeneous as to its constitutional makeup, ancient and feudal practices co-existed with distinctly modern tendencies. One of the latter was the desire of the dominant ministers at court to break down the divisions between the various lands of the Hapsburg family with their separate and independent diets, and incorporate them into a state which could be comparable in its organic unity to the western European powers, France and England, and could, if centralized, hold its own with an aggressive and growing Prussia. But centralization met with determined opposition. Maria Theresa at several stages in the development of the policy apparently doubted whether it could be carried out and showed a disposition to accept some compromise solution. But her son, Joseph II, who had grown up during the full flowering of the Enlightenment, refused to attenuate in the slightest degree his program for centralization and uniformity. Historical traditions and sentimental cares for the past meant nothing to him. The transformation of a loose congeries of provinces, some inherited, others gained by conquest, into a centralized and absolutistic monarchy was a program which had to be carried out to the last detail and in the shortest time possible, so that the disparity between Austria and other European powers might be diminished. But the program met bitter resistance in Hungary, where the nobility were anxious to defend their ancient prerogatives and disliked everything that came from Vienna. In order to make any progress in Hungary at all Joseph had to make many exceptions and concessions.

In Bohemia and Moravia, however, the reforms went into effect with clocklike precision. All power of resistance seemed completely gone. There appeared to be no reason to think that the once independent Bohemia and Moravia could not be changed into administrative units of a centralized state with perfect ease by a simple royal declaration. It looked as if even the peasant population were willing to give up its language and what cultural traditions it still held, and accept German, the language of commerce and culture, for its mother tongue. On ground long since cleared of almost everything recalling the Hussite period and the ancient glories of the Czech kingdom, there appeared the germ of a new life looking toward Vienna and grafted onto the Austrian branch of German culture.

Joseph II and his advisers were firmly convinced of the eventual success of their rapid reorganization of the Austrian lands. In their enthusiasm for a "new order" they did not see that novel measures, introduced in the interests of future development, may awake hidden powers of resistance and may revive forces long dormant or moribund. Some of the decrees, stemming from an enlightened interest in the condition of the common people and motivated by an awakened social conscience, undoubtedly improved the situation among the peasantry in Bohemia and Moravia in many ways. In 1781 Joseph II issued the Patent of Toleration which brought to an end the period of the Counter-Reformation. Both Calvinists and Lutherans were allowed, with some limitations, the free exercise of their faiths. But the real effects of this apparently liberal measure were relatively limited. There were very few changes in declared faith in Bohemia or Moravia after the publication of the Patent. The remnants of Protestantism among the Czechs were so weak that they could not attract to themselves any large numbers of the nation. No other creed save that of Calvinism and Lutheranism was to be allowed, and Joseph and his ministers were particularly severe against any re-vival of Hussitism in any form. This situation persisted essentially unchanged until 1918.

The Protestants remained an inconsiderable minority in the land of Hus. Yet Catholicism, in spite of the fact that it was the faith of the great majority of the people, never be-came identified with the national tradition as strongly as in other lands, particularly in the neighboring Slav land of Poland. It is not strange, therefore, that Liberalism was welcome in Bohemia. In the latter part of the nineteenth century, and in the years before the World War, perhaps the most striking manifestation in the spiritual life of the Czechs was the general indifference to the Catholic church and its doctrines, and a definite tendency toward scepticism and free thought. This twofold tendency was furthered by resentment at the close co-operation of the church with the court at Vienna and the persistent efforts of the nobility, whether German or dubiously national, to monopolize the higher and more lucrative positions in the hierarchy. The Czech of the nineteenth century was more likely to identify the Hussite movement with loyalty to the nation than with pure religion. Credit must be given to Masaryk and his pupils for drawing the attention of Czechs and Slovaks in the years just before the first World War to the primarily religious content of the Hussite reformation. But even the great influence of Masaryk was not sufficient to effect any great increase in the participation of the average Czech in the life of the Catholic church.

Decrees were issued from the chancery of Joseph II which granted greater personal freedom to the peasantry, restricted the extent of the work they were obliged to do on the land of their overlord, limited the tax-rates, and assured the peasants some guarantee of protection from the capri-ciousness of the powerful nobility. The older generation remained attached to the soil and made no noticeable effort to take advantage of their new privileges. But for the younger generation the way was now open to join the movement toward the cities, where they found employment in industry or business, or could attend school.

The schools, however, were completely German. Joseph planned to use the school system to speed up the uniformization of the varied populations of the several lands of his realm by insisting upon the sole use of the German language in instruction. German usurped the place of the local vernacular in the upper grades of the elementary school and in the high schools, and in the university displaced Latin. At the University of Prague, which, after the expulsion of the Jesuits in 1773, passed into the control of the government, German was used exclusively. It was not until 1791—after the death of Joseph—that a chair of Czech language and literature was established, and that only as a concession to Bohemian (not necessarily Czech) patriotic sentiment. But there awoke among a part of the Czech students in these schools an interest in the past of their people, in their language and literature. If an enthusiastic teacher praised German in comparison with a dead language like Latin, there was no reason why a Czech pupil should not think that the language which he had learned at home before coming to school was also capable of the same superiorities over a dead and difficult tongue. Thus in an atmosphere of systematic germanization, the sons of Czech and Moravian farmers and the artisans in the towns were born and reared and all unconsciously prepared for the crucial days that lay ahead of them. A national consciousness, previously limited to the very lowest and culturally most isolated stratum of the Czech people, the peasantry, began to spread through a higher, more mobile and increasingly powerful class, the bourgeoisie, recruited in increasing numbers from the peasantry, who moved to the towns and joined the ranks of artisans and small shop-keepers.

Events in Bohemia were somewhat paralleled in the other Hapsburg lands and even beyond their boundaries in central and southeastern Europe. But there was in these other lands a fundamental difference from Bohemia and Moravia. Here, as we have pointed out, the urban population, though predominantly German in speech and culture, offered very little resistance to the centralism of Vienna during the reign of Joseph. The nobility, on the other hand, pacified for a while by the concessions granted by Maria Theresa, opposed with all the greater determination the efforts of Joseph to weaken its prerogatives and upset the traditional relationships between the Czech lands and the Vienna administration. This nobility spoke German as a matter of course, and was connected with the nobility in the rest of the Hapsburg lands by marriage and social ties. In its unwillingness to give any encouragement to an impatient and reckless innovator, whose ministers and advisers were at least partially of bourgeois origin, the nobility was disposed to support any measures which would accentuate the separateness of Bohemia and Moravia from the rest of the Empire. The Czech language itself, now just beginning to be studied by the younger generation of German liberals, Czech literature of earlier centuries, and the history of the Czech kingdom, served as symbols of the new national feeling. It is not difficult, therefore, to understand why that portion of the Bohemian (not Czech alone) nobility which was opposed to Joseph's reforms made common cause with the bourgeois and intellectual leaders of the national revival. The work thus undertaken was effective and enduring, based as it was on a union of class and national aspirations. But even under these circumstances the situation in Bohemia was different from that in Poland or Hungary where the nobility had been for centuries the leaders of national life. In Bohemia and Moravia the nobility during the seventeenth and eighteenth centuries had been too mixed with foreign blood recently settled in the land to have any national sense. Some of them did identify themselves with their new homeland, but there was no deep-seated community of national feeling between the nobility and the rest of the native population. As soon as it became clear that the new movement among the people was assuming an exclusively Czech complexion, and that the line of demarcation between the Czechs and the surrounding Germans was being more sharply drawn as the movement progressed, the distinction between the nobility and the new force in Czech history became more sharply drawn.

A portion of the nobility remained faithful to its German connections, and thus helped to retain for the German party those positions in social and political life which had been won during the period of the eclipse of Czech nationalism. Another part of the nobility remained aloof from the struggle that was brewing and strove to act the role of mediator in the ensuing decades. Yet a third part joined forces with the Czech popular party, but this group was, numerically, the weakest of the three sections of the Bohemian nobility. Thus by reason of the fact that the great majority of the Bohemian nobility was either openly antipathetic to the national aspirations of the Czech people or was not sympathetic to the popular hopes, there developed a rift which was finally to result in a radical curtailment of the privileges of the nobility after 1918, and an obligatory land reform which reduced the nobility's importance in the new republic to a minimum.

The Czech nationalistic movement did not receive the support of the Czech nobility as a whole. The loss of that support was the harder to bear in that the nobility had fully as much as the popular cause to lose from Hapsburg centralization. The nobility might therefore be expected to make the people's cause its own, as Polish and Hungarian nobles had done under somewhat similar circumstances. But there were compensations for this loss. Support for the Czech nationalistic movement began to grow in the towns spread throughout the Slav districts of the country. Wherever the countryside was German, the towns remained German, but elsewhere the tide began gradually to flow in the direction of the cause of Czech nationalism. The towns and the country surrounding them came closer together in their social and cultural outlook and their national political program was the expression of a common patriotism. Owing probably to the fact that the national movements in Poland and Hungary were dominated by the nobility, the urban populations never played a leading role in those countries. The feudal nobility ruled the peasantry and dominated the towns. But because the Czech nobility refused the leadership which it might have had for the taking, that leadership devolved upon the middle and lower bourgeoisie. This explains why Czech nationalism throughout the nineteenth century and on into the twentieth was a democratic movement. Whatever the national cause gained was gained for the most part without the aid of the upper classes, by the initiative and courage of the people themselves. There is inscribed on the National Theater (Národní Divadlo) in Prague the motto "The Nation's Gift to Itself" (*Národ sobě*). The beautiful edifice was built by popular subscription, without the help of any powerful nobleman or rich industrialist. The motto could well apply to the whole struggle of the Czechs for their own national life.

But it was not until half a century after the humble beginnings of the national movement that the Czechs achieved any participation in their own political life. The liberal régime which Joseph had tried to establish in all of his lands did not survive his death. After the short reign of his brother Leopold II (1790-1792) there followed the long reign of Francis I (1792-1835). For anyone with liberal ideas it was a long, cold winter. Francis was a nephew of Marie Antoinette whom the French people had treated summarily, and he had good reason to suspect that the ideas of the French Revolution, if allowed to spread, might prepare for him a similar fate. He took upon himself the leadership of the hosts of righteousness against the armies of destruction—and subjected his lands to several decades of war and devastation. At home security against the virus of new ideas was the principal aim of government. Every person suspected either of a lingering sympathy for the program of the late Joseph or of that equally pernicious crime, Jacobinism, was removed from any governmental office, school or political post of any consequence as soon as the Emperor's ministers could make out the papers. All progressive and liberal ideas were soon banished from the Hapsburg lands (called the Austrian Empire from 1804). Peace descended like a pall.

Even after the end of the Napoleonic wars and after the Congress of Vienna in 1815, there was no change for the better. On the contrary, the vigilance of the court and the central offices was more enthusiastic than ever before. Of Prince Metternich we have had something to say in connection with the Germans in Bohemia in the nineteenth century. The effect of his antipathy to new ideas upon Czech nationalism should be remarked upon. He was concerned to preserve peace and order in the Empire. The best guarantee of internal order, he thought, was a well-trained police force empowered to protect the populace from the infection of any new idea. No meeting could discuss public questions, no newspaper could take the liberty of informing its readers of the true import of national politics. Metternich also entrusted his police force with the task of preventing the entry of dangerous ideas into Austria from the rest of the world. The frontiers were zealously guarded and petty spying and delation fattened many a pocketbook. In comparison with more modern dictators Metternich may have had an easy time, for there was no radio to reach so quickly beyond political borders, but he had his troubles with the pamphlets and leaflets criticizing his government which were printed outside the Austrian borders and brought into the country secretly and spread among the people. Because of their fugitive character and the frequent anonymity of their authors and distributors, this underground opposition press was more difficult to control than the established journals. Though it is true that for over thirty years, from 1815 to 1848 there was no open revolt against the Metternich government, the success of the system was more apparent than real. It was an unhealthy one, possible only because recuperation from the exhaustion of the Napoleonic period was slow. It crumpled like a house of cards at the first determined blast of liberalism from outside.

The Czech lands had been firmly integrated into the unity of the Hapsburg lands in Central Europe and shared all the benefits of the Metternich régime. If other lands of the Austrian Empire could not legislate for themselves in their national diets, neither could Bohemia and Moravia. From 1790 to 1848 they were relieved of the onerous responsibilities attendant upon governing themselves. It was a period when national vigor and the undercurrents of a national consciousness were gathering momentum for the exigencies of the trying times ahead.

There is one feature of this inner growth that is particularly worthy of note. It is the almost perfect sublimation of all the forces of the Czech people into literary expression in the widest sense of that term. Excluded from political activity of any sort, they bent their energies toward rebuilding the spirit of national unity which had been lost during the seventeenth and eighteenth centuries. Lost spiritual ground is always difficult to regain. But writers and teachers found a common solid ground on which to build in the brilliant past of the Czech kingdom and its people. The tactical significance of this appeal to history must not be overlooked. This was the only way in which the nineteenth century demands for national and political emancipation could be put in their true perspective. The leaders of the movement were not asking for novel and unjustified privileges, but could say in all truth that they were working for a freedom which their land had won and enjoyed during many centuries. Palacký voiced this Czech conviction when he said of his people: "We were in existence before Austria, and we will still be here after she is gone."

What distinguished the Czech struggle for independence, even in its earlier stages in the nineteenth century, from some otherwise similar crusades was the unusually high level of informed historical understanding displayed by the whole Czech people. This consciousness of historical realities marked post-war Czechoslovakia as well. Every Czech felt that the Republic of 1918 was the logical conclusion of centuries of war and peace, successes and failures, disappointments and dreams. The foreign observer may easily fail to sense this deep-rooted confidence of the Czechs in the logic of history, and yet it is the most important psychological fact in the Central European scene. No prophecy of the ultimate settlement of Danubian problems dare overlook it.

The foundation for this firm national faith was laid by the little circle of leaders of the Czech movement at the end of the eighteenth century. Though at first small in number, and without wide influence, their earnestness and persistence won more adherents among those who were able to spread books among the lower classes. In this task the work of the rural priesthood was notable. It is not without significance that in its first period the leaders and spokesmen were philologists. To a casual traveler through Bohemia at the beginning of the ninteenth century it might have appeared to be a completely German province, but we now realize that Czech was far from being a dead language even at its lowest ebb. It still lived among the peasant population for whom the Jesuits wrote and printed books as a missionary enterprise. But the Czech that was given to the peasants was a sorry travesty of the classic language of the sixteenth century. Inaccuracies and colloquialisms, in addition to a sadly depleted vocabulary, made it imperative that the language be purified, standardized and forged anew into a suitable tool for the work it had to do—the unification and elevation of the Czech spirit.

This recreation of a vital and inspiring Czech language was accomplished by two Czech scholars: Josef Dobrovský (d. 1829) and Josef Jungmann (d. 1847). A comparison of the work of the two men shows how rapidly the revival of the Czech language went on in their time. The older of the two, Dobrovský, wrote in Latin or German; he would have found few readers of his scholarly work if he had written in Czech. Jungmann went farther, compiled a German-Czech dictionary, and then began to mold the Czech language into a literary medium. By publishing translations from several literatures he furnished those who wanted to write in Czech a solid grounding in grammar, enriched the native vocabulary, and raised literary criteria immeasurably. One of his most notable contributions to Czech literature was his translation of Milton's *Paradise Lost*. The effects of his initiative were far-reaching. Poets, novelists and essayists hurried to satisfy the growing demand for works written in Czech.

The drama soon felt the same demand. The professorate, that part of it which was of Czech descent, began to try, tentatively and without much enthusiasm, the new medium. The University of Prague, which in the days of John Hus had been the center of the nationalistic movement, was still in German hands, and the Vienna court did its best to see that the control remained there. Realizing that the University would be likely to stay German, the Czech patriots decided to create their own cultural foundations which would serve as foci and standard-bearers in the struggle for cultural autonomy. In 1818 the Museum of the Bohemian Kingdom was founded by a group of patriotic scholars and noblemen, among the latter of whom the leaders were Counts Klebelsberg and Kolowrat, and twelve years later there was joined to it a society of Czech scholars, the *Matice česká*. Their aim was to encourage science and scholarship and especially the use of Czech in spreading a desire for learning among the people. The society and its meager treasures were housed at first in a small townhouse of Count Sternberg. It was a modest foundation, but a step in advance of the first efforts of Jungmann had been made.

These patriotic scholars were painfully aware of the great decline their nation's spirit had experienced in the preceding centuries. Their correspondence had that deplorable state as its principal undertone. They followed a twofold policy in their effort to re-establish the nation's awareness of and confidence in itself. On the one hand they built up connections with other Slavic peoples whose spiritual and intellectual life was less advanced than in Bohemia, particularly with Poles and Russians; and on the other hand they broadened and deepened their knowledge of the past of their own people, so that they might have increasingly convincing support for the new structure they hoped to erect. This desire for co-operation with other Slavic nations, frequently known somewhat inaccurately as Pan-Slavism, and a predilection for scientific history, which we might call historism, are the two most characteristic traits of Czech cultural life in modern times.

The age in which this revival began was a period of enthusiasm for the simpler things of life, of which an artificial civilization had robbed mankind. The Romantic movement, of which Jean Jacques Rousseau was the John the Baptist, crying in the wilderness, "Repent ye," was in full swing. Rousseau had a German disciple, Johann Gottfried Herder, a native of East Prussia. Herder regarded the Slavic peoples as the least corrupted of all nations, and predicted for them a glorious future. At this late date it is hard to realize what vitalizing effect these words of a German writer had upon the Czech patriots. By grouping all the Slav nations together and contrasting them with the Germanic peoples, he had virtually called upon the Czechs to seek the support of related peoples, match strides with their Germanic neighbors, and march forward to the future that was theirs. But in addition to these somewhat unrealistic generalities, there were also some practical aims to be considered. Czech language and literature, neglected for several centuries, were badly in need of an increasing vocabulary and a more flexible grammatical structure. The logical place to seek for help in filling these wants was in the related Slavic tongues, spoken by neighboring Slavic peoples. The general similarity of vocabulary and syntax made the borrowing of words and forms between the related tongues a simple matter. Slavonic studies were the fashion of the hour, and Prague became the capital of the western Slavic intellectual and scholarly world. The tradition of comparative Slavic studies begun thus in the early years of the nineteenth century, maintained itself steadily and grew even more after 1918.

The reason for the great popularity of the historical sciences in the Czech revival have been pointed out above. Scientific history got into its full swing in the 'twenties of the nineteenth century. Its supporters may be divided into two groups. There were the members of several noble families, whose interest in history was motivated in large part by a desire to find historical justification for their independence from the despotic rule of Vienna. At this distance from the struggle, when the facts of the virtual independence of the Bohemian Estates in the centuries before the White Mountain are generally admitted, it may seem incongruous that supposedly intelligent nobles had to support a whole nationalistic movement to discover these facts, but such was the case. The campaign for political centralization with its concomitant censorship had involved robbing the Czechs of a knowledge of their own past, and the campaign had been successful in a remarkable degree.

The other group of supporters of Czech historical science might almost be said to have consisted mainly of one man, the young František Palacký. His family seat was in Moravia, not far from the place where the Moravian Church sprang up in the eighteenth century. His parents had subscribed to the Augsburg Confession under Joseph II, but their tradition had for many generations been one of sympathy with the tenets of the Bohemian Brethren (*Unitas Fratrum Bohemorum*). His writing reflects this leaning to Hussitism. He shared with the nobles who supported the Czech revival the conviction that a monumental and authoritative history of the Czech people should be written, and he set about writing it himself. From this point his path diverges from that of the conservative Catholic Czech nobility. They were interested in proving their independence from the Hapsburg court. Palacký, a son of the people, saw much more in the history of Czech freedom than the prideful position of the Estates. He found, as he pursued his studies, how important the wars of the spirit and of faith had been to the whole Czech nation. The period of Czech history that attracted him most was the period of the glory

161

of the nation, the fourteenth and fifteenth centuries, when all Europe had looked to Bohemia in admiration for the heroism of her people and the high spiritual ideals of her leaders. There was little glory in that age for the nobility of the land. They had only too willingly sold their Czech birthright for the comfort of the Hapsburg court. Palacký was compelled, therefore, to make it clear that, as he read the past, the greatest epoch of Czech history was the work of the native Slavs, with only negligible help from a germanized nobility. The powerful appeal of such a thesis to those struggling for national existence in an atmosphere of Romanticism can easily be imagined. Palacký's *History of the Czech People*[1] became one of the pillars of modern Czech life and thought. The five-volume work was indispensable to the specialist, and was devoured by the layman as well. It was the *vade mecum* for all Czech political leaders, and Palacký's own later political activity would be incomprehensible without his *History*, from which he drew continually in his efforts to clarify for the nation the significance of contemporary events. In his earlier years Palacký had written a biography of Jan Amos Komenský (Comenius), a fellow-Moravian who was one of the leaders of the later phase of the Hussite reformation, and he had declared himself Komenský's heir and successor. A modern fellow-Moravian of Komenský and Palacký, Thomas Garrigue Masaryk, shared their concept of the meaning of Czech history, and the continuity of its spirit from the time of Jan Hus through Komenský and Palacký into our own days. The work of Palacký can thus be regarded as the medium through which the spirit of the Golden Age of the Czech people has been transmitted to the post-War Czech nation. No other work of this period of national revival,

[1] The Czech edition of his *Geschichte von Böhmen* was called *Dějiny českého národu*, of which this English title is a literal translation.

1815-1848, can be compared in ultimate importance with his *History*.

Because the history of the Czechs was the essence of their political struggle, the great historian of the nation became the leader of their political life. The critical moment for his leadership came upon him before he had reached in his *History* the Hussite period. The revolutionary movement which broke out all over Europe in 1848, after a first explosion in Paris, overthrew Metternich and the whole rotten shell of reaction which he had set up. The path to freedom in public life in the Hapsburg Empire, particularly for those like the Czechs who had hitherto been obliged to play a passive role, seemed open.

The news of the February revolution in Paris had the effect of an earthquake in the lands of the Hapsburg monarchy. Under the circumstances that was only to be expected. Nowhere in Europe could a régime have been more hateful than the Metternich government just before the outbreaks of March 1848. Not even the nobility as a body was consulted in matters of imperial policy. The diets of the various lands, though nominally still in existence as relics of the medieval Empire, met only to go through the motions of approving governmental demands for more taxes. No one was under any delusions that it would have made any difference whether the diet approved or disapproved. The taxes would have continued to mount and be collected, Diet or no Diet. Only one diet showed any signs of demanding some of its ancient rights—the Hungarian—and this had become an issue just on the eve of the March revolution.

Of the general need for a complete reorganization of the monarchy after the revolution and the fall of Metternich there was no doubt in the mind of any thinking person within the Empire. But as to the nature and details of that reorganization there was no agreement at all. The Poles, who had been added to the Hapsburg territory by the partitions of the eighteenth century, were unconcerned as to any future for Austria: their goal was the re-establishment of an independent Polish state. In Hungary, opposition to the centralism of the Vienna court was strong, because the Hungarian nobility had managed to maintain the nationalistic and separatist spirit of the Estates; and the revolutionary movement of 1848, in so far as it was anti-Austrian, had the support of all classes. There was general agreement among the Magyars that the hitherto strong bonds uniting their country to the other Hapsburg lands should be relaxed, and that officialdom within their land should be Hungarian in origin. The fact that this was a common desire was responsible for its realization. The liberal German bourgeoisie who supported the revolution in Vienna and in the German regions of the Empire regarded Austria as a German state and had every intention of maintaining that national character. This group, probably in a majority, regarded the movement for the unification of Germany with sympathetic interest. Some of the national groups in the Empire were as yet suffering from a retarded national consciousness, or were not yet sufficiently integrated to be able to present a developed program with which they might be able to bargain with the government or exchange support with other related groups. The Rumanians, the Croats and the Slovenes had in 1848 to accept the continuance of the Austrian Empire in lieu of a more viable alternative.

The attitude of the Czech leaders was determined both by the facts of the history of their nation and by a careful estimate of their power and the possibilities of their existing position. Their demands for a revival of the Czech state with at least those boundaries which it had after the loss of Silesia to Prussia in the eighteenth century derived from the study of Czech history. There was at this time no inclination to go farther back in that history than 1526. Complete independence was not the issue. At least the better advised among the Czechs were aware of the realities of their situation, and saw that the regeneration of the Czech people had not made such substantial progress that they could assume the difficult task of maintaining an independent state in so delicate and dangerous a region as Central Europe. For all these reasons, therefore, the continuance of Austria was accepted in 1848 as necessary and even desirable.

The most striking evidence of these ideas is the letter which Palacký dispatched to Frankfort as his answer to the invitation sent to him and the Czechs in general to participate in the elections for the coming Parliament of Frankfort. The invitation of itself indicated that the German nationalists lacked even an elementary understanding of the national aspirations of the Czechs, as well as any real knowledge of the historical relations of the Czech kingdom with the German Empire. We have elsewhere quoted from this remarkable letter (see above, p. 44 f.), but certain relevant sections are too significant to be passed over without extensive quotation here.

The object of your assembly is to establish a federation of the German nation in place of the existing federation of princes, to guide the German nation to real unity, to strengthen the sentiment of German national consciousness and in this manner expand the power and strength of the German Reich. . . .

The second reason which prevents me from taking part in your deliberations is the fact that, according to all I have so far learnt of your aims and intentions as publicly proclaimed, it is your irrevocable desire and purpose to undermine Austria as an independent empire and indeed to make her impossible for all time to come—an empire whose preservation, integrity and consolidation is, and must be, a great and important matter not only for my nation but also for the whole of Europe, indeed for humanity and civilization itself. . . .

You know that in the Southeast of Europe, along the fron-

tiers of the Russian Empire there live many nations widely dif-
fering in origin, in language, in history and in customs—Slavs,
Wallachians, Magyars, and Germans, not to speak of Turks and
Albanians—none of whom is sufficiently powerful of itself to
offer successful defiance to the superior neighbor on the East
forever. They could only do so if a close and firm tie bound
them all together as one. The vital artery of this necessary
union of nations is the Danube. The fulcrum of power of such
a union must never be moved from this river if the union is to
be effective and to remain so. Assuredly if the Austrian state
had not existed for ages it would have been incumbent upon
us in the interests of Europe and indeed of humanity to endeavor to create it as soon as possible. . . .

. . . in the unhappy blindness that has long afflicted her,
Austria has long failed to recognize the real juridical and moral
basis of her existence, and has denied it; the fundamental rule,
that is, that all the nationalities and all the religions under her
sceptre should enjoy complete equality of rights and respect in
common. The rights of nations are in truth the rights of nature.
No nation on earth has the right to demand that its neighbors
should sacrifice themselves for its benefit, no nation is under an
obligation to deny or sacrifice itself for the good of its neighbor. Nature knows neither dominant nor subject nations. If
the bond which unites a number of diverse nations in a single
political entity is to be firm and enduring, no nation must have
cause to fear that the union will cost it any of the things it holds
most dear. On the contrary, each must have the certain hope
that in the central authority it will find defence and protection
against possible violations by neighbors of the principles of
equality. Then will every nation do its best to delegate to that
central authority such powers as will enable it successfully to
provide the aforesaid protection. I am convinced that even now
it is not too late for this fundamental rule of justice, this *sacra
ancora* for a vessel in danger of foundering, to be publicly and
sincerely proclaimed in the Austrian Empire and energetically
carried out in all sectors with the consent and support of all. . . .

. . . If Europe is to be saved, Vienna must not sink to the role
of a provincial town. If there exist in Vienna people who ask to
have your Frankfurt as their capital, we can only cry: Lord,
forgive them, for they know not what they ask! . . .

. . . I am ready at every moment to give with pleasure a

helping hand in all activities that do not endanger the independence, the integrity and development of the power of the Austrian Empire. . . .

It was the hope and conviction of the Czech leaders that the monarchy would be radically reorganized and made into a constitutional state, firmly rooted in concepts of law and justice so as to guarantee to all its members the safe and free exercise of their human and civic liberties.

Federalization and decentralization were basic conditions for the realization of this hope. So much was admitted by all liberals, but it was no easy matter to decide whether the principle of reorganization should be that of historical political organisms or that of nationality. At first most of the Czech leaders felt that the ancient kingdoms, Bohemia and Hungary, should be restored as members of the new monarchy. Obviously there would then be a considerable mixture of peoples within the boundaries thus established. But as time went on, and the implications of the revolution became clearer, the nobility, save in Hungary, ceased to exercise much influence, and the principle of nationality began to appear more logical than a sentimental appeal to traditions long since dead. In the summer of 1848 a constitutional convention met in Vienna, and Palacký brought forward the outline of a constitution which provided for the federalization of the Empire. The convention was transferred to Kroměříž (Kremsier), and Palacký brought before the session of January 23, 1849, a plan for the division of the Austrian Empire into eight provinces:

1. German-Austrian
2. Czech and Slovak
3. Polish
4. Illyrian (Slovene and Croatian)
5. Italian
6. South Slav (Serbian)
7. Magyar
8. Rumanian

It will be seen that this was a division according to ethnographic lines so far as that was possible. The whole effort was to provide each of these ethnic groups as full a national existence within the framework of the Austrian Empire as would be consonant with political realities. Palacký's plan had its imperfections, not entirely to be laid at his door, but rather to be partially excused because of the short time in which he had to prepare a revision of the whole Empire which would satisfy the national aspirations of many peoples. So soon, however, after the outbreak of the revolution no one could have prophesied the final outcome of so radical a development, particularly in view of the fact that the various nationalities were unevenly advanced both in political and in national consciousness. But Palacký's plan was in itself prophetic, in that it envisaged and provided for eventualities which were to be realized only many years later, such as the union of the Czechs and the Slovaks in one political body, and a similar union of the South Slavs in one state.

With all its imperfections, and Palacký was quite aware of the fact that his plan did not satisfy all legitimate national demands, it must be maintained that if it had been accepted and supported by all those who would have profited by the perpetuation and peaceful development of the Empire, it would have effected a fundamental change in the nature of the Hapsburg state from a patriarchal monarchy into a state supported by the mass of the population. Such a peaceful transformation at this early date would without doubt have prevented the violent dissolution which took place at the end of the last world war. Palacký insisted that the essential parity of the various nations as integral political and cultural groups should be proclaimed as a fundamental dogma of the whole Empire. This insistence was dictated not only by his desire to assure the autonomy of the Czech people but also by the conviction that only on that basis could a modern state maintain internal and external peace.

The propagandist for Palacký's program among the Czechs was the brilliant publicist Karel Havlíček (1821-1856), who may be properly considered the founder of modern Czech journalism. Largely as a result of the work of his active pen, the majority of Czech opinion approved Palacký's demand for autonomy within a federal state. Only a very inconsiderable number of radicals went so far as to ask for complete and unconditional independence. The ancient hatred between the Hapsburg house and the Czech people was for the moment softened: Palacký and his followers saw in the dynasty the most effective means of binding together the Danubian lands and their peoples. They were hopeful that the new ruler, Francis Joseph, who had ascended the throne in November 1848, would understand the needs and long-repressed desires of the nations of the Empire and would decide in favor of a constitutional federal empire.

But these rosy hopes soon faded. The imperial army had been unaffected by the revolutionary movement, and the new Emperor almost immediately chose to place his reliance upon the military, selecting his advisers from the most conservative and reactionary groups in the government. After he had quelled the revolution in Hungary with the aid of the Czar, he turned his attention to the liberals in the rest of the Empire. Palacký's program was summarily rejected, and a rigid and centralized absolutism was re-established. For a whole decade, thanks to an alert police force and a strict censorship, this malodorous disease of absolutism was maintained in the long-suffering body of the Austrian Empire. Anyone with constructive ideas for the vitalizing of any genuine cohesiveness within the Empire was more than unwelcome. Palacký was kept under police surveillance. Havlíček was persecuted and fined, and his journals suppressed. He was finally sent into exile to Brixen. His health was undermined, he was not allowed to return to Prague to visit his dying wife, but his spirit was unbroken. He had become a symbol of the national resistance to Hapsburg despotism, and the news of his death shocked into certainty the feeling among the Czechs that the Austrian régime had shown itself incapable of recovery. From this time, in the later 'fifties, the ultimate issue comes into clearer focus: the Czech people must prepare themselves for the day when the Austrian monarchy will fall, and they will be able to build from its wreckage their own independent state.

The decade from about 1860 to 1870 was a fateful period in Central Europe. The events of 1918 are directly connected with the happenings of that time. In 1860 Francis Joseph came to the conclusion that the absolutistic centralism of the preceding decade had at least partially failed. Opposition to it had become so vocal and persistent that he proclaimed a return to a constitutional system. But there is slight reason to believe that he or his advisers had any sincere wish to initiate any real change in the administration of imperial affairs. All our evidence goes to show that the Emperor had not the faintest intention of building an Empire with only the interests of its people in view. He was unwilling to forego participation in the affairs of Germany, and so long as the German states were only loosely bound together a large and centralized Austrian Empire could easily maintain its primacy among them. But the rivalry of a growing Prussia began to be a serious matter, particularly after Bismarck became chancellor and assumed control of foreign affairs. In the light of this ominous development, Francis Joseph was faced with two alternatives. He could either accept the fact that there was no place in a purely German union of states for a heterogeneous agglomeration of peoples such as Austria, or he and his ministers could bend their energies to giving the Austrian state at least the outward appearance of being a German state. The first alternative demanded more courage and imagination than Francis Joseph or his advisers possessed. The second alternative was accepted. But in retrospect it is tragically clear that vital interests of the monarchy and of the whole Danube region were sacrificed in order to maintain an illusion which could last only so long as Bismarck refrained from taking the logical and decisive step which would mean the beginning of the end for the Hapsburg Empire.

For a whole decade the efforts of the court party at Vienna to maintain the precarious position of Austria as a member of the German Confederation and prevent Prussia from dominating German politics were pitifully obvious. In the first constitution which was elaborated in 1860 (generally known as the October Diploma), every effort was made to preserve the hegemony of Germans within the Empire. This strategy was greeted by a storm of indignation from all quarters where non-German national aspirations were thus disregarded. The most determined opposition came from the Magyars, whose political and national unity was so effective that the Vienna court was obliged to make considerable concessions, incorporated in the so-called February Patent of February 26, 1861. But even this arrangement was rejected by the Hungarian Diet, which made no secret of its willingness to defend itself from Austrian oppression with armed force. The diplomatic and military reverses suffered by the Empire in the next few years put the government in the position of having to choose between Hungary and the rest of the Empire. If Hungary were given autonomy the government could deal more successfully with the lesser national groups, perhaps with Hungary's support. In 1866, as a result of Prussia's victory in the short Austro-Prussian War, Austria was excluded from the German *Bund*; in 1867 Hungary was granted autonomy, and the Hapsburg monarchy had another chance to make a fundamental change in internal policy.

Czech leaders were hopeful that Francis Joseph and his advisers would recognize the legitimacy of the claims of the Czech nation for the same rights the Magyars had just regained. But the Emperor was unable or unwilling to see the seriousness of the situation, and the Czech demands for the historical privileges of the Bohemian kingdom fell on deaf ears. In the succeeding months and years after the conclusion of the Compromise with Hungary the Czechs bore the brunt of the struggle to bring about a reconsideration of the treaty so as to free from the oppressive rule of the Magyar aristocracy the Slavs of the lands east of the Leitha.

The opposition of the Czech leaders to the newly established Dualism was still consistent with their position in 1848 and 1849. In 1865, while the projected Compromise was still being debated, Palacký had written a series of articles, later published as a small book under the title *The Idea of the Austrian State*, which should be regarded as one of the most significant modern treatments of Austria as a political necessity. He made it clear that, without defending the administration of the Empire, he still felt that the legitimate aspirations of the Danubian peoples could be reasonably satisfied within the framework of a federalized imperial structure. If, however, such an aim were not sincerely pursued by the government, he left no doubt as to the alternative which would have to be faced. His own words will best indicate the moderate tenor of responsible Czech thought at this crucial period of Danubian history:

As for myself, I have always desired the existence of the Austrian state. I have always envisaged an Austria which would be just to all its peoples, an Austria which would wish to be a mother to all those it governed, and not a step-mother. In other words I have always hoped that Austria would have a government that was neither German nor Magyar nor Slav nor Roumanian, but only Austrian, in the highest and broadest sense of the term, by which I mean a government which would be equally just for all under its jurisdiction.

In the course of the argument it becomes evident that he has been driven to the conclusion that it is useless to expect that the Emperor or his advisers will ever realize the paramount necessity of readjusting national relationships in the Empire on a basis of historical justice and legitimate aspirations of its peoples. He no longer emphasizes the thought that, if the Austrian Empire had not existed it would have been necessary to create it, as he had freely said in 1848. He had then envisaged a federal Austria organized according to ethnographic lines of division. His suggestions had been completely disregarded. In 1865 he had modified the purely ethnographic division to one which could better be called historico-geographical. He saw the danger of dualism, which he called simply double centralism. Such a perpetuation of the worst evils of Hapsburgism meant simply the destruction of all national life throughout the Danubian region.

In the closing paragraph of the pamphlet Palacký puts the issue of the fate of the Empire squarely up to the government, then planning the Compromise with Hungary.

The day of the declaration of dualism will, with inevitable and natural necessity, be the birthday of Pan-Slavism in its least desirable form. Its parents will be the authors of the dual system. What will then happen anyone can readily imagine. We Slavs will face such an eventuality with sincere regret, but also without fear. We were in existence before Austria and we will still be here after she is gone.

The defiant ring of the last sentence of his pamphlet was destined to re-echo in the political thought of the Czech people and its leaders for decades.

173

≺ 9 ≻

Czech Nationalism in the Pre-War Years:
1867 to 1914

THE Compromise (*Ausgleich*) of 1867 had shown that the Czech nation could expect little consideration from the Austrian government. It would have to look elsewhere for help in its uneven struggle for national autonomy. A group of Czech political leaders, consisting of Palacký, his son-in-law, F. L. Rieger, Brauner and Julius Grégr, joined the Slav deputation to an Ethnographic Congress called to meet in Moscow in the spring of 1867. The Czech delegation was received by Czar Alexander II at Tsarskoé Sélo on May 26, and much enthusiasm for the idea of Pan-Slavism was generated in Bohemia and Moravia when the report of this friendly gesture was circulated. But the results of the efforts of the Czech delegates to sound out and perhaps interest Pan-Slav sentiments among Russian statesmen were certainly unfavorable. Two years later Rieger approached Napoleon III in the interests of a strong and federalized Austria as a counterweight to an aggressive Prussia. The indignation of the court party in Vienna at the interference of amateur statesmen in foreign affairs can easily be imagined. The immediate net result of these maneuvers of the Czech leaders was a more strict repression of civic liberty, and a wave of imprisonments for political offences throughout Bohemia.

But the pendulum soon swung in the other direction, and in 1870-1871 the Czechs regained confidence in a more liberal Vienna. Hope burned anew that Prague and Vienna might come closer together, and the Czechs gained momentarily substantially what the Magyars had won by the 1867 Compromise. But the Magyars, who feared that the

174

dualism which was so favorable to them might be disturbed by any readjustment in favor of the Czechs, and the Austrian Germans, who felt that their privileged position in the Austrian half of the Empire would be lost, objected vociferously to any liberalizing of the governmental attitude toward the Czechs.

In an imperial rescript of September 12, 1871 Francis Joseph had declared:

Mindful of the constitutional position of the Czech crown and being aware of the glory and might which that crown has brought to Us and Our predecessors, and, furthermore, remembering the extraordinary faithfulness with which the people of that kingdom have always supported Our throne, We take pleasure in recognizing the privileges of that kingdom and declare Ourselves ready to renew that recognition by a coronation oath.

On October 10, pursuant to encouragement from the Hohenwart ministry, the Bohemian Diet passed unanimously the so-called Fundamental Articles, which provided for the equalization of Czech participation in the political life of the kingdom along democratic lines, but the pressure from German and Magyar "liberals" was too great for the Emperor to withstand, and on October 25 the Hohenwart ministry, which had encouraged the Czechs to formulate their national demands in the form of articles to be approved by the Emperor, resigned, and was succeeded on November 6 by the reactionary Beust. Francis Joseph had showed himself a weakling, and the Czech people held him in ill-concealed contempt for his craven submission to the badgering of Beust and Andrássy, the anti-Slav premier of Hungary. The old story told by the fourteenth century chronicler Dalimil about the traditional Hapsburg disregard of their solemn oaths was revived and retold with nineteenth century footnotes. Little adulation was offered the Emperor from the Czechs in these days. Some printer in Prague with a sense of barrack-room humor printed on toilet paper the Emperor's Rescript of September 12, in which he made such glowing promises, in both Hungarian and German. The streets of Prague were then strewn with this evidence of imperial fidelity.

Some far-sighted Czech leaders were not too regretful of the failure of the Fundamental Articles. If they had succeeded and been accepted, the Czech constitutional position would still not have been equal to that of the Magyars, for the equality achieved would have been only within the Austrian half of the Empire; their brothers, the Slovaks, would not have shared any of the political or cultural gains, and the centuries-old division of the Slavs in the Empire would have been perpetuated. Palacký's plan had from the first called for the autonomy of the Czechs and Slovaks together as one nation within a federal Empire. On the other hand, there would have been definite guarantees against disproportionate German influence within Bohemia, and hopeful provisions for the participation of the Czechs in matters of common interest such as foreign affairs and the army. But the opponents of Czech nationalism would not hear of even such a limited gain, and brought every possible influence to bear upon the vacillating monarch to induce him to disregard his promises.

This proposal of the Hohenwart ministry in 1871 was the last attempt at a settlement of the dispute between the Czech nation and the court at Vienna. Thenceforth the government was mostly in the hands of Germans and Magyars. In the western (Austrian) half of the Empire the Poles had more influence than other national minorities; in the Hungarian half of the Empire, the Croatians were able to achieve a degree of autonomy. Imperial policies were accommodated in an increasing degree to the policies of Germany. Francis Joseph forgot his ideas of revenge for the defeat of 1866 and accepted the leadership of Prussia, and finally approved plans for close co-operation in international affairs. From the moment that an alliance between the German Empire and the Austro-Hungarian monarchy was concluded in 1879, it was obvious that Germany was the leading partner in the concern. In the light of later events it is also clear that Austria occupied a weak position on the Danube from 1879, or even from 1867. The leaders of the government, whether German or Magyar, had no desire for an independent Austrian policy which might irritate a powerful and aggressive German Empire. There were occasional conservative efforts to follow a purely Austrian policy, but as a general rule the dependence of Austrian policy upon German leadership in the decades before the last World War was an accepted fact. In compensation Germany permitted Austrian penetration of the Balkans. In 1878 Austria occupied Bosnia and Herzegovina, two purely Slav principalities. But this territorial gain was not accomplished without some political loss, both immediate and subsequent. Russia regarded this attack upon fellow Slavs and co-religionists with open disfavor, and Austrian efforts to dominate Balkan politics were to meet persistent Russian counter-moves until the shooting of the Archduke Francis Ferdinand in Serajevo on June 28, 1914. The close Austro-German alliance of the first World War was rooted in the events of 1879, and could have been clearly prophesied by anyone conversant with internal Austrian affairs during subsequent decades.

During the inconclusive negotiations of 1871 with Vienna, the Czech conservatives, led by Rieger, dominated the scene in Bohemia. They determined to co-operate with that part of the Czech nobility who, though not in general nationally conscious, yet were opposed to the centralism of Vienna and desired to maintain the lands of the Czech crown (Bohemia, Moravia and Silesia) as an autonomous unit within the framework of the Empire. Indicative of the change in Czech political thinking since the publication of Palacký's *Idea of the Austrian State*, the reasoning of the conservatives was based upon historical and not ethnic categories. But after the negotiations with Vienna were broken off, certain shifts in Czech public opinion took place, and these must be explained before we can understand fully why the Danubian monarchy broke up in 1918 and how the Czechs played so important a role in the last phase of that dissolution.

After the failure of the negotiations with Vienna in 1870-1871, the conservative party, known as the Old Czechs, steadily lost prestige. They were acting as the responsible leaders of the Czech people, and yet three obvious facts combined to discredit them completely with the Czech people: they had made too great concessions to Austrian centralism, then failed even to secure the greatly diminished demands that they had made, and even worse, had made an alliance with the ultra-conservative Czech nobility. The nobility as a political factor soon lost what little influence it had thus far possessed. It had either openly moved into the German liberal camp, which was strongly opposed to Czech nationalism, or had tried to maintain an opportunistic neutrality. A very few Czech nobles supported the cause of the Czech people, but they were so few as to have no influence in their class or in the process of germanization even in their own regions. The virtual absence of any ties of sympathy between the Czech nobility and the Czech people during the nineteenth century accounts for the fact that after 1918 most titles of nobility and the extensive privileges of the class were abolished, and the provisions of the land-reform laws effected a more equal distribution of arable land at the expense of the hitherto highly favored aristocracy.

Under these circumstances, the course determined upon by the moderate and conservative Czech political leaders was that of passive resistance to Vienna. It was widely felt that the hope of the Czech cause lay in the inevitable fall of the monarchy. The now venerable Palacký, popularly known as the "Father of his People," had given up all hope of a revitalized Austria, and had reconciled himself to its certain dissolution. In 1874, just two years before his death, he wrote:

> "Even so late as twenty-five years ago, Austria was commonly regarded as holding the leading position in European affairs. Now it is a serious question whether she is any longer a great power, in view of the fact that under Hapsburg leadership she has had to submit to Prussian 'protection.' . . . I simply cannot understand how Austria, with even an iota of common sense and good intentions, could have got herself into such a hopeless mess."

Palacký gave much thought in his last years to the problems that would face the Czech people in their very delicate situation in the middle of Europe after the inevitable collapse of the Austrian monarchy. He foresaw that their land might be the battlefield between Germany and Russia.

But the monarchy was destined to endure another forty years before these anticipations of Palacký became actualities. As the Old Czech leaders went into eclipse because of the failure of their program in 1871, there developed a new tendency among the younger generation which looked toward an acceptance of their situation. In a few years they decided to participate in imperial politics, accepted seats in the Vienna Reichsrat, in the several diets and in other public and imperial institutions. Dualism was thus virtually recognized. But there was much bitter criticism of this *volte-face* and it was commonly spoken of as a victory of cheap opportunism over national principles. As a matter of fact, an impartial observer would have to conclude that Czech political life in the period 1871 to 1914 furnishes few examples of heroism. Even Francis Joseph must have had a poor opinion of Czech courage. But if we were to take an optimistic view of the matter the Czech policy might be called either one of considered moderation or of watchful waiting, on the assumption that, national and international conditions being what they were, the best plan to follow was one by which the Czech position was consolidated in minor details, and the whole Czech people prepared for the decisive struggle that was sure to come.

The power in the government at Vienna was divided between the court party, the German-speaking Austrians and the Magyars. Obviously the Czech deputies were able to exercise no influence upon foreign policy, particularly with regard to the close alliance with Germany. The Czechs had furthermore no voice in the appointment of officers in the army or in its administration. There were occasionally Czech members of ministries, but no Czech was ever a premier or a minister of foreign affairs or of the army. The Emperor was quite aware of the fact that the Germans and Austrians would offer the most bitter opposition to any such appointment. Fundamentally he shared their feelings. The Royal Castle on the Hradčany in Prague was allowed to deteriorate sadly, for it was seldom occupied by anyone save obscure members of the royal family. The visits of Francis Joseph to Prague were very infrequent, and were marked by cool reserve on the part of the Emperor and his entourage, and open antipathy on that of the people of the city.

The activity of the Czech delegates to the Vienna Parliament (Reichsrat) which functioned as the legislative body for the Austrian half of the Empire, was for the most part of little consequence. The Czech delegates were so few in number that they could gain a hearing for their claims only with the support of another group. Sometimes they gained some scattered German support, but this was exceptional and their help came predominantly from non-German deputies. The Yugoslavs were to be found frequently on the side of the Czechs, and thus a basis was laid for Czechoslovak-Yugoslav co-operation in the post-war period. On the other hand, co-operation with the Polish deputies almost never occurred. The Poles were in favor at court, and their support of the government was taken more or less for granted, particularly when the government found it necessary to oppose the liberal Germans. But it was not until the last two years of the World War that the non-German groups in the Reichsrat worked together consistently. Nationalistic aspirations had developed in all the Slavic parts of the Empire so far that they were agreed that it was expedient to show the outside world that the Vienna government could no longer count upon the support of its Slavic peoples.

As a consequence of their relatively weak position in the Reichsrat, the Czech deputies had to give up any hope of altering the constitution of the Empire toward their federalized ideal, and they restricted their efforts to measures of a less fundamental and more practical nature. One very important result of their activity was the division of the Prague University, the oldest in Central Europe, into two separate institutions in 1882. By this arrangement, a division into a Czech (Charles University) and a German (Deutsche Universität in Prag), a compromise was reached which had both satisfactory and unsatisfactory features for the Czechs. On the one hand, the way was now open for research and publication in Czech, with attendant increase of interest in Czech culture, and the heightened value of Czech language and literature. On the other hand, the government had made such irritating restrictions upon the exercise by the new Czech university of its functions that there was no doubt that the German institution was regarded by the government as the heir of the medieval university. The mere fact that the Czechs constituted more than two-thirds of the population of the lands of the Bohemian crown seemed to be of no importance to the Vienna government. Apparently there was to be no departure from the now traditional policy that the Czechs were to get nothing which they did not absolutely force the government to give them, and even then the grant was to be so hedged about with "ifs" and "ands" and "buts" that the actual benefit to the Czechs would be as far as possible nullified.

But in spite of this Hapsburg policy and its patient pursuance the Czechs made substantial progress in the years 1871 to 1914. Slowly but steadily the weak spots in their cultural and social structure were strengthened, and their economic and political position vastly improved. It was their period of training and preparation for the critical struggle for political independence during the war and its exercise after the fall of the monarchy.

Several features of this developmental process can be noted as typical of the Czech nation in its entirety. During this period democratic principles spread their roots so deep among the people that it is difficult to envisage any possible circumstance—whether conquest, oppression or national humiliation—that would uproot this passionate devotion to the dignity and rights of the individual. The estrangement between the majority of the nobility, bound to the German nobility by ties of blood and class consciousness, and the Czech people made necessary the unification of the lower classes in a common cause. This widening of the base of the national movement in the long run more than compensated for the lack of support by the aristocracy. The upper bourgeoisie, the farming and the laboring classes were won over to the national program by a systematic campaign. The most effective work was done through the schools, and where the government refused to establish Czech schools the Czechs built them with their own meager resources. The press, low-priced books, the theater and all civic enterprises also made their intangible but powerful contribution to a growing national sentiment. As a result there was no part of the land, no social or economic group, no class in which there did not rule the idea that the Czech nation would win its rightful place among the states of Europe by the united efforts of all its people, and that the present tribulations were but training and preparation for an independence which was sure to come.

In these same years, 1871 to 1914, the general standard of living among the Czech people had materially improved. Nature had been gracious to the Czech lands, and the Czech farmer, even after the importation of foodstuffs from overseas had lowered prices in Europe, was comparatively well off. He had to meet the competition of the large-scale production of the extensive farms of the nobility, but by determination, hard work, and economy he managed to maintain his position. In these years, and indeed after the war, the Czech farming class was one of the most reliable supports of the social and economic stability of the land.

In these critical decades when, following the lead of the rest of western Europe, industry made great strides in the Czech lands, the ill effects of the centuries of oppression and consequent backwardness among the Czechs lingered on. These ill effects were accentuated by two circumstances. In the first place, the Vienna government followed a consistent policy of encouragement to Germans in industry and commerce in Bohemia in order to have their support for the program of germanization. In the second place, the majority of the Jews in these same pursuits, for easily understandable reasons of opportunism, identified themselves with the Germans. In competition, therefore, with the large established German firms, Czech industrialists and bankers labored under serious handicaps. The Czech struggle for economic parity was no less difficult and complicated than that for political autonomy. But though the tactics the

Czechs chose to employ in this struggle brought no sudden and stunning victories, yet the cumulative effect of the small gains steadily won was remarkable. The largest Czech financial institution is the Živnostenská Banka (Industrial Bank). It was founded in this period and supported by the smaller industrial concerns and the trades connected with them. In these years of growth a typical evidence of Czech economic maturity was the small or medium-sized factory, the well-organized workshop, and the savings banks which kept the savings of small depositors and made loans to this same group. These beginnings were modest but solid, and growth was steady. The strains of the war period and the post-war uncertainties only served to show how sound this financial and industrial structure had become, and how loyally the Czech people supported it. But one very important thing was lacking to the Czech financier and industrialist. He was unable to establish European connections: Vienna was the financial and industrial capital of the Empire and he had to do his trading through German agents and jobbers. Under such circumstances personal connections are even more important than among diplomats and politicians.

During these decades the native population increased rapidly. This excess was absorbed in several ways. A part found occupation in the new or expanded industries in Bohemia, creating thus a large class of skilled workmen whose competence was easily comparable to that in other lands where the industrial revolution had come earlier. The Czech has always found the arts and crafts congenial to him. Many others left Bohemia for Vienna or for other parts of the Empire wherever opportunity beckoned for advancement or steady employment. Still others heard the call of the New World and, without losing their love for the homeland, cast in their lot with other immigrants to the United States. In Nebraska, Iowa, Minnesota, Wisconsin

President Masaryk

and Texas there are large settlements of Czechs on the land. In New York, Cleveland, and particularly Chicago and nearby urban centers, Czech skilled laborers found jobs and a new home. Even before this last wave of emigration, during the seventeenth and eighteenth centuries when their land had lost its freedom, many Czechs left Bohemia to find outside its boundaries a liberty that no longer existed in their native land.

Along with this improvement in their economic situation went further cultural development. The work which the Czech patriots had begun under such great difficulties at the end of the eighteenth century and early in the nineteenth, was now bearing fruit. Czech literature was at all times extremely sensitive to the literary currents of the rest of the western world. It would be difficult to exaggerate the importance to Czech literature of the vast amount of translation from English, German, Italian, French and Russian into Czech that was so popularly received in the latter half of the nineteenth century. The dramas of Shakespeare were translated into Czech from 1855 to 1872. In 1872 the well-known poet J. V. Sladek, who had lived in America from 1868 to 1870, translated Longfellow's *Hiawatha* into Czech verse. The most prolific of all Czech pre-War poets, Jaroslav Vrchlický, translated the poems of Walt Whitman into Czech. Mark Twain, Goethe, Schiller, Gibbon, Selma Lagerlöf, Dostojevsky, Ruskin, Oscar Wilde, Shelley and many others were made available to the Czech people in cheap and yet authentic translations. As a general rule Czech literary lights were not able to maintain themselves by writing alone, and could devote only part of their time to the pen, but they felt that they were fulfilling a mission of education and elevation of the highest moment for their people. Very little of Czech literary production, however, ever became known in the rest of Europe.

The case was much different with Czech music. It was

185

during this same period that the soul of the Czech people found voice through its music. The musical bent of the people had a long history, and besides their own folk songs and religious music there was sincere and impartial appreciation of the great music of other peoples. But with Bedřich Smetana Czech music became both an outlet for national feeling and the property of the rest of the world. Smetana's genius lay in his true discernment and representation of the deeper emotions of the heart of his people, love of country, enjoyment of its beauties, closeness to the soil, whimsical humor, intensity of feeling, and throughout an independence of foreign models. His best known opera, *The Bartered Bride* (*Prodáná nevěsta*), first produced in Prague in 1866, has since been frequently produced in England and America. Smetana had a worthy successor in Anton Dvořák, who lived for a few years in the American Middle West and there was inspired to compose his famous New World Symphony. He has been perhaps better known internationally than Smetana, but this might be because his work is less typically Czech.

Czech painting, sculpture and architecture suffered not so much from a lack of talent, as from a lack of philanthropic patronage. The flowering of these arts needs some artificial stimulus. But it would be incorrect to assume that the Czechs were inactive in these branches of creative art. The galleries of modern art in Prague contain many works by Czech painters and sculptors of the past two generations, and these will not suffer by comparison with the art of the rest of Europe. Throughout the lands of Bohemia and Moravia, as well as in Prague itself, there are countless excellent examples of Gothic and Baroque art and architecture which have served later Czech artists for a laboratory.

The Sokol movement may be credited with making the most vital contribution to the focusing of Czech national life in this period of preparation. In the early 'sixties of the nineteenth century two Czech patriots, Miroslav Tyrš and Jindřich Fügner, conceived the idea that physical education might provide an outlet for hitherto untouched and perhaps unrealized national energies. They began to organize groups of men—later on women were organized along the same lines—who wanted to use their spare time for sport or physical exercise to promote their general health. But bodily exercise was not the ultimate goal to Tyrš, who had studied Greek literature and culture for many years. Mechanical drill and perfection in set exercises was less important to him than the balanced integration of all the capacities of the human mechanism. Fraternities of the Sokol (which means "falcon") were founded in Prague and in the provinces, and soon spread over the whole land. Members of the Sokol were also patriotic Czechs, and their patriotism soon permeated the whole movement. The periodic conventions of the Sokols in Prague became gala occasions, and Czechs from the whole of Bohemia and Moravia took great pride in their physical prowess and in the achievement of a united national spirit. The leading ideas in the Sokol movement were the equality of all members and the obligation of comradeship with every other "brother" and of loyalty to the nation as a whole. In addition to raising the level of health and general well-being throughout the land, the Sokol movement was a school for democracy, preparing its members for participation, either in their own villages and towns, or later in more trying times on a wider field, in the final struggle for their national liberties and their maintenance in a troubled world. The Sokol movement from its very beginning met with enthusiastic popular support and from many points of view was more important in unifying the nation than the activity of political leaders.

Czech political leaders had in general a common aim during the four decades preceding the outbreak of the World War: to assure the undisturbed development of the nation within the Austro-Hungarian monarchy. In matters of detail, however, there were many divergent opinions, so that the unified front was soon broken. In 1871 the Old Czechs were still the dominant party. But the failure of their negotiations with the Vienna government lost them popular support and the Young Czechs came forward as the national party. They commanded support from the bourgeoisie, the agrarian class and from labor. Yet their position at home and vis-à-vis the imperial ministries was weakened in the early 'nineties by the rise to prominence of other parties. The new parties had grown up on a basis either of class interests or of divergent political and cultural programs. In this political confusion the Czechs shared the fate of the Sudeten Germans, who were also interminably divided among themselves in this same period. The bargaining power of the Czech members of the Reichsrat was naturally substantially weakened by this division among the Czech electorate. Labor was the first group to withdraw from the united front, hoping to find more effective assistance in their struggle for better living conditions from their class in other countries than from participation in a national political action at home, directed largely by bourgeois elements of the population. Another party was composed of members of the working class who refused, for nationalistic reasons, to ally with the Social Democrats whose constituency cut across national lines. Their hope was the formation of an independent party free of the odium attached to the leisure class. A third considerable group was the farmer class which was likewise organized as a separate political party by the end of the nineteenth century. After these class movements had grown into political parties, the Young Czechs could recruit only from the bourgeoisie, which included the industrial classes, businessmen, the highly skilled artisans and the professions, and in addition the very influential intelligentsia. The Roman Catholics had early realized the need for political action, and a Centrist party, dissatisfied with liberalism in all its pernicious manifestations, was one of the earlier recognizably cohesive groups.

The larger and more responsible Czech parties were immersed in the problems of current politics. Problems arose almost daily which demanded immediate treatment, regardless of the makeup of the government or of the imminence (or distance) of the collapse of the Empire. Anyone studying pre-1914 Czech history who obtains his information from the official publications of the respective political parties and their spokesmen, or from the daily press and even reports of open discussions, might easily gain the impression that the relation of the Czech nation to the dynasty and the whole imperial system was perfectly regular and that the question of political independence had ceased to be of any importance. That impression would be completely false. Party manifestoes were at all times controlled by a censorship which even in periods of political tranquillity watched the press closely. It was impossible to give any open support to the idea of independence, for it was tantamount to treason and was severely repressed. But though the larger parties were scrupulous in the correctness of their public statements, several of the smaller parties, ably led and carefully organized, kept up a propaganda in the press and by pamphlet which, though within the letter of the law, kept alive by skillful innuendo the desire for independence. Even more significant and effective than any open campaign which can be traced in published writings and speeches was the relentless determination in all branches of the national life to win their nation's freedom and to be prepared to exercise it when it should come.

In these decades the Czech people had a number of exceptionally able leaders who organized and maintained the struggle with Vienna. But in only a few cases were they known outside the boundaries of the Empire. For the most part they were engrossed in the peculiar problems of their own situation and had little occasion to make contacts with foreign statesmen. As a consequence of this relative isolation few persons in the outside world knew of the struggle the Czech nation was waging for its freedom. Whereas in the case of the Poles in these years there was a numerous emigration of intelligentsia and political agitators who were able to publicize the oppression under which the Polish nation was suffering, there was almost no political emigration of articulate Czechs from Bohemia. The Czech political situation was not, therefore, widely known in western Europe. The political leader who had any connections with foreign statesmen was the rare exception, and the maintenance of such connections was likely to result in open disfavor in government circles.

So long as the Old Czech party was at the helm of Czech political action, F. L. Rieger was the generally recognized spokesman of the nation. He was a man of universally acknowledged integrity and ability, but his acquaintance with Napoleon III and leading French politicians in the years 1867 to 1870 cost him the confidence of Francis Joseph and the whole court party, whose jealousy of their exclusive prerogatives in the field of foreign affairs is not difficult to understand. The conservative tendency of the party, however, cost it its popular support, and the elections of 1889 marked the end of its dominance. Its place was taken by the more radical and aggressive Young Czechs. In the early years of this movement it could boast of no leader of international importance, but after the turn of the century when both the Agrarians and the Social Democrats had gained a more numerous following, Karel Kramář, the Young Czech leader, somewhat belatedly came to be known among the statesmen of western Europe as the leading figure on the Czech political scene. He was the representative of the Czech bourgeoisie, and leaned rather to Czarist Russia and a Pan-Slavist program than to the western democracies. In articles in the French press Kramář expressed the conviction that a federal union of the Danubian countries should take the place of the Austrian monarchy, and that an alliance between France and Russia was necessary to prevent the expansion of the Hohenzollern power to the Bosphorus and beyond. This challenging position was much discussed in French journals after 1900 by André Chéradame, René Henry, Louis Leger and Ernest Denis.

Czech labor belonged to the Second Internationale, and their leaders thus had the opportunity to become acquainted with the leaders of labor throughout the western world. The recognized leader of the nationally-minded Czech labor organizations was Václav J. Klofáč, who maintained close relationships with progressive elements in the other Slav nations, particularly in the Balkans.

If we were to attempt to characterize the separate periods of modern Czech political growth by the leading personalities of those periods we should without any hesitation choose for the first period, beginning with 1848, František Palacký, historian, political theorist and revered leader. The second period, beginning in the early 'seventies of the nineteenth century, is inevitably bound up with the name of Palacký's son-in-law, František Ladislav Rieger. After Rieger there was no comparable leader for some years, until there arrived upon the scene the majestic figure of Masaryk, whose political genius did not find its proper scope until he was, in his own words, "a superannuated university professor."

Thomas Garrigue Masaryk was born in 1850 in Moravia, the son of a Moravian father and a Slovak mother. Slovakia was then an integral part of the Hungarian kingdom. He grew up in Moravia, far from Prague, the growing center of

191

Czech national hopes. He went to the University of Vienna for his education and began his teaching career in the capital of the Empire. In 1882, when the Prague University was divided into a Czech and a German institution, he was named professor of philosophy and sociology at the Czech University, and transferred his activities to Prague.

Before turning to national politics he had become a national figure in another field, and had ardent followers as well as bitter opponents. Early in the nineteenth century certain Czech patriots had attempted to heighten the pride of the people in their glorious past by the publication of poems which the editors claimed had been found in the Zelenohorský (Grüneberg) and Kralovédvorský (Königinhof) manuscripts. It was asserted and widely believed that these poems had been written in the tenth and thirteenth centuries. Soon after their initial publication some scholars had expressed doubts as to their genuineness, but public indignation quieted such sacrilegious qualms. But a few unrepentant souls refused to accept the dictation of sentiment over scholarship. The question thus remained open, and as national strength grew and national aims became more coherent, the school of critics felt more keenly the incongruity of founding so important a thing as patriotism upon documents which at best were of dubious authenticity. The period of the first publication of these poems was the age of lush romanticism, and there was little so repulsive to the conscious scientific attitude of the end of the century as the naïve dreams of its early decades. In the belief that the truth, though it might hurt, could not injure the cause of the nation, Masaryk set himself to determine beyond any possibility of doubt whether the manuscripts were genuine or forged. He came to the unequivocal conviction that they were bald forgeries. In giving the results of his investigations to the public, he went into the whole complicated question of the place of Czech literature—partic-

ularly in the Golden Age of Czech nationalism, the period
of the Hussite reformation—in Czech life. His work aroused
a storm of rebuttal, but his position was so sound that it
soon found general acceptance, and Czech publicists were
quick to see the significance of the new approach for the
future development of the Czech political program.

Masaryk, however, remained active as a university professor until the beginning of the first World War. It was
naturally impossible for him to remain completely aloof
from political activity, and he was in fact for a time a
deputy to the Reichsrat at Vienna (1891-1893). At the beginning of his political career he had worked with the
Young Czechs. Later (1900) he broke away from them and
founded his own party, known variously as the People's
Party, the Progressives, or the Realists. Though this party
was not numerous, it had representation in the Reichsrat,
to which Masaryk himself was elected for a second time in
1907. His active participation in imperial politics was an
important factor in the development of his political philosophy. When he first went to Vienna he was of the opinion
that the monarchy was essentially a sound organism, and
needed only to be reformed and made more responsive to
the needs of its population. But the more he studied the
problems of the peoples of the Danubian basin and became
familiar with the functioning of the Hapsburg administration the more he felt that any adequate regeneration of the
ancient system was impossible. A few passages from his
Making of a State will show the cast of his thought as to the
Czech-Austrian problem.

In my study on "Palacký's Idea of the Czech People" I recognized the fundamental contradiction between the Czech idea
and the Hapsburg Austrian idea. Unlike Palacký, I had already
reached and expressed the conclusion that, if democratic and
social movements should gain strength in Europe, we might
hope to win independence. In later years, especially after 1907,

the better I got to know Austria and the Hapsburg dynasty, the more was I driven into opposition. This dynasty which, in Vienna and in Austria, seemed so powerful, was morally and physically degenerate. Thus Austria became for me both a moral and a political problem. (p. 46 f.)

In our special case, it was chiefly the monarchy of the Hapsburgs that estranged us from the Central Powers. It had carried through the violent Counter-Reformation, it had broken political faith with our people, restricting their independence, Germanizing them, and becoming, after the French Revolution, the chief inspirer of Reaction. Once the proud rulers of the Holy Roman Empire, the Hapsburgs had sunk to the level of being a mere vanguard of the eastward march of Pan-Germanism. But German pressure upon the Slavs, and the fact that behind the Hapsburgs stood the Hohenzollerns, contributed also to determine our attitude towards Germany. (p. 378)

The Germans and we were at war, yet we respected each other, as the agreements at Bachmatch and other minor incidents prove. Our resentment of Austro-Hungarian oppression was more direct, more personal; and, for this reason, our political relationship to the new republican and democratic Germany may well be other than it was to the old Austria-Hungary and to Prussia. For my own part I may say that, though I was working for our political independence even before the war, I never showed hostility to the Germans of Germany or even to the Germans in Austria. Then and afterwards I took a definite stand against Austrian Hapsburgism and Prussian Germanism, siding openly with the Allies during the war, but saying no word of insult to the Germans or to the Austrians as a nation. My bearing, as I have good ground to know, was recognized and respected even in German official circles. Nor was my policy affected by the knowledge that the Austrian military authorities and some circles in Germany wished to suppress my adherents by force and, above all, to have me arrested, even before the war, because they thought me dangerous. (p. 379)

Resistance to absolutism is characteristic of democratic progress throughout the modern era which has been marked by a long series of religious, literary, social and political revolutions. Even in the Roman era dictatorship was rightly limited to war time, because, in war, one leader is better than a dozen; and in so far as revolution resembles war, it, too, gives rise to dictatorships. They are, however, unsuited to normal times. Political leaders are not infallible. Four eyes see better than two, as I have learned by experience and study. . . . Democracy needs to be especially on its guard against political upstarts, for none but the uncultured or the half-cultured hold themselves infallible. (p. 418)

His precise discernment of the approaching dissolution of the monarchy and his insistence that the Czech people should look forward to the time when they would rule themselves marked Masaryk as the leader of the nation in the last phases of its struggle with Austria. His wide travel and penetrating knowledge of the diverse currents of both western and eastern European political and philosophical thought made his pre-eminence over all other Czech leaders all the more evident. His marriage to an American woman, Miss Charlotte Garrigue, had quickened his interest in English and American literature and philosophy and had given him some familiarity with a new world of ideas which had thus far been completely unknown to leaders of Czech cultural and political life. His university rostrum gave him great influence with the youth of the land, and as these young people grew up and assumed their places in commerce and society, the older generation of politicians and office-holders was obliged to explain where they stood with regard to Masaryk and his ideas as to the present and future of the Czech nation. And, finally, it was extremely important that Masaryk, almost alone among the successive leaders of Czech thought, had a very clear idea as to the necessary co-operative relationship between the Czechs and the Slovaks. This was a problem as old as the forceful separation of the two branches of the family, and a sound and permanent solution of it was imperative before there could be any successful outcome of the struggle for political freedom.

⤙ 10 ⤚

The Slovaks

MOST of our discussion thus far has been concerned with the western half of Czechoslovakia and its inhabitants. The reason for this disproportionate emphasis is obvious. The peoples in the western part of the country have been more active in the affairs of Europe and have left more and fuller records of their life and thought than their brothers to the east. Yet it is necessary to trace the history of these eastern brothers and explain, so far as is possible within the framework of this book, the course of their development until 1914. Without such a preliminary sketch it would be impossible to understand the Czechoslovak struggle for independence in the war years 1914-1918, as well as the development of the Czechoslovak Republic until its destruction in March 1939.

In earlier chapters we have brought various parts of the story up to 1914. We must now retrace our steps to the early centuries of the Middle Ages. The roots of most European problems are to be found in the dim obscurity of distant centuries. It is still a truism, though at times a tragically disregarded truism, that only by a close study of origins can we understand the modern manifestations of any fundamental problem. Nowhere in European history is this more true than in the case of the Czechs and Slovaks and their respective developments and interrelations.

The history of the Slovaks has apparently been of slight interest to historians of the rest of the world, and perhaps for that reason deserves more emphasis here. Unlike the history of most of the other peoples of Europe, that of the Slovaks is not a record of wars of expansion, rather is it the story of an uninterrupted struggle for existence. In this

prolonged struggle we can sense, more clearly than anywhere else in Europe, how powerful a factor in human history nationalism may be. We may also see how stubbornly
a relatively weak national unit, given the slightest encouragement from circumstances, can resist external pressures.
For almost a thousand years the struggle of the Slovaks for
national existence went on against overwhelming odds, to
be crowned at last with victory at the end of the first World
War. Such a gallant struggle and such a hard-won victory
are well worth our study. We will then have some idea of
the significance of the active co-operation of Czechs and
Slovaks in a joint struggle for independence and subsequent
political union.

If we had a map of Central Europe ten and a half centuries ago we should notice, just north of the Middle Danube, a territory in some degree similar to the modern
Republic. To the historians of the Middle Ages that territory was known as the Great Moravian Empire, to which
we have referred above (p. 10 ff.). Nothing is definitely
known of the territorial extent of the Empire, though it is
fairly certain that the central portion of the modern Republic, that is the watersheds of the rivers of Moravia and of
the Vah River, formed a part of this Empire. Somewhere
in this region was the seat of the rulers of Greater Moravia,
which bore the suggestive name of Velehrad (Great Castle).
At this period the eastern and mountainous part of Czechoslovakia was sparsely settled and of slight political significance. The rolling plains and lowlands along the Middle
Danube constituted a much more important area, because
there the inhabitants were in contact with peoples related
to them in race, though subjects of alien rulers. Though it
cannot be said that the boundaries of Greater Moravia
coincided with those of modern Czechoslovakia, it must be
pointed out that the central section of the modern state

was an important territorial element of the Moravian Empire.

The people of Greater Moravia belonged to the large Slavic group of peoples and had just begun to develop politically with the disappearance of the characteristic Slav divisions into tribes and families. But the Moravian Empire lasted hardly a century, and in that time any real feeling of unity and community of interest could not take root. The administrative effectiveness of a primitive and imperfect political organization was bound to be negligible. There was little commerce between parts of the Empire, and consequently little or no occasion for the various sections to become acquainted with each other. There was, however, one unifying element: the work and influence of the brothers Cyril and Methodius in the ninth century, to which we have referred in an earlier chapter.

As we examine the situation relative to other European embryonic states at this early period, it is evident that the Moravian Empire had neither more nor less political stability than, let us say, England or the Frankish kingdom. Its misfortune was that it bordered on one side upon the plains of Hungary and the lands between the Danube and the Theiss, fertile territory over which bands of marauding warriors from the far eastern steppes of Asia had roamed from earliest times. In the early Middle Ages the Huns and the Avars had made it their temporary home, and after them, in the ninth century, the Magyars took it over. These latter were similar in origin and in manner of life to their predecessors, but in one important aspect they differed. Whereas the Huns and Avars, after a sudden and meteoric conquest of most of Europe, disappeared entirely from recorded history, the Magyars, changing their manner of life from nomadic to agricultural, settled in the Hungarian plains and have remained there to this day.

Greater Moravia was the object of repeated Magyar raids

long before the newcomers had decided to settle down, but so long as the Empire was strong these sporadic invasions had no serious consequences. But by about the year 900 the Moravian Empire was rapidly disintegrating. The attacks of the Magyars were sufficient to complete its dissolution, and Greater Moravia disappears from the northern Danube valley as a purely Slavic state. Two medieval states were to arise from its ruins, Bohemia and Hungary. It was only natural that political dualism should prevent amalgamation of populations. A decisive factor was Magyar military superiority. The former Moravian Empire was thus divided up in this fashion: in the west the Slavic population, unconquered by the Magyars, grew into the Czech nation; the eastern part under Magyar rule came to form an integral part of the growing Magyar state. If Greater Moravia had been able to survive the vicissitudes of several more centuries, it might well be that we would today speak of the Slavs of Central Europe as Moravians. Instead, because of a decisive military conquest and consequent bisection of Greater Moravia by a non-Slavic people we speak of Czechs and Slovaks and the state which they formed when reunited as Czechoslovakia.

The nature and extent of the Magyar conquest of a part of the Moravian Empire early in the tenth century has further significance. If Greater Moravia had been allowed to fall apart of itself, there would in all probability have been formed, in the course of the next century or so two separate and independent states, Czech and Slovak. The two peoples were originally so closely related as to be almost indistinguishable, but geography and distance could easily have induced a separate political existence. The Magyar conquest made any such natural development impossible. The Slavs in the eastern part of what had once been Greater Moravia were not allowed to develop as an independent unit, but were incorporated into a state whose Magyar rulers were the conquerors of the previous Slav state. The Slovaks therefore had no opportunity to develop their own culture, written language, political institutions or social concepts in any independent way. Their relationship with the Czechs, their brothers to the west, had, for all practical purposes, ceased to be a reality for them. This situation lasted for nine centuries. Many circumstances of the past twenty years can be understood only in the light of this basic fact. Indeed this early and complete separation must be borne in mind throughout the following discussion.

For centuries after the Magyar conquest of Greater Moravia there is almost no mention of the Slovak people; a silence which, in view of their subjugation to a non-Slav people, is not surprising. Medieval chronicles went into elaborate detail concerning the life at court, and the deeds of valor of knights and warriors. Documents which are left us from royal or episcopal chanceries mention kings, nobles and prelates, great properties and feudal finance. But in Slovakia all the upper strata of society were Magyars. The Slovak, reduced to serfdom, interested no one whose business it was to write chronicles and transcribe feudal charters. No Slovak became a political personage, and because he had no social status he was of no military consequence. By and large he was a hewer of wood and drawer of water for his Magyar lord. For over two centuries this was the situation.

In the thirteenth century a slight modification of this completely subservient position may be noticed. That century witnessed a general increase of population in all parts of Europe. The Slovaks began, imperceptibly, to move in increasing numbers into the mountain sections of central and eastern Slovakia. Simultaneously, and for the same reason—increase of population—there came into the country German miners, craftsmen and merchants. Slovakia was a part of south and eastern Europe which became the haven of great numbers of Germans who had found the economic situation in Germany discouraging. Favored by the feudal Magyar overlords because they brought skills and goods from foreign lands, these Germans established themselves in Slovakia as a privileged minority. With the rise of capitalism and the increase of the power of money, the German minority found itself in a position to exercise a dominant role in Hungarian politics. For the Slovaks the influx of the Germans and their position of economic privilege meant simply that now there were two ethnic groups above them in their own land instead of one. The task of gaining any kind of economic or social independence thus became doubly hard.

But the situation was not impossible. Town life tends to be more individualistic than a feudal agrarian society. So long as there were only the two elements: the feudal Magyar ruling class on the one hand and the Slovak serf-peasant on the other, there was no possibility of a Slovak crossing the line that divided the two races. With the arrival of the German merchant and industrial immigrant, a middleman enters the picture. In the course of time, as they acquired wealth, Germans married into the nobility. At the other end of the social and economic scale, Slovaks, at first in small numbers, later in more considerable proportions, were able to enter the commercial and industrial world of the towns. This Slovak infiltration into the higher classes was an exceedingly slow process, but, once started, maintained itself steadily. Our information concerning the details of this process is relatively meager, but all the more valuable for that reason. The town book of Žilina, dating from the fourteenth century, listing the citizens, shows Germans and Slovaks living as neighbors and engaged in similar businesses and crafts. It was soon quite apparent that the Slovaks had won a position of influence in the town life of Slovakia, and the ruling Magyar classes were unable to nullify these gains.

The part played by religion in the early history of Slovakia cannot be disregarded. When the eastern part of Greater Moravia came under the rule of the Magyar conquerors, there was a vital difference between the new masters and the Slav subjects. Christianity had come to Greater Moravia from Byzantium, but the Magyars were still faithful to their pagan deities. But, as so often happens in history, the faith of the vanquished people subdued the victors, and the Magyars became devoutly militant Christians. To this day many Magyar words concerned with religious life are of Slav origin and bear witness to the fact that Christianity came to the Magyars from their Slovak subjects. However, when the Magyar state was ready to consider the adoption of an official religion, it turned away from the East, whence Christianity had come to the Slavs, and gave its allegiance to Rome and the western rite. Latin became the language of the court as well as of the church to a greater extent than in the rest of Europe. The languages of the various ethnic groups which lived under Magyar rule, unable to overcome the handicaps imposed upon them by the favored position of Latin, did not develop as rapidly as the vernaculars in other European countries. Reduced to a subordinate place, they became the property of peasants and servants. This was even the lot of the native tongue of the ruling race. The first written monuments of the Magyar tongue do not go farther back than the end of the thirteenth century. By this time French, German, Italian and Castilian were languages with a long and honorable history behind them.

Certain striking similarities in political development between the Hungarian and the Czech kingdoms in these early centuries are of great importance for the history of the Slovaks—subjects of the former, bound by blood and language to the latter. In both Bohemia and Hungary the native dynasties died out at the beginning of the fourteenth century. In Bohemia the dynasty of the Přemyslids, legendary in its origins, could point to its centuries-old labors to unify all the Slavic tribes in Bohemia and Moravia into one nation and protect its independence. In Hungary the dynasty of the Árpáds could rightfully claim a similar achievement. Every Magyar knew that Árpád had led the people in their conquest of the land, and his heirs had organized the state and maintained it triumphant in the face of their many adversaries. There was thus a similar national attitude toward the respective native dynasties.

After the extinction of the two lines there was a further similarity between the two states in the choice of a succeeding dynasty. Both peoples chose new dynasties which were essentially western and bred in the tradition of a Latin civilization. For two states which bordered on the East and were in constant touch, either by reason of race, language, or geographical situation, with eastern European civilization, this step indicated that a definitive alliance with western Latin Europe had been decided upon. The dynasty of the Luxemburgers, which ruled in Bohemia from 1310 to 1437, was closely related to the ruling house of France. The new Angevin kings of Hungary were closely connected both with the ruling house of France and with the royal house of Naples and Aragon.

Until recently it has been generally accepted that there was no intellectual activity among the Slovaks until well into the fifteenth century. This view was held by the great French Slavist, Ernest Denis, as late as 1917, when he published his *Les Slovaques*. But more recent studies by Czech and Slovak scholars have brought about a revision of this thesis by showing that there were Slovak students at the newly founded University of Prague soon after its foundation in 1348. For some decades it was the only university in

Central Europe. The Emperor Charles IV was desirous of providing higher education for those of his subjects in the Empire who would otherwise have to go either to Paris or to Italy. In its beginnings, therefore, this university was international. The renaissance of letters at the Prague court, for which Charles was in large part responsible, was cosmopolitan in its nature, but was also a contributing factor in the growth of Czech nationalism. As might be expected from the close connection between language and nationalism, the Czech language blossomed in these same decades.

We are not accurately informed as to the number of Slovak students in attendance at the University of Prague at any one time, but that they were numerous enough to be noticed, and that many of them were actively interested in the Czech nationalistic revival is now clearly established. It is only reasonable to suppose that on their return to their homes in Slovakia they took positions of leadership among their own people, and some of them, because of their superior education, must have become town officials. Their influence should have been considerable. The fact that Hussitism became widely known and less widely professed in Slovakia soon after the death of Hus would indicate that the ground had been prepared and the spread of Czech ideas was neither difficult nor unwelcome. On these general facts there is but slight disagreement among Czech and Slovak historians, though concerning the exact extent of the spread of Czech nationalistic ideas among the Slovaks there is more difference of opinion.

Some importance should be attached to the fact that early in the fifteenth century a member of the Luxemburg family, Sigismund, became King of Hungary, and that, at the end of his life, he was also in possession of the Czech crown. The rule of both lands was thus united, for a short while, in the hands of one Luxemburger. Any such dynastic union, however short, brought some interchange of official personnel with its concomitant commercial and social effects.

We have elsewhere emphasized the strongly feudal nature of the Hungarian kingdom under which the Slovak peasant lived. But the growth of population, commerce, nationalism, and town life which marked the fifteenth century all over Europe and particularly in the Danubian area brought with it a definite weakening of the power of the feudal overlord. The shifting of social prestige and political power may have been less noticeable in Hungary than in the rest of Europe, because of the high class consciousness of the Magyar magnates. But the lesser nobility had come to stay and grow in influence, and, as a newer social and political group, acted as another means by which the Slovak people might improve their position. If a Slovak could enter commerce, he might become a person of wealth, and if he became reasonably wealthy, he might marry his daughter into the family of a country squire who was in need of money. It does not take much imagination to understand how the owner of a small domain, living in a modest castle completely surrounded by Slovaks with whom he had continually to deal for the common things of life, would be influenced by his milieu more than a powerful lord, living in a great castle, insulated against any Slavic influences by an elaborate and numerous body of retainers of his own Magyar race.

Added to this environmental difference between the greater and the lesser nobility, we should remember that the great magnates had a sense of their mission to keep the common folk in their place, determined for them by generations of Magyar rulers. The Magyars have never denied that they were particularly fitted to rule an "inferior" people like the Slovaks. But in the fourteenth and still more in the fifteenth century a certain amalgamation with the native population took place within the ranks of the lesser nobility which had settled in Slovakia. A similar change occurred in the towns and among the lettered classes. It was by no means a complete absorption, but it was, for the native Slovaks, a remarkable improvement over the earlier situation. The bonds which had earlier kept them in complete subservience were beginning to loosen. Though even yet the highest places in church and state were closed to Slovaks, no matter how able or educated, nevertheless there were rewards to be won for individual enterprise and ability.

Throughout the fifteenth century the similarities between the kingdoms of Bohemia and Hungary continue to be striking. For a while after the death of Sigismund and after the untimely end of his son-in-law and heir there was an interregnum in both states; then for a few short years Sigismund's grandson ruled in both lands. But the similarity does not end there. After a short period of uncertainty in both lands, each chose a native nobleman to rule. In Bohemia it was George of Poděbrady, the Hussite king; in Hungary it was Matthias Corvinus. On the death of the latter in 1490, the occupant of the Czech throne, the Polish Jagellon King Vladislav II, was elected to the Hungarian throne. This situation has been referred to in an earlier chapter but it is mentioned again in this connection to show the closeness of the texture binding the histories of the three states of Poland, Bohemia and Hungary.

The great similarity of the vernacular languages furnished an additional bond between the peoples of Bohemia and Slovakia. Agitation within the church in Bohemia, arising out of the Hussite controversies, had its repercussions in other areas of Czech life. The national language was especially activated and enriched by the animated pamphleteering of several generations. When the dust of battle had settled, Czech was found to have invaded and occupied territory hitherto the exclusive property of Latin: theology, philosophy and the royal chancery. Within an incredibly short time the native tongue had so enriched its vocabulary and regularized its syntax and morphology that it was now possible to express in Czech any idea or fine distinction in thought which previously would have had to be conveyed in the formalized Latin of the schools and the law-courts. Political and military prestige combined with purely linguistic flexibility to make Czech rather than Slovak the *lingua franca* of a considerable region outside Bohemia. Written Czech became the language of the educated Slovaks, particularly if they had studied at Prague, and remained such until the end of the eighteenth century. Official documents were written in Czech in those towns in Slovakia where the native Slovaks had been able to rise to positions of responsibility and leadership. The few Slovak lesser nobility executed their official documents and correspondence in Czech, and as soon as printing came to the country books were printed in Czech for the Slovak reading public. This public may not have been large, but it was important for Slav race-consciousness out of all proportion to its numbers. It would be difficult to exaggerate the influence of this wide acceptance of Czech as the written language of the Slovaks during a period when Bohemia was free and Slovakia was ruled by Magyars. The dialectal peculiarities that appear here and there in Slovak documents did not alter the fundamental fact that Czech was accepted as the basic tongue of the two peoples.

Volumes have been written on the question of the influence of Hussitism upon Slovak spiritual and cultural life. Until recently opinion was divided along confessional lines, Catholic writers claiming that Hussitism had had no beneficial effect upon Slovak life, Protestants insisting as loudly that the Hussite movement was responsible for awakening among the Slovaks a consciousness of their common national and cultural heritage with the Czechs. More recent critical and objective studies by both Czech and Slovak scholars (e.g. V. Chaloupecký and B. Varsík) have clarified the issues. It is now established that few Slovak clergy embraced the Hussite teachings and made any effort to spread them among the people. Traces of Hussite teaching are found in only a few places, and even there its spread was very limited. Hussite armies did spend some time in parts of Slovakia both during the reign of Sigismund as King of Hungary, a bitter enemy of everything Hussite, and later when Hungary was torn by internal dynastic strife. There is no doubt that the presence of Hussite warriors, deeply religious, faithful to the ideals of Hus, led by their priests who used Czech instead of Latin in their services, had some influence upon the Slovaks. We hear of Slovak *zemany* (lesser nobles) who were influenced by the teachings of Hus to confiscate church properties when these were in the possession of immoral clergy. The fact that the noble increased his landholdings by this righteous act should perhaps not be held against him too strictly. But the end result of the sojourn of the Hussite armies was not very considerable. In the first place their stay in Slovakia was relatively short, and in the second place we have incontrovertible evidence that the organization and power of the Catholic Church in Slovakia was not noticeably disturbed at any time in the fifteenth century.

But after 1517 the situation was quite different. Martin Luther had started a movement that was to win fervent allegiance wherever there were Germans. In both Bohemia and Slovakia the German minorities, in town or in the country, immediately adopted the new teachings. In Bohemia large numbers of Czechs who had been nurtured on Hussite doctrines of anti-clericalism found Lutheranism congenial to them. The German movement thus lost some of its exclusively German character, and when it appeared in the towns of Slovakia the German preachers could say to the nationalistic Slovaks that thousands of Czechs had become Lutherans. As a result, by the end of the sixteenth century Slovakia as well as Bohemia was predominantly Protestant.

Indeed it was during this century that Bohemia and Slovakia were closer together culturally and psychologically than at any time from their early separation until the first World War. Many illustrations of this rapport might be cited, but we shall mention only one. Between the years 1579 and 1593 the famous translation of the Bible into Czech known, from the place of printing, as the Bible of Kralice (Bible Kralická), was printed and published. Kralice lies in Moravia, within the boundaries of the Czech kingdom, but by the nature of the population and its proximity to Slovakia, it is actually as much Slovak as Czech. Both Czech and Slovak Protestants adopted this translation as a common medium, and education, religious and devotional literature, hymnody—and consequently a large proportion of home and social thought—drew their vocabulary as well as their inspiration from a common Czech version of the Scriptures. Had this cultural *rapprochement* between the two peoples been maintained for only a few more generations there is little doubt that the divisive effects of the fall of Greater Moravia would have been completely obliterated. The fact that there was a political boundary between the two lands would have been of small moment in view of the fact that a single monarch, of the family of the Hapsburgs, ruled over both Bohemia and Slovakia.

After the battle of the White Mountain in 1620 aggressive Hapsburg catholicization of the land forced the rural population to accept the Roman faith, and those nobles and upper bourgeoisie who were unwilling to abandon their Protestantism had to flee. Many of them fled to Slovakia, where the power of the Catholic Hapsburgs was much less centralized than in Bohemia. Many of the Magyar nobles were Protestants, and the immigrant Czech Protestants were for a while not unwelcome. But this favorable situation did not last long, and after 1670 Catholic persecution was partially successful in reducing the number of Slav Protestants in Slovakia. There is ample evidence, however, that Czech Protestant books continued to circulate among the Slovaks, and that the memory of the time when the two lands, Bohemia and Slovakia, were spiritually united in greater or less degree, from the fourteenth through the sixteenth century, was never completely dimmed. The persistence of these traditions of an earlier political and religious affinity was to have far-reaching consequences in later years when the revival of national consciousness among the Czechs heightened the favor with which any ancient tradition joining them with their Slovak kinsmen was regarded.

The Catholic Counter-Reformation had been increasingly active in Bohemia since the arrival in Prague of the first Jesuits, 1556. After the Hapsburg victory at the battle of the White Mountain the order dominated the religious and educational life of the lands of the Czech crown. Until recently it has been a commonplace that almost all the Jesuits were foreigners and consequently by instinct inimical to everything that was typically Czech. But this view can no longer be maintained in the face of researches of Czech scholars. Although the first Jesuits that came to Bohemia were foreigners, Spanish, German and Italian in origin, the order very soon adopted a policy of increasing substantially the proportion of native members. By 1620, a considerable majority of the whole order was of native blood and speech, prepared for their missionary work at colleges in Germany or Italy. Quite correctly the order sensed that one of the greatest obstacles to the success of its missionary program in Bohemia was the prevalence of the native Czech literature, almost completely Hussite in temper. Only native missionaries could combat such deeply rooted traditions. The earlier Czech literature had to be effaced, not because it was in the native Czech tongue, but because it was Hussite and anti-Catholic.

But effacement of the native Hussite literature without replacement by an equivalent substitute would have been ineffective, and the Jesuit order has never successfully been accused of lack of perspicacity. It now became obvious why so many native Czechs had been taken into the order. It was to be their task to assume the education of the Slavic youth and produce a literature that would supplant the Hussite tradition with a Catholic and pro-Hapsburg attitude. The Hapsburgs maintained a nominal suzerainty over those parts of Hungary that were not occupied by the Ottoman Turks, that is the north and west of the ancient Hungarian domains. This was precisely the territory of Slovakia. The Jesuits, once Bohemia was well on the road to re-catholicization, turned their attention to Slovakia and established a college and an administrative center at Trnava, whence close relations were maintained with the Jesuit college at Prague. Books published by the Jesuits in Prague for the use of the native population in Bohemia and Moravia were now also used by the Jesuits in Slovakia, and the unity in language which had been crystallized by the union between Czech and Slovak Hussites and Lutherans was continued by those who set out to eradicate their teachings. It should not, however, be concluded that the Jesuits had any conscious desire to further the spirit of national unity between the Czechs and the Slovaks. A common literary language was used simply because it was ready to hand when the order began its missionary work in Slovakia.

But this condition which was so favorable for the spread of a common national feeling between Czechs and Slovaks was not destined to last for long. A radical change was imminent, and it is necessary to see how it came about. After the loss of political independence and the reduction of its nobility and bourgeoisie to virtual extinction, the Czech nation, in its social structure, was comparable to the Slovak. In both cases the body of the population was the peasantry, remnants of the lower bourgeoisie, some of the lower knighthood and the petty nobility which, by daily contact with the native peasantry, succeeded in maintaining their national feeling and traditions. It was among these classes that the Jesuit missionaries labored so effectively. Each time the Jesuits were able to destroy a Hussite or Lutheran book, written in the language that had become common to both Czechs and Slovaks, the knowledge of the common tongue lost some of its hold. As the Jesuits were able to fill the void thus created they adapted the written language to local dialectal tendencies. The language, hitherto in process of coalescence, began to take two separate paths.

Though this was an important source of separateness between the two kindred peoples, by itself it would hardly have led to complete separation had not another factor entered. It was indeed much more important for the course of this process of separation that during the second half of the seventeenth century and throughout the eighteenth century Prague ceased to have any significance comparable with that which it had enjoyed in the three preceding centuries. Even in Moravia, for long closely connected with Bohemia and Prague, the feeling of separatism from the erstwhile capital of the lands of the Bohemian Crown made itself felt. The situation in Slovakia, politically a part of a separate kingdom, was even more serious. The Jesuits in Slovakia, working from Trnava, followed the same procedure their brethren in Prague had adopted. In their preaching to the people and in their tract writing they used dialectal expressions so as to be more easily understood by the people. In the course of time it was only natural that the previous trend toward unity of the spoken and written language in the two regions should be reversed. The existence of separate political and social institutions in Austrian-dominated Bohemia and Magyar-dominated Slovakia made the differentiation in language only the more marked. By the eighteenth century this dualism had become so deeply rooted in Slovakia that it has been impossible, up to the present time, to eradicate it completely. But here and there, where there still persisted small groups of Lutheran Protestants, undimmed memories of the days of the Reformation lived on—memories of the close concord between Czech and Slovak evangelicals. Books dating from the days when one written language was used in both regions were still read, and it is now known that in these circles a conscious effort was made to trace the collaboration of Czech and Slovak evangelicals back to the Hussite reformation. But wherever the new Catholic faith struck root, under the influence of the Jesuit missionary activity, the earlier connections with Czech religious life were broken, and Slovak life and thought were reoriented toward Hungary to which they were bound by political, institutional and juridical ties.

Literary, linguistic and religious factors were not the only ones which affected the fortunes of the Slovak people in the period after the Reformation. During the sixteenth and seventeenth centuries the Hungarian state was put in turmoil both by the struggle against the Turkish conqueror and by internal strife. But in the eighteenth century—after 1711—Hungary appears again on the map of Europe much as she was during her period of greatness under the vigorous Matthew Corvinus. The Hapsburg court at Vienna was the focal point of political and social life in the Danube area, but the Hungarian nobility sturdily refused to allow their land to relapse into the condition of subservience to Vienna

which it had suffered after 1620. In this struggle for autonomy the nobility from the various regions of Hungary took
the lead and a feeling of national unity arose among them.
It is usual to refer to this patriotic sentiment as *Hungarismus*, because it was a loyalty to a geographical and political
unit, the Kingdom of Hungary, the home of Magyars, but
also of Slovaks, Rumanians and other smaller minority
groups. Some few Slovaks, either of the native nobility or
of the higher bourgeoisie, identified themselves with this
movement. Any such thing as a national or racial state was
at this time quite inconceivable, and it was only natural
that in an established and relatively peaceful kingdom the
attention of the urban and literate population throughout
the land should be turned toward the capital city, Budapest. This new focus of social, economic, and political life
inevitably heightened the differences between the Czechs,
outside the kingdom of Hungary, and the Slovaks, residing
within its borders.

There still remain some unsolved mysteries with regard
to the course of the development of Czech-Slovak relations,
in spite of the considerable amount of research into the
questions by both Czech and Slovak historians during the
past several decades. One of these questions is why Czech
and Slovak Catholics found no common ground in the years
1918-1938; and its corollary, why one of the bitterest attacks
upon the unity of the republic was led by the radical Catholic wing. We make no pretense to having the certain answer
to these questions, but light may be cast upon the problem
if we point out some historical connections. By the rupture
of the growing linguistic unity of which we have just
spoken, the atmosphere in which the Czech and Slovak
Catholics were coming together was hopelessly vitiated.
The evidence in this regard is still somewhat vague, but the
general situation was certainly conducive to divisiveness.
Later on, during the nineteenth century, the picture be-

came much clearer, for by that time Bohemia had absorbed the liberal ideas of western Europe, and the spirit implanted among the people by the Jesuits in the era of their greatest influence had begun to disappear. Among the Czechs memories of Hussitism and their anti-Catholic past came to life again. There was no return to the Bohemia of the fifteenth century, but the spread of a knowledge of their past and of the close relationship of the Catholic Church to their Hapsburg oppressors tended to make the Czech Catholics somewhat indifferent to the religious and dogmatic aspects of the faith and draw their attention to programs for social betterment, the general uplift of the nation and political independence. In Slovakia there was no similar development, at least in any discernible measure. Thus Catholicism in Bohemia and in Slovakia presented completely different programs and aims, whose differences had been steadily growing for over a century and a half.

There is an additional factor, partly political and partly religious, which must be taken into consideration. We have spoken above of *Hungarismus*, a patriotism centered around the geographical and political entity of the kingdom comprising many peoples. The Catholic organization, in spite of its universality, was closely identified with this all-inclusive state throughout the eighteenth century. But with the spread of ideas of nationalism after the French Revolution the various peoples of Hungary began to feel the racial distinctions between them. The Magyars, the dominant political group in the kingdom, began to emphasize their racial superiority. *Hungarismus* began to change into *Magyarismus*, and the less powerful groups—Slovaks, Rumanians, Croatians and Germans—were made to feel that they were inferior to the Magyar rulers. The Catholic Church, far from opposing this change, allied itself with the Magyar nobility and lent its support to the newly oriented state. At the same time the lower nobility in Bohemia and Moravia had joined with the masses in refusing to further Hapsburg-Catholic reactionary centralization.

It should occasion no surprise, in view of this, that there came from the Catholic camp a deliberate effort to substitute for the written Czech then in use in Slovakia a language based upon a local dialect. A Catholic priest, Antonin Bernolák (d. 1813), after some preliminary studies, published in 1790 a *Grammatica Slavica* intended to be the basis for a new written tongue. But he made the tactical error of relying upon the dialects of western Slovakia, where the spoken tongue was most like the language of Bohemia and Moravia, and was consequently unfamiliar to the Slavs of central and eastern Slovakia. The resultant language was thus neither Czech nor, for the majority of the Slovaks, was it Slovak. About the only followers Bernolák had were Catholic writers, and even among them the vogue for his grammar and dictionary soon died out.

At the very time that Bernolák was trying to bring into being a new literary language there was developing in other regions of these Slavic lands a movement which had its roots in the ancient traditions of Czechoslovak literary unity. It was an effort to unite Czechs and Slovaks on a new basis. The movement has been described as the Czechoslovak renaissance, worthy to be compared with the first effort at a common life at the time of the Great Moravian Empire and even more with the organic and close co-operation of Czech and Slovak Protestants in the sixteenth and early seventeenth centuries.

This Czechoslovak renaissance is not an isolated phenomenon, but is only one manifestation of the growth of national consciousness so prevalent in post-Napoleonic Europe and particularly in Central Europe. For long it had no political aims at all, and consequently the political boundaries between Bohemia and Moravia on the one hand and Hungary on the other were no barriers to free interchange of ideas and expression between leaders on both sides of the frontiers. As we examine the movement more closely it is interesting to observe slight differences in emphasis between the Czech and the Slovak branches. It will be recalled that in Bohemia the Jesuits were able to eradicate the literary remains of Hussite and Reformation times. After several decades of their energetic missionary work the heirs of the Czech Protestants survived only surreptitiously and in small numbers. When Joseph II issued his Patent of Toleration in 1781 a relatively small proportion of the population of Bohemia and Moravia declared their adherence to Lutheranism or Calvinism, and a large part of these were of foreign origin. Protestantism played but a minor role in Czech spiritual life in the period with which we are dealing. Interest in the glorious past of the country was centered around its departed political independence, the deeds of its rulers and leaders and similar secular themes. The ancient literature was studied, but with an eye to form and language rather than to content and ideology.

In Slovakia, on the other hand, the strands of history had been woven into a different texture. A predominant majority of the people had grown up in an atmosphere of Protestantism. In spite of every kind of restriction from the end of the seventeenth century and continuing through the eighteenth, Hungarian Protestantism had not been undermined as it had been in Bohemia. The past for the Slovaks was essentially the story of their Reformation, and they were able to study it in the books which survived plentifully from earlier centuries, written in the same language—Czech—to which the attention of Czech patriots was returning in the early nineteenth century. The renaissance which we have called Czechoslovak had thus a national character, and the leaders from both sides of the border had a powerful bond of union—a language that had been used by both their peoples in their age of glory and independence. Many Slovak patriots worked for shorter or longer periods of time in Bohemia, while others had intimate literary connections with patriotic circles in Prague, Brno and Pilsen. The Czech Reformation had stemmed from Prague and certainly traveled to Slovakia from the west, but by the late eighteenth century the current has begun to flow in the opposite direction and the traditions of the Reformation were carried from Slovakia to the west, and the urge for national unity drew upon these ancient traditions for much of its strength. There was no explicit return to sixteenth century Protestantism as such either on the part of the Czechs or of the Slovaks, but the effect of this revaluation of their past was to minimize the missionary and educational work of the Jesuits in the intervening century and a half. Czech Catholics were being weaned away from a universal, supra-national church by the more immediate promptings of an awakening national consciousness.

Thus far we have remarked how the various factors tended to bring the Czechs and Slovaks together again. But in the second quarter of the nineteenth century new elements of a contrary nature made themselves felt and in the sequel were to be more seriously divisive than the abortive efforts of Bernolák. Nationalism was a universal phenomenon in nineteenth century Europe. The Magyars, no less than the Slovaks, felt the flattering impulsion of the new doctrines, and the Hungarian state rapidly became a Magyar state. That same social group—the nobility—which had been loyally Hungarian in the eighteenth century now became loudly Magyar and lent its powerful support to the conversion of the multi-racial state into a national Magyar state.

As an illustration of this altered policy we may take one single development. From the Middle Ages to the end of the eighteenth century the language in use in governmental courts and bureaus was Latin. But the days of medieval scholasticism were over, and Latin became an increasingly obsolescent tongue; those who could use it adequately became fewer with the passing of the years. In Vienna, German was substituted for Latin. In Hungary, it was felt that something should be done, but the nobility refused to adopt German, the language of their hated Austrian neighbors; and Magyar, the native tongue of the upper and ruling classes in Hungary, became the official language of the whole kingdom. The remaining nationalities of the kingdom, Slovaks, Rumanians and Croatians, had had no objection to surrendering the right to speak their mother tongues in governmental and official matters, so long as it was a surrender to a universal language, Latin. They recognized that there was a practical need, in a state consisting of several nationalities, for a common tongue. They would have had no objection, even, to accepting Magyar as an "official" tongue. But when it became evident that the ruling Magyars intended to give Magyar the dominant position in all spheres of national life and to reduce the languages of the other nationalities to the level of patois, the non-Magyars were resentful and determined to resist. This attempt to magyarize the less powerful peoples in the Hungarian kingdom by degrading their languages is only an illustration of the conscious tendency on the part of the ruling race to denationalize the minorities.

As soon as it became clear that the nobility almost to a man supported these measures and identified themselves with the Magyar majority the other nationalities faced a definitely unfavorable situation. In the Diet, still constituted as it was in the Middle Ages, the nobility held a dominant position and brooked no opposition. From its decisions there was no legal or legislative appeal. But the days of appeal to the pressure of public opinion were in sight, and the lesser nationalities set about preparing themselves for the time when their united front would oblige the entrenched Magyars to make concessions to national aspirations. Support for these aims had to be won among the common people. The middle classes and the peasants had to be reached by the spoken word and the printed page. But among the Slovaks it was not so easy to put these aims into effect. The Czech language as it had been known to the Slovaks for several centuries from Bible translations and other devotional works was so different from the spoken vernacular that it was read and written with increasing difficulty. This was true not only in Slovakia but even in Bohemia and Moravia; the Czech language of the early nineteenth century had grown far beyond the Czech of the sixteenth century. If Slovakia had been united to Bohemia at that time, there is little doubt that nineteenth century Czech would have soon won its way as the written and spoken vernacular in Slovakia within a few decades and would have served to bring the two Slav regions together. But the political and administrative separation of the two regions by their respective incorporation into Austria and Hungary crystallized a cultural and linguistic divergence which had grown only slowly until that time. Under these circumstances a large part of the Slovak patriots felt that it would be best to accept the linguistic dualism as inevitable. At a time when modern Czech was winning favor rapidly because of its adaptability to every kind of literary creation in Bohemia, an influential group of Slovak writers came to the conclusion that some one of the various dialects should be adopted as a written tongue so as to lessen the discrepancy between written Slovak and the language in common use by the people.

The introduction of this written Slovak in the 'forties of the nineteenth century is bound up with the name of the Slovak patriot and *littérateur* Ludovit' Štúr (1815-1856).

Of the younger generation of Slovak patriots, he grew up in the atmosphere of Romanticism which drew upon the writings of Rousseau and Herder for its idealization of the common people. Štúr was strongly influenced by German Romanticism and studied Herder and Hegel carefully, searching for a way to apply their conclusions to his own people. He was a restless spirit and temperamentally unsympathetic with the leaders of the older generation of Slovak writers such as the poet Jan Kollár and the learned archeologist Pavel Josef Šafařík. Soon after returning, in 1840, from two years of study at the University of Halle, he became the leading spirit among the younger generation of Slovak patriots at Bratislava, where he held a minor teaching post. When he finally decided to launch a distinctive written Slovak language, the youth of the land rallied to his support in spite of the efforts of the older generation of Slovak writers to prevent the growth of dualism. As so often happens under similar circumstances, the issues split families and pitted son against father, but victory in the struggle rested with the militant younger generation.

The year 1834-1835 is usually given as the date of the rise of written Slovak, although, strictly speaking, Štúr did not make his first formal declaration until 1846. The basis for the written language which he introduced was the dialect of central Slovakia, which differed from written Czech more than that of western Slovakia which Bernolák had used. It is of some interest that the new language was more popular with Protestant writers than with Catholic. The line of demarcation between the older and the younger generations was made more clear by the emergence of different literary motifs. The older generation drew their themes from the history of their people; the younger writers enthusiastically appealed to the now fashionable romantic philosophy.

In Germany and surrounding lands the Nation and its

individuality had by now become almost deified. By the Slovaks, a people conscious of their separateness from their rulers, this deification was even more deeply felt. Every act and manifestation of power on the part of the Magyars only increased the devotion of the Slovaks to their own ethnic group. Their determination to maintain their nationhood was heightened by the repeated assertions of their leaders who told them that, of all the subject Slavs, they had retained most faithfully the elemental traits of the Slav nature and that by the revival and spread of these traits to the other Slavs a better and brighter future for all their Slav brethren was assured. But while the Slovaks were enjoying the roseate dreams of a glorious Slav future, contrasting so sharply with reality, and doubly endangered by the growing aggressiveness of the Magyars who ruled over them, they were drawing farther apart from the Czechs in at least one important matter, their common literary language. This estrangement, unlike the political separation, was not destined to be healed. The century following upon Štúr's activity until the political union of 1918 sufficed to cement and perpetuate a difference which might conceivably have disappeared in the same period of time under more favorable circumstances.

It should also be borne in mind that relations between Czechs and Slovaks after the rise of the new written Slovak language did not depend solely upon the will of the two Slav groups. Neither the Czechs nor the Slovaks were masters in their own homes and could not make any final decisions as to their political or cultural future. After the fall of the absolutist régime in 1848 there arose the all-important question as to the reconstruction of the Hapsburg monarchy. There were several possibilities. One of these, uppermost in everyone's mind, was federalization, which would certainly bring into clearer light the national consciousness of the various ethnic groups of which the population of the monarchy was made up. Another possibility was further centralization, which would mean the concentration of all offices and governmental agencies at Vienna. A third possible solution was dualism, a division of the monarchy into two quasi-autonomous parts, one of which would be predominantly German, the other Magyar.

Palacký's plan for federalization of the Empire, submitted in 1848, it will be remembered, called for the union of the Czech and Slovak regions into one administrative whole. Another such unit was to be the German portion of the monarchy, another the Magyar, and so on. If this plan had been adopted there would surely have emerged a solid basis for the co-operation of Czechs and Slovaks, not only in literature and culture, but also in political life, public administration and business. The split which began to widen after the well-intentioned but perhaps unfortunate activity of Štúr would have been arrested and both groups would quickly have grown together into one living and harmonious organism. The older generation of Slovak scholars who opposed the militancy of the followers of Štúr were still strong enough to have been able, with a little outside support, to nullify the radical separatism that was gaining ground. But Palacký's plan was proposed at an unpropitious time and the oblivion that engulfed the rest of the work of the Kroměříž congress was also its fate.

The reactionary decade, 1849-1859, was a period of German ascendancy throughout the Empire. Even the Magyars who had been so strong in their own kingdom and eager for independence from Vienna, were obliged, by a display of force, to submit to the new régime. The Slovaks were even less able to make any progress, or indeed to hold their position in the face of a determined Austrian centralism.

If this centralizing policy had been fully maintained for much longer than these ten years, the lines of demarcation between the separate lands of the Empire would certainly have grown dim, and the various peoples would in all likelihood have lost some of their distinctness. That part of the population which spoke German would have held a privileged place, and other languages and peoples would have had to be content with subsidiary roles. If this condition had been realized the Magyars would have been in the same relative position as the Czechs. There is little doubt that under these circumstances the Czechs and the Slovaks would have come closer together in the realization that a common danger threatened their language and their national life. It is significant that, if we understand the intention of the government in this decade, the union of the Czechs and the Slovaks would have been welcome to Vienna. The ministry of education opposed the separation of the two tongues, Czech and Slovak, and insisted that written Czech be taught in the lower schools in Slovakia. Official publications, proclamations, and even the decrees of local officials were issued in Czech throughout Slovakia.

But this highly centralized system fell. It was unable to show results, either in domestic or foreign affairs, which would have justified the oppression to which the various national groups felt themselves subjected. Another solution had to be attempted: dualism. The Compromise of 1867, referred to in an earlier chapter, satisfied only two of the many elements in the monarchy: the Germans in the Austrian half of the Empire and the Magyars in the Hungarian territories. F. L. Rieger, Palacký's son-in-law, in a speech before the Bohemian Diet preceding the ratification of the Compromise by the German representatives from Bohemia, protested against the injustice of the new arrangement: "In the establishment of a Cisleithanian and of a Hungarian Parliament I clearly discern an effort to subjugate the Slavic peoples in both parts of the empire. Over one part the Germans, over the other the Magyars will rule. It is our conviction that such a division of rights that belong to others cannot endure." There was apparently no intention of considering the rights of the other, more numerous, nationalities in the empire, either on the part of the Emperor or of his advisers. The Compromise lasted fifty years, that is, until the collapse of the Empire in 1918. Dualism was not only unjust to many nationalities in the Empire but disastrous for the whole monarchy. Nevertheless, no one had the courage to face that fact and discard a ruinous system in favor of one which would have placed the monarchy on the natural and safe basis which Palacký had suggested in 1848, a basis which would have guaranteed equality to all the nationalities in the empire.

The possibility of normal and many-sided co-operation between Czechs and Slovaks which Palacký's federal plan would have assured and which even the centralism of 1849-1859 provided, though in a much more limited degree, was substantially nullified by the Compromise. The lands of the Bohemian Crown—Bohemia, Moravia and Silesia—remained, along with other provinces, a part of the Austrian half of the Empire. The Slovaks were incorporated into the Magyar half of the Empire. More than ever before, the Slavs within the Empire had, after 1867, to reconcile themselves to the twofold difficulties of enforced division and subordination to different masters. The Germans and the Magyars were so solidly entrenched in their stations of power that the Czechs and Slovaks, far from having any hope of being able to overthrow an unjust system, were barely able to defend the weakened positions remaining in their possession. The Slavs now faced two foci of danger: Vienna and Budapest. What might have been a unified defence had now to be split, and, consequently, weakened. The Czechs and Slovaks were thus forced into the embarrassing position of having to fight a war on two fronts. Their whole plan of campaign had to be altered to fit the changed conditions of their struggle for existence which had, from their point of view, definitely deteriorated.

The half-century from 1867 to 1914 was in many ways one of the most difficult periods in the history of the Slovak people. In that period may be found the roots of all the troubles that emerged in the post-war years, from 1918 to 1938. A major cause of Slovak distress was the fact that they were cut off from contact with any political force that might have lent them support or sympathy. The Compromise of 1867 was built upon the tacit understanding that the court at Vienna would keep its hands out of internal affairs in Hungary. This was the price that had to be paid for the consent of the Magyars to leave foreign affairs and a few other common matters in the control of the Emperor.

In the period of attempted centralization—from 1848 to 1867—the Emperor had shown favor on several occasions to the non-Magyar peoples of Hungary so as to gain their support as a counterpoise to the Magyars. The Slovaks had fallen in with this strategy and had adapted their program and aims to the desires of the court. Their rewards were generally in the form of minor concessions. In 1862, for example, on the occasion of the founding of the *Matica Slovenská* (Slovak Foundation), an institution intended to promote the cultural efforts of the Slovaks, Francis Joseph made a contribution of 1,000 gulden. But any petitions for protection against the growing aggressiveness of the Magyars toward the Slovaks in all departments of public and private life found their certain way into the darkest cubbyholes of the bureaus at Vienna. The effectiveness of their interment was final. But after 1867 there was no longer any need to drop these few crumbs which came from the sumptuous imperial table. Under the Compromise the Slovaks stood face to face with the Magyars, their masters.

The economic position of the Slovaks was as weak as their social position. They were mostly peasant and hill-folk, dependent upon the bankers in Budapest and upon the more prosperous Magyars in the rich plains of Central Hungary. They had little with which to bargain with their powerful masters for political concessions. Their only hope was some sort of common action with their fellow non-Magyars in the kingdom, the Serbs, the Croatians or the Rumanians. But it was a slender hope, as these three groups were hardly better situated economically or politically.

After 1867 the Magyars were so strong that they could proceed to put into effect an idea which had been developing since before the days of Joseph II: the transformation of the Hungarian state into a Magyar state as a legal and institutional fact. The new Hungarian constitution was so carefully constructed that it gave the appearance of a typical liberal document. Public opinion in the western world was misled by the fair words of the text and the legislation which put it into effect, and failed to understand the significance of the preamble which virtually nullified the liberalism of the text of the nationality law of 1868: "According to the fundamental principles of the Constitution all the inhabitants of the kingdom form, from a political point of view, a single people, the Hungarian people, one and indivisible. Each inhabitant of whatever nationality is equally a citizen of this people and enjoys the same rights as every other citizen. This equality of rights, in so far as it applies to the several languages in use in the country, may be modified by special dispositions only so far as these comport with the unity of the state, the practical necessities of government, and the administration and requirements of justice." In the right hands such an interpretative preamble to the law could make its administration mean almost anything. In 1887 a Magyar deputy, Louis Moczary, was moved by indignation to say on the floor of the Diet: "The law of 1868 exists only on paper and no one of its clauses is observed." Moczary's honesty forced him out of politics the next year. The position of the Slovaks under a chauvinistic Magyar government was worse than that of the Rumanians and Serbs in Hungary. These latter were members of peoples which, outside Hungary, had national states. But the Slovaks had no such outside help. Under more favorable circumstances the Czechs might have been of some assistance, but there were obstacles to help from that quarter. The Magyar government made every possible effort to prevent the growth of any common feeling between Czechs and Slovaks. Even so commonplace a thing as railroad communication between Bohemia and Slovakia was kept at an extremely low level of efficiency. The Hungarian railway system was pointed toward Budapest, and the roads to the west from Slovakia were consistently disregarded.

Another obstacle in the way of Czech help for oppressed Slovaks in Hungary was the coolness between the two peoples which had been growing more acute since the split in the languages became crystallized by Štúr's reforms. Both sides must share responsibility for this estrangement, and it is at this distance almost impossible to judge which was the more culpable of the two. Among the Czechs there had been growing a reaction against the principle of nationality which lay at the basis of Palacký's plan for a federalized empire enounced in 1848. Because the Magyars justified their demands for independence of Vienna on historical grounds, the Czech leaders came to think in terms of the ancient autonomy of the Bohemian kingdom. Intent upon their own difficulties, they soon forgot about the Slovaks, and excused their poor memories by appealing to the strict application of historical principles which would have decreed that Slovakia was a part of the Hungarian kingdom. In a struggle for constitutional rights the Czechs saw themselves in the same position with regard to the empire as the Magyars, and their blood relationship to the Slovaks slipped into the background for the time being. On the other side of the frontier the Slovaks were so occupied with the immediate problems of protecting their own interests within the framework of the Hungarian constitution that the need for maintaining contact with their Czech brethren was eclipsed.

In the 'seventies of the nineteenth century the Slovaks suffered severe losses all along the line. Slowly but surely the few high schools which they still kept open were closed. In 1875 the *Matica Slovenská* was dissolved, and its property, accumulated by voluntary contributions, was confiscated by the government and used to magyarize the Slovaks. In these years Koloman Tisza, minister of the interior, roundly declared that there was no such thing as a Slovak nation. The Slovaks had no defenders, either at the court at Vienna or outside the monarchy. In the Hungarian Diet they did not have a single representative. Hungarian elections, which long before the war in 1914 had become proverbially cynical, had prompted one of the most eminent students of Central Europe, R. W. Seton-Watson, to make an independent study of the Slovak question. In his book, *Racial Problems in Hungary* (1908),[1] he adduced incontrovertible evidence that these elections were even then the exact opposite of what they pretended to be, liberal and free elections.

Under these difficulties, which were painfully evident to every Slovak at every step, it is no wonder that, though they became somewhat less acute in the 'eighties, resignation should have become the refuge of the people. They did not have the heart to set about doing the few small things that would have restored their confidence and at the same time increased their strength. It is likewise understandable that

[1] This book is almost impossible to obtain. It is reported that the Hungarian government found the evidence Seton-Watson amassed so damning that it bought up all available copies. I cannot vouch for the truth of the report.

the Czechs, oppressed by Vienna and fighting an uphill battle for their own national existence, could not extend the Slovaks any help. But beyond the boundaries of the monarchy there was a great and powerful state, Russia. Official Russia never had had any interest in the Slav peoples within the Hapsburg empire. The Slavophiles who frequently gave utterance to their enthusiasm for Slav solidarity usually had in mind the Slavs of the Balkan area who were of the Orthodox faith and bound to Russia by a long cultural and confessional tradition. The problems of the western Slavs were seldom of any interest to them. The size and might of Russia, compared with the numbers and problems of the small Slav peoples to the west and south, particularly those within the Austro-Hungarian territories, could well raise doubts as to whether Russia might be expected to concern herself with such inconsequential affairs. There was always an element of the unreal and the naïve in Pan-Slavism. In Slovakia after 1867, where we find Pan-Slavism we are likely to discover that it was largely a counsel of despair and resignation, rather than a program of actual work. But in the realm of literature, it was more significant. The Russian classics were translated and avidly read among the Slovaks. Yet this hunger for Slavic literary themes and models had no political consequences in a positive sense, though the Magyar officials saw fit to regard Russophilism of any sort as a justification for petty persecution and the imposition of further cultural and linguistic restrictions.

In the last decade of the nineteenth century the situation began to improve for the Slovaks. The older generation of Slovak patriots, among whom the poet Svetozar Hurban Vajanský held a leading place, cultivated the Slovak language and literature and lived on hopes of help from their powerful Russian brother. But the younger generation was much more realistic in its plans and aspirations. Refusing to limit themselves to purely literary creation as the effective means of improving the position of their people, they turned their attention to economic life. They judged correctly that any amelioration in the material conditions of life, whether in town or country, would have a salutary effect upon other aspects of national existence and would strengthen a national consciousness that showed signs of withering under consistent pressure from the Magyar overlords.

It was only natural that leading members of this energetic newer generation of Slovaks should find kindred souls in Masaryk and his followers in Prague. By blood and temperament Masaryk was as much Slovak as Czech. He had little sympathy for the principles of so-called historical rights upon which the Czech conservatives had, for some time after 1867, built their case. Rather, he sought deeper foundations for a national movement in the inner vitality of the people themselves. He was therefore convinced that the Czechs, if they were joined by the Slovaks, could make for themselves a unified group capable of independent existence either within or without the framework of the monarchy. He steadfastly opposed movements in Bohemia that were based on sentiment rather than on realities, warning the public against high-sounding plans and vain imaginings, and reiterated his conviction that the patient and efficient performance of the commonplace tasks of every day could add infinitely more to the store of national strength than all the dreams of castles in Paradise. This realistic doctrine was in line with the thought of the leaders of Young Slovakia, and Masaryk's leadership was quickly and gladly recognized.

Thus, toward the end of the nineteenth century and in the early years of the twentieth, the Czech and Slovak generation which was to take the lead in the struggle for independence from 1914 to 1918 and thereafter in the formation of the first Czechoslovak Republic, began to grow together, gain mutual confidence, and find in each other complementary reserves of strength and idealism. Now at last, after long and sad years of separation, the two sister peoples begin to draw together again in the person and work of Masaryk. A new period in their history, which we can again call Czechoslovak history, opens. The key theme of this period is active co-operation in the maintenance of gains already won and the ultimate achievement of complete independence as one nation.

Yet it would be a falsification of the situation to assert that this new program of co-operation was supported by the majority of the Slovak population. In actual numbers those who actively supported the new movement were few, but intelligent and determined. On the other hand, the dissipation of forces caused by indifference and lack of imagination as to the real issues behind these efforts to co-operate with Czech realists was confusing to the masses of the Slovak people and had the effect of lending support to the Magyar government at Budapest. Fortunately for the cause of national independence, mere numbers were not to be the deciding factor either as to the justice of the program or as to the actual strength of the movement. The important thing was the measure in which the program of renewed co-operation with the Czechs answered the needs of the time and, what is more important, was consonant with the spirit of the history of the nation. It would have been helpful if the program had been able to count on a larger number of active supporters, particularly in view of the increased vigilance of the Magyar government and the sharp measures taken to stamp out the new spirit and all its fruits; but the spark had been struck and the fire was certain to flame up at the first opportunity. That opportunity could not come until the war broke out in 1914, and even then in Slovakia, because of governmental surveillance, it had not been possible for the leaders of the movement to spread its philosophy among large sections of the population. The events of the war, with their manifold effects upon the minds of the common people, made it possible for the idea of a common cause with the Czechs to become more widely spread. But the Slovaks were even then behind the Czechs in political preparedness, though their leaders were fully as anxious to co-operate with the Czechs as the Czechs were to have them. It was necessary, for the success of the movement, that the Czechs should take the lead in such a significant and decisive action as the securing of independence for their combined peoples.

⪦ 11 ⪧

The Struggle for Czech and Slovak Independence: 1914-1918. The Beginnings

THE eve of the World War of 1914 to 1918 found the Czechs divided in their views concerning the future of their nation. During the last decade of the preceding century many parties had come into existence, and opinion generally followed the lines of party programs on social, economic and political issues. But as this tendency developed rapidly, some of the leaders began to be disturbed over the prospective loss of the fundamental national unity which had been won at such cost during the nineteenth century. Consequently, warning voices were raised, crying out that the Czech people were playing into the hands of their Austrian rulers by setting up so many cliques and fostering such serious lines of cleavage within the nation. The annexation of Bosnia-Herzegovina by Austria-Hungary in 1908 and the subsequent accentuation of Hapsburg subservience to the ambitions of Berlin sharpened the doubts harbored by the more far-seeing Czech politicians as to the permanence of the Austro-Hungarian empire. Members of the radical parties, making their appeal to the historic rights of the kingdom of Bohemia and supported by some Realists[1] and National Socialists, proclaimed the lack of logic in a Hapsburg empire which, at the same time that it was growing internally weaker, was expanding its territory. The solution to this anomalous development, they declared, was an organic separation of the Bohemian crown lands from the Empire.

After the Serajevo incident (June 28, 1914) the Austrian ultimatum to Serbia and the subsequent declaration of

[1] See above, p. 193.

234

war, the Czechs could do little else than feel that Hapsburg Vienna was joining forces with Hohenzollern Berlin in a German crusade against the Slavs. The natural Czech reaction, in view of their own long history of Hapsburg oppression, was one of lively sympathy for Serbia and bitter resentment against the government at Vienna and the whole German ruling caste throughout the Empire. The attack on Serbia was interpreted by the Czech populace as the first action of a concerted assault on all the smaller Slav peoples. Such an attack could only elicit their sympathy, and eventually, in self-defense, their active antagonism.

General mobilization in the Empire was ordered on July 26. The Czech soldiers who were called to the colors made their sentiments known immediately. Some few refused to obey the order, and the great majority sang Slav songs interspersed with anti-German cries as their trains pulled out of the Prague stations. The civilian populace was openly and vociferously of the same mind. Such cries as "Russia is with us, and France will mop up anyone who is against us," and "Maria Theresa lost Silesia, Francis Joseph is going to lose everything," reflected the deep-rooted conviction of the Czech people that the stupid aggressiveness of a Berlin-dominated Hapsburg court would unite all the Slavs, East and West, and result in a great Russian-led victory over the Central German powers.

The German population of Austria and Bohemia, however, felt equally sure that the Central Powers would crush the Entente in a few months at most. Thus far it was a conflict of hopes and beliefs only. But the government at Vienna could not allow this openly revolutionary sentiment to continue, and a policy of repression of Slavic anti-Austrian opinion (and, of course, action) was immediately adopted by the military dictatorship set up in Prague (*Kriegsüberwachungsamt*). The Czech press, though some of it was at the beginning either pro-Austrian or compliant, was muzzled by a rigid censorship. Scores of daily papers and periodicals were completely suppressed, and those that were permitted to continue publication were obliged to print as unsigned editorial material the official statements given out by the censor's office. Civil courts were supplanted by military tribunals, and civil law suspended. In Slovakia, all newspapers appearing in the Slovak language were suppressed. The leader of the National Socialist party in Bohemia, V. Klofáč, was imprisoned on charges of high treason, and in Slovakia the Hungarian government proceeded with even more determination, if possible, than the Austrians showed in Bohemia. Several of their most prominent leaders were thrown into prison and forced to make declarations against Russia—to whom the Slovaks, more than the Czechs, looked for succor from Magyar oppression.

In such grim circumstances the Czech political leaders may be excused for hesitating to make any categorical pronouncements as to either Czech loyalty or reserve toward the government. Their hesitation was partly due to obvious political opportunism and partly to the fact that petty party divisions had so obscured the fundamental line of Czech political development that scarcely any of the leaders knew what course to follow in the present crisis. But the Czech soldiers called to the Austrian colors and Czechs living abroad felt no such inhibitions, and anti-Austrian demonstrations in Paris, Kiev, Petrograd and Moscow were numerous. The instinct of the common people was surer than the experience of the politicians.

The early successes of Russian arms in Galicia and the Carpathians heightened the hopes of the Czechs and Slovaks in the autumn of 1914. The Russian commander, Grand Duke Nikolai Nikolaievich, promised the Slavs of the Austro-Hungarian empire that Russia would soon liberate them from their oppressor, and, in the course of the war, 300,000 Czech and Slovak soldiers deserted to the Russians from their Austrian and Hungarian units. But the fond hopes thus aroused at the beginning of hostilities were destined to be disappointed at the loss by the Russians of the gains they had made, and their further withdrawal in the face of better organized Hapsburg and German armies. On the southwestern front, toward Serbia, over 70,000 Austro-Hungarian soldiers surrendered to the Serbians. Of this number over half were Czechs, who were glad to give themselves up to brother Slavs. But the Austrian and Hungarian military took severe measures to break this spirit of revolt. Many sentences of death were passed upon Czechs and Moravians in the winter of 1914-1915 for having in their possession copies of the manifesto of Czar Nicholas II promising the people of Bohemia the restoration of their freedom. Though some of the sentences of death were commuted to life imprisonment, at least thirty-five persons were executed for this crime.

But the anti-Austrian and anti-Magyar feeling among Czechs and Slovaks was too deep-rooted to be so simply eradicated. Resistance was indeed driven underground, but it became no less bitter for that reason, and ultimately it became even more dangerous. The need for organization of this body of resentment and a clearly articulated program of opposition came to be felt among most of the leaders. There were still a few—among them Dr. Šmeral—who regarded any clear anti-Hapsburg policy on the part of the Czechs as inopportune and even certain to react unfavorably against the nation. Others, for various reasons, were non-committal. After some indecision most of the Czech parties and their leaders agreed that in the interests of national existence they would have to take a united stand in opposition to the Hapsburg government in the present conflict. The more prominent among these leaders who looked in general terms toward the realization of Czech national autonomy were Antonín Švehla, high in the councils of the

Agrarian party and later Prime Minister; Dr. Hajn, a leader of the Radical Progressive party; Dr. Scheiner, head of the Sokol organization; Dr. Jan Herben, editor of the journal *Čas*; Dr. Šámal, Dr. Eduard Beneš, then a young lecturer in sociology at the Czech university; and Professor Thomas Masaryk.

This group of like-minded men, with a few others, formed the nucleus of what was soon to become, under pressure of changing circumstances, a revolutionary movement. At first they met separately by twos and threes, but soon held informal and secret meetings of all or most of the group at the home of Dr. Bouček, a practicing lawyer and active member of Masaryk's Realist party. At these meetings the aims of ultimate Czech independence and the methods to be employed to gain those ends were decided upon after careful discussion of the meaning of the course of the war and the political maneuvering behind the scenes both east and west. The united conclusion was that the future of the Czech people depended upon a victory of the Entente over the Central Powers. Obviously, then, they had to make themselves and their cause known to the political leaders of the Entente nations if they wanted to profit by such a victory.

Their reasoning was simple. A victory of the Central Powers, Germany and Austria-Hungary, would be essentially a German victory, since Austrian foreign policy had been dictated from Berlin for decades. A German victory would mean an open road for the German *Drang nach Osten* at the expense of the smaller Slav peoples lying in the path of this expansion, and they would be worse off than before. As they saw it, German domination of the Danube basin meant Slav slavery. A victory of the Entente was the only possible hope of the peoples of the Hapsburg empire. Unfortunately, the Entente statesmen were too inadequately aware of the realities of Central European politics to realize the importance of these elementary facts for their own cause until well over two years of the costly war had gone by.

Masaryk's profound researches into the social and political structure of Czarist Russia obliged him to reject the ardent Russophilism of Kramář and the Young Czechs from the very beginning of the war. Fortunately for the whole movement, this enthusiasm for Russia and the hope of incorporation into the Russian Empire was cooled by the military disasters to the Czarist armies in the winter of 1914-1915; and the Young Czechs thereafter, as a general rule, loyally supported Masaryk's more radical program of complete independence of both branches of the Czechoslovak people from the rule of the Hapsburgs. This program was the keystone of the whole movement, and ultimate success was a vindication of the soundness of Masaryk's reasoning.

The last meeting of the whole group, later with some important additions to be known as the "Maffia," was held late in December 1914. Masaryk announced then his plans to go abroad in order to establish connection with influential individuals in the Entente capitals and set up an organization able to maintain the necessary communications between Prague and the outside world. It was understood that the outside action should be closely integrated with the work of the group remaining within Bohemia. At this time Masaryk planned to return once more to Prague before leaving the land for the duration of the war, but it was realized that such a return might not be possible, and arrangements were made to meet that contingency so that no break in the continuity of direction might occur. He left Prague on December 17, 1914, and arrived in Rome on December 22. He did not again set foot on Czech soil until he returned four years later as President of the Czechoslovak Republic, December 21, 1918.

In the meantime Czechs and Slovaks residing in Russia, France, Switzerland, Italy, England and America were showing both by word and action where their sympathies lay. When the war broke out there were 70,000 Czechs and Slovaks living in Russia and Siberia, concentrated mostly in Petrograd, Moscow, Kiev, Warsaw and Odessa, as craftsmen or skilled mechanics, or engaged in business or the professions. At the same time the number of Czechs and Slovaks in France was much smaller. In Paris there were about 2,000 in the whole Czech-Slovak colony, mostly skilled craftsmen and laborers. They had an active Sokol, and were quite conscious of their nationality. In all the rest of France there were perhaps several thousand more. The number of Czechs and Slovaks resident in Italy and England at the beginning of the war was considerably less, and they were so scattered that they had no organization and no coherence. But in the United States there were a million and a half Czechs and Slovaks, with extensive patriotic organizations, newspapers, churches and Sokols. They were particularly strong in and around Cleveland, Pittsburgh, New York and Chicago; and throughout the Middle Western states there were numerous colonies and settlements engaged in farming, in industry and in the professions. Their natural Slav love of freedom had become more intense under the fostering protection of the American flag, and their generous support of the work of Masaryk and Beneš for the liberation of their homeland was destined to be a decisive factor in the crucial years that lay ahead.

A considerable number of the Czechs and Slovaks in Russia had become subjects of the Czar, and those who had not were strongly pro-Russian in the conflict. Yet the outbreak of war quickened still more their nationalistic yearnings, and the Czechs of Petrograd obtained an assurance of support for the cause of the Czechs in Bohemia from Maklakov, Minister of the Interior. Sazanov, Minister of Foreign Affairs, suggested that they send a memorandum clarifying their problem to the Czar. This note, composed by Jiří Klecanda, was presented to the Czar early in August, 1914. On August 20 Czar Nicholas received sympathetically a deputation of Czechs in Moscow. A month later, on September 17, a deputation of Czechs and Slovaks told the Czar in Petrograd that they looked forward to the day when the crown of St. Václav should be joined to the crown of the Romanovs. News of these diplomatic successes filtered back to Bohemia, and the Russophiles among the Czech leaders felt that their battle was half won. But events were to belie their hopes, and it should here be suggested that grave doubts of the sincerity of Sazanov and the Czar may justly be entertained. Expressions of sympathy were not expensive, and the pro-German clique at the Romanov court was at all times powerful.

The persistent demand of the Czechs did, however, succeed in gaining the government's permission to form a volunteer corps to fight beside the Russian army in the Galician campaign. Russian official circles planned to use the corps thus formed in fomenting a revolution among the Slavs of Bohemia and Slovakia to facilitate the purely military conquest of the Austro-Hungarian empire. This corps took the name of the Czech Legion (*Česká Družina*). Formed late in August 1914, it was officered mostly by Russians and placed under the command first of Lieutenant Colonel Lotocky and later of Lieutenant Colonel Sozentovich with headquarters at Kiev. Within a few days more than 800 volunteers had joined. The regimental flag was the Russian tricolor with the crown of St. Václav superimposed. The oath of allegiance to the Russian Czar was administered on September 28, 1914, and the Legion took part in the Galician campaign, attached to the Third Army. Individual soldiers from the Legion were sent into the Austro-Hungarian lines and induced the desertion or surrender of whole platoons and companies of Czechs and Slovaks to the Russians. The whole 28th Regiment of Prague followed these Russian Czechs to the Russian lines, and the 35th Regiment of Pilsen surrendered within half an hour of reaching the front lines. As a result of these wholesale surrenders the number of Czech and Slovak soldiers in Russia was immeasurably increased, and the leaders of the Legion obtained permission to expand it by taking in volunteers from the newly arrived Czech and Slovak prisoners. The Legion grew to almost three thousand soldiers. Among the new members was Bohdán Pavlů, former editor of the influential newspaper *Národní Listy*; he was henceforth to assume a leading role in guiding the policies of the Czechoslovak movement in Russia.

In the spring of 1915 the appalling inefficiency of the Russian military organization became evident, and the Austrians, aided by German troops, forced a withdrawal of the demoralized Russian forces from Galicia. The enlarged Legion, however, distinguished itself in several rearguard and local engagements during the withdrawal, and Czechoslovak prestige grew greatly among the Russian people and also in official circles. After the spring campaign the Legion, now commanded by Lieutenant Colonel Trojanov, was transferred to the army of General Brusilov on the Volhynian frontier (September 1915).

The continued ineffectiveness of the Russian army disillusioned many of the Czechs and Slovaks living in Russia who had pinned their hopes on their powerful Slav brother. At the same time it accentuated the differences between the Kiev and Petrograd Czech and Slovak colonies. The latter was more conservative, as it was naturally more susceptible to the atmosphere of the reactionary court, which in turn was strongly Germanophile. There is small doubt that the court at Petrograd had little desire to see Austria-Hungary dismembered. Its ambitions would have been fully satisfied with a slight increase of Russian territory by the annexation of Austrian Galicia and Volhynia. The more radical solution of the war issue, the dismemberment of the Hapsburg empire by the creation of independent Slav states, was repugnant to the dynastically-minded advisers of the Czar. Of pure and thorough-going Pan-Slavism there was almost no vestige at the Romanov court. The Czech colonies in Petrograd, and to a lesser extent in Moscow, could not fail to be influenced by this atmosphere. At Kiev, on the other hand, where the Czechs and Slovaks, because engaged in industry and commerce at some distance from the court, were able to form their own opinions, a more radical temper prevailed. Here Czechoslovak independence was felt to be inevitable and unconditionally necessary.

In spite of these differences of outlook, however, serious attempts were made to bring all the Czechs and Slovaks in Russia into some organic political group. After early abortive efforts in this direction there finally resulted a constituent assembly of the "Federation of Czechoslovak Associations in Russia" (*Svaz československých spolků v Rusku*) which met in Moscow early in March 1915, attended by thirty-four delegates. A weekly, *Čechoslovak*, was founded in Petrograd in June 1915, with articles not only in Czech and Slovak, but also in Russian, and other journals soon appeared in Moscow and Kiev. A principal aim of these efforts was the formation of a large Czechoslovak army from the thousands of Czech and Slovak prisoners in Russian prison camps to fight against Austria-Hungary.

But questions of organization and jurisdiction were very complicated, and the Russian government refused to allow the formation of a Czechoslovak army which would have any semblance of independence of Russian control. Czech and Slovak prisoners, however, were gladly given permission to volunteer for work in industry and even in munitions factories. Coming from a highly industrialized country, their skilled services were more than welcome to a Russian government harassed by the impending threat of a complete industrial breakdown. Many others of the prisoners enlisted in the volunteer army of Serbian prisoners, formation of which, because Serbia was already a recognized state, the Russian authorities found no difficulty in allowing. The "Federation" (*Svaz*) very early sent emissaries to Paris to gain the support of the Council there for political action, and to plan a comprehensive campaign for Czechoslovak liberation from Hapsburg oppression. Yet, because the Russian Czechoslovaks were less united among themselves as to the alternatives to Hapsburg rule—union with Russia, a new Czech monarchy, or a democracy—their voice carried little weight in the councils of the Czech leaders in Paris.

At the same time, the Russian military failure had its immediate effects on the anti-Austrian movement in Prague. The whole Russophile section of the Czech population was completely discredited, and those who thought in terms of Pan-Slavism no longer had any grounds for argument. This disappointment brought a temporary depression, yet in the long run it was salutary that the disillusionment should have come so early in the struggle. A clearer concentration of attention and action upon the struggle in the west, whence alone their eventual salvation was to come, was now possible. But the proud optimism of the German and Magyar ruling classes was heightened by the certainty of Russian failure, and they openly boasted that the Czechs and Slovaks would henceforth have even less participation in the political life of the Empire than they had had before the war. Persecution of the Slavs, direct and indirect, increased in severity. Dr. Kramář and Dr. Scheiner were imprisoned on May 21, 1915, and Drs. Rašín, Červinka and Zamazal on June 12. The price of living mounted rapidly, and Bohemia and Slovakia were robbed to an alarming extent of their supplies of food and provisions throughout the year 1915.

In France, even before her actual entry into the war, large crowds of Czechs and Slovaks living in Paris demonstrated before the Austro-Hungarian Embassy on July 26, 1914. This was followed by the enlistment of hundreds of Czechs and Slovaks in the Foreign Legion. The publicity attendant upon these events made it possible for some eminent French citizens—Sansboeuf, the deputy Garat and Professor Ernest Denis—to arrange for Czechs and Slovaks to be exempted from the classification of enemy aliens as Hapsburg subjects. The idea soon gained ground that a special Czech and Slovak military unit might be organized from volunteers among the colony, to fight on the side of France. In August 1914 over 300 volunteers were in training at Bayonne, as a unit of the Foreign Legion. This unit was known as the *Nazdar* company. On October 23, 1914, it went into the front lines near Rheims. A total of 471 Czechs, later joined by many more from Great Britain, enlisted in the French Foreign Legion in the first year of the war. So early in the war, obviously, the political aims of the volunteer company were vague. The period of articulate political organization was some distance in the future. Nevertheless the symbolic value of a company of Czech and Slovak volunteers whose standard bore the historic emblem of Bohemian freedom, the Lion of the House of Luxemburg, cannot be overestimated.

A Franco-Czech journal, *Nazdar*, was launched in October 1914, and Professor Denis wrote for the first number his famous article on "The Crucifixion of the Czechs." Copies of the journal were smuggled into Bohemia and widely read, creating a profound impression. But owing to inept leadership *Nazdar* died almost immediately. The work of publicizing the Czech cause was taken up in January 1915, by another journal, *L' Indépendance Tchèque,* founded by Koníček-Horský, just arrived from Russia, and edited by V. Crkal. The tone of this journal was, however, too Russophile and reactionary to suit most of the Czechs in France, who were strongly democratic. A sharp and apparently irreconcilable division of opinion within the Czech colony in Paris developed and was not quieted until the arrival of Masaryk in March 1915. Koníček-Horský was discredited, and in place of his journal another bi-monthly review, *La Nation Tchèque*, initially under the editorship of Professor Denis, was established May 1, 1915, representing the opinion of the vast majority of thinking Czechs at home and abroad.

The arrival of Masaryk in the spring of 1915, and the later arrival of Beneš in September of the same year, made Paris the virtual center of the Czechoslovak campaign on foreign soil. We shall return to that story soon. The complete story of the winning of Czechoslovak independence is immensely complicated. Chronology cannot be followed without the intrusion of factors of political geography. The movement pursues a different course in Russia from that in France, and in Italy from that in America or England. Yet it comes to be bound together by a dominant concept, personified in Masaryk, and a dominant technique, guided by Beneš. Therein lies its unity, for these two men worked together with remarkable singlemindedness. It will be our task to trace the threads of the movement in order to show how they all are finally woven into a unified and integrated whole. We shall first bring the story of Czechoslovak action in Italy, America, France and England to the time of the Paris Declaration of November 1915, when a unified organization came to public notice. This is the first step. We shall then trace the second step: the successful effort to create a Czechoslovak military organization recognized by the Entente nations as an independent unit. The third step was the winning of political recognition by the Entente governments of the Czechoslovak National Council. When the Council was recognized diplomatically as the *de facto* government of the Czechoslovak people fighting against the Central Powers, the real victory was won.

There were few Czechs or Slovaks in Italy before the entry of that nation into the war against Austria-Hungary on May 23, 1915. Even then Italy's participation in the hostilities was not what could be called active in the months immediately following her declaration of war, and the primary interest of Italian policy seemed to be directed toward a maintenance of a balance of power on the Adriatic slightly in Italy's favor. On this basis the Yugo-Slavs could not be allowed to gain prestige or territory at the expense of Austria, and Italy could hardly be expected to welcome the dismemberment of the Hapsburg dominions, particularly if such dismemberment meant strengthening Serbia, or any strong grouping of Yugo-Slavs. This predisposition of Italian policy was to make more difficult the problem of the Czechoslovak National Council in gaining recognition for its national aspirations. Understanding of the Czechoslovak problem, however, grew in official circles during 1916 and 1917, and several prominent Italian politicians and publicists, particularly di Cesare, Torre, Salvemini, and the Socialist minister Bissolati, openly advocated the independence of the Czech and Slovak peoples. In 1917 Benito Mussolini supported the claims of the Czechs to an independent national existence in his paper, *Popolo d'Italia*.

The situation among the American Czechs and Slovaks was, at the beginning of the war, somewhat parallel to that in Russia, in that there was some difference of opinion between conservative and radical elements within the various colonies. But the reactionary influence of the Czarist court was lacking. In its place there was considerable Catholic opposition to the radical democracy of the rank and file of the whole group. There were already in existence a number of Czech and Slovak newspapers, and the media for propaganda were thus well established. As early as 1907 the Slovak League had been founded, and early in 1915 the Czech National Union represented the Czech element. The Old World backgrounds of the two elements were different, but the impact of the war brought the two peoples together. In October 1915, representatives of the Slovak League and the Czech Union met in Cleveland and proclaimed the inevitable necessity of a "Union of the Czechs and Slovaks in a confederation of states with complete autonomy for Slovakia." The idea of a federalized Danubian state was still regarded as the best they could hope for. Before America's entrance into the war the active propaganda of the Central Powers kept American opinion somewhat divided between the Entente and the German-Austrian Alliance, and this division may have been partially reflected among americanized Czechs and Slovaks. But the work of Karel Pergler, editor of the New York *Spravedlnost*; of Emanuel Voska whose counter-espionage organization was so vitally useful to the Entente powers; of Francis Kopecký, who, as an official of the Austrian consulate in New York, furnished to Voska and the Allied agents information of incalculable value; and of Vojta Beneš, an older brother of Dr. Beneš, who, having previously been in America, was chosen as the most suitable person in Prague to present the case for the liberation movement—all contributed to swing American Czechoslovak opinion wholeheartedly behind the program of the Paris Council. The energy of Joseph Tvrzický and Dr. J. L. Fisher in organizing the Czech National Association was also of great importance. A campaign of moderate and intelligent publicity through newspapers, pamphlets and books acquainted the American public with the Czechoslovak people and its aims.

Though there were some volunteers from America for military service, either through Canada or direct to France, the greatest contribution of the colony in the United States was of a financial nature. Masaryk in his *Making of a State* tells that in 1914-1915 he received $37,871 from America, in 1916, $71,185, in 1917 (to April 30, 1918) $82,391, and in 1918 (from May 1 on) $483,438—a grand total of $674,-885. It may not seem a large sum in these later days of astronomical finance, but with careful use it was enough to bring the work to a successful conclusion.

In England the number of Czechs and Slovaks was small and their military significance was very little, but the cause had some informed and influential friends. Professor R. W. Seton-Watson, an expert in Hapsburg affairs, and Wickham Steed, foreign editor of the powerful London *Times* gave unsparingly of their time and influence to the Czechoslovak cause, opening doors for Masaryk to politicians in high positions, informing the British people through the press of the justice of the cause and the ultimate benefit that would accrue to Britain from the dissolution of the Austro-Hungarian empire. The professorship in the University of London which Seton-Watson procured for Masaryk was a post of unequalled opportunity—an opportunity of which Masaryk most ably availed himself in the inaugural lecture on October 19, 1915. Asquith, then Prime Minister, had consented to preside, but was prevented by illness from attending, and Lord Robert Cecil took his place. The good will of Asquith and Cecil was in itself a diplomatic victory, but Masaryk's lecture, "The Problem of the Small Nation in the European Crisis" was a sensation, and strengthened the logical foundations of the movement in the British mind.

In the meantime the Austrian and Hungarian repression

of the Czechs and Slovaks had become almost unbearably severe. There were many executions of soldiers and civilians. The press, art, education, food and all economic life were rigidly controlled by the imperial army in the interests of the ruling races at the expense of the subject peoples.

The story of the daring and successful work of the Maffia in the first half of 1915 has been graphically told by Beneš himself in his *War Memoirs,* and it will not be necessary to repeat that story here. But it must be remarked that for coolness, resourcefulness and sustained courage of a considerable number of habitually honorable and law-abiding men who knew that their own lives and the cause of a whole people depended upon their wiliness and successful circumvention of the law, there is nothing to match it in modern times.

Beneš made two trips on false passports to Switzerland to meet Masaryk and report on the internal situation at Prague and to bring back messages and instructions from him. Three leading members of the Maffia were arrested: Kramář (May 20), Scheiner (May 21) and Rašín (July 12). But the fears of the other members that their organization was known and that their game was up were unfounded. The arrests were ordered simply because the three men taken into custody were considered too dangerous to be left free. Nevertheless it was decided in July and August 1915 that the scene of aggressive anti-Hapsburg action would have to be shifted to the lands of the Entente. Masaryk, thinking that the time had come for an open declaration of Czechoslovak aims, expressed a desire to have a number of active Czech politicians get to Switzerland and thence to France, but for one reason and another only Beneš was able to escape. After making detailed arrangements for future communication between the Maffia at home and the offices in France, Beneš reached Switzerland on September 3, 1915, and went immediately to Paris, where Masaryk was awaiting him. The Austrian police continued to take a strong line, and soon Masaryk's daughter Alice, Madame Beneš, Dr. Soukup and many other persons of national importance were also in prison, either under sentence of indefinite detention, or awaiting a trial which, if it ever came, would certainly be a travesty even on Hapsburg justice.

The arrival of Beneš in Paris marks the beginning of a new and decisive phase in the Czechoslovak struggle for independence. The framework of a widespread organization was set up. Sychrava, an experienced journalist, remained in Zurich, a focal point of intrigue for both the Entente and the Central Powers. Beneš, already known in academic circles in France, headed the general secretariat established in Paris. Dürich, a prominent Agrarian who had escaped from Prague in May 1915, was temporarily in Switzerland, but plans were already being laid for his trip to Russia to bring order out of the misunderstandings existing between the several colonies at Moscow, Kiev and Petrograd. Masaryk was thus left free to go to England to take up the work there. The task of informing and convincing British official opinion concerning the Czechoslovak cause could not possibly have been done by anyone else. Thus the whole Czechoslovak organization was based upon an ideal division of labor.

The Maffia, it should be recalled, was an exclusively Czech organization and naturally thought and planned in terms of Czech freedom from Austrian misrule. For the Slovaks, who were living under a harsher Magyar oppression, such a spirit of revolt headed by such an organization was an absolute impossibility, at least until much later in the war. The action of the Czech and Slovak colonies in Russia, France and America had been on a broader basis. Whereas at home they could not work together at all, abroad the two branches of the nation could make common cause. Their close ethnic and cultural relationship became of more importance once they were cast among non-Slav peoples, or even among a branch of the Slav race (e.g. the Russians) which differed from both of them much more than Slovaks differed from Czechs. It had been more evident, therefore, to leading Czechs living abroad, with the clearer perspective that distance gives, that they and the Slovaks should join their efforts. To Masaryk, himself perhaps more Slovak than Czech, such a united effort had been a self-evident necessity from the beginning of the war.

On November 14, 1915, the Czech Foreign Committee issued a proclamation in Paris which was a virtual declaration of war against the Hapsburg state. It announced the alliance of the Czechs and the Slovaks with the Entente powers and voiced the demand for the establishment of an independent Czech-Slovak state within the historical boundaries of the two peoples. The form of the declaration had been approved by the leaders in Prague, and was signed by representatives of the Czech and Slovak colonies in France, Russia, England and America. It bears the names of Dürich, Masaryk, Bohumil Čermak (Russia), Antonín Veselý (Paris), Ludvik Fisher (Chicago), Karel Pergler (Chicago), Františék Kupka (Paris), Emanuel Voska (Chicago), Jan Sýkora (England) and Františék Kupecký (England). Though Beneš may almost be said to have written the declaration, it was thought better for him not to appear as a signatory.

Soon after the publication of this document the forces of the central organization, now called the Czechoslovak National Council, were greatly strengthened by the addition of Milan Štefánik and Štefan Osuský. Štefánik, a former pupil of Masaryk at Prague, had come to Paris in 1902, gained a reputation as an astronomer, become a French citizen and volunteered in the French air service where he served with distinction. He was able to secure for the Czechoslovak Council, and particularly for Masaryk and

Beneš, interviews with prominent French politicians. The first hearing Briand gave Masaryk, arranged by Štefánik, on February 3, 1916, was very sympathetic, and Briand never thereafter wavered in his open advocacy of Czechoslovak independence. For many months he was alone among responsible Entente statesmen in this position. Štefan Osuský was a Slovak who had been for some years in America. In addition to serving as a liaison officer between American Slovaks and the Paris Council, he was well versed in Hungarian affairs. His knowledge of Hungarian politics was to be extremely useful to the Council in planning for the liberation of Slovakia from the Magyars.

By the beginning of the year 1916 the first step on the road to the creation of an independent Czechoslovakia had been taken. A representative political organization had been formed whose authority was tacitly if not yet openly recognized by responsible Czech leaders at Prague as well as by Czech and Slovak colonies throughout the world. Its policy and demands upon Austria-Hungary had been publicly declared. All this was an important move in the right direction, but it was still only the first step. At least two other steps—assuming the victory of the Entente in the war —would have to be taken before independence would be realized. First, in a world at war, in order that the claims of the Council to speak for Czechs and Slovaks all over the world might be proved valid, a considerable military organization, recognizing the undisputed authority and control of the Council, would have to be set up. Once this was done, the final step, political recognition of a *de facto* and *de jure* existence of a Czechoslovak government would have to be gained from all the Entente powers. Each of these steps would certainly involve all kinds of difficulties.

The establishment of a central Czechoslovak military authority was a very delicate and involved matter. The eagerness with which Czechs and Slovaks, whether already living in Entente countries and the United States in 1914 or prisoners of war from units of the Austro-Hungarian armies, volunteered to fight against their oppressors has already been mentioned. But they were scattered and relatively not numerous.

In Russia the pro-German party at court effectively discouraged any thought of a disruption of the Magyar-German Hapsburg empire. When Russian statesmen, furthermore, spoke of Pan-Slavism they had in mind only those Slavs who were of the Orthodox faith. Czarist Russia cannot be said to have entertained at any time serious thoughts of aiding in the creation of an independent Czechoslovak state out of the Hapsburg dominions. The balance between the three empires, Russia, Germany and Austria-Hungary, was too convenient to be lightly disturbed.

From the summer of 1915 to the spring of 1916 the differences between the Petrograd (Russophile) Czechs and Slovaks and the Moscow and Kiev (Nationalist) groups came to a head, and a new assembly of the Federation (see above, p. 243) met in Kiev in April 1916, established an interim Czechoslovak governmental council of ten members, functioning in Russia and recognizing the supreme authority of the Paris National Council. This was a tactical defeat of the Russophile Petrograd group, but it did not bring complete harmony. Personalities as well as differences in fundamental policies kept the Czechoslovak colonies in Russia in turmoil for some time to come. In particular the Russophile group led by Koníček-Horský objected strenuously to the leadership of Masaryk, which was, they contended, leading their nation away from its natural Slav orbit into close political and cultural connections with the western nations. This alliance they deprecated as unnatural and ultimately destructive of their Slav heritage. In addition, the position of the Czechoslovaks within the territory of a nation at war—though only half-heartedly so—was at best delicate. The composition of their group, partly resident Czechs and Slovaks, and partly prisoners of war, complicated by the uncertain vagaries of an intrigue-riddled imperial court, make the doubts and vacillations of the Czechoslovaks in Russia somewhat understandable.

Early in June 1916, Czar Nicholas approved a proposal made by Dr. Vondrák, President of the Federation, that Czechoslovak prisoners of war be freed to form a Czechoslovak army. But the conservative Boris Stürmer, the new Prime Minister, blocked the execution of the decree, and Czech and Slovak prisoners who wanted to serve against the Central Powers had to be content with following some of their fellows who had previously joined the Serbian army.

The leaders of the Federation were greatly discouraged by this setback. There was also unrest and deep dissatisfaction among the Czech and Slovak prisoners whose hopes had been so cruelly dashed. It is not surprising, therefore, that the arrival of Dürich from Paris was looked forward to by all sections of Czechoslovak opinion in Russia with relief and hope. He spoke Russian, and was known to be close to Kramář and therefore probably acceptable to the Russophile section of the Czechoslovak colonies in Petrograd and Moscow. On the other hand, he came as the representative of the National Council in Paris and was consequently thought by the radicals to be favorable to independence. His first démarches augured well for the success of his mission. He was received in audience by the Czar and seemed to be co-operating satisfactorily with Štefánik who had come to Russia a month after Dürich. But it was not long before it became perfectly clear that the strongly reactionary party at court and the Russophiles among the Petrograd Czechs had won Dürich over to their view. In connection with the party of Koníček-Horský he broke with the Federation, and headed a so-called "Czechoslovak National

Council in Russia" which was nothing more nor less than a puppet in the hands of the reactionary party at the imperial court. Štefánik, after communication with Masaryk and Beneš, was obliged to disown Dürich, and declare him no longer a member of the National Council (February 1917). This radical move was fortunately supported by the great majority of Czechoslovaks in Russia. They had by now come to the conclusion that Russia would never willingly aid them in their struggle for independence, and realized the tragic consequences of several years of indecision.

The outbreak (March 8, 1917) and rapid development of the Russian revolution in Petrograd and the increased instability of Russian political direction only fortified the resolution of the Czechoslovaks to break their ties with Russia and cast in their lot with the Entente. The chaos of the early months of the Russian revolution kept Russian political leaders too busy to pay much attention to the Czechs and Slovaks. These latter took advantage of the situation to strengthen their organization, and they gained permission to increase the size of their Legion to four regiments (June 13, 1917) by admitting numbers of prisoners and volunteers. The battle of Zborov in Galicia (July 1-2, 1917) was about the last flare of Russian military activity, and the Czechoslovak brigade participated in this action with cool courage and eminent success, capturing 4,200 prisoners and much matériel. Russian military circles were duly impressed, and Kerensky was induced to approve the organization of a Czechoslovak army independent of the Russian military. But Russian bureaucracy and the conservative army leaders put many obstacles in the way of the execution of these concessions.

Masaryk arrived in Russia from England in May 1917, hoping to be able to bring an effective unity into the thought and action of the discouraged Czechoslovak colonies, but he had to spend months in patient negotiation to counteract military and political obstruction of his plans. His labors bore some fruit, and by October 1917 he felt he had won his first point, permission to create an independent Czechoslovak army. General Dukhonin agreed (October 9, 1917) that the Czechoslovak army should be an independent unit under French command, not to be used save against Austria-Hungary and Germany, and to be under the political control of the Paris National Council. This very principle of independence was later to be of great significance when Red Russians, Czarist Russians and the Entente powers all wanted to use the Czechoslovak army as a pawn in their struggles for power.

The work of recruiting, in the meantime, had gone on at an increased tempo. By September there were over 22,000 volunteer members of the army. By the end of the year another 10,000 soldiers were enrolled and in training. The Czechoslovak army now consisted of two divisions, made up of eight active regiments and two reserve, each provided with artillery units.

The second principal object of Masaryk's trip to Russia was the transference of the Czechoslovak army to the western front. He foresaw the complete retirement of Russia from active participation in the war, and wanted to get the Czechoslovak units to France where their presence would have some definite political significance. On June 13, 1917, Masaryk had engaged with M. Albert Thomas, Minister of Munitions in the Ribot cabinet, to arrange for the transportation of 30,000 Czechoslovak troops from Russia to the French front. In accordance with this agreement 1,200 Czechoslovak troops were sent to France in October 1917, and in the spring of 1918 another transport loaded with a similar number left Russia for the western front. But under the chaotic conditions of Bolshevik Russia in 1918 no more such moves were practicable.

The position of the remaining 30,000 Czechoslovak troops was made more delicate by the conclusion of peace between Bolshevik Russia and the Central Powers, December 1917 to March 3, 1918, at Brest-Litovsk. From this time on the Czechoslovak army in Russia and Siberia is of relatively little significance in the struggle of the Czech and Slovak peoples for independence. The Anabasis of the Czechoslovak troops across Siberia is a thrilling story of cool courage and discipline, but it merits treatment more complete than it is possible to give here. Events on the western front, both military and political, finally determined the fate of the Czech and Slovak peoples. We shall therefore return to the West and take up the story where we left it, in the spring of 1916.

The Struggle for Czech and Slovak Independence:
1914-1918. Final Phases

IN THE SPRING MONTHS of 1916 Masaryk was in London,
laying the groundwork for British recognition of Czech and
Slovak aims. Beneš and Štefánik were in Paris at the headquarters of the National Council on the rue Bonaparte.
Bohdán Pavlů had recently arrived from Russia (March 16,
1916) by way of London, and almost all friends of the cause,
Czech, French and Russian, were vainly trying to dissuade
Dürich from going on his ill-fated Russian trip. But his
determination was much greater than his wisdom. As a last
resort Štefánik was sent after him to try to repair the damage he was certain to do.

Beneš was then alone as the representative of the Council
in Paris. His task was the management of the details of the
campaign for military and political recognition at the center of Entente political activity. The whole campaign had
been mapped out on the assumption that the war would
last for four or five years. Masaryk had come to this conclusion early in the war after learning that Lord Kitchener
and other competent military analysts had expressed such
an opinion. Consequently the persistence of rumors from
the summer of 1916 onwards that the Central Powers, and
particularly Austria, were putting out unofficial peace feelers was a source of considerable perturbation to the Council. An early peace would undoubtedly be postulated on
the continuance of the Hapsburg monarchy, and all the
hopes of the Council were focused on the collapse of that
Empire. More disturbing than the peace feelers themselves
was the possibility that most of the Entente statesmen
seemed to feel at this time and well into 1917 that it was

sound strategy to encourage the Hapsburg ministers to envisage a separate peace. If Austria-Hungary were weaned from the alliance with Germany, Germany alone would be easier to defeat. Both Beneš and Masaryk labored with every resource at their command to convince the French and British statesmen that a victory gained over Germany alone would leave the basic problems of European political stabilization unsolved.

Their task was not made lighter by the death of the eighty-six-year-old Francis Joseph and the succession of Charles in November 1916. Charles let it be known immediately that he wanted peace. The Entente powers welcomed the possibility of a face-saving peace, and the days were dark for the Czechoslovak Council. Their burden of discouragement was increased by the news from Prague. Nine leading political parties had united in the "Czech Federation" (*Český Svaz*) in November 1916, and immediately issued a declaration to the Czech people expressing loyalty to the Hapsburg dynasty. This was, as it stood, a virtual repudiation of Masaryk and his co-laborers abroad, and Beneš was hard put to it to convince the Quai d'Orsay that this action at Prague in no way represented the dominant sentiment of the Czech people, but had in reality been extorted from the party leaders by Count Czernin, Austro-Hungarian Foreign Minister. Nevertheless, the embarrassment was real and might easily have become tragic, had not the peace terms proposed by the Central Powers been so completely unacceptable as to cause a reaction in favor of the Czechoslovak thesis of destruction of the Hapsburg empire. Yet this reaction, definitely discernible, after a quarter of a century, from a study of the documents, was some time in making itself felt. The revised attitude of the Entente is most clearly seen in the note of January 10, 1917, in reply to Wilson's request for a statement of the aims of the belligerent powers. The Entente powers publicly proclaimed for the first time as one of their principal aims "the liberation of the Italians, Slavs, Rumanians and Czecho-Slovaks from foreign domination." Still, various peace pro-posals throughout the year 1917, emanating mostly from Vienna, kept the members of the National Council on tenterhooks lest their long-term program be nullified by an early conclusion of hostilities.

The 1917 revolutions in Russia, by removing their east-ern ally from the field, forced the Entente leaders to give some tangible expression to the logic of the earlier and more general declaration in the reply to Wilson's request for terms of peace. By now Austria-Hungary was seen as an obstacle to a stabilized Europe, and the thesis of the Na-tional Council appealed with greater force. A further step toward full political recognition was taken. This was the agreement referred to above between M. Albert Thomas, French Minister of Munitions, and Masaryk of June 13, 1917, providing for the transfer of 30,000 Czech and Slovak troops from Russia to the French front. This amounted almost to a *de facto* recognition and gave the National Council a much stronger tactical position. Beneš concluded further detailed arrangements for the organization and recognition of a Czechoslovak army during the summer and early autumn. These additional agreements were initialed August 4, 1917, and finally signed under date of December 19, 1917, by President Poincaré, Clemenceau, then Pre-mier, and Pichon, Foreign Minister. Though not yet com-plete political recognition, the signing of these agreements implied a long step in that direction, and was a signal dip-lomatic victory for the Council; a victory compounded of nearly equal parts of political sagacity, patience in nego-tiation, and, on a larger scale, an understanding of the logic of national development in Central Europe.

Of the three nations, France, England and Italy, the situation in Italy, at least in the critical years 1916 and

1917, was the most delicate for the Council. Italy did not enter the war until May 1915, and her geographical proximity to the eastern coast of the Adriatic, then part of the Austro-Hungarian empire, had considerable influence upon her attitude toward the thesis of Czechoslovak independence, as it was postulated upon the disruption of the Dual Monarchy. Italian war aims envisaged only the transfer of certain Adriatic coastal districts to Italy. The maintenance of the Dual Monarchy, slightly reduced in size and power, was an express aim of Italian policy from the first. The ambitions of the Yugoslavs for the creation of a large Adriatic national state rivalling Italy were regarded with a distrust bordering on fear. The net result of these two factors was that Slav nationalism applied to the Hapsburg monarchy was anathema to Italian thinking.

The Czechoslovak thesis on the other hand, was based on avowedly nationalistic assumptions. All Czech and Slovak leaders were warmly sympathetic toward the aspirations of the Yugoslavs. Consequently, it was only natural that the efforts of the National Council to win Italian support were received with coolness by Italian statesmen. But from the point of view of Czechoslovak policy Italian support was necessary. Neither France nor England was in direct contact with Hapsburg armies, and consequently took no Czech or Slovak prisoners. The Czechslovak army in France, if it could not recruit from prisoners, would never be of sufficient numbers to be a political or military factor; and recognition depended in the last analysis upon a demonstration of effectiveness in the field and usefulness as an ally. The supply of Czech and Slovak troops from Russia, because of transportation difficulties, would certainly be small. Italy, on the other hand, was fighting directly against Austria-Hungary and thousands of Czech and Slovak troops could easily pass into Italian hands. If the National Council could succeed in persuading Italian statesmen of the justice and expediency of their anti-Hapsburg thesis, they could use these prisoners to form a large army and become a factor in an Entente victory. Obviously, then, Italian support was of paramount importance to the Council.

Little was known in official Italian circles, or even among the better informed public, of the Czechs and Slovaks— their history, culture or aspirations. The beginnings of their action in Italy were therefore difficult. After the ground had been somewhat prepared, Beneš went to Rome in January 1917, and had some conferences with officials in the Foreign Office. Forewarned as to the natural bias of Italian leadership against both Slavs and nationalism, he endeavored with a measure of success to point out that the interests of Italy and the Czechoslovaks with regard to the liquidation of the Dual Monarchy were identical: the nationalization of the Hapsburg domains would, he argued, be a profitable development from the Italian point of view. The clear implication which he left the Italians to draw was that Italy would be in a more favorable position if the nations facing her littoral, and therefore her natural rivals, were more in number, and smaller in size. She could never fulfil her obvious destiny if she had to face and compete with an Austria-Hungary much larger than herself. The implications seemed to be understood, but only slowly. Several prominent Italians came out openly for the Czechoslovak position, and opinion gradually but appreciably began to veer in that direction.

Meanwhile the thousands of Czech and Slovak prisoners from the Austro-Hungarian army in Italy, concentrated mostly in a camp near Naples, began their own agitation for active association with the Paris Council. Baron Sonnino, Italian Foreign Minister, was impressed by the French recognition of the Czechoslovak army implied in the Thomas-Masaryk agreement of June 13, 1917; and recognized (September 1917) the right of the Paris National Council to represent the Czechs and Slovaks in Italy, of whom 4,000 had already volunteered to fight with the Entente against the Central Powers. Thereafter he permitted formation of labor battalions of Czechoslovak prisoners, but rejected Beneš's request for the recognition of military units under control of the National Council. But the disaster of Caporetto (October 24-November 1, 1917) made Italian political leadership less sure of itself, and, after much preliminary negotiation, Štefánik concluded a treaty with the then premier, Orlando (April 21, 1918), which allowed formation of an independent Czechoslovak army in Italy to be commanded by General Andrea Graziani, officered partly by Italian, partly by Czech and Slovak officers, but under the political control of the National Council in Paris. This was the first treaty concluded by the National Council which clearly recognized it as a sovereign political body. The diplomatic victory was all the more significant in that an initial prejudice against the Czechoslovak cause had to be overcome. The number of Czechoslovak troops soon rose to 22,000 volunteers. All seasoned veterans, they soon saw action, were cited for conspicuous bravery by General Diaz, and in the official Italian communiqué of September 22, 1918. This division also participated in the battle of the Piave in late October. All Czechoslovak statesmen are at one in pointing out that, once the Italians understood the aims of the National Council, they were uniformly sympathetic. Furthermore, if it could be said that they were not easy to convince, it should also be added that the Italians were always as good as their word.

It has been pointed out above that the first step in the program of the National Council, the establishment of a central political authority, was taken by the summer of 1916. The second step—the organization of an army recruited (1) from Czechs and Slovaks residing abroad at the outbreak of hostilities or (2) from Czech and Slovak soldiers who had fallen into the hands of the Entente powers as prisoners of war—has been partly described with reference to Russia and Italy. Few Austro-Hungarian units saw action on the French front, and consequently few Czechoslovak prisoners were taken. But one considerable group of Czech prisoners was added to the small volunteer company formed at Bayonne in the autumn of 1914. Approximately 25,000 Czech and Slovak troops had been taken prisoners by the Serbians in the early months of the war. At the time of von Mackensen's drive against Serbia in the autumn of 1915, these prisoners straggled along with the retreating Serbians into Albania; thence, with Italian help, they took refuge on the island of Asinara. Those that arrived, however were but a sorry remnant of the number that had begun the desperate retreat. Only 11,000 of the original 25,000 survived the ravages of hunger and disease on the way. Once on the island, their plight was, if anything, worse. Only 4,000 of this number lasted long enough to be taken to France to form there a nucleus of the Czechoslovak army on French soil.

Thus in the spring and summer of 1916 the National Council had a larger number to recruit from than it could have hoped for from activities on the western front, and it hastened to make the best of the new situation by a press campaign among the prisoners. At the same time the Council intensified its campaign among the French, and by conferences and interviews with highly placed French officials and influential personalities outside official circles the validity of the Czechoslovak thesis, that the dissolution of the Dual Monarchy was imperative, was brought home to a wider public.

But so long as undercover negotiations for peace initiated by Austria-Hungary were being carried on, that is, from the fall of 1916 until late in 1917, any effective encouragement of the Czechoslovak cause on the part of England or France was not to be expected. The National Council, therefore, feeling sure that the Entente statesmen would come to see the futility of a separate peace, bent their energies to consolidating the organization and training of the military units in Russia, Italy and France. When the peace tentatives failed to materialize, the whole Czechoslovak movement was in a stronger position than ever, partly because its actual organization was vastly improved, and partly because the Entente statesmen had been obliged by the logic of the situation to accept the Czechoslovak thesis with regard to Austria-Hungary. It was not long, therefore, after the agreements recognizing the Czechoslovak army as an independent military unit were reached, before full political recognition was accorded the National Council as a treaty-making government.

It was not long in time, but there were considerable obstacles to be overcome before that final step could be taken. It could hardly be expected that the Council would be given further substantial encouragement unless the Entente statesmen could be convinced that the desire for the destruction of the Hapsburg monarchy was actively shared by the other minorities of the Empire. For this reason the "Congress of Peoples Oppressed by the Hapsburg Monarchy" which met in Rome early in April 1918 was an event of great political significance. It was a tangible demonstration to Western Europe of how united the racial minorities in Austria-Hungary—Poles, Yugoslavs, Czechs, Slovaks, Rumanians and Italians—had become in their determination to re-form the territory of the monarchy into a collection of national states. The spirit animating the Rome Congress lived on through the ceremonies attending the semi-centennial celebration of the founding of the Czech National Theater in Prague on May 16 and 17, 1918. In patriotic speeches representatives of the various peoples in the Empire demanded, as a right shared by them all, freedom of their several nations from the Hapsburg yoke. Very significantly the Slovak poet Hviezdoslav brought greetings "from that branch of the Czechoslovak nation that lives in Hungary." In the final resolution of the meeting the pledge of mutual help was made: "All nations represented are determined to help each other, since the victory of one is also the victory of the other." The cumulative effect of the Rome Congress and the Prague demonstrations was of no little weight in the decision of the Entente powers to increase their tangible aid to the Czechoslovak National Council. Beneš and his co-workers now represented a vigorous and growing movement of revolt against the authority of the Dual Monarchy which could only be of advantage to the enemies of the Central Powers.

While Masaryk was in Russia, Beneš obtained from Lord Robert Cecil and A. J. Balfour in May and June 1918 specific commitments which assured the National Council *de facto* recognition as the responsible agents of the Czechoslovak cause. Balfour's letter of June 3, 1918, makes quite clear how the recent course of events had led Britain to grant more than either France or Italy had conceded separately until this time; and shows how the way had been paved for complete political recognition by all the Entente powers. The letter, as printed by Beneš in his *War Memoirs* (p. 376), was as follows:

Foreign Office
Sir,   *June 3, 1918*

In reply to the memoranda with which you were so good as to furnish me on the 10th and 11th instant, I have the honour to assure you that His Majesty's Government, who have every possible sympathy with the Czechoslovak movement, will be glad to give the same recognition to this movement as has been granted by the Governments of France and Italy.

His Majesty's Government will thus be prepared to recognize the Czechoslovak National Council as the supreme organ of the Czechoslovak movement in Allied countries, and they will also be prepared to recognize the Czechoslovak Army as an organized unit operating in the Allied cause, and to attach thereto a British liaison officer as soon as the need for this may arise.

His Majesty's Government will at the same time be prepared to accord to the National Council political rights concerning the civil affairs of Czechoslovaks similar to those already accorded to the Polish National Committee.

I have to add that the above decisions have been communicated to the Allied Governments concerned.

I am, sir,

Dr. Beneš,   Your obedient servant,
   Thanet House,   ARTHUR JAMES BALFOUR
    231, Strand, London

This strong letter without doubt encouraged the French policy-makers to clarify their position. On June 30 Pichon, French Foreign Minister, sent Beneš a letter in which, *inter alia*, he said:

. . . the Government of the Republic, in recognition of your efforts and your attachment to the Allied cause, considers it just and necessary to proclaim the right of your nation to its independence and to recognize publicly and officially the National Council as the supreme organ of its general interests and the first step towards a future Czecho-Slovak Government. . . .

Faithful to the principles of respect for nationalities and the liberation of oppressed nations, the Government of the Republic considers the claims of the Czecho-Slovak nation as just and well founded, and will, at the proper moment, support with all its solicitude the realization of your aspirations to independence within the historic boundaries of your territories at present suffering under the oppressive yoke of Austria and Hungary. . . .

. . . I tender my warmest and most sincere wishes that the Czecho-Slovak state may speedily become . . . an insurmountable barrier to Teutonic aggression and a factor for peace in a reconstituted Europe in accordance with the principles of justice and rights of nationalities.

268

Five weeks later, August 9, the British Foreign Office issued a statement:

Since the beginning of the war the Czecho-Slovak nation has resisted the common enemy by every means in its power. The Czecho-Slovaks have constituted a considerable army, fighting on three different battlefields and attempting, in Russia and Siberia, to arrest the Germanic invasion.

In consideration of their efforts to achieve independence, Great Britain regards the Czecho-Slovaks as an Allied nation and recognizes the unity of the three Czecho-Slovak armies as an Allied and belligerent army waging a regular warfare against Austria-Hungary and Germany.

Great Britain also recognizes the right of the Czecho-Slovak National Council as the supreme organ of the Czecho-Slovak national interests, and as the present trustee of the future Czecho-Slovak Government to exercise supreme authority over this Allied and belligerent army.

On September 2, the State Department of the United States issued a statement over the signature of Secretary Lansing which makes the same points:

The Czecho-Slovak peoples having taken up arms against the German and Austro-Hungarian empires, and having placed in the field organised armies, which were waging war against those empires under officers of their own nationality and in accordance with the rules and practices of civilised nations, and Czecho-Slovaks having in the prosecution of their independence in the present war confided the supreme political authority to the Czecho-Slovak National Council, the Government of the United States recognises that a state of belligerency exists between the Czecho-Slovaks thus organised and the German and Austro-Hungarian empires.

It also recognises the Czecho-Slovak National Council as a de facto belligerent government, clothed with proper authority to direct the military and political affairs of the Czecho-Slovaks.

The Government of the United States further declares that it is prepared to enter formally into relations with the de facto government thus recognised for the purpose of prosecuting the war against the common enemy, the empires of Germany and Austria-Hungary.

On September 11 the Japanese Embassy in Paris followed suit. It is worth remarking that all these declarations emphasize the existence of the Czecho-Slovak military forces in actual combat against the Central Powers.[1] There could hardly be a more explicit justification of the plan of campaign worked out and so tenaciously adhered to by the Paris Council than this repeated reference to the reality of their war effort. They built well.

The defeat of the Central Powers had by this time been accepted as inevitable for several months, and it was clear to everyone that the polyglot Hapsburg empire was in actuality already ancient history. Final *de jure* recognition of the Czechoslovak state was, after these significant pronouncements, only a matter of a few formalities. The whole National Council had every reason to feel proud of its achievements when, alone of the succession states, Czechoslovakia was represented by Beneš in the plenary session of the Supreme War Council at Versailles on November 4, at which armistice terms were drawn up.

In America the movement had progressed slowly but steadily during the years 1915 and 1916. Recruiting of volunteer soldiers presented some difficulties so long as the United States was neutral, but the financial and moral support of the Czech and Slovak colonies was of supreme importance. Štefánik came to America in May 1917, but after America's entrance into the war, April 1917, Czechs and Slovaks with American citizenship were not free to volunteer for service in a foreign army. About 2,500 newer immigrants, however, who were not yet subject to military service of the United States joined the Czechoslovak army and saw service on the western front. But the American public and political leaders were becoming more aware of the logic of the Czechoslovak thesis of the dismemberment

[1] Masaryk estimated the Czechoslovak military forces at 182,000.

of the Dual Monarchy along national and historical lines, and sympathy for the aspirations of the Czechoslovaks became increasingly vocal. The works of Thomas Čapek, a New York lawyer of Czech extraction—*The Slovaks of Hungary* (1915) and *Bohemia Under Hapsburg Misrule* (1915), were widely read and were very influential in changing American ignorance and indifference into active sympathy for the cause. Masaryk arrived in Vancouver from his months of work with the Czechs and Slovaks in Russia and Siberia on April 20, 1918; and on his way across the United States was enthusiastically welcomed by the American population as well as by all branches of the oppressed Slav peoples.

Through the friendly offices of Charles R. Crane, a wealthy American industrialist who had for long been interested in the western Slavs, and upon whose judgment President Wilson was inclined to rely, Masaryk had interviews with Secretary of State Lansing and, on June 19, 1918, with Wilson himself. He was able to convince the President that the tenth of his fourteen points (demanding a federalization of the Austro-Hungarian Empire) could not ultimately be satisfactory to the peoples of the Hapsburg lands; and the State Department issued on June 28 a clear statement of the American government's conviction that all the Slav peoples living under Austrian or German rule should be completely free. This note was intended to clarify a statement which Lansing had given out on May 29 in which the proclamation of the Rome Congress of Oppressed Peoples under date of April 8, 1918, demanding freedom from Hapsburg domination, was approved in somewhat general terms.

The Czech and Slovak colonies in America were widely dispersed, and as a consequence many shades of opinion concerning the government to be established were freely voiced. Masaryk felt the necessity of bringing some harmony into this diversity. But traditional Slovak yearnings for autonomy within the Magyar state tended to be transferred to the projected new Czech-Slovak state. Some agreement between American Czechs and American Slovaks would have to be reached before the Council could count on the continued support of both sections of opinion in America. At Pittsburgh on June 30, 1918, an agreement in fairly general terms was arrived at by representatives of American Czech and Slovak societies. So much has been said about this Pittsburgh declaration that it seems best to give the authentic text *in toto*.

The representatives of the Slovak and Czech organisations in the United States, the Slovak League, the Czech National Alliance and the Federation of Czech Catholics

deliberating in the presence of the Chairman of the Czechoslovak National Council, Professor Masaryk, on the Czechoslovak question and on our previous declarations of program, have passed the following resolution:

We approve of the political program which aims at the union of the Czechs and Slovaks in an independent State composed of the Czech lands and Slovakia.

Slovakia shall have her own administrative system, her own diet and her own courts.

The Slovak language shall be the official language in the schools, in the public offices and in public affairs generally.

The Czechoslovak State shall be a republic, and its Constitution a democratic one.

The organisation of the collaboration between Czechs and Slovaks in the United States shall, according to need and the changing situation, be intensified and regulated by mutual consent.

Detailed provisions touching the organisation of the Czechoslovak State shall be left to the liberated Czechs and Slovaks and their duly accredited representatives.

Several remarks should be made with regard to this document so that its later use may be correctly judged. In the first place, it is a resolution made by *American* Czechs and Slovaks and not by residents of Bohemia and Slovakia.

272

The signatories were in no way representatives of any native Czech or Slovak organizations. In the second place, it is not a treaty, but simply the proclamation of a program which the signatories were willing to support. There is no claim in the document that there was any sort of bargain entered into with Masaryk, but merely that it was done in his presence. In the third place, "autonomy" is not so much as mentioned. Finally, there is an explicit statement that the new Czechoslovak State is to be organized by representatives of the liberated Czechs and Slovaks. By this statement the American Czechs and Slovaks eliminate themselves from the task of setting up the new State in its detailed mechanism. The statement that is often repeated, that the Czechoslovak Republic was founded in Pittsburgh, obviously has no foundation in the facts. The organization of Czechoslovak sentiment and war effort proceeded harmoniously and enthusiastically under the guidance of Masaryk from this time on until independence and union of the two peoples in their native land were achieved.

Military as well as political affairs were going so badly for the Central Powers after the beginning of the Entente counter-offensive in July 1918 that the Vienna government began feverishly to seek peace with the Entente, and, at home, to hold out the bait of autonomy for the subject peoples within a federalized Empire. It was a crucial time, and the National Council could not afford to be caught napping. A separate or premature peace would nullify all the work done, and blast all their hopes for Czechoslovak independence. After advising with Masaryk and conducting urgent negotiations with the proper authorities in Paris, Beneš informed the Entente governments on October 14 that the National Council had constituted itself a Provisional Government, with its seat in Paris. Pichon accorded this Provisional Government *de jure* recognition on October 15, and the other Allies followed suit almost immediately. On October 18 Masaryk published from Independence Hall in Philadelphia a Declaration of Independence, reminiscent in many details of the American Declaration of Independence. That same day, Wilson, in his reply to Austria-Hungary's request for peace terms, specifically recognized the right of the Czechoslovak Provisional Government to make its own terms with the Dual Monarchy.

The National Committee in Prague had been kept fully advised of all these steps taken by the National Council, was in complete agreement with the program of Masaryk and Beneš, and was accommodating its own activities to the tempo of the action of the Paris Council. This close coordination will explain the neatness and bloodlessness of the ultimate complete success.

Thus far we have laid most emphasis upon the work of the National Council in Paris, London, Russia, Italy and America, largely because it was there that political and military recognition had to be gained. But all the work of the National Council would have been in vain if there had not been parallel action in the homeland. We must therefore retrace our steps to the autumn of 1915 in order to pick up the thread of events in Bohemia and Slovakia after the final escape of Beneš in September 1915.

The trials of Kramář, Rašín, and a number of less prominent patriots (Scheiner had been freed soon after his arrest for lack of evidence) began in November 1915, and the court proceedings lasted over six months. Naturally the Czech people followed the trial with consuming interest. The whole nation felt that it was on trial. Four of the accused, the two political leaders, Kramář and Rašín, and two of their lieutenants, Červinka and Zamazal, were condemned to death for high treason. The judgments were appealed but sustained in November 1916. The sentences were ready for the signature of Francis Joseph, but his death supervened, and his successor, Charles, commuted the sentence of Kramář to fifteen years of hard labor, Rašín's to ten years, and Červinka's and Zamazal's to lighter sentences of six years each.

A sustained war and the British blockade of the Continent had their effects upon living conditions in Austria and Bohemia. Food was scarce, prices were high, and government regulations were multitudinous, harshly enforced and altogether insupportable. Human nature being what it is, some opportunism was inevitable. This was the time chosen (January 1917) by nine Czech parties, under pressure from the new Austro-Hungarian Foreign Minister, Count Czernin, to amalgamate and proclaim their loyalty to the dynasty. This ill-starred proclamation was to cause the National Council serious embarrassment in their dealings with the Allies, until it could be explained that it was extorted under threat of duress by a Hapsburg minister who was partly of Czech blood. Fortunately for the Czech cause, the outbreak of the Russian Revolution diverted attention both at home and abroad from this pitiable demonstration of "realist" politics.

The nation as a whole openly resented this weakness, and, under the leadership of patriotic men of letters, a movement grew to repudiate those political "leaders." In April 1917, Jaroslav Kvapil, beloved poet and dramatist, wrote a manifesto, addressed to the Czech deputies in the Reichsrat, calling upon them to stand firm for the democratic traditions of the Czech nation. In it he says:

A democratic Europe, a Europe of free and independent peoples, is the Europe of tomorrow and the future. The nation demands of you, gentlemen, that, in this great moment of history, you bend all your energies, forego all other considerations, and act as free men, unbound by any thought of personal gain—as men of high moral and national sense.

The words of the manifesto were carefully chosen so as

to avoid any open treason, but the intent was clearly revolutionary. In the form in which he wrote it, the manifesto was signed by the leading Czech poets, novelists, artists and intellectual leaders of Bohemia; among them Alois Jirásek, the most popular novelist of Bohemia, F. V. Krejčí, literary critic and essayist, Jan Herben, essayist and influential journalist of Slovak blood (born in Moravia), Fr. X. Svoboda, psychological analyst in many literary genres, František Kvapil, poet, Antal Stašek, novelist of patriotic themes, Václav Novotný, historian and biographer of John Hus, and many others whose names were bywords in Bohemia. The effect was immediate, and at the next meeting of the Reichsrat (May 30, 1917) the Czech deputies took a strong position, demanding a federalization of the Empire, but especially a democratic Czech state along the lines of its historical rights. It is not hard to imagine how indignant the German and Magyar majority became at this Czech temerity and outright insolence.

The Writers' Manifesto came to be regarded as the expression of the national will. It was soon known almost by heart by every patriotic Czech. The memorandum to the Czech delegates to the International Socialist Conference at Stockholm which met from May to November 1917 was substantially identical with the Writers' Manifesto. This memorandum voiced the demands of the Czech people: an independent democratic state consisting of Bohemia and Slovakia, formally existing within the loose framework of a federal Danubian system.

But opportunism, or perhaps we should say the vestiges of pro-Hapsburg sentiment, did not easily disappear from the Czech political scene. Nevertheless the radicals, whose fundamental thesis was a conviction that the Hapsburg monarchy was a political and social anachronism which must be quickly hurried off the stage, were gaining in confidence and in power. The soft character of the Emperor

Charles and the knowledge that Austria-Hungary was seeking peace seemed omens of coming disaster. In an effort to woo Czech opinion Charles amnestied Kramář, Rašín and Klofáč on July 2, 1917. The effect was not what he had hoped for. A great impetus was given to the radical, anti-Hapsburg movement. The opportunists were outvoted in the Czech National Committee, never again to regain their position of power. Gradually, during the closing months of 1917, a nationalistic realignment of parties and influential newspapers took place that left only the Clerical parties on the side of the Vienna government.

To accentuate the growth of a spirit of political independence, the increasingly severe rationing of food, resulting in hunger and disease, particularly among the poorer classes, brought on riots and angry demonstrations. German and Magyar troops were brought into Bohemia to quell the disturbances, and Prague took on the air of a beleaguered city. For a proud people who had already seen the first rays of their day of liberation, this added insult served only to make the injury they had already suffered seem the more bitterly cruel. And then, to cap the climax, workers in a factory in Vitkovice were fired on by German troops in July 1917. Five Czech workmen were killed and martial law proclaimed in the whole region of Moravská-Ostrava. If there were still any Czechs who had a lingering affection for the Hapsburg monarchy, this attack reduced them to a stunned silence and united the nation in its bitterness against the oppressor.

News of the diplomatic and military successes of the Czechoslovak Council in Paris and its armies in Russia, France and, later, Italy, had been widely disseminated among the people throughout the latter half of 1917. This news strengthened the hand of the radical and revolutionary leaders at home. Count Czernin, perhaps impressed by the success of the arms of the Central Powers at the Brest-

Litovsk negotiations, made a statement late in December 1917 declaring the relations of the various peoples within the Austro-Hungarian empire an internal matter, of concern to the imperial government alone. The statement was greeted by the Czechs with an uproar of angry resentment, and on January 6, 1918, all the Czech deputies signed and issued a proclamation demanding a free, democratic and sovereign Czech state, and unconditional liberation of the Slovaks from Magyar tyranny. This was memorable as the first unequivocal pronouncement of the Czech revolutionary thesis made within the Empire which was definitely unreconcilable with the continuance of the Hapsburg monarchy. Yet in retrospect we can see that it was only the logical development of ideas clearly implicit in the Writers' Manifesto of May 30, 1917. The Austrian Prime Minister, von Seidler, suppressed publication of the statement in the daily press, but it was spread far and wide in Bohemia by handbills, and its moral effect was tremendous.

The last desperate offensive of the Central Powers was begun in March 1918, and some Austro-Hungarian troops were used on the western front. Czech units in the Austrian army stationed at Rumburk mutinied, and the air was electric with thoughts of revolution. Count Czernin, as usual tactless, issued another of his statements (April 2, 1918) in which he asserted that the vast majority of the Czech people were loyal to the dynasty. The stirring answer to this slander was a great demonstration on April 13, led by the beloved Jirásek, in which the whole assembly joined in a solemn oath, ending with these words:

> Faithful in work, faithful in our fight, faithful in the midst of suffering and privation, faithful unto death, we shall endure until we win, as win we must. We shall endure until our nation's freedom is in our grasp.

During the spring and summer of 1918 the economic structure of the Empire was crumbling. Poor crops, inadequate transportation and communication, aggravated by a demoralized public opinion, resulted in widespread hunger and despair, made more terrifying by outbreaks of typhus. And the government was helpless to prevent further deterioration. At the same time, as if prospering on adversity, the sense of unity among the Czechs was noticeably growing. A remarkable feeling of national solidarity, transcending party, class and, among the common people, even religious lines, spread like wildfire through the whole nation. On July 13 the National Czech Committee was reconstituted as an interparty council with Kramář as president, Švehla and Klofáč as vice-presidents, and Soukup as secretary. Its primary purpose, in collaboration with the National Council in Paris, of course, was to prepare for the political exigencies of the collapse of the Empire which they now saw as a proximate certainty. Though they were in constant communication with like-minded Slovaks, the threat of persecution by the Magyar government prevented any Slovak from participating openly in the work of the Committee.

The mention of the peculiar position in which Slovak radicals found themselves in 1918 demands some explanation. In a previous chapter we have shown how the Hungarian government had followed for centuries a policy of assimilation (magyarization) of the Slovaks, reducing them to a state of political impotency. The great mass of the Slovaks were kept in feudal illiteracy. If any Slovak wished to enter a profession or politics his only path lay through Magyar schools, and these schools were so conducted that with hardly an exception the Slovak youth came out of them "politically reliable." A minority so debased was easily controlled. During the war this repression had been even more severe than before. For the first two years of the war there was no revolutionary movement worth the name, though there were a few individuals who braved prison and persecution to arouse the Slovak people to make an effort to attain freedom. Abroad, with wider horizons before them, Slovaks were active in the revolutionary movement in all its phases, from the beginning of the war, but at home we look in vain for any integrated or concerted program for Slovak independence until late in 1917.

It was not until May 1, 1918, three weeks after the Meeting of the Oath, led by Jirásek (April 13, 1918), that a representative group of Slovak Socialists and Social Democrats, brought together by Dr. Vavro Šrobár, at Liptovský Sväty Mikulaš, demanded "self-determination for all nations, including also that branch of the Czechoslovak nation which lives in Hungary." Šrobár was imprisoned for his part in organizing the demonstration, but Slovakia, finally aroused, had spoken and publicly united her cause with that of the Czechs. This proclamation had received the hearty approval of the Prague Maffia before publication. The close co-ordination between Czech and Slovak action from this time on—though the Slovak action was perforce mostly subterranean—was an important factor in the completeness of the Hapsburg collapse. The Magyar government was able to repress, by severe police measures, any further public expression of a revolutionary spirit; and, apart from the activity of individuals who escaped to Vienna or Prague, little happened in the province until the formation of the Slovak National Council in October 1918.

Between July and October 1918 events moved with the speed and violence of an avalanche. Czech deputies dared to demand Czechoslovak independence, as we have seen, on the floor of the Reichsrat. The British government had given, in June, formal recognition of the Paris Council as a provisional government of the united Czechoslovak state, fighting as an ally against the Central Powers. The United States government gave formal *de facto* recognition to the National Council on September 2, Japan on September 11, and France and Italy followed soon with complete political recognition. That much of the task was accomplished, and the Committee in Prague, apprised immediately of every advance, knew that the tide of battle was flowing rapidly in their favor. Last-minute desperate diplomatic efforts of the Emperor Charles to forestall disruption of the Empire were foredoomed to failure. The Hapsburg monarchy was about ready to give up its already superannuated ghost. The final chapter of the story was being written in the forests and fields, and on the roads of northern France where German troops were retreating; and in the plains and ravines of the Veneto along the Piave, where Austrian and Hungarian units were in full rout before the Italian and Allied drive. Such a final chapter was too definitive to be rewritten by belated diplomacy.

A group of radical Czechs, the Socialist Council, met on October 12 in Prague and planned to foment demonstrations on October 14, in the course of which, they hoped, a republic would be proclaimed. The National Committee, however, felt the move premature and labored to prevent a revolution which would justify harsh reprisals by the Austrian military. The planned demonstrations did not take place, and the government thought that, because of the failure of the *putsch*, the revolutionaries had been discredited among the people. But therein they deceived themselves. The Czech leaders had not lost control of the situation. Indeed the fact that they had been able to prevent the demonstrations of the extreme radicals should have shown the government how strong the real leaders were. On October 16 Emperor Charles published an Imperial Manifesto declaring that the Austrian realm—not Hungary —should be reconstituted as a federal state. But closing the stable doors after the horses had gone must have given the Emperor little satisfaction. Masaryk had anticipated the intent of this desperate move and published his declaration of independence in Philadelphia on October 18 (see above,

p. 274). The nations of Austria, seeing that full independence was in their grasp, paid not the slightest attention to the Emperor's Manifesto.

On October 25 a number of the National Committee, led by Kramář, left Prague for Geneva, to meet Beneš and Osuský of the National Council, now recognized by the Entente as the provisional government of the Czechoslovak people. There was full agreement between the two groups on every important point concerning the future of their state. At the conclusion of their deliberations the Prague Committee returned home and Beneš went back to Paris, where much remained to be done.

The Prague Committee had left, on October 25, a Prague under the Austrian double eagle. They returned on October 31 to a Prague proudly flying its new tricolor and the Bohemian Lion, the emblem of their ancient and glorious Bohemian dynasty. On October 28 the members of the National Committee remaining in Prague, Švehla, Rašín, Stříbrný and Soukup, augmented late in the day by the Slovak leader Šrobár, had taken advantage of the capitulation of Austria to Wilson's terms to issue a terse declaration of the fact of independence, consisting of a preamble and five articles. It began: "The independent Czechoslovak state has come into being." The Czech Sokol societies acting under orders from Scheiner took over the task of maintaining order. A casual visitor to Prague on the 28th and the 29th of October 1918, would have thought that they were festival days. There was little evidence of the fact that one of the oldest empires in the history of Western Europe was crumbling before his eyes. The news of the great events spread immediately to the rest of Bohemia and Moravia, and, more slowly, to Slovakia.

The Slovak National Council knew, through Hodža at Vienna who was in frequent communication with the

Prague Committee, that the iron was hot, and it assembled at Turčiansky Svätý Martin on October 29, and the next day issued a declaration proclaiming that "the Slovak nation is a part of the Czechoslovak nation, one with it in language and in the history of its civilization. . . . We also claim for this, the Czechoslovak nation, the absolute right of self-determination on a basis of complete independence." The declaration found instantaneous support from patriotic societies throughout Slovakia. Among other eminent Slovaks, Father Andrej Hlinka expressed joy and satisfaction at the achievement of a common independence.

By the exigencies of war, so manifold in their developments, two branches of one people, separated for almost a thousand years, again joined their fortunes. It is one of the anomalies of which Central European history is so full, however, that the real union of their forces had not been realizable at home during the war, but rather among colonies of emigrants spread over thousands of miles beyond the seven seas. The spirit of a people that wills to live knows no bounds of time or place.

≺ 13 ≻

Building a State: Internal Affairs
1918-1938

THE Czechoslovaks were now masters in their own house. Independence had been won largely through the inspired labors of a few men. But a few men, however inspired and able, do not make a nation, and late in 1918 it remained to be seen if the people for whom these few had labored so successfully would be able to appropriate the gains and build upon the foundations thus laid.

The task ahead of the leaders and the people of Czechoslovakia in these fateful early months and years was both simple and tremendous. After being ruled for centuries in all aspects of their life by Austrian overlords, they had now not only to take over the reins of government and determine all lines of their domestic and foreign policies, but they had to assume these obligations in a time when the whole world was suffering from the catastrophic effects of a long and devastating war. The Czechoslovaks had not only to build their own state in a sick world, without the help of any benevolent neighbors, but they had also, as it turned out, to help in the rehabilitation of surrounding states weaker than themselves—all this with very little practice in the world of affairs. Their brilliant success is universally recognized, yet that success will only be enhanced by a calm recital of the steps in its attainment.

We shall turn first to the organization of the state within the borders allowed it by the several peace treaties: Versailles, Trianon, Neuilly and the Teschen award of the Council of Ambassadors, and see how problems that would have taxed the resources of the most experienced and far-

seeing politicians were met and solved with candor, coolness, patience and a complete absence of fanfare.

The National Committee which, with the full consent of
the National Council in Paris, had proclaimed the independence of Czechoslovakia on October 28, 1918, after
hardly more than a fortnight of preliminary work, adopted
on November 13 a provisional constitution which provided
for a parliamentary republic with a strong executive and a
responsible cabinet. In accordance with this instrument,
the National Committee transformed itself on the following day into a larger National Assembly of 256 (later 270)
Czech and Slovak members (November 14). This National
Assembly was not elected by the people but it was none the
less representative, in that it was constituted from the
principal Czech political parties according to their 1911
Reichsrat membership, with 55 co-opted Slovaks, and enjoyed the full confidence of the people. This Assembly
elected Masaryk President *in absentia* and a coalition government was named of which Kramář was Prime Minister,
Beneš Foreign Minister, and Dr. Rašín Minister of Finance.

The immediate task confronting the new and untried
government in its first days and weeks was the winning of
public confidence. The ministry bent all its energies to
securing the adequate distribution of the depleted food-
supplies. More far-reaching in its consequences was the
matter of the currency. In the early post-war chaos and the
uncertainty involved in the transfer of sovereignty from the
Hapsburg empire to an independent state it was only
natural that there should be serious concern as to the value
of Austrian currency still circulating in a Czech state. Dr.
Rašín was given wide powers by the National Assembly and
adopted a very conservative policy which might be more
accurately called deflationary. The whole people were
called on to make sacrifices and rallied loyally to the spar-
tan régime Rašín demanded of them. But as Austria was

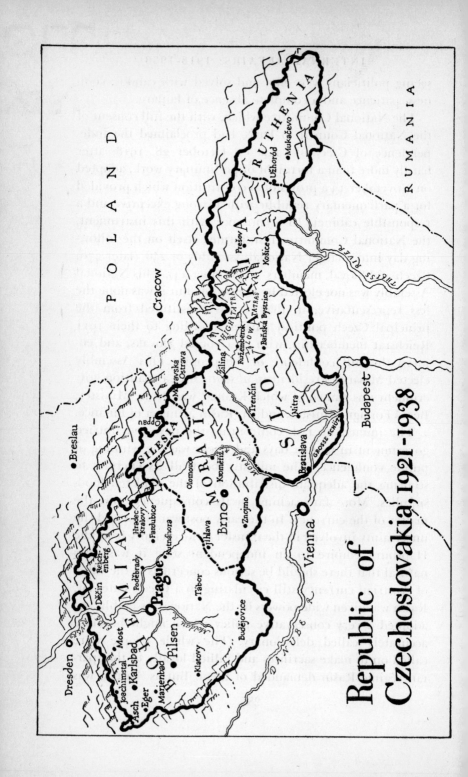

Republic of Czechoslovakia, 1921-1938

apparently going in the opposite direction—toward inflation —Rašín was compelled to separate the currency of the new state from that of Austria (February 25, 1919). In April the Czechoslovak crown (koruna) was adopted as the monetary unit, a forced loan of one per cent was levied upon reissue of banknotes, and the banknote circulation limited. The whole financial policy looked toward a fixed metal basis. In an era when inflation was the order of the day throughout all Europe, this conservative procedure demanded vision on the part of the leaders and courage on the part of the people. Both these qualities were present in the young republic. Though the state budget was not balanced until the fourth year of independence, the soundness of the policy of financial conservatism was made clear when the fifth year brought a surplus. Rašín has been called a financial genius, but he would have said that financial genius consisted in not spending more money than the state could, on reasonable grounds, expect to have.

In the later phases of the struggle for independence there had never been any serious doubt among the leaders of the movement, either at home or abroad, that the form the new state would take would be that of a democratic republic. In the proclamation of Czechoslovak independence by the National Council in Paris on October 18, 1918, the general features of the projected democratic state were briefly summarized—universal suffrage, minority rights, proportional representation, land and broad social reforms. The National Assembly, therefore, adopted in its first sessions a provisional constitution envisaging such a constitutional structure, and established a commission to work out the details of the definitive constitution. Though this formal document was not adopted until February 29, 1920, its main features were assumed and assured from the first days of independence.

This Constitution has some interesting features which

may be briefly touched upon. The people are declared to be the sole source of all power in the state. The legislative power of the whole republic rests in a bi-cameral parliament: a chamber of deputies to consist of 300 members elected for a six-year term, a senate of 150 members elected for eight years. The members of parliament are to be chosen according to the principle of proportional representation by recognized political parties. The President must summon parliament in session twice each year, spring and autumn. Extraordinary sessions may also be called, by the President, by the Chairmen of the two chambers, or by two-fifths of either chamber. In the interim between full sessions of Parliament an elective committee of 24—16 deputies and 8 senators—was delegated to exercise plenary parliamentary power, save for a few specifically reserved cases such as election of the President or Vice-President, amendment of the Constitution, or declaration of war.

The President is elected by the National Assembly (i.e. both chambers meeting in joint session) for a term of seven years. The first president was declared eligible for re-election indefinitely, but otherwise only one successive re-election is permitted without an intervening seven-year term. The President's powers are wide but specified, and what is not specified resides in the Parliament. Provision is made for the independence of the judiciary from political pressure by permanent appointment. Freedom in religion, language, the press and assembly, the right of petition and the inviolability of postal matter and the ownership of property are guaranteed, though restrictions may be imposed by specific acts of Parliament in the national interest.

The Constitution is particularly emphatic in the matter of guarantees to the national and language minorities. This provision was emphasized in pursuance of the voluntary commitments of Beneš and Kramář at the Paris Peace Conference. The right of every citizen of the republic to use his own tongue and to have instruction for his children in that tongue is specifically provided for.

The constitutional and political structure of the country, especially Bohemia and Moravia, was less changed by the coming of independence than might have been expected. Independence had been preceded by decades of political activity under Hapsburg rule; and the party allegiances, based on fundamental social and economic interests, had become sufficiently stabilized for patterns of political ideologies to be generally recognizable.

After a preliminary swing of adjustment from right to moderate left in the years 1919 and 1920, there ensued a period of relative parliamentary stability, when the Agrarian party with the support of the Social Democrats, the Czech National Socialist and National Democratic parties, with occasional support from the Catholic Centre, led the government along conservative socialist lines. The German minority was divided along parallel political lines, but refused to join the government until 1926, when the German Agrarian and German Christian Socialist parties decided to give up their negativistic attitude toward the government and accept posts in the cabinet. Dr. Franz Spina and Dr. Robert Mayr-Harting, respectively representing these two parties, accepted important portfolios in the Švehla ministry which was formed in October 1926. On the other hand, the Magyars, enjoying full proportional representation on the floor of Parliament, and likewise divided along similar lines of political divergence, steadfastly remained in the opposition. Frequently during these early years the government's majority was precariously small and the tact and patience of President Masaryk was needed to avert many a parliamentary crisis.

An illuminating commentary upon the fundamentally conservative character of Czechoslovak democracy is the course of the communist wing of the Socialist parties. In

December 1920 a general strike was proclaimed by the radical wing of the Social Democratic party and a *coup d'état* was attempted, but the attempt was a quick and decisive failure. These radicals, now calling themselves Communists, continued as a political factor, and reached the high point of their power in 1925, when they polled over 900,000 votes. There had never been any serious talk of reprisals for the attempted *coup d'état*, or of suppressing the extreme radical wing of the party. The conservative majority felt that the electorate could be relied upon to maintain their equilibrium under the most uncertain conditions. After reaching their peak in 1925, the Communists steadily declined in prestige and significance. The Czech and Slovak peasant, artisan, and small shopkeeper was too tenacious of his hard-won property rights to have any real affinity for communism. As elsewhere in Europe communism was vocal, but at no time in the history of the republic was there the slightest chance that communism would make any considerable appeal to more than a very small minority of the Czechoslovak people. The later rapprochement with Soviet Russia was rather in spite of its communism than because of it. After 1933 it suited the German Propaganda Ministry to make much of the association with Russia. The credence given this propaganda in Great Britain was founded in ignorance of the facts, which was unnecessary and inexcusable, or in vicious misconstruction of the facts, which was worse.

For almost a decade and a half, from 1922 to 1935, the general pattern of political life in the republic was hardly disturbed. The steadying hand of President Masaryk and the political maturity of the Czech people, now increasingly matched by a Slovak populace rapidly learning how to use its franchise and political power, made a consolidated public opinion and deepened the roots of Czechoslovak democracy. During much of this time—from 1926 to 1935—a large section of the German population, which may well be called the more enlightened part, collaborated sincerely and effectively with the government. This spirit of collaboration lasted through the most trying years of the world-wide economic depression which were unusually severe upon a small country so largely dependent upon the export of industrial products for its life. During these years of stress these open-minded leaders of the German parties realized perfectly well and did not hesitate to declare in public that the Czechoslovak government was doing all it could to alleviate the suffering among the Sudeten Germans, even at the expense of the Slav population. Numerous minor shifts of political alignment from the right and from the left took place in these years, reflecting the pressures of public opinion as it was influenced by both domestic and foreign matters. If one of the lesser parties withdrew from the government another would take its place. But the basic assumption that a satisfactory coalition government could be maintained was not questioned in these years.

In the years 1935 to 1938 when the tempo of the approaching world crisis was accelerating and the strongly nationalist Sudeten German movement, goaded and guided from Berlin, presented the government with a desperate problem whose end result the Czechs—though apparently no one else—saw quite clearly, the solid nature of Czechoslovak democracy became clearer than ever before. At the 1935 elections the Czech and Slovak parties maintained their strength, and the electorate betrayed no sign of political panic. Their political convictions had been tested by years of free and open discussion, and they were not easily thrown off balance.

It has been pointed out above (Chapter X) that the Slovaks had been much less prepared for the responsibilities of independent political existence than the Czechs. Centuries of Magyar repression had made of the Slovaks a peasant, virtually serf, and illiterate people. Only a few leaders were politically minded. There was therefore no large group of trained and educated citizenry from whom schoolteachers, publicists, public officials, or even minor political leaders could be chosen. This kind of personnel cannot be trained in a short time. This tragic lack of preparation for the tasks of self-government among the Slovaks posed a delicate problem for the government of the republic. With the full approval of the Slovak leaders, the government decided that in the interests of efficiency and safety against Magyar subversive activity in Slovakia it would be necessary to send numbers of trained Czechs to fill those positions in the public service in Slovakia for which there were no native Slovaks available. It was the intention of the government that these Czechs should be withdrawn as soon as competent Slovaks could be trained to displace them. It is not hard to understand, however, that such a condition might easily lead to resentment on the part of many Slovaks, nor can it be said that all these interim Czech officeholders in Slovakia were careful to avoid giving offense by their attitudes and actions. Opposition to the Prague government certainly existed, in a more or less acute form, in many circles in Slovakia. But the government's policy of withdrawing Czech administrative and educational officials as soon as practicable was adhered to, and up to 1932 a substantial proportion of Czech officeholders had returned to Bohemia. On the other hand, some of these Czechs had married Slovak wives and had virtually become Slovaks.

The Slovak "problem" was not, however, restricted to this local matter of a number of Czechs holding offices in Slovakia. It was complicated by the injection of religious issues and by appeals to the so-called Pittsburgh agreement (See above, Chapter XII). Though no larger proportion of Slovaks are Roman Catholics than of the Czechs, it can safely be said that their allegiance to their faith is more unquestioning. Clerical participation in political affairs is direct and not always disinterested. The Slovak clergy feared that the Czechoslovak state would completely secularize education in Slovakia, and no convinced clerical would willingly surrender a control of education once exercised. The many new educational institutions springing up in Slovakia, erected and supported by the state, boded ill for the dominant position of the clergy. The Slovak Populist party, led by Monsignor Andrej Hlinka of Ružemberok, maintained a position of steady opposition to the Prague government until January 1927, when two leaders of the party, Tiso and Gažik, accepted posts in the Švehla coalition. On several occasions in later years Father Hlinka publicly reaffirmed his loyalty to the republic, thus discrediting the claims of some vociferous dissidents that Slovakia wanted either to be free or to return to Hungary.

This Slovak opposition to the Prague government did not at any time represent more than a minority of the Slovak population, and so long as it existed was never considered a leading problem within the republic where the local conditions in Slovakia were generally known. The active and wholehearted participation of such Slovak statesmen as Vavro Šrobár, Milan Štefánik, Ivan Dérer, Ivan Markovič and Milan Hodža in successive governments up to 1939, and the important positions occupied by Slovaks in the diplomatic service such as Štefan Osuský (Paris) and Col. Vladimir Hurban (Washington), went far to make the Slovak "problem" seem something like a tempest in a teapot. Vital separatism in Slovakia between Versailles and Munich can be dismissed as a fantasy. At the present time (1943), no serious student of Central European affairs thinks of the "independent" state of Slovakia as a creation based upon the will of the Slovak people.

It was to be expected that in a country so largely agricultural the question of ownership of land should be of paramount importance. The obvious urgency of this question was accentuated by the fact that every Czech knew that, following the tragic defeat of the White Mountain in 1620, the land and estates of Czech Protestants had been confiscated by their Hapsburg conquerors. In Slovakia the Magyar rulers had held almost all the land for centuries. Throughout the territory of the republic there were many great estates held by a few large German or Magyar families. The Schwarzenberg family, for example, had 187 estates covering almost half a million acres of the best land in Bohemia and Moravia. In the whole republic the aristocracy (mostly German) held 55 per cent of the arable and forest land and the Hapsburg family another 10 per cent. To that should be added 8 per cent of the land in the possession of ecclesiastical persons and corporations, leaving to the native small holder about one-fourth of the land. Almost all of the 75 per cent owned by the great landholders was worked by Czech or Slovak peasants on a lease or share basis, leaving them each year at the mercy of the landlord. In Bohemia and Moravia alone 71 per cent of the total number of landowners, with less than five acres each, owned only 6.5 per cent of the total area of the land. The disproportion was too great to be endured. Now that the Czechs and Slovaks were again masters in their own house they immediately set about equalizing the centuries-long injustice which had been the measure of their subservience to foreign conquerors.

On December 9, 1918, a law was passed by the National Assembly "freezing" the larger estates. By this law no estate of 375 or more acres of arable, or of 625 acres of *both* arable and forest land, could be sold or in any way transferred or hypothecated. On April 27, 1919, a Land Reform Act was passed governing the expropriation and redistribution of all agricultural land in the republic in estates of over 375 acres of arable land and 250 acres of forest or pasture land—a maximum total of 625 acres being allowed. All forest or pasture or agricultural land in excess of this amount was subject to expropriation by the newly established Land Office. About nine and a half million acres came under the provisions of the Act. Compensation to the former owners was fixed at the 1913-1915 level. Because of the change that had taken place as the Austrian currency gave way to the new Czechoslovak currency, this looked like a sharp devaluation. Yet, the owners had only to look across the borders, both to Austria and to Germany, to feel relieved that they would be paid in a currency that was stable. The laws provided that the land, once in government hands, should be made available for purchase by those who had insufficient land from which to make a livelihood. Preference was given to those tenant farmers who had lived on these expropriated estates for the longest periods, to disabled soldiers, legionaries and their widows, and to co-operative enterprises—particularly if made up largely of former tenants. Because of the fact that few of the former tenants had been able to lay aside any reserves with which to purchase the land, the government provided for generous state loans. The Land Office moved slowly in executing the provisions of the land law, desirous of avoiding any serious injustices, and made further provisions allowing exemptions from expropriation when the land was being operated in a highly efficient way or where local conditions made the continued unit operation of an agricultural industry (e.g. a brewery or sugar refinery) with its tributary territory a generally useful and socially profitable connection. For obvious strategic reasons the state kept in its own hands a large amount of forest land along the borders—over one million acres were thus taken from the total land available for redistribution among private landowners.

By the end of 1937 over four and a half million acres had

been redistributed according to the terms of this law to about 650,000 applicants, and the totals would have reached respectively five million and 700,000 by 1940 if international events had not deprived the Czechoslovak people of their freedom of action. The firmness, tact and poise with which the Czechoslovak government acted in effecting this fundamental reform over a period of almost two decades served to unite the agricultural classes, both Czech and Slovak, in loyal support and confidence in the good faith of their leaders.

The attitude of the government toward labor, as might have been expected in a land whose leaders had exalted the dignity of work, was confidently liberal. One of the first laws passed by the National Assembly after the Land Reform was the eight-hour day (December 19, 1918), which made additional provision for collective wage agreement in certain specified cases. This law was followed by others of the same intent, demonstrating the deep-rooted desire among the people and their leaders to bring social justice from the realm of theory into that of actuality. Within a very short time legislation was adopted providing sickness and unemployment insurance, government aid to housing, pensions for old soldiers and their dependents, the protection of the renter from ejection, an effective system of wage arbitration courts. It is worth noting that though these problems were eagerly considered from the very first, definitive solutions were not regarded as reached until thorough and expert examination into the capacity of the nation's economic structure gave assurance that the law was not only viable but indeed salutary. Early legislation was therefore subjected to frequent subsequent revision and amendment.

The co-operative movement, begun in the middle of the nineteenth century, was congenial to the democratic Czech and Slovak temperament and, encouraged by the state, went forward by great strides under the republic. In the two decades following 1918 the membership, and with it the breadth of interest and function, of the co-operatives increased many fold. By 1938 there were almost 12,000 co-operative societies with essentially agricultural interests alone; dairies, building associations, cattle-raising associations, distilleries, mills, power-stations, banks and other similar enterprises. It is estimated that over 11 per cent of the total population (that is over one-third of the agricultural population) belonged to at least one of the 17,021 co-operative enterprises of all sorts in the republic. The enlivening social effect of such a widespread movement upon the initiative and prideful economic interest of the whole population can hardly be exaggerated.

Complex problems of economic readjustment faced a small nation which had previously formed part of a larger producing and distributing unit. Because of political boundaries newly established, tariff boundaries began to grow into high walls. New markets had to be found for finished as well as raw products that had previously been marketable in other parts of the Austro-Hungarian empire. International financial obligations of pre-war Austria-Hungary had to be shouldered proportionately by the Succession States. A currency which would be independent of the Austrian crown had to be established and maintained in a period when the international money market was being shaken by inflation and national bankruptcies. It was a delicate situation, fraught with many possibilities for disaster. But it is universally conceded that the people of Czechoslovakia, ably guided by their political and economic leaders, succeeded in utilizing to the fullest extent their resources, natural and industrial, so that a recent writer was able to speak of her two decades of independence as effecting "one of the greatest economic achievements in Central Europe after the World War."

Within the boundaries of the republic much fruitful soil and great forest tracts favored extensive agricultural activity. Of the land devoted to agricultural crops, almost two-thirds is used for the production of grains of various kinds—wheat, barley, rye, oats and maize. More than one-sixth of the total agricultural land is given over to sugar-beets and potatoes, the former being especially important for its manufactured export product, beet-sugar. To co-ordinate its grain production the government established in 1934 a corporation to regulate the sale and prices and indirectly the production of its grains, with a view to a wider economic collaboration with the other members of the Little Entente. The Czechoslovak Grain Company was extended, in 1936, to June 1940.

The mineral resources of the country are very important, and the high degree of industrialization of the western parts of the republic reflects this natural wealth. All of the gold, silver, tungsten, tin, uranium and radium produced in pre-1918 Austria came from Bohemia. Over 67 per cent of all mining and metallurgical industries in the Austro-Hungarian Empire were to be found in Czechoslovakia.[1] The most considerable mine-products are coal and lignite, the former found both in Bohemia and Moravia in the mountain areas, the latter found almost exclusively in Bohemia. Of both coal and lignite there was always a substantial excess of exports over imports. The superior quality of Bohemian lignite caused a steady demand for it both in Germany and Austria, where it was widely used in heavy industry. There was a sharp drop in the production of both coal and lignite during the years of the world depression, and even as late as 1938 the high levels of 1929 had not

[1] It is interesting to note the percentage of pre-1918 Austro-Hungarian industries that remained in Czechoslovakia: sugar 92 per cent, glass 92 per cent, cotton 75 per cent, jute 90 per cent, shoes 75 per cent, china 100 per cent, chemicals 75 per cent, malt products 87 per cent, brewing 57 per cent, wool 80 per cent, leather 70 per cent.

again been reached. Austria and Germany, the two best customers, had increased their own production and domestic Czechoslovak industry had not been able to take up the slack in the demand.

Most of the pig-iron produced in Czechoslovakia was used for domestic purposes precisely because of the great demand in the rest of the world for the manufactured iron and steel goods produced by Czechoslovak heavy industry. The Škoda works, in particular, have produced for export, in addition to armaments, great quantities of highly specialized iron and steel goods for shipping needs, agricultural implements, motor-cars, railway rolling-stock, and all sorts of manufacturing technical equipment. Though there would have been quite enough iron ore for domestic manufacture, the demand for the export of Czechoslovak iron and steel products was so great that much iron ore had to be imported, to be exported again as manufactured articles.

The textile industry in its various branches—cotton, wool, linen, jute and silk—was perhaps the most important industry in the whole republic, employing the largest number of hands (277,000 in 1920; 360,000 in 1935) and also having the largest total of export trade. Its inherent difficulty in a period of economic nationalism was that almost all the raw cotton and most of the raw wool, flax and silk yarn had to be imported. It was a milling industry, and consequently subject to the uncertainties of international politics. The fact that Czechoslovakia is an inland state, dependent upon transportation of the raw materials to her borders and of the finished products through the territory of her neighbors, thus being at the mercy of the good will of those neighbors, made this industry especially susceptible to dislocation in times of economic or political crisis. Most of the mills were in the mountain districts around the borders of the country where water power was abundant. The population in these mountain sections is predominantly

German and Austrian. This fact should be kept in mind in any consideration of the question of unemployment in the Sudeten districts in the period from 1929 to Munich. The connection between dependence of the textile industry upon easy access to world markets, its competition with the German textile industry and the location of the vast majority of the textile mills in Sudeten districts comes into clearer focus when we recall that Hitler denounced unilaterally that section in the Versailles treaty which gave Czechoslovakia certain rights of transport along the Elbe and at the port of Hamburg. Could it be that Hitler was not aware of the fact that his axe would fall most heavily upon the German-speaking inhabitants of Czechoslovakia, or that their cries of distress, for which he was largely responsible, would furnish him "grounds" for coming to their "rescue"?

The glass and porcelain industries in Czechoslovakia have a long history. Demanding special skills and the presence in quantity of quartz and fine clays as well as adequate fuels, these industries were particularly favored by the soil and artisans of Czechoslovakia. Large quantities of artistic glassware, plain and artistic crockery, as well as glass jewelry and novelties were steady exports during the two decades of the republic's existence. We have by no means exhausted the list of industries which flourished in the country, efficiently administered by energetic businessmen and manned by skilled craftsmen, many of whom were descended from generations of highly trained artisans. Nitrates, fertilizers, leather goods, especially shoes and gloves, cellulose, paper, dyes, are but a few of the products of Czech and Slovak industry with which the outside world has come to be familiar.

If we were to chart the course of agricultural and industrial production in Czechoslovakia during the two decades of its existence we should notice that its low point came in the years 1932 and 1933. As an exporting country it was dependent upon the international markets which were at their lowest in those years of the world economic depression. But the conservative currency policy of the government put Czechoslovak goods at a disadvantage in the world markets. After the devaluation of the American dollar, Czechoslovak goods suddenly became very dear, and, so long as Czechoslovakia remained on a gold parity, the future for her foreign markets looked very dismal. The implications for her internal economy, lowered standard of living, increased unemployment, were clear, and at the time, desperate. To counteract the effects of the world economic situation, therefore, the government devalued the crown by 16 2/3 per cent on February 17, 1934, the first of the Central European countries to make an official adjustment to the new price and exchange levels brought on by the depression. The effect of the devaluation was instantaneous and galvanic. The solidity of the Czechoslovak economic structure is shown by the fact that the increase in Czechoslovak trade after February 1934, was proportionately greater than the percentage of devaluation. Unemployment decreased, many factories that closed down resumed production, and the whole internal economic structure took up the new tempo. Czechoslovakia was one of the first countries in Europe to put the depression behind her.

Although the Czechs had undergone hundreds of years of indoctrination by the Hapsburg germanizing school system, they had been able to resist complete germanization. The Slovaks were not so fortunate. There was no way for a Slovak to rise from serfdom except by becoming magyarized. The only schools beyond the elementary level in Slovakia were Magyar schools. Advanced learning in Slovak was impossible. As a consequence, the Czechoslovaks em-

phasized the great importance of education. From the very
beginning of the republic the leaders insisted on more and
better free schools, not only elementary and academic, but
technical, professional, trade, experimental and opportunity schools. The system as worked out was centralized,
under a Ministry of Education, with a unified curriculum
presented throughout the republic. Considerable latitude
was allowed the individual teacher in presenting his subjects, according as the locality, town or district school board
might desire to diverge from the established curriculum.
The passion of the Czechs and Moravians for more education has been a byword in Central Europe, and it is not too
much to say that their cultural level was higher than that
of any of the surrounding peoples.

But the backward condition of Slovakia and Subcarpathian Ruthenia, because of the policy of the government
in Budapest, presented one of the two acute educational
problems in the early days of the republic. In Slovakia and
Ruthenia in 1915 under Magyar rule there were only
4,008 elementary schools (first six grades), of which only
about 300 were for Slovaks, who constituted about two-
thirds of the population—8 per cent of the schools for 65
per cent of the population. Illiteracy among Slovaks above
the age of six was 26.8 per cent, and in Ruthenia 57.6 per
cent, at the same time that in Bohemia the illiteracy was
2.12 per cent. By 1937, under the Republic, the number of
elementary schools had been increased to 5,378 at the expense of the government—an increase of 33.5 per cent, and
illiteracy had been reduced to a third of the 1915 figure.
Under Magyar rule there were no commercial schools for
Slovaks at all. Slovaks were not supposed to go into business
unless they magyarized themselves. In 1937 there were 20
such schools in Slovakia and Ruthenia. In 1915 there were
no secondary schools (high schools) for Slovaks; in 1937
there were 49. Under Magyar rule there was no university

for Slovaks; in 1938 there were two, Comenius University in Bratislava and Štefánik Technological Institute at Košice. Educational backwardness can hardly produce political maturity, and exceptional efforts had to be made by the Czechoslovak government in the post-war years to repair the ravages of the Hungarian policy of magyarization. In these twenty years the Slovak population received a larger proportion of school expenditures than their numbers would normally have justified, but the expenditure was imperative in view of the years of neglect to which the Slovak people had been subjected. In the process of redistribution of schools the Magyar population was not allowed to suffer. Over 94 per cent of the Hungarian school children were taught in Magyar schools in their own tongue by teachers of their own race, paid by the Czechoslovak government the same salaries as Czech and Slovak teachers of the same rank.

The second acute problem in the field of education was the matter of the minorities, and particularly the largest minority, the Austro-Germans. The Czechoslovaks had, with reason, complained that under the Hapsburgs they had been discriminated against in the inadequacy of schools offering instruction in the Czech and Slovak languages by Czech and Slovak teachers. The new government tried to right this injustice in a sense of fairness to all minorities. The figures tell the story of this effort: 95 per cent of all Germans in elementary and secondary schools were instructed in German by German teachers. Approximately the same figure applied to all other minorities where their grouping made it at all possible to build and support a school. It is interesting to see how the government applied the principle of proportional allotment of school funds. Each German elementary school was attended (on the average) by 188 pupils, whereas each Czechoslovak elementary school was attended by 239 pupils. There were thus more German schools per pupil than Czechoslovak, and the government spent more money per German pupil than it did on the Czech and Slovak children. The average class in the German school had 35.7 pupils; in the Czechoslovak there were 38.2. There were thus more teachers per pupil in German than in Czech or Slovak schools. The Ministry of Education spent more on each student in the German university in Prague than on the Czech or Slovak university student by a margin of 14 per cent. All along the line the Czechoslovak administration was scrupulous in its regard for the democratic principles in the sphere of education, rejecting sedulously the temptation to abuse its majority position, even leaning over backward to give the German minority the full benefit of a free country.

Such scrupulousness is not the creation of a few days or even of a few years. Persevered in for years, in the face of attack and misunderstanding, its roots must be looked for in the distant past. The Czechoslovak people had chosen Masaryk for their leader of their own free will. Masaryk has this to say of free education: "He who hinders a person or a nation in its education commits a mortal sin. Every individual has the same right to education as he has to live." The Czechoslovaks then, insisted on the right of all the constituent peoples of their republic to education in their own tongue, in spite of the fact that these various peoples had not granted it to the Czechoslovaks when it was theirs to grant.

≺ 14 ≻

Foreign Relations: 1918-1935

CZECHOSLOVAK foreign policy does not date from 1914, or indeed from 1918. It began to take definite shape in the middle of the last century. The revolutions of 1848 opened before all the hopeful leaders of the nationalistic cause visions of autonomy within the Hapsburg empire. There were, furthermore, some of these leaders who looked beyond mere autonomy to complete independence. But they realized full well that neither autonomy nor, *a fortiori*, independence could be won by their own efforts alone. They needed outside help. The question arose in the decades immediately subsequent to 1848 where such help could be obtained. It was clear that the aim of Prussian policy was to keep the Austro-Hungarian Empire intact but subservient to Berlin; hence no help could be expected from that quarter. Two other alternatives presented themselves. When the German-Magyar dualism was constitutionalized by the *Ausgleich* of 1867, the Czechs realized anew that their hopes for Slav autonomy within the framework of the Hapsburg monarchy were doomed to disappointment, and immediately cast about for help. The Ethnographic Congress in Moscow in May of that year offered an opportunity to present their case to their powerful Slav neighbor. But political results of the journey were not forthcoming. Then, as in 1914, Russia was not interested in the dismemberment of the Hapsburg domains.

When, in the spring of 1869, Rieger was granted an audience by Napoleon III, he presented a memorandum which pointed out the advantages to France inherent in a Slav as opposed to a germanized Bohemia:

If Bohemia, from which Austria obtains its most intelligent soldiers, becomes completely germanized, and then, in the inevitable course of events, is made a dependency of Greater Prussian Germany, it would be a sad and dangerous eventuality for her neighbors. If France desires to preserve the Austrian Empire as a great European power she should certainly not ally herself with the German-Magyar dualists who are hastening her destruction. If France does not desire to further the growth of Prussian power, she cannot afford to support the German party in Austria. A germanized Bohemia would be absorbed by Prussian Germany. A Slavic Bohemia would never be a Russian pawn. Her historic pride, independence, language and culture are too individual for that.

France was thus asked to lend her support to the efforts of the Czech patriots in their struggle for a federalized Danubian empire as against a German-Magyar dualism. Napoleon expressed warm sympathy with Czech aspirations, but the Franco-Prussian War of 1870-1871 put an effective end to Czech hopes for help from the West. Both these approaches, to France and to Russia, thus failed to materialize; but they are indicative of the alternative policies facing a Slav nation almost surrounded by Germanic peoples: should this people bind itself to the West, or should it declare itself primarily a Slav people and cast in its lot forever with its Slav kinsfolk to the East? Blood and language could not easily be denied, and Pan-Slavism was strong among the Young Czech leaders. Yet Karel Havlíček, after a trip to Russia in 1843-1844, declared: "The Russian frosts and other Russian things have extinguished the last spark of Pan-Slav enthusiasm in me. . . . The Slavs are not a nation, but four nations, as independent and unconnected as any other nations in Europe." Political realism had also to take account of geography, a factor favoring westernization, equally decisive with Russian disinclination to undermine the monarchial *status quo* in the Danubian area by supporting separatism of any sort among the lesser Slavic peoples of the Austro-Hungarian Empire.

For the four decades after 1871 these two concepts—Pan-Slavism and a western orientation—continued to struggle for dominance among the Czech leaders. Yet the real importance of the divergence of opinion on the matter of western or eastern orientation, was, during much of this period, obscured by other and less important issues. In retrospect it is clear that it remained the key to the problem of eventual independence. Dr. Karel Kramář became in the late 1890's the leader of those who struggled against the Austrian subservience to Germany and looked to Imperial Russia for support, in the hope that the situation of a Slavic Bohemia would be more favorable if Austria-Hungary were allied with Russia. But there was a reaction against this quasi-passive policy. Early in the present century Masaryk, who regarded himself as the political heir of Havlíček, came to be recognized as the leader of the political realists who were convinced that no impulse toward liberty could possibly come from an autocratic and backward Russia. It was his conclusion that the Czechs and their cousins, the Slovaks, should identify their future with the inevitable tendencies of political developments of Europe as a whole. Masaryk saw as early as 1908 the certainty of a general European war and was convinced that the Austro-Hungarian monarchy would collapse under the strain of such a conflict. Out of this collapse his people would surely gain their independence. The correctness of his analysis of political forces and currents is but one of the measures of his greatness.

Upon the outbreak of the war in 1914 Masaryk expressed to friends his conviction that the war would mean the defeat of Germany and the destruction of the Austro-Hungarian Empire. Final victory, he felt, would rest with the western powers. Kramář, on the other hand, still maintained his belief that the Slavs in the Empire should pin their hopes on Russia. Though the two leaders collaborated loyally in the movement for independence, Kramář at home, Masaryk abroad, the basic divergence of opinion indicates the persistence in some influential quarters of Czech opinion of deep-rooted Pan-Slavism. The young Beneš shared from the very beginning Masaryk's conviction that a western orientation of their country's policy was the only sound line to follow. Russia's early military failure nullified any leaning toward dependence on Russia, so that well before the end of the war, Czech and Slovak opinion was fundamentally united in looking to the West.

When the military decision of 1918 proved the western policy to be correct, it was only natural that 1919 and following years should find Czechoslovak foreign policy closely collaborating with the leading continental ally in the West—France. This orientation was often emphasized by Beneš in speeches to the Czechoslovak Parliament, though at the same time he made it perfectly clear that this was not orientation toward France as France, but the exponent of a policy which best represented the logic of European political development.

The independent existence of the Czechoslovak state had been recognized by all the Allied powers before the end of hostilities, and Beneš had been present at the meeting of the Supreme War Council on November 4, 1918, as the accepted representative of the new state to participate in the formulation of armistice terms. But much remained to be done before the relations of the new republic to its immediate neighbors and the rest of the outside world were stabilized. Its most pressing problem, early in 1919, concerned the delimitation of the new frontiers with Germany, Austria, Hungary and Poland.

Earlier conversations and memoranda had specified the frontiers of the historic lands of the Bohemian crown as the boundaries of the western half of the new state, and the Allied statesmen had no *a priori* objections to these frontiers. Indeed the French note of June 29, 1918, had specifically promised these ancient boundaries as the basis of the new state. But when it came to a detailed examination of boundary problems by the commissions of the Peace Conference some minor questions arose. In the north and west a simple declaratory settlement of the boundaries was complicated by the desire of the Sudeten Germans to join the German republic of Austria, and Austria's willingness to consider seriously this geographical fantasy. The Czech delegates had little difficulty in showing that such an arrangement would be completely unviable and would lead to serious economic and political maladjustments. On the other hand, Beneš wished to cede a part of the Asch-Egerland salient (where the population was almost entirely German in speech) to Germany in return for some territory in the county of Friedland, inhabited mostly by Czechs or Lusatian Sorbs. Though this exchange was not allowed, slight territorial adjustments, favorable to Bohemia, were made around Troppau in Upper Styria. The German delegation had no considerable objection to these slight modifications of the frontier. They were perhaps gratified that no more of Silesia, once for centuries the property of the Bohemian crown, had been returned to its heir, the new republic. Those parts of historic Bohemia inhabited by Germans had never formed a part of the territory of the German Reich. Therefore no logical or historical claim could have been made that they should be "returned to the Reich." At the Peace Conference Beneš's willingness to cede the Egerland (Chebsko) met the opposition of the French. M. Pichon remarked that it was unthinkable that territory should be taken from an ally and given to a people France must still regard as an enemy. At least it could not be said by the Germans that the Czechs tried to grab any German territory.

Austria was in a somewhat different position. The Sudeten Germans had, under Hapsburg rule, been the favored element in Bohemia. Under the new republic they would be in a minority, ruled by those whom they had ruled for centuries. It was only natural that Austria should try to protect them from those who would be expected to be vengeful conquerors. Appeal was therefore made to the principles of self-determination. But the Allied powers without any hesitation decided that, in this case at least, the principles of the magic phrase would have to give way to historicity, geographic realities, and economic practicability. Austria's claim to be the protector of the German Austrians resident in the new Czechoslovak republic was denied. Once this crucial question was disposed of, only minor differences between Austria and Czechoslovakia remained. The railway junction and bridge at Gmund, some distance from the town, were given to Czechoslovakia, and a few kilometers of territory along the border of Lower Austria were included in the new republic. Thus it is clear that the reasonable satisfaction of Czechoslovak demands *vis à vis* her two Germanic neighbors was not such as to give these neighbors grounds for bitterness. In the following years, in the absence of rancor on both sides, mutual confidence grew and a policy of amicable co-operation was not difficult to maintain.

With her two other principal neighbors, Hungary and Poland, the situation was regrettably otherwise. Slovakia was not, like Bohemia, an integral territory with a long history of political existence behind it. Slovaks lived mostly in "upper Hungary" and in the plains along the Danube and the Ipel, east of Bratislava, where they were interspersed with a large Magyar population. In much of this plains country the Slovaks were in a minority, but the population was so mixed that any boundary line on ethnographical principles would have been impossible. Beneš's preliminary demands for the southern boundary of Slovakia went further into Hungarian territory than the Allied Territorial Commission felt was justified. Count Károlyi, who became Hungarian premier after the Armistice, agreed to Allied occupation of northern Slovakia. In December 1918 and the first days of January 1919 French and Czechoslovak troops moved farther south to a line fixed by the Allied military authorities. And so matters remained until the overthrow of Károlyi's government by a Bolshevik group headed by Béla Kun (March 31, 1919). This government decided to try to retake some of the occupied parts of northern Hungary, and by early June the Hungarian forces had driven the ill-equipped Czechoslovak troops many miles north of the line they had held. Kun's defiance of the Peace Conference brought the threat of French troops, several ultimata, reluctant Hungarian withdrawal, and the eventual fall of the Communist régime (August 1, 1919). As a matter of course a "White" reaction followed. This border struggle left a residuum of ill-feeling between Czechoslovakia and Hungary which was destined unfortunately to be aggravated by the two attempts of Emperor Charles to regain the throne of Hungary, with the support, active or hopeful, of a considerable portion of Hungarian opinion.

The Boundaries Commission, in the meantime, set the definitive boundaries at the Ipel, which was much less than Beneš had demanded, but more than some members of the Commission thought necessary. The determinative factor was the east-west line of communication which would have been completely cut by a line any farther north. The Grosse Schütt, a large area southeast of Bratislava inhabited almost exclusively by Magyars, was also, on economic grounds, given to Czechoslovakia. The final line meant the inclusion of about 700,000 Magyars in Slovakia; a very considerable minority. Feeling ran high in post-war Hungary against what virtually all Magyars felt were unwarranted injustices imposed upon a proud nation by the Treaty of Trianon, and the seeds of later intransigent bitterness toward Czechoslovakia were plentifully sown. Yet all accounts agree that by comparison with the conduct of the Rumanian and Yugoslav military in their occupation of Hungarian territory the Czechs were restrained and temperate. Hungarian references to Czech "cleverness" in this early period of their relationship leave the reader, quite apart from questions of justice or injustice, with the strange feeling that what the Hungarians resented was the fact that the Czechs, an "inferior" people, showed greater political sagacity than the Magyar leaders themselves.

The friction with Poland was of a still different kind. Most of the borderline between the two Slav states was simple to fix, since the eastern Carpathian mountains formed a natural frontier. The bone of contention was a part of Austrian Silesia, known as the Duchy of Teschen (Těšín). Ethnographically mixed—Poles 54.8 per cent, Czechs 27.1 per cent, Germans 18 per cent—the territory around Teschen had had a checkered history, having belonged at various times to Poland, Bohemia and Hapsburg Austria. In addition to its ethnographic imbalance, it was a key railway junction, east and west between Bohemia and Slovakia, north and south between the Danubian area and the basins of the Elbe and the Vistula. Its strategic importance was clearly shown at the Battle of the Nations at Leipzig when Napoleon's disregard of this "Moravian Gate" brought him a crushing defeat. The rich coal mines of the district served the industrial area of northern Bohemia and Moravia. After several attempts to reach an acceptable voluntary settlement, the Council of Ambassadors determined upon a line which they felt was equitable, though it was certainly somewhat favorable to Czecho-slovakia. Other, though less significant, borderline disputes prolonged the tension between Poland and Czechoslovakia for several years until the Warsaw protocol of May 6, 1924, finally settled the matter.

This five-year disagreement was particularly unfortunate in that it embittered relations for years thereafter between two sister nations that should, logically, have labored side by side to bring confidence and order in post-war Central Europe. During all these prolonged and often painful negotiations Beneš labored for closer co-operation with Poland, but his efforts were reciprocated by only a small number of Polish statesmen whose influence was seldom dominant for long. On many occasions during these and subsequent years Poland was persuaded to work with the Little Entente for common aims at Geneva, but there was at no time any assurance that her support of the aims of the smaller states would be long maintained.

Subcarpathian Ruthenia, which had been kept in a shamefully backward condition by the Magyar landlords, was assigned to Czechoslovakia as a semi-autonomous territory by the decision of the Peace Conference. This territorial addition gave Czechoslovakia a common frontier with Rumania, and at the same time added heavily to her social and educational responsibilities.

Czechoslovakia's boundaries were thus not completely established until 1923, but her activity in European post-war political life had been increasing in extent and effectiveness under the able guidance of Beneš from the earliest days of independence. The broad lines of Czechoslovak foreign policy were succinctly enounced by Beneš in his several reports to the Czechoslovak Parliament, and after five years of action along those lines summarized in his speech of February 6, 1924. The principal points in that program were six:

1. A conviction that only class-hatred, terrorism and confusion could result from either a Bolshevist or a reactionary political régime in Czechoslovakia.

2. Support of the peace treaties which recognized their imperfection yet insisted that only by adherence to them could order be brought out of the chaotic aftermath of five years of war and destruction.

3. Amicable settlement of all questions in dispute with all neighboring states in order to bring domestic recovery and tranquillity.

4. Confidence in both the need for and the logic of a policy of peace and understanding among the nationalities within the state and a proper care that the rest of the world be informed of the honesty and probity of Czechoslovak intentions.

5. Furtherance of the idea of regional solidarity of states with similar interests, with particular emphasis upon the conviction that such regional groupings within the framework of the League of Nations could only serve to fortify the cause of peace and stability.

6. Reliance upon the democratic trend of European history and the deep-rooted need for peace and order—both given form and substance in the League of Nations.

Beneš, from the beginning of his activity as Foreign Minister of the new state, was confident that boundary questions were fundamentally minor matters that would find acceptable solutions with time and mutual good will. In consequence, from the first moment that Czechoslovak independence seemed assured, he had begun to lay the foundations of a new Central European order, predicated not upon a centralized rule such as that of the Hapsburgs, or upon the hegemony of a dominant Germany as envisaged by Schönerer, Naumann, the *Osterbegehrschaft* and others of that persuasion, but upon the free and willing collaboration of the several peoples of the Danube basin and adjacent areas.

Both Beneš and Masaryk knew perfectly well that, because of the nature of the geography, ethnography and economic organization of the Danube basin, there would have to be some ideological or quasi-political equivalent of the Hapsburg empire. With this realization in the forefront of their political reasoning they began conversations in the autumn of 1917 with Take Jonescu of Rumania, exploring the possibilities of some post-war integration of the policies of their two countries. Though it was not then possible to do more than prepare the ground, later negotiations in the autumn of 1918, which included M. Pašić, former Serbian premier, and M. Venizelos of Greece, brought their respective states closer together, and a program of parallel action at the coming Peace Conference was agreed upon. The Little Entente was founded on the realization of the existence of common interests and the need for common action.

This community of interests was brought to a sharp focus by tendencies and events in Austria and Hungary which had formerly ruled the peoples of the new states. In Austria, during 1919 and for many years thereafter, there was continued agitation in many quarters in favor of *Anschluss* with Germany. Otto Bauer, Austrian Foreign Minister, even broached the matter officially at Weimar and Berlin in the spring of 1919. Such a union would have brought an enlarged Germany into the Danube basin and jeopardized the whole structure of smaller independent states. For that reason these smaller states steadfastly opposed any such project.

On the other hand, the economic plight of Austria was pitiful and, in their own interest as well as in the interest of Austria, the Allies had to do something substantial to keep her people from starving, especially since they refused to permit her to join with Germany in a larger economic unit that would allow her to support herself. Beneš was one of the first to realize and point out the alternatives to Allied statesmen. Before the matter of aid to Austria could be adequately treated as a European question, Beneš arranged a loan of 130 million crowns (about four million dollars) and a credit of 500 million crowns (about thirteen million dollars) in February 1922. In May the problem of Austria came before the League of Nations and a loan of 650 million gold crowns (130 million dollars) was arranged, of which Czechoslovakia advanced 20 per cent. In return, Austria engaged to maintain her sovereignty, and thus *Anschluss* was for the time being ruled out. The relations between Austria and Czechoslovakia were thereafter generally cordial, though sporadic Austrian and German talk of *Anschluss* was an irritant that did not become serious until after the world economic crisis of 1929-1930.

In August 1919, a Hapsburg archduke, Joseph, seized power in Hungary, and Beneš sent a strong note to the Supreme Council of the Peace Conference, which in turn warned Hungary that a Hapsburg government would not be tolerated. Neither Rumania nor Yugoslavia could afford to allow a Hapsburg restoration any more than could Czechoslovakia. Thus the double threat of Austrian *Anschluss* and the return of the Hapsburgs precipitated the formal alignment of the three small states into what was at first known derisively but later with respect as the Little Entente. Its first juridical document was a treaty between Yugoslavia and Czechoslovakia signed by Ninčić and Beneš on August 14, 1920, providing for common political and military action "in case of an unprovoked attack by Hungary" on either. It was conceived of as an agreement within the framework of the League of Nations. Three days later Beneš was in Bucharest, and on August 19 Rumania declared herself ready to give "reciprocal military assistance" in case of an attack by Hungary on either Czechoslovakia, Yugoslavia or Rumania. The full and formal participation of Rumania in the Little Entente began on April 23, 1921.

Beneš regarded the tripartite agreement as only the beginning of an order of mutual confidence and collaboration in Central Europe. The attitude of all three countries toward Hungary was one of suspicion, particularly after the two unsuccessful efforts of the Emperor Charles to recover the throne (March 25-April 5, 1921 and October 20-November 1, 1921). In both cases Beneš, acting as spokesman for the Little Entente, stated the case of the Succession States against the Hapsburgs as a ruling dynasty and against Hungary as a factor retarding the establishment of peace and order in Central Europe. The dispatch, unity and cogency with which the Little Entente acted in these critical moments in Central European history drew favorable comments from the rest of the world, and the prestige of the three smaller states grew markedly as a consequence.

This heightened prestige was amply recognized at the Conference of Genoa (April 10-May 19, 1922). The great western powers had invited the Little Entente and Poland to confer with them on the question of the recognition of Russia and related problems of trade and finance. Though the Rapallo treaty between Germany and Russia, concluded secretly on April 16, made *de jure* recognition of Russia impracticable, Beneš's firm and able guidance of the policy of the Little Entente and Poland through the pitfalls of a conference in rather unstable equilibrium was recognized as further evidence that this bloc of small states must be treated with the respect due a single great power. Beneš was able to negotiate with Soviet Commissar of Foreign Affairs Chicherin a favorable commercial treaty which was the beginning of an era of closer *rapprochement* with Soviet Russia.

At this point there may be noticed the incipient coalescence of the two broad trends of Czechoslovak foreign policy we have noted above as so prominent in Czech thought of the nineteenth century: the western orientation, in the tradition of centuries of attachment to the West, in religion, art, literature and politics; and the eastern, more purely Slavic attraction, based on the undeniable factors of blood and language. From this time—1922—to the recent past these two trends have been maintained in Czechoslovak political and cultural life in an easy balance. Most of the credit for this evenhanded and realistic guiding of Czechoslovak political thought and action must be given to Beneš, though Masaryk gave him unqualified support and thus made the task easier.

The attitude of Czechoslovakia toward the League of Nations was consistently one of loyal support. Though its existence as a state antedated the League, yet the support of the League meant much for the young state. Beneš was never blind to the obstacles in the way of the League's fulfilment of its intended functions, nor to the faults in its internal functioning. Indeed he was a leader in all moves which would strengthen the League, broaden its support and make its work for peace and order more effective as well as more equitable. He had from the first envisaged the necessity of the active participation of both Russia and Germany in European affairs and was a leader in the movements which finally brought them both into the League—Germany in 1926, Russia in 1934.

The five years from 1923 to 1928 in Czechoslovak foreign policy constitute a period of further adjustment within the framework of the League of Nations. It is also a period of heightened understanding and co-operation within the Little Entente, of *rapprochement* with Poland, and, more significantly, of notable success in the search for security through a military alliance with France. In the rest of Europe this is the period of the Geneva Protocol (1924), the treaty of Locarno (December 1925), the entry of Germany into the League of Nations (1926), the Briand-Kellogg Peace Pact (1928) and the preparations for the Disarmament Conference which finally met in 1932. The atmosphere in which European politics moved was therefore apparently favorable to the voluntary consolidation of European peace.

In 1923 Beneš was elected a member of the Council of the League of Nations, of which he was thereafter to serve six times as chairman—a tribute both to his recognized qualities and to Czechoslovakia as a progressive and industrious nation. Preliminary discussions of collective security characterized this session of the League and the Czechoslovak delegates were active in furthering the idea. But when it became evident that the British, by their rejection of the Draft Treaty of Mutual Assistance, were reluctant to assume additional obligations in defense of boundaries far from their immediate spheres of interest, Beneš had to turn to France for a pact which would give Czechoslovakia necessary security. This Franco-Czechoslovak treaty (January 1924) but confirmed and formalized the friendship hitherto existing between the two countries—a friendship based on Czechoslovak gratitude for French aid in gaining her independence, and on French desire for substantial support on Germany's other front.

In the meantime Italian leadership was beginning to be anxious to assert itself in the Danubian basin, which was nearer to Italy than to France and was thus a natural economic market for Italian products and a logical area for the expansion of Italian political and cultural influence. Having already concluded a close alliance with France, Beneš was glad to enter into closer relations with Italy. A five-year treaty of friendship and co-operation between Czechoslovakia and Italy was concluded on July 5, 1924. In the conversations with Mussolini, Beneš endeavored to make it quite clear that the treaty with France did not in any way mean that it was the desire of Czechoslovakia, or indeed of any member of the Little Entente, to make any alliance with a single one of the larger powers to the exclusion of any other. Czechoslovakia had no intention of becoming the satellite of any power. There was another very important thought in Beneš's mind in concluding with Italy a treaty very similar to, if not so radical as, the military alliance with France. He saw that the relations between the two former allies had cooled considerably in the years since the war, and felt that Czechoslovakia might serve as a nexus between them, and in so doing contribute to the stabilization of European order. The treaty with Italy called for mutual support of the *status quo* in the Danubian area as fixed in the treaties of St. Germain, Trainon and Neuilly.

Thus, when Beneš came to the 1924 session of the League of Nations, late in August, he carried in his briefcase the signatures of the two continental allies to treaties guaranteeing the *status quo*. The Geneva Protocol, voted on October 2, 1924, by delegates of forty-eight states, was in large measure the work of Beneš who, as *rapporteur* of the Third Committee, charged with this task, had formulated its comprehensive provisions and presented them to the Assembly. The Protocol, providing for pacific settlement of international disputes and the outlawry of aggressive war, and consequently for eventual disarmament, was nullified by Great Britain's refusal, in March 1925, to ratify it. This was a severe blow to Beneš and his plans for the rational consolidation of European peace, but he was nevertheless willing to work along other lines if he was convinced there was any reasonable chance that success might be achieved.

Germany made several suggestions in February 1925 for a western peace pact and treaties of arbitration with her neighbors, and Czechoslovakia indicated her general willingness to accept the conditions as outlined by France and Great Britain. The result of eight months of deliberation along these lines was the Locarno Peace Pact, initialled October 16, 1925. Germany was admitted into the League, accepted the Versailles boundaries, and engaged herself, in separate treaties, to arbitrate all disputes with Czechoslovakia, France, Belgium and Poland. As a part of the total agreement, Czechoslovakia and Poland were given absolute guarantees of their boundaries and independence by France. Thus, with the Franco-Czechoslovak treaty of January 1924 made more explicit, Czechoslovakia's quest for security seemed to have ended in success.

An important domestic by-product of the conclusion of the Locarno treaties was the early decision of two leading Sudeten German parties, the Agrarians and the German Clericals, to give up their negative attitude and become active participants in the Czechoslovak government. Their reasoning was quite simple: if Germany had given up all thought of revisionism, as her signature to the Locarno Pact seemed to indicate, Sudeten Germans within the boundaries of Czechoslovakia were wasting their time hoping for inclusion in any species of *Grossdeutschland*. The relations of Czechoslovakia with Germany were thereafter, until 1933, of the most cordial, in spite of several recurrences of the question of Austro-German *Anschluss* or its diluted counterpart, a customs union.

Poland, somewhat concerned lest France, after having come to terms with Germany as a result of the negotiations under way at Locarno, might draw nearer to Soviet Russia, now sought stronger ties with Czechoslovakia, and arbitration and commercial treaties were concluded between Beneš and Skrzynski in the spring of 1925, to the gratification of public opinion in both Slav states. Though never a Pan-Slavist, Beneš had always felt and unhesitatingly declared that the evident community of interests in many aspects of foreign relations between Poland and Czecho-slovakia rendered their ultimate co-operation imperative. So far as lay in his power he had endeavored to guide the policy of the Little Entente so that Poland would be encouraged to find bases for common action with the states to the south of her. In this endeavor he had been fairly successful. The treaties of 1925 he regarded as the fruit of this consistent policy of understanding founded on common needs and interests. These treaties certainly marked the high point in cordiality between the two states. After 1926, Pilsudski's unconcealed hope that Slovakia might revert to Hungary so that Poland and Hungary and Rumania might have a common frontier strained relations with Czechoslo-vakia, and complete frankness could not thrive in such an atmosphere.

At the beginning of 1926, Europe as a whole was breathing easily, and it appeared as if the spirit of Locarno had a real basis in fact. But the arrest of Prince Windischgrätz and a number of other highly placed Hungarians on January 4 of that year on charges of counterfeiting French 1,000-franc notes threw Central Europe into an uproar. The fact that the counterfeiting was done in a government building with the full knowledge and complicity of the Hungarian Chief of Police made the whole sordid affair most serious. In Czechoslovakia it was remembered that, between 1919 and 1921, 30 million crowns of Czechoslovak banknotes had been forged by Hungarian "patriots," and this new scandal gave the Czechoslovak public reason to feel that peculative irredentism in Hungary was a habit. At the trial in Buda-pest the defendants protested that their actions were dictated by patriotic motives. Though this defense might have had some mollifying effect upon the Hungarian public, it raised the question in the rest of Central Europe as to the connection between "patriotism" and international crime. The sentences finally meted out to the participants in the "incident" seemed unduly light to the rest of the world and particularly to Czechoslovakia. The unhappy effects of this episode were only aggravated by the discovery (January 2, 1928) of an attempt to smuggle five carloads of arms from Italy to Hungary in violation of the terms of the Treaty of Trianon. In this matter Yugoslavia was as disturbed as Czechoslovakia at the evidence of Italo-Hungarian "friend-liness," and the Little Entente brought the matter before the Council of the League. Though definite responsibility was difficult to fix, the Little Entente had every reason to doubt the good faith of Italy in the whole affair and more reason to maintain an attitude of watchful suspicion toward Hungary. A commercial treaty regularizing necessary trade between Hungary and Czechoslovakia had been concluded in May 1927, but mutual distrust virtually nullified any hoped-for benefits.

On February 2, 1928, Pope Pius XI ratified the *modus vivendi* between the republic and the Holy See, thus ending in a compromise a dispute of many years' standing which had had its repercussions in internal affairs. Though a majority of the population were Roman Catholic, yet the feeling was general that the papacy, long closely attached to the Hapsburgs, disliked the new and democratic order. Other issues also arose: the borders of some dioceses which had been determined under the Empire crossed the new boundaries between Hungary and Austria in the south and Czechoslovakia, so that some Magyar and Austrian bishops exercised ecclesiastical jurisdiction—which also included control of considerable property—within the republic; under the Land Reform law the government had expropriated some church lands, which the church felt was unwarranted.

Masaryk and other leading government officials had been present at the celebrations in the Old Town Square of John Hus day, July 6, 1925, and, as Hus was still regarded as a heretic by the church, this was seen as an affront to the Holy See. The nuncio left Prague for Rome on the same day. The Czechoslovak Clericals, in spite of their sympathy with the papal point of view, did not feel that a complete rupture was justifiable and did not leave the cabinet. Beneš, openly supported by Masaryk, remained firm in his stand that the whole matter was an internal affair; and, as the Curia does not readily recede from a diplomatic position, it was three years before a workable settlement which was a victory for neither side could be arrived at. The boundaries of the dioceses were to be redrawn so as not to cross state lines; all bishops exercising jurisdiction within the republic should be Czechoslovak citizens, and freedom of worship was guaranteed to all creeds. As a seal of friendly relations, a high papal decoration was conferred upon Masaryk in September 1929. For a state whose religious tradition had for centuries been non-conformist and nationalistic to come to a satisfactory *modus vivendi*, though not a concordat, was a triumph of patience and realism for which both Masaryk and Beneš deserve much credit.

The ardent desire of Italy to play an important role in Central European affairs led her to make several moves which had effects opposite to those for which she had hoped. The illegal export of arms to Hungary in 1928 raised the suspicions of the states of the Little Entente whose cardinal policy was directed against Hungarian irredentism. Yugoslavia felt particularly nervous at what looked to her like a conscious effort on the part of an inimical Italy to encircle her. In 1927 and the following years the virtual protectorate over Albania assumed by Italy, coupled with her treaty with Hungary and wooing of Bulgaria, made Yugoslavia increasingly aware of her dangerous position. This threat to one of the members of the Little Entente was a cause of grave concern to all, and Czechoslovakia, while having no cause for alarm for herself, was yet careful to give to the next meetings of the Council of the Little Entente every appearance of complete unanimity and untroubled solidarity.

In these years Beneš was active at Geneva, promoting a system of bilateral treaties of arbitration between states whose interests might possibly clash. Nor did he limit himself to this program. He supported every significant move which tended to bring the nations of the world together in peaceful intercourse, and the proposals embodied in the Kellogg-Briand Peace Pact received his enthusiastic and unqualified advocacy. Public opinion in Czechoslovakia was unanimous in approval of Beneš's sponsorship of the Pact, and that country was one of the first to ratify the treaty (January 23, 1929). The fact that the Pact was soon a dead letter was no fault of Beneš or of Czechoslovakia.

In the late 1920's, in an atmosphere of hopefulness and stable economy, men of good will throughout the world looked forward to the coming Disarmament Conference as the culmination of the long and arduous efforts for a permanently peaceful world. Commissions of technical experts had been at work since 1925. The position of Czechoslovakia was such that though she had had to threaten military action in the early post-war years to maintain peace in the Danubian area, yet her interests as an industrial nation demanded permanent peace and relief from the heavy tax burden of armaments. Because Czechoslovakia's desire for peace was recognized to be both sincere and based on her own interests Beneš was named *rapporteur général* of the Conference that convened in February 1932. But high and noble as its aims were, the Conference failed for a variety of reasons. Its program was too broad, the economic crisis of 1929 and subsequent years had caused too much general uneasiness for it not to be reflected in international relations; the sabotaging of many proposals by the British delegation and the withdrawal of Germany in September were

—separately and cumulatively—blows too heavy for any such conference, from its beginnings in very delicate balance, to sustain. Instead of disarmament, rapid and renewed armament was to follow upon this elaborate effort to pacify the western world.

The world economic crisis that broke upon Europe in 1930 transformed the work of most of the foreign offices in Europe into bureaus of trade and finance. Czechoslovakia was perhaps more affected than any other of the small states. Foreign trade dropped from 21 billion crowns in 1928 to 7.4 billion in 1932 and 5.8 billion in 1933. The internal repercussions, as might have been expected, were commensurately serious. Unemployment grew from 88,000 in 1929-1930 to 920,000 in 1932-1933. In the train of unemployment, the Sudeten German question became more acute. The German population of the republic was, in larger proportion than the Czech and Slovak, engaged in industries that competed with industries in Germany. Because Germany felt obliged to protect its own production, Czechoslovak export to its largest market was cut off, and the workers engaged in those industries naturally suffered most severely.

Though it is certain that there were cases where the economic dislocation incident upon lost export markets worked hardships upon large numbers of Sudeten Germans, no reliable evidence has been adduced that there was any systematic discrimination as such by the Czechs against the German population in the republic. On the other hand, it is a matter of indisputable record that the government increased its aid in these crucial years to the Sudeten areas proportionately more than to Czech unemployed. But the current of dissatisfaction had set in. The strident voices of Hitler and his apostles carried far and wide in the Sudeten lands. An internal problem, precipitated by a world economic catastrophe, made more critical by protective measures taken in a neighboring state, was to be exploited by that state as an excuse for aggression. Few of the Sudeten Germans realized that the gravity of their plight was in a considerable measure brought on by the selfish action of that very state to which they sought to be joined, in the fond delusion that they would there find peace, quiet and plenty.

Another early result of the world economic crisis was the revival of agitation for *Anschluss* between Austria and Germany. This came to a head in the sudden agreement of March 1931 between Curtius and Schober for a Customs Union. Austria's situation was undoubtedly serious and simple palliatives were not enough. But to the Little Entente the implications of the Austro-German move were more far-reaching than the simple matter of Austria's economic stress. Though quite willing to render Austria any substantial aid in their power, in self-defense the states of the Little Entente could not permit any sort of union between Austria and Germany. They saw quite clearly that the presence of Germany on the Middle Danube, however disguised at first, would certainly mean the end of their independent existence. As Beneš reported to the Czechoslovak Chamber of Deputies on April 23, 1931: "A customs union was only the first step toward complete economic and political union," and should that eventuate it was obvious that the equilibrium in Central and Southeastern Europe, so hardly won, would be fatally destroyed. Germany and Austria pointed with some pride to the clauses in the treaty in which other powers were invited to join the Union. But if Czechoslovakia, for example, were to join this Customs Union she would certainly lose all her economic freedom. And the loss of her political freedom would not be far behind. The only policy Czechoslovakia could conscientiously follow was one of absolute refusal to permit the Union to take place. The other members of the Little

Entente followed the same line, both to support Czecho-slovakia, the state most immediately concerned, and in their own ultimate interest.

At this very important crisis the Little Entente was the more anxious to make its own position and determination effectively clear and unmistakable, because of the fact that the League of Nations had lost prestige by its confused diffi-dence in the Sino-Japanese affair. A League that could not act with decision in such a clear case of aggression had for-feited much of the not too secure confidence it had previ-ously enjoyed. It might, reasoned the Little Entente, be even more diffident, that is to say, "diplomatic," in a dis-pute involving a great power like Germany. The states of the Little Entente would then be at Germany's mercy. Of the correctness of these fears the history of the next decade was to give ample proof. But after the Little Entente had made its firm resolve not to permit any sort of union be-tween Austria and Germany, sentiment at the League of Nations followed suit. Austria and Germany, faced with universal opposition, withdrew the plan and for the mo-ment the issue was dead. The time for *Anschluss* was not yet.

The dynamic changes that supervened in Germany after the National Socialists came to power in January 1933 so profoundly affected the life of the Czechoslovak republic that it may be said that the story of Czechoslovak foreign relations from that time until Munich are the story of her relations with Germany and Hitlerism on the one hand, and on the other, of her efforts to strengthen her own posi-tion in the face of certain German expansion into the Danubian area.

Apart from the question of *Anschluss*, with regard to which Czechoslovak policy, in accord with the rest of the Little Entente, was adamant, Czechoslovak relations with Germany had been consistently cordial from the time of the Paris Peace Conference. Beneš had repeatedly acted as intermediary between Paris and Berlin and had made numerous friendly gestures toward Germany. He had made it clear to every French government that Czechoslovakia was anxious for a genuine *rapprochement* between France and Germany. In general this policy of benevolence had been appreciated by the Weimar republic, though no open acknowledgment of it was ever made. All this is a matter of record as well as of fact. In times past Bohemia had had very few quarrels with the Germans north and west of her mountains—her quarrel had been with the Austrians under Hapsburg rule—and there was neither inconsistency nor weakness in her policy of amity for her powerful northern and western neighbor.

¶ But Hitler was determined to crush Czechoslovakia, and the campaign of vilification of the Czechs in the press and over the radio found fertile soil among the hard-hit Sudeten German population. By methods now familiar to the whole world the embers of Pan-Germanism among the German minority were fanned into a consuming fire; union with the Third Reich was promised as a solution of all their ills; and the leaders of the separatist movement, artfully guided from Berlin, took every possible advantage of the democratic freedoms—of speech, the press, organization and public meeting—allowed by the Czechoslovak constitution and protected by the Czech police. The Czechoslovak leaders were not deceived by the repeated declarations of Henlein, Frank, and the other Sudeten *Heimatfront* leaders that they were completely loyal to the republic, knowing full well that their funds, their uniforms, their firearms and their strategy were imported from Munich and Berlin.

At the elections of 1935, after two years of National Socialist propaganda within the republic, the *Sudetendeutsche Partei* polled almost a million and a quarter votes, over 62 per cent of the total German vote, gaining many from the German Catholics, the Farmers' Party and perhaps less from the German Social Democrats. Whether this sudden increase of votes represented conviction or reluctant assent to an aggressive program was probably not clear even to most of the Sudeten Germans.

Events in Austria had, in the meantime, shown to what lengths the new leadership in Germany would go. The Chancellor, Dollfuss, had been murdered by Austrian Nazis (July 25, 1934), and even after that Nazi agitation in Austria did not cease. Within a year Mussolini, who had in July 1934 sent troops to the Brenner Pass as a preventive of *Anschluss*, changed his direction again and was making overtures to Hitler's representatives—and the Axis was on the way to actuality. If the interests of both Italy and Germany in Austria could be reconciled, the road to full collaboration on a larger scale was open. Surrounded by evidence of the determination of Hitler's Germany to absorb Austria and foment destructive dissension in Czechoslovakia on any possible pretext, Beneš, on May 16, 1935, signed a mutual-assistance pact with the Soviet Union, contingent upon the action of France in pursuance of the terms of the Franco-Soviet mutual assistance pact of May 2, 1935. Thus Czechoslovakia brought together the two traditional points of her political compass—the West and Slavdom. This Soviet-Czechoslovak treaty was approved by the Little Entente and was, of course, within the framework of the League of Nations. In the face of militant German expansionism it was an effort to guarantee stability and ensure peace in the Danubian area. The German reaction to the two pacts was naturally one of bitter resentment.

From this time events move with such dizzying speed as to make any coherent account of them almost impossible. Indeed if it were coherent it would misrepresent the facts, for there was no reason or intelligible pattern to be found in the whole course of events. The German press and radio campaign, turning on and off its blasts, thus increasing the confusion; Hitler's own intermittent professions of a deep desire to live at peace with all his neighbors; the kaleidoscopic scene in western Europe, with France and England blowing both hot and cold in the Ethiopian and Spanish "incidents"; the change in Yugoslav orientation under the guidance of Stoyadinović who leaned toward the Axis; the certain acceleration of impending Austrian chaos—all these factors made any policy for Czechoslovakia save one of watchful waiting quite impossible. Yet foreign observers frequently observed that in these frenetic years Prague was the coolest capital in Europe.

The Czechs realized the paramount importance of their state in any shift of political forces in Europe. In a speech before the Committee on Foreign Affairs of the Czechoslovak Senate and Chamber of Deputies on November 5, 1935, Beneš reiterated what every Czech knew concerning the place of his country in European politics:

. . . our state is the key to the whole post-war structure of Central Europe. If it is touched either internally or internationally, the whole fabric of Central Europe is menaced, and the peace of Europe seriously infringed. It would not be long before all Europe would be grievously conscious of the fact.

The Czechs never lost sight of the brute fact that they were *the* obstacle, physical and ideological, to German expansionism. There was little likelihood that Nazi Germany would *not* try to move into the Danubian area, and to do so she would have to exterminate or absorb Czechoslovakia. There was not a Czech in the whole republic in 1936 who would have disagreed with the phrase "After Austria, it is our turn next." Yet they showed remarkable coolness and confidence that they would give a good account of themselves if it should come to the trial of force. Their boundary defenses had been strengthened continuously since 1934, and their army, both as to equipment and personnel, was near peak efficiency by late in 1935. And then the double alliance with France and the Soviet Union seemed a further guarantee of their security.

The communiqué issued by the Council of the Little Entente at the end of August 1935 recognized the gravity of the international situation, and reaffirmed the solidarity of the alliance and its firm allegiance to the League of Nations, the idea of a Danubian Pact, and a common and unalterable opposition to a Hapsburg restoration. But no member of the Council deceived himself as to the frailty of the props of peace. Dubious Franco-Italian relations, German rearmament, Italo-German *rapprochement*, the political fatuity of British leadership, and Nazi economic and propaganda penetration of Austria, Hungary, Bulgaria, Rumania and Yugoslavia, all constituted a whole closet full of very active skeletons which might jump out at any moment and frighten all of Europe into war.

≺ 15 ≻

Munich and After

BECAUSE of his feeling that a younger hand should be at the
helm during the storm which he saw approaching, Masaryk
resigned the presidency in December 1935. Beneš was immediately elected by Parliament to succeed him. This
change, generally anticipated throughout Europe for some
time, brought with it no noticeable modifications in either
foreign or domestic policy. Professor Kamil Krofta, the
eminent historian who had been Beneš's aide in the foreign
office for almost a decade, was chosen (March 1936) to carry
on in his place.

The new administration was not allowed any respite for
adjustment to its tasks by the German propaganda office.
In February 1936 the false story of Soviet airfields in Czechoslovakia was blazoned in the German press, and Czechoslovakia was branded as a Communist-Jewish tool. The campaign against the Czechoslovak-Soviet treaty of 1935 was
kept up for two years. It must have been intended for local
consumption, for the rest of the western world paid little
attention to it. When this story wore thin and had to be
discarded, the Nazi press and radio had recourse to tales of
Czech discrimination and cruelty to the Sudeten Germans
in every department of life. The protestations of the Czechoslovak government that the facts should be investigated
on the spot; and the accounts of neutral observers and journalists who had first-hand information and impressions that
the German minority in Czechoslovakia was by all odds
the best treated in all Europe and in some respects favored
over the Czechs themselves, had little effect beyond causing
the tone of Nazi screeching to go even higher.

Through 1936, 1937, and 1938 Henlein followed a consistent policy, engineered and timed from Berlin, of stating certain conditions which ostensibly would satisfy Sudeten demands for justice; then, when the Czechoslovak government showed a willingness to meet these demands within more than reasonable limits, of increasing them. The Czechoslovak government was in full possession of evidence that Henlein was in continual and direct contact with Nazi emissaries and the Wilhelmstrasse and acted on their instructions, even in the earlier years when he was loudly protesting his loyalty to the republic. Of these facts there is not, nor indeed ever can be, any shadow of doubt. Even Lord Runciman was aware of them in the summer of 1938, and he took good care to know as little of the realities of the situation as possible. In view of this indisputable state of affairs, there is hardly any point in following in detail the development of Henlein's various programs, from his Prague speech of February 23, 1936, to the eight-point speech at Karlsbad, April 24, 1938, and the counter-suggestions of the Hodža ministry. In actuality, there was never the slightest possibility that a complete acceptance of Sudeten demands at any point in the period of tension would have meant any permanent alleviation of the crisis. Nazi Germany was seeking a pretext to make an international incident out of Czechoslovakia and would certainly have found it in some way or other. Beneš, Hodža, Krofta, Jan Masaryk and Osuský were perfectly aware of this determination on the part of Hitler and his advisers, and the foreign offices at London and Paris were told the facts and shown the evidence. Leading publicists, French, English and American, were also aware of the true situation. But foresight and courage were wanting in the right places in these tragic years.

The Nazi march into Vienna, March 12-13, 1938, was the signal for the Sudeten demands to be raised again. In his Karlsbad speech (April 24, 1938) Henlein demanded the virtual break-up of the Czechoslovak state. France and England urged Hodža and Krofta to settle the Sudeten problem peacefully, and France renewed her polite assurance that she had every intention of living up to her treaty obligations if Czechoslovakia were attacked. In London there was no secret of British unwillingness to support France in any such military action as her treaty with Czechoslovakia called for. No one should be so naïve as to think that Beneš was unmindful of the real intention of Chamberlain as early as the first week in May, when American newspapermen in London had accurate ideas of official British willingness to sacrifice Czechoslovak independence to Germany.

Yet Beneš did not let his knowledge of that intention prevent him from guarding his country's frontiers and integrity as long as possible. The "routine" concentration of German troops on the northern Czech borders during the weekend of May 21 looked to him like an action similar to that which led to the occupation of Austria. The Czechoslovak army was mobilized quietly and within a few hours. Hitler was taken by surprise. Foiled by Beneš's quick and courageous action, Hitler never forgave him or the Czechs, but he covered his chagrin by dismissing the whole incident as an illustration of Czech bellicosity.

Defeated for the moment in the direct military approach, Hitler tried another tack, suggesting through his aide, Captain Wiedemann, whom he sent to London to confer with Lord Halifax, that an English "mediator" be sent to Czechoslovakia to "advise" the Czechoslovak government as to how to accede to Sudeten demands. The mission of Lord Runciman is one of those sordid affairs best openly admitted as such and then forgotten. Czech opinion recognized it for what it was—ill concealed blackmail—and was indignant. It is not so easy to forget that the British Prime Minister told Parliament (July 26) that the Czechoslovak government had asked that such a mediator be sent. The fact is well known, attested from a multitude of sources, that the suggestion originated with Mr. Chamberlain and was communicated to the French Foreign Office by Lord Halifax during the visit of the British sovereigns to Paris during the week of July 19.

Negotiations between the Czechoslovak government and Sudeten leaders were intermittent during June and July, but the Hodža cabinet put forward on July 26 a Nationality Statute giving a large measure of local autonomy and complete proportionality in state employment, education and contracts for public works. Conversations between Runciman, who arrived in Prague on August 3, Henlein, his lieutenant Kundt, Hodža and Beneš, separately and in groups in Bohemia, and between Henlein and Hitler at Berchtesgaden and Berlin, made newspaper headlines but little real progress toward a settlement of any sort.

The month of August was taken up by jockeying for diplomatic position. The Sudeten districts were thrown into turmoil by threats and violence, induced, as all the reliable evidence goes to show, by Henlein's Nazis, aided, financed and armed by Nazis from across the border. The support accorded the secessionist agitators by the German inhabitants of the Sudeten areas, however, was far from unanimous. During the months of July and August an increasing number of Sudeten Germans, many of them prominent in the *Heimatfront* movement, took occasion to advise members of the Czech government of their loyalty to the republic, and their deprecation and disavowal of the now radically separatist policy of Henlein. The outside world was then and unfortunately remains years later too little aware of the fact that there were many diverse currents of thought and tradition within the so-called Henleinist party, and that its apparent unity was a very precarious and artificial thing. Only pressure from Germany kept it even superficially intact. Runciman, so far as we can judge from his actions and published reports, had no realization of this important fact.

Border incidents were used by the German press to prove that the Czechs could not keep order, whereas the fact was that these disturbances were precipitated by Henlein's "Black Guard" who usually disappeared like a morning mist when any small body of Czech police came into view.

On September 4 Georges Bonnet, French Foreign Minister, declared in a public speech in the presence of American Ambassador Bullitt that France would under all circumstances remain faithful to the pacts and treaties which she had concluded. Other official and semi-official sources revealed that Germany had been repeatedly warned by France that unpredictable consequences might result from German military intervention in the Sudeten dispute. But the fact that Germany paid not the slightest attention to the warnings has led many informed observers to deduce that this firm front was not intended to deceive the Wilhelmstrasse as to the real French and British intentions. The partial mobilization of the French army to about one million men by September 1 had, viewed in this light, little or no significance.

It now appears that Runciman's mission was that of a mediator between the Czechoslovak government and Hitler, rather than between the Sudeten leaders and the Czechoslovak government—the original intention. Henlein made no decision without going to Berchtesgaden. If Runciman asked Henlein a question of any consequence at all he knew he would have to wait until Henlein could get Hitler's answer. It would have been simpler for Runciman to listen to Hitler directly.

On September 5 Beneš gave the Sudeten leaders the government's "Fourth Plan," granting most of the Karlsbad eight points—providing, beyond provisions for equality in education, language and the sharing of police jurisdictions, for cantonization; but still maintaining some semblance of unity of the Czechoslovak state. It is now known that many of Henlein's lieutenants were more than satisfied with this plan, and so expressed themselves to Beneš and Hodža. But Henlein had received instructions from Hitler not to make any agreement with the Czechs before his speech at the Nürnberg meeting of the Party, which was scheduled for September 12, when Hitler would announce his terms to the world. On very flimsy grounds, therefore, discussions were interrupted, drawn out and confused by new and irrelevant issues.

On September 11 Bonnet flew from Paris to Geneva and had conversations with M. Litvinov and the Rumanian Foreign Minister. The Soviet minister emphatically assured Bonnet that Russia would fulfil her treaty obligations to Czechoslovakia and had secured Rumanian consent to the passage of Soviet troops to aid the Prague government.

Hitler's bellicose if vague speech on the evening of September 12 was the signal for an attempted Nazi *putsch* in the Sudetenland. It is one of the strange aspects of the whole crisis that so little attention was paid to the ease with which the Czech government put down the attempted rising without extraordinary measures, within thirty-six hours, and how relieved most of the Sudeten Germans were that order was quickly restored and the Reich Nazis had fled back across the border almost as quickly as they had come. These facts were broadcast to the world, but apparently any sense of proportion had long since departed from the minds of British and French leaders. Henlein fled to Germany the afternoon of September 15, leaving behind a melodramatic proclamation to the Sudetens and the whole civilized world.

But this quick pacification, received with unconcealed satisfaction by most Sudeten Germans, was precisely what Hitler could not endure. Having failed to intimidate the

Czechs, he applied pressure where he knew a combination of pressure, confusion and lack of information would be of most immediate benefit to Nazi expansion. It is quite likely that the whole crisis would have dissolved into thin air, or at least this acute phase of it would have, if Chamberlain had not already made up his mind that, regardless of its effect upon the Czechoslovak people, the cession of the Sudetenlands to the Reich was necessary in order to maintain European peace. He was in Berchtesgaden conferring with Hitler as to ways and means of making this cession at the very moment that Henlein fled into Germany because the *putsch* had failed.

Czechoslovakia's firm and efficient handling of the Henleinist *putsch* made a favorable impression upon everyone but those who had decided to force her to accede to Hitler's demands. Chamberlain, Daladier and Bonnet, at a meeting in London on September 18, arranged the terms of the proposed cession, which were presented to the Czechoslovak government in Prague the next day. The Anglo-French proposals suggested direct transfer to Germany of areas "with over 50 per cent of German inhabitants." Great Britain was thereupon prepared to join in an international general guarantee of the independence of the remaining Czechoslovak state.

Czechoslovak indignation knew no bounds. The ears of British and French politicians and diplomats must have crisped during these days. The true and bitter things the Czech populace was saying about them, if preserved, would make heartening reading for posterity. Yet, much of this indignation was superhumanly restrained. Outsiders then in Prague and elsewhere in the Republic were impressed with the intelligent comprehension of the real significance of the ignoble surrender for the immediate future of Europe. A common Czech observation was: "How shortsighted of the 'democratic' countries not to realize the strategic importance of the loss of Czechoslovakia in the war that is certain to come!" As to the proposed guarantee the Czechs remarked: "Why, from a selfish point of view, should England refuse to guarantee boundaries which geographically and by formidable fortification are defensible, and then offer to guarantee a frontier which is completely indefensible?"

A sovereign state, the only one in Central Europe to have a record of consistent honor in international relations during the difficult post-war period, had, in the words of the Czechoslovak minister to Paris, Štefan Osuský, "been condemned without a hearing" by those who called themselves its friends. Poland interjected a jackal-ish note into the crisis by demanding the return of the Teschen district which had been awarded to Czechoslovakia by the Council of Ambassadors in 1920 and confirmed by the Warsaw Protocol of 1924; and Hungary expressed a desire to participate in the "readjustments" that were *en train*. Soviet and Rumanian policies were the only ones that preserved any vestige of honor.

On the evening of September 20 the Czechoslovak rejection of the terms of the Anglo-French proposals was relayed to Paris and London. This dignified and closely reasoned document[1] was not published in either the French *Blue Book* or the British *White Book*. The text of the note, containing an appeal to unabrogated treaties of arbitration between Germany and Czechoslovakia, is well worth careful reading in view of subsequent events.

Within a few hours of the receipt of the note in Paris and London, Beneš was got out of bed (2:15 a.m., September 21), and told by the British and French ministers in Prague that the proposals of their governments must be accepted or Czechoslovakia would have to bear the consequences alone.

[1] The text is printed in full by Hubert Ripka in his *Munich: Before and After* (London, Gollancz, 1939), pp. 74-77.

It was during this meeting that Beneš asked the French minister, M. de Lacroix (who at the time made only a verbal statement of France's "disinterestedness" in any Czechoslovak-German war) for a written statement of the attitude of his government. Under such circumstances did the leaders of France repudiate a treaty obligation which had been publicly reaffirmed less than a fortnight previously as a sacred engagement of the French nation. It has since become known that this shameful repudiation was decided by only three men: President LeBrun, M. Daladier, the Premier, and M. Bonnet, the Foreign Minister. The exact story of how the treachery was engineered, certainly against the will of a very considerable section of enlightened French opinion, is not yet, and may never be completely known, but the fact and the tragic consequences are only too clear.

At 9:00 in the morning of September 21, after long deliberation from 6:30 on, the Czechoslovak cabinet decided to submit. The bitter humiliation was made necessary by the threat of Poland to join Germany and attack Czechoslovakia on her flank. If Poland had marched from the north, Hungary would have attacked from the south. Czechoslovakia would have been willing to make a stand against the might of Germany, but the added danger from Poland and Hungary, both anxious to take advantage of her hour of greatest distress, would have been too great.

Thousands of Czech citizens thronged the Václavské Náměstí demanding a government that would resist. Popular demand for the elimination of the extreme rightist Agrarians was particularly insistent. It was inevitable that the Hodža cabinet, which had accepted the humiliating proposals, should fall; and General Jan Syrový, the one-eyed hero of the Czech Anabasis across Siberia, took the helm, supported by a cabinet of experts. Beneš and Syrový appealed to the people to maintain calm and confidence, and the response, though militant, was admirable. On that same day, September 22, Chamberlain, with the Czechoslovak acceptance of the Anglo-French proposals in his pocket, arrived in Godesberg to arrange with Hitler details of the transfer of Czechoslovak territory to the Reich.

But Hitler made demands for so rapid a timetable of occupation of the Sudetenland that even Chamberlain could not accept it, and on the afternoon of September 23, before Chamberlain left Godesberg, word was sent to Prague that the British and French governments could no longer take the responsibility of advising Czechoslovakia not to mobilize. This apparent change of front had a galvanic effect not only upon the atmosphere in Czechoslovakia but also upon all Central European countries. It looked now as if the western democracies might after all stand up to Hitler. Hungary suddenly became less anxious to press her claims to Slovakia.

Among the Czechs depression and bitterness gave way to relief and exultation. Mobilization was effected more rapidly than the army expected. Every reservist, whether called or not, hurried to his station. A vast majority of Sudeten Germans obeyed their summons to the colors with a readiness which would have astonished those who had been taken in by Nazi propaganda. Slovaks of all shades of political belief rallied to the support of the Republic. This spontaneous demonstration of Czechoslovak national unity —German, Czech, Slovak and Ruthene—had a most salutary effect on opinion in nearby states. In Rumania and Yugoslavia street demonstrations, volunteers offering themselves to Czechoslovakia for military service, and an enthusiastic press all echoed this tribute to courage. Soviet assurance of military help, even beyond the terms of the Franco-Soviet-Czechoslovak treaties, was quickly given. It is significant in this connection that, because of certain British predispositions with regard to Soviet Russia, this source of help could not be used by Prague without ranging Britain on the side of an anti-Bolshevist Germany. Even powerful elements in the Czech Agrarian party threatened to invite Hitler to take over the republic if Soviet Russia were asked for help. Yet, in the face of this complication, Russia could still be of some assistance to Czechoslovakia. On September 23 Russia informed Poland that she would denounce the Soviet-Polish Non-Aggression Pact if the latter took military action against Czechoslovakia. As it turned out, Russia's will to help the Prague government was nullified by Franco-British refusal to invite the Soviets to participate in the negotiations at any point. At the same time, Rumania and Yugoslavia had reminded Hungary of the purposes and provisions of the Little Entente treaties. The Czechs felt that at last the western powers had come to realize the importance of a stand against Hitlerism. It was reported that on September 23 M. Daladier had reiterated, in the presence of a delegation of Radical Socialists, France's firm determination to go to Czechoslovakia's aid if she were attacked by Germany. That same night a partial mobilization of the French army was ordered and a token mobilization was ordered in England on the next day.

On the 24th hope ran high in Prague. The government radio station announced that Czechoslovakia's allies and friends, France, Russia, Yugoslavia and Rumania, had reiterated their promises of support. Hitler's Godesberg demands were received by the government. His new ultimatum demanded many districts which were completely Czech and set a short time limit of October 1 for withdrawal of all Czech officials and police. The new frontiers cut main roads and railways in such a way as to put the rest of the country completely at Germany's mercy. Though the details were not immediately made public, everyone sensed the nature of the ultimatum. Rejection was taken as a matter of course, and popular support of the government was unanimous. Slovak autonomists offered wholehearted co-operation, burying their differences with the Czechs in the hour of stress, and two Slovaks joined the cabinet. All foreigners in the republic were deeply impressed by the universal and sincere feeling of loyalty to the state from all classes and elements—Sudeten German, many Magyars and Poles, as well as Czech, Slovak and Ruthenian.

The formal refusal of the Godesberg ultimatum was conveyed to the British government on September 25 by Jan Masaryk.

In the meantime, beginning about the 20th, a new series of border incidents had broken out. Czechoslovak customs houses were dynamited or burned, post offices and public buildings attacked, policemen captured or shot and private citizens shot at and many killed. The perpetrators of these acts of brigandage and violence were partly Henlein's *Freikorps*, Sudeten Germans who had fled across the border after the earlier *putsch* had failed, and partly Reich German Nazis. These incidents increased in frequency and seriousness until after the Munich "Accord." It was no longer a conflict between Sudeten Germans and Czech police, but between those who professed allegiance to Hitler and those loyal to the Czechoslovak state. Chamberlain seems not to have recognized this altered situation. It is difficult to discover precisely what significant changes of opinion were taking place in the French Foreign Office. The initiative had long since been abandoned to Chamberlain. While still at Godesberg, Chamberlain suggested to Hitler that the border districts be policed by Sudeten Germans, as if all Sudeten Germans were supporters of Henlein. Either Runciman or Mr. Newton, the British Minister at Prague, must have been very careless analysts of a situation obvious to everyone else, or else Chamberlain wilfully disregarded their reports.

Hitler's speech at the Sportpalast at eight o'clock in the

President Beneš

evening of September 26 was blatant, threatening, confident and insulting to the democracies and particularly to
Beneš, all at one and the same time. The next day Great
Britain engaged to stand by France "if, in spite of all efforts
made by the British Prime Minister, a German attack is
made on Czechoslovakia." That evening announcement
was made of the mobilization of the British fleet. The Little
Entente declared itself ready to march if Hungary should
attack Czechoslovakia. Russia's determination to live up to
her treaty obligations was openly reavowed. A general war
seemed imminent. Chamberlain was, in the meantime,
after several days' conversations with Daladier and General
Gamelin in London, making a "last effort" to avert war. He
sent his confidant, Sir Horace Wilson, to Berlin, asking for
an orderly settlement of the crisis by a conference of Germany and Czechoslovakia, with British representatives if
desirable.

French opinion in these trying days was profoundly
confused. Many prominent leaders of the Right and Center favored peace at all costs, and through the press and
proclamations made the public feel that a peaceful settlement of the crisis was possible if only the Czechs would
accept the German terms. Put in that way it seemed absurd
that France should engage in a large-scale war just because
the Czechs insisted on being stubborn on a few matters of
procedure. The responsibility of France for the subsequent
débâcle is, in some ways, greater than that of Britain: both
by reason of her solemn treaty engagements and, what is of
equal importance, because her own fate hung in the balance and her leaders deliberately failed to recognize it.
There can be no question of French fear that Soviet Russia would not take immediate military action against Germany in fulfilment of both the letter and the spirit of her
treaty with France and Czechoslovakia. M. Litvinov cate-
gorically reiterated Russia's certainty of action in this even-

tuality to both French and British officials at Geneva on September 25 and 26. This ghastly failure was not the fault of the French people, which has never lacked courage, nor directly of French "democratic" political organization, but purely of French political leadership. Another French Revolution might have been a good thing for French honor.

From this point the tragedy rapidly reaches its climax. The intention of both the British and the French governments to accept Hitler's conditions was evident to Prague in the evening of September 27, when Beneš was told that, unless Czechoslovakia accepted the British timetable of German occupation, an invasion would certainly follow on the 28th, and Czechoslovakia, as a result of the war thus precipitated, could never hope for restoration of its frontiers. The Czech reply was an acceptance in principle of the British (and French) timetable; but the unworkability of some of the conditions was explicitly pointed out, as well as the fact that this new ultimatum was much more severe than the previously accepted Anglo-French proposals.

Ostensibly as a result of a personal message from Chamberlain to Hitler, the night of September 27-28, in which the former declared that he felt certain Hitler could "get all essentials without war and without delay," and of a message from Mussolini to Hitler, German military action was postponed twenty-four hours. President Roosevelt's urgent message (3:00 a.m., September 28), proposing a conference of "all the nations directly involved" was evidently disregarded, and indeed it was not even welcomed in France.

In the midst of his speech to the House of Commons on the 28th, giving an account of his recent dealings with Hitler, Chamberlain was dramatically presented at about 4:00 p.m. with a copy of a telegram from Hitler inviting the Prime Minister and M. Daladier to meet with him and Mussolini the next day in Munich. The House broke into enthusiastic applause. The timing of the presentation of this invitation could hardly have been more effective. But the story was repeated among members of the diplomatic corps in London, and seriously accepted, that this message had been on Chamberlain's desk at 10 Downing Street since about noon. The cynicism that would dictate such a cheaply dramatic scene would easily be capable of the Munich "Accord." If this whole sordid story is true, the accusations levelled at Chamberlain by many well-informed journalists and students of international affairs at home and abroad are only too justified.

Though previously Chamberlain had suggested that the dispute be ironed out between representatives of the German and the Czechoslovak governments, no mention was now made of Czechoslovak representatives at the four-power conference set for the next day. Nor did the French government insist that Czechoslovakia should have anything to say about the disposition of her own territory. Chamberlain, in a note to Prague through the British minister, insisted on having "wide discretion." As the event was to show—whether "discretion" was the correct term or not —whatever it was, it was certainly wide.

The two Czechoslovak delegates, Drs. Mastný and Masařík, were lodged at the same hotel as the English delegation, but were at no time accorded the right of offering any factual observations as to the minimal vital interests of the republic. They were told simply that the great powers did not expect an answer from Czechoslovakia but regarded the arrangement as accepted. At the last meeting, at which the terms of the settlement were communicated to the Czechoslovak delegates (1:30 a.m., September 30), Chamberlain was obviously bored and made no effort to conceal his yawns.

Any pretense that the Munich "Accord" was an improvement upon the Godesberg ultimatum is naïve. If anything, the effect of its provisions were more severe upon the republic than the Godesberg terms would have been, precisely by reason of the so-called International Commission, which gave to Germany whatever Czech territory her delegate demanded. The French and British members of the Commission gave the German member a blank check. In addition to almost 3,000,000 Sudeten Germans, about 800,-000 Czechs were included in the territory given to the Reich. The rump Czechoslovakia was obviously incapable of independent economic or political existence, which, of course, was so planned by Hitler. The promised loans from France and England, ostensibly $150,000,000, turned out, on examination, to be worth about $30,000,000, and that was not forthcoming until after three tragic months had passed. The guarantee of the new frontiers of the republic, pledged in paragraphs 1 and 2 of the "Annex to the Agreement" by all four signatories, was soon ignored by Britain and France.

The words of Dr. Krofta to the French and British ministers in Prague when he notified them officially of his government's acceptance of the Munich "Accord" (noon, September 30), are worth quoting because of their prophetic accuracy:

I do not intend to criticize, but this is for us a disaster which we have not merited. We surrender and shall endeavor to secure for our nation a peaceful existence. I do not know whether your countries will benefit by these decisions which have been made at Munich, but we are certainly not the last; after us there are others who will be affected—and who will suffer from these decisions.

September 1939 and June 14, 1940, were not very far away.

The bitterness of heart and the depth of poignant grief felt by the whole Czechoslovak people cannot be described. While peasant women, strong soldiers, men of letters, merchants, teamsters, mechanics, legionaries of the march across Siberia were seen on the streets of Prague shaken with the sobbing that only deep despair can bring, Daladier and Chamberlain were being greeted by wildly cheering throngs at Le Bourget and Croydon. Daladier at least had the grace to realize that his own country's honor had been besmirched almost beyond repair.

The march of events during the four months after Munich could have been prophesied with amazing accuracy—and indeed there were many, both inside and outside the British and French governments, who read the signs clearly. The Czechs themselves, than whom as a people there is none in the world more politically aware, knew perfectly well what was going to happen around them.

A weakened and deserted state could not resist Polish and Hungarian claims when these were fomented and supported by a Germany which had just received carte blanche in Central Europe from Great Britain and France. Poland by October 10 had taken the 76,000 Poles in the Teschen district and also more than 125,000 Czechs. Hungary, after making extravagant demands during October, had to be satisfied with the terms of the Vienna award of November 2, by which she received the 504,000 Magyars scattered along the southern boundary of Slovakia, including enough of Subcarpathian Ruthenia to give her a common frontier with Poland, and also 290,000 Slovaks, giving her a total Slovak minority of about 470,000; that is, almost as many Slovaks as there had been Magyars in Slovakia during the republic. There were left over 350,000 Sudeten Germans in the truncated republic, and these were, according to the Munich agreement, to be allowed to opt for the Reich. But they were too useful to Germany as irritants to be allowed to leave Czechoslovakia, and were ordered to remain in the country. They claimed and obtained extraordinary political and cultural privileges and were a convenient mouthpiece for Hitler's further demands.

Seeing that the republic he had helped create and main-

tain was dead, and realizing that his continued presence at
the head of the government would only provoke the next
step in the tragedy, Beneš, on October 5, resigned the presidency and soon (October 21) left the country for London.
The government of General Syrový carried on, with such
modifications as the new situation, calling for "co-operation" with the Reich, demanded. The important post of
Foreign Minister was filled by Dr. Chvalkovský, an Agrarian who had previously held the posts of minister at Rome
and Berlin, where he was supposed to have sympathies and
some influence. On November 30 Dr. Emil Hácha, an
elderly and distinguished jurist, without active political
experience, was agreed upon for the presidency; and Rudolf Beran, also an Agrarian, became Premier, taking office
on December 1.

After Munich the only hope for the country's survival
lay in complete reorientation toward Nazi Germany. The
Soviet pact of 1935 was denounced (October 21). The internal reaction from the democratic traditions of Masaryk
and Beneš was sudden and apparently complete. The parties of the left were dissolved. Almost overnight officeholders who were known to have been convinced followers of
the two founders of the republic were obliged to give up
their posts, and, where possible, more "reliable" persons
were put in their positions. A gesture of conformity with
the Nürnberg anti-Semitic laws was made. The Czechs
remarked bitterly that "At least the Germans never pretended to be our firm friends." The Slovak autonomists
gained the vocal ascendancy in Slovakia, though they had
never previously been able to command more than a third
of the Slovak votes. The Czechoslovak Parliament, in order
to avoid another open appeal to Hitler by an apparently
dissident group crying "persecution," granted the demands
of the Slovak Catholics led by Monsignor Tiso, Hlinka's
deputy, for autonomy (October 7). Ruthenia became an

autonomous unit under the presidency of M. Andrej Bródy, who was removed on October 26 for treasonable dealings with Hungary. Monsignor Augustin Vološín, a Ukrainian, replaced him.

Both Slovakia and Ruthenia became centers for disturbing Ukrainian propaganda, furthered and partially financed from Berlin—disturbing particularly for Poland with its large and not too happy Ukrainian minority. The Prague government was unable to give satisfaction to Polish protests, because of the decentralization forced upon the republic by the Munich terms and its consequences. The government of Slovakia became totalitarian, with the Catholic Party of "National Unity," representing hardly more than 30 per cent of the population, imitating, even to S.A. and S.S. uniforms and concentration camps, the National Socialist Party in Germany. Czech officials, teachers and public employees to the number of 9,000 were immediately dismissed. Extreme separatism, undoubtedly fostered by Nazi agents, grew in intensity during the early months of 1939, reaching its culmination in early March 1939, when Tiso, deposed and imprisoned for treason at the orders of President Hácha (March 10), appealed to Hitler to take Slovakia under his "protection." Since March 15, 1939, Slovakia has been a comic opera "independent" state, showing its independence by doing exactly what the local Nazi Gauleiter has ordered. The Ruthenian "autonomous" state was also organized by Nazi agents, and anti-Semitism, as in Slovakia, flourished.

The Sudeten Germans soon found that their new "freedom" was quite different from what they had been led to expect. Their Prussian "brothers" turned out to be severe taskmasters. In a matter of several months many of them wished to be back in a Czechoslovak state. As in Austria the political and civil posts were soon in the hands of Reich Nazis, and the last state of the Sudeten Germans was worse than the first. But this inconvenience was less basic than that which resulted from the economic dislocation brought on by the impossible new frontier adjustments of the Munich "Accord."

In the domain of economics the maimed state was completely at the mercy of Germany. The few industries that were still on Czechoslovak territory were unable to command the raw materials which previously came from the areas given to Germany. Railway and supply systems were completely and irrationally disrupted. The Sudeten areas themselves were, if anything, in worse plight than ever before. They, too, had prospered throughout history from the logical and permanent give-and-take with the more central lowland areas along well trodden routes. This stable relationship was now completely disarranged and there was no natural route of exchange with Reich Germany to take its place. As early as December 1938 the German economic authorities felt obliged to re-establish something of the older economic free flow by disregarding the frontier lines themselves and forcing the Czechs to disregard them as customs barriers. The fact that this was ironic proof of the contention of the Czechs in their remonstrances to Chamberlain and the whole world before Munich was naturally lost on those who had brought the anomalous situation to pass.

Not content with having forced from the now defenseless state as much "co-operation" as possible under the Munich terms, broadly construed, Germany was determined to absorb the remnant. Nazi *agents-provocateurs* in Slovakia, Subcarpathian Ruthenia, and in sections of Bohemia and Moravia incited riots and disturbances which were announced in the German press and to the world as palpable evidence of the inability of the Prague government to maintain order. The Prague government was told that maintain order it must. The "or else" was a clear implication. But the Czechs were not so easily intimidated as the Germans had hoped, and by late in February order had been restored by firm and decisive police action. After the Germans had created what seemed an impossible situation for the Czech government, the Czech determination to be masters in their own house apparently foiled the Nazi plans.

When Tiso and some of his co-separatists were deposed and imprisoned, on well-authenticated grounds of encouraging the separatist movement in the direction of Hungary, at the orders of the mild Dr. Hácha on March 10, 1939, they appealed to Hitler against the action of the President as unconstitutional. The German press and radio took up the cry, and the Czechs were condemned as stubborn, insolent, unco-operative, dictatorial terrorists, and as obstacles in the path of Central European peace and progress. On the 14th it was reported from Berlin that Hitler had presented the Prague government with an ultimatum demanding partition of the former republic into three independent units: Bohemia-Moravia, Slovakia and Ruthenia, and the acceptance of a virtual Reich protectorate over the whole. That same day large concentrations of German troops were observed on the northern, western and southern borders of Bohemia and Moravia, obviously awaiting the order to occupy the country. Acting on orders from Berlin, the Slovak Separatist Parliament proclaimed complete independence from the Prague government.

After President Hácha's request for a consultation with the German *chargé d'affaires* in Prague, Herr Hencke, had been disregarded, the Czech president was summoned to Berlin. He arrived, with Chvalkovský and several secretaries, late in the evening of the 14th. A conference with Ribbentrop preceded the meeting with Hitler which began about 1:00 a.m. (March 15). The German press in midnight editions was already announcing the end of the re-

public. All efforts by Hácha to moderate the drastic decision of Hitler were in vain. The strain of the situation was
almost too much for an aged man of Hácha's temperament
and training, and it was necessary for attending physi-
cians, thoughtfully provided by Ribbentrop, to use restora-
tives twice during the long ordeal. The bombardment of
Prague by 800 planes was mentioned by Göring as one of
the first alternatives to a refusal to acquiesce. The President's signature was finally gained (3:55 a.m.) to a strange
document which had long been prepared for this occasion.
It read:

The Führer today, in the presence of the Reich Minister for
Foreign Affairs, Herr von Ribbentrop, received the Czecho-
Slovak President, Dr. Hácha, and the Czecho-Slovak Minister
for Foreign Affairs, Dr. Chvalkovský, at their request in Berlin.
At the meeting the serious situation which had arisen as a result of the events of the past week on what was hitherto Czecho-
Slovak territory was closely and frankly examined. Both sides
gave expression to their mutual conviction that the aim of all
efforts in this part of Central Europe should be the safeguard-
ing of calm, order and peace. The Czecho-Slovak President
declared that in order to serve this purpose, and in order to
secure final pacification, he placed the destiny of the Czech
people and country with confidence in the hands of the Führer
of the German Reich.

The Führer accepted this declaration and expressed his determination to take the Czech people under the protection of
the German Reich and to guarantee to it an autonomous development of its national life in accordance with its particular
characteristics.

More than an hour before this document was signed,
however, German troops, in several columns, were on
Czech territory. About 9:00 that morning the vanguard of
the motorized columns reached the outskirts of Prague.
Hitler himself came to Prague that afternoon and spent
the night in the ancient castle on the Hradčany in the

apartments in which the Liberator-President Masaryk had lived for seventeen years.

The next day Hitler issued a proclamation specifying the juridical changes that German occupation entailed. There was now the "Protectorate of Bohemia-Moravia" with a Reich Protector (von Neurath) acting for Hitler, and, directly or indirectly, in complete control of life and property within the Protectorate. The German occupation and establishment of the Protectorate was recognized only by the satellites of Germany. Great Britain, France, the Soviet Union and the United States refused to recognize the occupation, and immediately and specifically issued statements condemning the unjustified violation of a solemn treaty engagement and, on broader lines, of international law and practice.

The full story of what took place within the country in the following months is a matter about which it is not yet possible to write with adequate documentation. The history of German occupation of the territories of the Republic of Czechoslovakia must await freer times. The immediate installation of the Gestapo with its accompaniment of concentration camps and "executions"; the pillaging of the land; the rigid application of the Nürnberg anti-Semitic laws; the murder of thousands of peaceful Czech and Moravian students and teachers, artisans, army officers and public officials; the systematic spoliation of the cultural treasures of the country; the effective germanization of all industry, business, education, religion, art, music and thought, these are all known in broad outlines. But the full details will be revealed only gradually.

Though the blow of March 14-15 was sudden, and to all appearances crushing, it did not catch Czech democratic leadership completely unprepared. Beneš had left the country in October for England, and several months later came to America for a series of lectures. The Czechoslovak diplomatic service throughout the world was unanimously loyal to the ideals of Masaryk and Beneš. The German *coup* had been anticipated by Beneš and his advisers, whose information concerning the plans of the Nazi inner cabinet was amazingly accurate. The groundwork was thus laid early for the reconquest of their country's independence out of the travail of a second world conflict, similar to the successful effort made by Masaryk, Beneš and Štefánik in 1914-1918.

Only a month after the German attack on Poland that began the Second World War, a convention was signed between a committee of responsible Czechs and Slovaks in exile and the French government (October 2, 1939) providing for the organization and training of a Czech army on French soil for service on the western front. Soon thereafter, Dr. Beneš, returning to England from America, organized a Czechoslovak National Committee of five Czechs and three Slovaks. This Committee was recognized on November 17 by the French government as a provisional government in exile. The more prominent members of the Committee were Monsignor Jan Šrámek, a former Prime Minister; Dr. Juraj Slávik, Ambassador to Poland; Rudolf Viest, deputy head of the Czechoslovak Legion; and Štefan Osuský, Minister to France. The status of the Committee was not completely satisfactory, as the Quai d'Orsay seemed lukewarm in its attitude toward the Czechoslovak cause. But in London the situation was somewhat more favorable, and, on December 2, this Committee was given a qualified recognition which allowed it to function as a cobelligerent with the Allies.

Czechoslovaks of all stations of life were escaping from the Protectorate in increasing numbers: soldiers, particularly aviators, politicians, business and professional men found their way across the frontiers through Rumania to the Near East and across Poland to Scandinavia, and thence to England or France. The Czechoslovak army and air force was growing in size and military potentiality to such an extent that it formed a welcome addition to the Allied military effort.

The fall of France in June 1940 enhanced the value of the Czechoslovak military contribution to the Allied cause, and Dr. Beneš was able to gain from the British government on July 21, 1940, a political and diplomatic recognition of a Czechoslovak Provisional government. The government set up at that time was as follows: Prime Minister, Monsignor Jan Šrámek; Minister for Foreign Affairs, Jan Masaryk; State Secretary for Foreign Affairs, Dr. Hubert Ripka; Minister of National Defense, General Sergěj Ingr; State Secretary in Ministry of National Defense, General Rudolf Viest; Minister of Finance, Dr. Edward Outrata; Minister of Social Welfare, Mr. František Němec; State Secretary in Ministry of Social Welfare, Mr. Ján Bečko; Minister of Home Affairs, Dr. Juraj Slávik; Ministers of State (i.e. without portfolio), Dr. Štefan Osuský, Dr. Ladislav Feierabend, Mr. Jaromír Nečas. Of these twelve ministers four were Slovak by birth, three were born in Moravia and the remaining five were Czech by birth.

This Provisional Government functioned smoothly for almost a year, with minor adjustments in personnel to make room for new arrivals who had succeeded in escaping from the Protectorate. One of the most significant acts of this government was to sign (November 11, 1940) with the Polish government in exile a declaration of intention to unite their two countries in some sort of close political and economic union after the war. The general terms in which this declaration was phrased, as later developments were to show, were notably modest:

The two Governments consider it imperative to declare solemnly even now that Poland and Czechoslovakia, closing once and for all the period of past recriminations and disputes, and taking into consideration the community of their fundamental interests, are determined, on the conclusion of this war, to enter as independent and sovereign States into a closer political and economic association, which would become the basis of a new order in Central Europe and a guarantee of its stability. Moreover both Governments express the hope that in this co-operation, based on respect for the freedom of nations, the principles of democracy and the dignity of man, they will also be joined by other countries in that part of the European continent. The two Governments are resolved already now to co-operate closely for the defence of their common interest and for the preparation of the future association of the two countries.

On July 18, 1941, provisional recognition was changed to full *de jure* recognition by Great Britain and Soviet Russia, and an exchange of diplomatic representatives was arranged. Twelve days later the United States government took similar action. A treaty of alliance with the Soviet Union was concluded at about the same time. With a Czechoslovak army and air force in action on the western front and another with the Soviet and Polish armies on the eastern front, the successful and determinative phases of the 1914-1918 struggle for independence were being paralleled and even surpassed in the crucial years of 1941 and 1942.

Now that the Czechoslovak government had full *de jure* recognition, the intentions of the Polish-Czechoslovak declaration of November 11, 1940 could be carried out. Committees of experts from the two countries wrestled with the problems of effectual union for over a year. The results of their labors was the more detailed and specific declaration of January 23, 1942, comprising fourteen points. This declaration forms a confederation of the two states, providing for a common foreign policy, a common general staff with unified supreme command, co-ordinated foreign trade, tariffs and financial policies. Social policy, education, transportation and the democratic freedoms are to be worked out in complete co-operation. Such a comprehensive and far-reaching confederation, voluntarily arrived at by two sovereign states, constitutes a revolution in European diplomatic and political history. The importance of the pact has not been adequately emphasized in the rest of the world.

In spite of the full recognition accorded the Czechoslovak government headed by Dr. Beneš in July 1941, the shadow of the Munich "Accord" hung over their heads. There was no doubt in anyone's mind that the British government under Mr. Churchill's leadership was profoundly opposed to the policy of appeasement so disastrously followed by Mr. Chamberlain. But the "Accord" was still in existence. The Czechoslovak government continually urged upon the British government in the later months of 1941 and through the spring of 1942 that some public denunciation of the Munich agreement be made, so that the record might be clear. Notes were exchanged between the two governments on August 5, 1942, in which Mr. Eden made specific this denunciation. After mentioning the formal recognition of Dr. Beneš's government, Mr. Eden said:

The foregoing statement and the formal act of recognition have guided the policy of H. M. Government in regard to Czechoslovakia, but in order to avoid any possible misunderstanding, I desire to declare on behalf of H. M. Government in the United Kingdom that as Germany has deliberately destroyed the arrangements concerning Czechoslovakia reached in 1938, in which H. M. Government in the United Kingdom participated, H. M. Government regard themselves as free from any engagements in this respect. At the final settlement of the Czechoslovak frontiers to be reached at the end of the war, they will not be influenced by any changes effected in and since 1938.

The juridical gain for the Czechoslovak cause was obvious. The moral effect upon the people in the homeland could only be tremendous. On August 8, in a broadcast that must have been widely heard and reported in the Protectorate, Dr. Beneš quoted a formal statement which M. Molotov had authorized him to make public, in which the position of the Soviet Union toward the Munich Agreement was reiterated. M. Molotov had said:

The Soviet Government never had anything to do with Munich. It was against the policy which led to Munich and it therefore does not recognize anything which took place there in relation to Czechoslovakia, nor any consequences of the Munich policy in 1938 and 1939. Neither does it recognize any change of the Czechoslovak frontiers in 1938 and 1939. It takes its stand on the pre-Munich frontiers.

As the United States had never given any recognition to the changes arising out of the Munich "negotiations" the legal position of the Czechoslovak state was now everywhere firmly re-established.

In almost every way the present situation is more hopeful than that prevailing during the greater part of the earlier struggle—1914-1918. Internally there have intervened twenty years of trying but solidifying political, social and economic experience. The peoples of the whole area of the republic have come to have confidence in themselves, their leadership, their institutions and the philosophical foundations of their state. These are great confidences to achieve in a short period of only two decades. Many nations have failed to gain them in as many centuries. Externally they have every reason to hope that the course of the war has convinced western Europe and America that the existence of such a state as Czechoslovakia, allowing for the modifications of sovereignty contemplated in the Polish-Czechoslovak agreement of confederation and such others as may flow from it, is a necessary bulwark of peace and stability in Central Europe. It is perhaps too early to judge whether this hope will be disap-

pointed by a reaction toward complacency and isolationism
in Great Britain and America when the present war is over.
No one is more aware of the possibility of such a reaction
than the Czech and Slovak leaders and peoples themselves.
They have good cause to remember that not long ago they
were spoken of by a responsible statesman of a great western power as a distant people of whom nothing was known.
Krofta's answer to that attitude (see above, p. 348) will be
as true in 1960 as it was in 1938.

But if the United Nations are again victorious—as there
is every reason to think they will be—there is no doubt that
Komenský's familiar apostrophe to his beloved people,
written when he too was an exile in London from his native land, will once again come true:

> ... after the tempest of God's wrath shall have passed,
> the rule of thy country will again return unto thee,
> O Czech people.

BIBLIOGRAPHY AND INDEX

RULERS OF THE LANDS OF CZECHOSLOVAKIA[1]

620-657 Samo (a Frank)   846-870 Rostislav   896-906 Mojmir II
830-846 Mojmir I   870-896 Svatopluk

Cosmas of Prague lists, without dates, the following early dukes of Bohemia: Přemysl, Nezamysl, Mnata, Vojen, Unislav, Křesomysl, Neklan, Hostivit. *The last named had a son Bořivoj, and with him we enter upon surer ground. His son was Duke Spytihněv I, 895-905, whose rule was recognized in the western part of the crumbling Moravian Empire.*

BOHEMIA		SLOVAKIA	
905-921	Vratislav I	from *ca.* 906 to 1918 under Hungarian rule.	
921-929	Václav I (Saint)	From 907 to 1526 Hungary had the follow-	
929-967	Boleslav I	ing princes and kings.	
967-999	Boleslav II		
999-1034	Boleslav III	907-947	Zsolt
1002-1003	Vladivoj (Polish prince)	947-972	Taksony
1003-1004	Boleslas Chrobry (Polish king)	972-997	Géza
1034-1055	Břetislav I	997-1038	Stephen I, king from 1000
1055-1061	Spytihněv II	1038-1046	Peter Orseolo
1061-1092	Vratislav II (king 1085-1092)	1046-1061	Andrew I
1092-1110	Břetislav II	1061-1063	Béla I
1110-1120	Bořivoj II	1063-1074	Solomon
1120-1125	Vladislav I	1074-1077	Géza I
1125-1140	Soběslav I	1077-1095	László I (Saint)
1140-1174	Vladislav II (king 1158-1174)	1095-1114	Kálmán
1174-1180	Soběslav II	1114-1131	Stephen II
1180-1189	Frederick	1141-1162	Géza II
1191-1192	Václav II	1161-1172	Stephen III
		1171-1196	Béla III
		1196-1204	Imre
	Kings of Bohemia	1205	László III
1198-1230	Přemysl Otakar I	1205-1235	Andrew II
1230-1253	Václav I	1235-1270	Béla IV
1253-1278	Přemysl Otakar II	1270-1290	László IV
1283-1305	*Václav II	1290-1301	Andrew III
1305-1306	Václav III (last Přemyslid)	1301-1305	*Václav II (of Bohemia)
1306-1307	Rudolf of Hapsburg	1305-1308	Otto of Bavaria
1307-1310	Henry of Carinthia	1308-1342	Charles Robert of Anjou
1310-1346	John of Luxemburg	1342-1382	Louis the Great of Anjou
1346-1378	Charles I (IV of the Empire)	1382-1387	Mary of Anjou
1378-1419	Václav IV	1387-1437	*Sigismund of Luxemburg
1419-1437	*Sigismund	1437-1439	*Albert of Hapsburg
1437-1439	*Albert of Hapsburg	1440-1444	Vladislav I (Jagiello)
1439-1457	Ladislas Posthumous	1445-1457	*Ladislas (László) V Posthumous
1458-1471	George of Poděbrady	1458-1490	Matthew Corvinus
1471-1516	*Vladislav II	1490-1516	*Vladislav II
1516-1526	*Louis I	1516-1526	*Louis II

RULERS OF BOHEMIA AND HUNGARY, 1526-1918

1526-1564	Ferdinand I	1711-1740	Charles II (VI of the Empire)
1564-1576	Maximilian I (II of Empire)	1740-1780	Maria Theresa
1576-1612	Rudolf II	1741-1743	Charles Albert of Bavaria
1612-1619	Mathias	1780-1790	Joseph II
1619-1620	Frederick of the Palatinate	1790-1792	Leopold II
1619-1637	Ferdinand II	1792-1835	Francis I
1637-1657	Ferdinand III	1835-1848	Ferdinand IV (I of the Empire)
1657-1705	Leopold I	1848-1916	Francis Joseph
1705-1711	Joseph I	1916-1918	Charles III (I of Aust.-Hung.)

PRESIDENTS OF CZECHOSLOVAKIA

1918-1935	Thomas Garrigue Masaryk	1938-	Emil Hácha (of Protectorate of
1935-	Eduard Beneš		Bohemia-Moravia)

[1] Some of the early dates are approximate. Contested reigns, counter-kings, etc., are generally not so indicated. An * indicates that a ruler before 1526 was king both in Bohemia and in Hungary.

⤙ General Bibliography ⤚

The following titles are concerned with the general history of Czechoslovakia and its component lands. For the most part they will not be listed in the special bibliographies for particular chapters. It should be understood that neither this nor the later bibliographies are more than selective lists of the vast literature, particularly in German and Czech, that has appeared on the many periods and aspects of the history and culture of the peoples of Czechoslovakia.

Bachmann, A., *Geschichte Böhmens* (*bis 1526*), 2 vols., Gotha, 1899-1905

Bretholz, Bertold, *Geschichte Böhmens und Mährens bis zum Aussterben der Přemysliden* (*1306*), Munich, 1912

——, *Neuere Geschichte Böhmens* (*1526-1576*), Gotha, 1920. A continuation of Bachman's *Geschichte Böhmens*

——, *Geschichte Böhmens und Mährens*, 4 vols., Reichenberg, 1924

Chaloupecký, V., *Staré Slovensko*, Bratislava, 1928

Denis, Ernest, *Huss et la guerre des Hussites*, Paris, 1878

——, *La fin de l'indépendence bohême*, 2 vols., Paris, 1890. A Czech translation with copious notes and corrections by J. Vančura, *Konec samostatnosti české*, 2 vols., Prague, 1932

——, *La Bohême depuis la Montagne-Blanche*, 2 vols., Paris, 1903

——, *Les Slovaques*, Paris, 1917

Dudik, B., *Mährens allgemeine Geschichte* (*bis 1350*), 12 vols., and an index, Brünn, 1860-88

Fischel, A., *Das tschechische Volk*, 2 vols., Breslau, 1928

Frind, A., *Kirchengeschichte Böhmens*, 4 vols., Prague, 1862-1878

Hassinger, Hugo, *Die Tschechoslowakei*, Vienna, 1925

Jakubec, Jan, *Dějiny literatury české*, 2 vols., Prague, 1929-34

Krofta, Kamil, *A Short History of Czechoslovakia*, New York, 1934

——, *Das Deutschtum in der tschechoslowakischen Geschichte*, Prague, 1936

Lades, Hans, *Die Tschechen und die deutsche Frage*, Erlangen, 1938

Lippert, J., *Socialgeschichte Böhmens*, 2 vols., Prague, 1896-98

Lützow, Count Francis, *Bohemia, an historical sketch*, Everyman's edition, revised, New York, 1939

——, *Lectures on the Historians of Bohemia*, London, 1905

——, *Bohemian Literature*, London, 1907

——, *The Life and Times of Master John Hus*, London, 1909

——, *The Hussite Wars*, London, 1914

Martel, René, *La Ruthénie Subcarpathique*, Paris, 1937

Nosek, Vladimir, *The Spirit of Bohemia*, London, 1926

Novotný, V. and Urbánek, R., *České Dějiny*, 9 vols. thus far, Prague, 1912—. Since the death of Professor Novotný in 1932, this monumental project is under the editorship of Dr. Kamil Krofta, with the co-operation of numerous Czech historians

Novotný, V., Odložilík, O., Dobiaš, J., Urbánek, R., and Prokeš, J., vol. 4, *Dějiny*, in the series *Vlastivěda*, in 2 parts, Prague, 1932-33

Novotný, V., *Sborník to*, under title: *Českou Minulostí*, Prague, 1929

Palacký, František, *Geschichte Böhmens* (to 1526), 5 vols. in 10, Prague, 1864-67. Czech edition, *Dějiny českého národu*, Prague, 1908

——, *Würdigung der alten böhmischen Geschichtsschreiber*, Prague, 1830

Pekař, Josef, *Smysl českých dějin*, Prague, 1936

——, *Sborník to*, under title: *Od pravěku k dnešku*, 2 vols., Prague, 1930

Prokeš, J., *Histoire tchécoslovaque*, Prague, 1927

Schranil, J., *Die Vorgeschichte Böhmens und Mährens*, Leipzig, 1928

Tobolka, Z., *Politické dějiny československého národa od 1848 až po dnešní doby*, 5 vols. Prague, 1932-37

Tomek, V. V., *Dějepis města Prahy*, 12 vols., 2nd ed., Prague, 1892-1901, Vol. 1 translated by Tomek appeared as *Geschichte der Stadt Prag*, Prague, 1856

Weiszäcker, W., "Das Nationalbewusstsein als Faktor der böhmischen Geschichte" in *Zeitschrift für sudetendeutsche Geschichte* II (1938), 155-160

Winter, E., *Tausend Jahre Geisteskampf im Sudetenraum*, Leipzig, 1938

Though the reader of this book is to be spared the annoyance of elaborate footnotes, something should be said as to the scholarly journals in which specialized articles treating the history of Czechoslovakia may be found. The best known, though not the oldest, is the *Český Časopis Historický*, which for high standards of scholarship and competence of reviews has no superior among professional journals in Europe or America. The oldest similar organ is the *Časopis Českého Musea*, which, though less wide in its appeal, is in no wise inferior to the *ČČH*. The *Časopis Matice Moravské* is the outlet for specifically Moravian history. These may be regarded as the leading Czech historical journals, though there are many more. German scholarship in Bohemia has been ably represented since 1862 by the *Mittheilungen des Vereins für Geschichte der Deutschen in Böhmen*. It has been supplanted by the *Zeitschrift für Sudetendeutsche Geschichte* since 1937. The *Zeitschrift des Vereines für Geschichte Mährens und Schlesiens* (1897-1914) as well as the *Mitteilungen des Instituts für Österreichische Geschichtsforschung* (1880-1915) and the *Archiv für Österreichische Geschichte* (1866-1915) are rich in material bearing on the history of the lands of the Bohemian crown.

Chapter II

Bachmann, A., *Böhmen und seine Nachbarländer unter Georg von Podiebrad 1458-61 und des Königs Bewerbung um die deutsche Krone*, Prague, 1878.

———, *Deutsche Reichsgeschichte im Zeitalter Friedrich III und Maximilian I*, 2 vols., Prague, 1884

Bryce, James, *The Holy Roman Empire*, London, 1907

Flieder, R., *Corona regni Bohemiae*, Prague, 1908

Gindely, A., *Rudolf II und seine Zeit*, Prague, 1868

Hauck, A., *Kirchengeschichte Deutschlands*, 7 vols., Leipzig, 1904ff.

Kalousek, J., *České státní právo*, Prague, 1892

Kapras, J., *Právní dějiny zemí koruny české*, 2 vols., Prague, 1913

Krofta, K., *Bílá Hora*, Prague, 1913

Pekař, J., *Smysl českých dějin*, Prague, 1936

Peterka, O., *Rechtsgeschichte der böhmischen Länder*, Prague, 1923

Rezek, A., *Zvolení a korunování Ferdinanda I za krále českého*, Prague, 1877

Toman, H., *Das Böhmische Staatsrecht und die Entwickelung der osterreichischen Reichsidee vom Jahre 1527 bis 1848*, Prague, 1872

Uhlirz, Karl, *Handbuch der Geschichte Österreichs und seiner Nachbarländer Böhmen und Ungarn*, I, II, i, Vienna, 1927, 1930

CHAPTERS III-V

Balbín, B., *Dissertatio apologetica pro lingua slavonica praecipue bohemica*, Prague, 1775

Bibl, V., *Maximilian II*, Prague, 1930

Bilek, T. V., *Dějiny konfiskací v Čechách po r. 1618*, 2 vols., Prague, 1882-83

Coxe, W., *History of the House of Austria*, London, 5 vols., 1820

Fontes rerum bohemicarum, 6 vols. ed. Palacký and Emler, Prague, 1873-1907

Gindely, A., *Geschichte der Gegenreformation in Böhmen*, Leipzig, 1894

———, *Rudolf II und seine Zeit*, Prague, 1868

———, *Dějiny českého povstání*, 4 vols., Prague, 1870-80

———, *Der Majestätsbrief*, Prague, 1868

Huber, A., *Geschichte Österreichs (bis 1648)*, 5 vols., Gotha, 1885-96

Kerner, R. J., *Bohemia in the Eighteenth Century*, New York, 1932

Lindner, T., *Deutsche Geschichte unter den Hapsburgern und Luxemburgern* (1273-1437), 2 vols., Berlin, 1890-1893

Rezek, A., *Dějiny Čech a Moravy Nové Doby*, 6 vols., Prague, 1892-98

Rieger, B., *Zřizeni Krajské v Čechách*, 2 vols., Prague, 1889, 1893

Schulte, A., *Geschichte der Hapsburger in den ersten drei Jahrhunderten*, Innsbruck, 1887

Tieftrunk, K., *Odpor českých stavův proti Ferdinandovi I. léta 1547*, Prague, 1872

Tomek, W. W., *Dějepis Rakauský*, Prague, 1858. German ed. same year

BIBLIOGRAPHY

CHAPTER VI

Bittner, K., *Deutsche und Tschechen*, Leipzig, 1936

Cosmae Pragensis Chronicon Bohemorum, ed. Pelzel and Dobrovsky, Prague, 1783

Dalimil, *Kronika*, modern Czech ed., Prague, 1920

Frind, A., *Die Geschichte der Bischöfe und Erzbischöfe von Prag*, Prague, 1873

Herder, J. G., *Ideen zur Geschichte der Menschheit*, ed. Kuhnemann, Stuttgart

Kerner, R. J., *Bohemia in the Eighteenth Century*, New York, 1932

Klik, J., *Národnostní poměry v Čechách od valek husitských do bitvy bělohorské*, Prague, 1922

Kristen, Z., ed. of *Soběslavum* in *ČČH* XXVIII (1922)

Mendl, B., *Sociální krise a zápasy ve městech čtrnactého věku*, Prague, 1926

Naegle, A., *Kirchengeschichte Böhmens*, 2 vols., Prague, 1915

Novotný, V., *Náboženské hnutí ve XIV. a XV. století v Čechách*, Prague, 1914

Palacký, F., *Die Geschichte des Hussitentums und Prof. Constantin Höfler*, Prague, 1868

Rádl, E., *Válka Čechů s Němci*, Prague, 1928

Schránil, J., *Die Vorgeschichte Böhmens und Mährens*, Leipzig, 1928

Weiszäcker, W., "Das Nationalbewusstsein als Faktor der böhmischen Geschichte," in *Zft. für Sudetendeutsche Geschichte* II (1938), 155-160

Winter, Z., *Dějiny řemesel a obchodů v Čechách v XIV. a XV. století*, Prague, 1906

Wolkan, R., *Die Geschichte der deutschen Literatur in Böhmen und in den Sudetenländern*, Augsburg, 1925

Wostry, W., "Ein deutschfeindliches Pamphlet aus Böhmen aus dem 14. Jhdt." in *Mitteilungen des Vereins für Geschichte der Deutschen in Böhmen*, LIII (1915), 193-238

CHAPTER VII

Auerbach, B., *Les races et les nationalités en Autriche-Hongrie*, 2nd. ed., Paris, 1917

Fochler-Hauke, G., *Deutscher Volksboden und Deutscher Volkstum in der Tschechoslowakei*, Berlin, 1937

Kraus, A., *Die sogenannte Tschechische Renaissance und die Heimatdeutschen*, Prague, 1928

Krofta, K., *Das Deutschtum in der tschechoslowakischen Geschichte*, Prague, 1936

Lehmann, E., *Der Sudetendeutsche*, Potsdam, 1925

Molisch, P., *Die Sudetendeutsche Freiheitsbewegung*, Vienna, 1932

Pfitzner, J., *Das Erwachen der Sudetendeutschen im Spiegel ihres Schrifttums bis 1848*, Augsburg, 1926

——, *Sudetendeutsche Geschichte*, Reichenberg, 1937

——, *Sudetendeutsche Einheitsbewegung*, Leipzig, 1937

——, "Nationales Erwachen und Reifen der Sudetendeutschen" in *Das Sudetendeutschtum*, ed. Pirchan, Weiszäcker and Zatschek, Leipzig, 1939, pp. 439-471

——, "Die Entwicklung des Gesamtbildes sudetendeutscher Geschichte" in *Zeitschrift für Sudetendeutsche Geschichte*, II (1938), 273-292

Schmidtmayer, A., *Geschichte der Sudetendeutschen*, Leipzig, 1938

Schneefuss, W., *Deutschböhmen*, Leipzig, 1938

Uhlirz, Karl and Mathilde, *Handbuch der Geschichte Österreichs und seiner Nachbarländer Böhmen und Ungarn*, II, i, Vienna, 1930

Winter, E., *Tausend Jahre Geisteskampf im Sudetenraum*, Leipzig, 1938

Wolkan, R., *Sudetendeutsche Literaturgeschichte*, Augsburg, 1925

Wostry, W., "Die geschichtlichen Grundlagen des Sudetendeutschtums" in *Zft. f. Sudetendeutsche Geschichte*, II (1938), 1-30

Chapters VIII-IX

Bibl, V., *Der Zerfall Österreichs*, Leipzig, 1932

Černý, J. M., *Boj za právo. Sborník aktů politických u věcech státu a národa českého od r. 1848*, 2 vols., Prague, 1893

Charmatz, R., *Oesterreichs innere Geschichte von 1848-1895*, Vienna, 3rd. ed. 1918

Denis, E., *La Bohême depuis la Montagne-Blanche*, vol. 2

Domanovszky, A., *Die Geschichte Ungarns*, Leipzig, 1923

Heidler, J., *Čechy a Rakousko v politických brožurách předbřeznových*, Prague, 1920

BIBLIOGRAPHY

Jelinek, H., *La Littérature tchèque contemporaine*, Paris, 1912

Kazbunda, K., *České hnutí roku 1848*, Prague, 1929

Masaryk, T. G., *Palackého idea národa českého*, Prague, 1912, 1926

——, *The Making of a State*, London, 1925

Odložilík, O., "A Czech Plan for a Danubian Federation—1848" in *Journal of Central European Affairs*, Oct. 1941

Palacký, F., *Gedenkblätter*, Prague, 1874

——, *Oesterreichs Staatsidee*, Prague, 1866

——, *Drobné Spisy*, 3 vols., Prague, 1901, 1902

Prokeš, J., *Základní problémy českých dějin*, Prague, 1925

Raupach, H., *Der tschechische Frühnationalismus*, Essen, 1939

Srbik, H. v., *Metternich, der Staatsmann und der Mensch*, 2 vols., Leipzig, 1925

Tobolka, Zd. and Kramář, K., *Dějiny české politiky nové doby*, Prague, 1909

Tobolka, Zd., *Politické dějiny československého národa od r. 1848 až po dnešní dobu*, 5 vols., Prague, 1932ff.

Traub, H., *Poslední český pokus o vyrovnání s Rakouskem 1871*, Prague, 1919

CHAPTER X

Botto, Julius, *Slovaci*, Turčiansky Sv. Martin, 2 vols., 1906, 1910

Capek, Thomas, *The Slovaks of Hungary*, New York, 1906

Chaloupecký, V., *Staré Slovensko*, Bratislava, 1923

Denis, Ernest, *Les Slovaques*, Paris, 1917

Eisner, Jan, *Slovensko v pravěku*, Bratislava, 1933

Hodža, Milan, *Československý rozkol*. Turčiansky Sv. Martin, 1920

Horák, Jiří, *Slovenská vlasť*, Prague, 1921

Klima, St., *Slovanská vzájemnost*, Prague, 1938

Kvačala, Jan, *Dějiny reformacie na Slovensku 1517-1711*, Lipt. Sv. Mikulaš, 1935

Krofta, Kamil, *Čtění o ustavních dějinách slovenských*, Prague, 1924

Locher, Th. J. G., *Die nazionale Differenzierung und Integrerung der Slovaken und Tschechen in ihrem geschichtlichen Verlauf bis 1848*, Haarlem, 1931

Medvecký, K. A., *Slovensky prevrat*, Bratislava, 1927

BIBLIOGRAPHY

Pražák, Albert, *Dějiny spisovné slovenštiny po dobu Štúrovu*, Prague, 1922

Rapant, Daniel, *K počiatkom maďarizacie*, Bratislava, 1927

Škultéty, Joseph, *Sketches from Slovak History*, Middletown, Pa., *Sto dvadsat-pät rokov zo slovenského života*, Turčiansky Sv. Martin, 1920

Szana, Alexander, *Die Geschichte der Slowakei*, Bratislava, 2 vols., 1930-31

Szekfü, J., *Der Staat Ungarn*, Berlin, 1918

Tourtzer, H., *Louis Stúr et l'idée de l'indépendance slovaque (1815-1856)*, Cahors, 1913

Weingart, M., *Slovanská vzájemnost v minulosti a přítomnosti*, Bratislava, 1925

CHAPTERS XI-XII

Beneš, Edvard, *Bohemia's Case for Independence*, London, 1917

———, *My War Memoirs*, New York, 1928

———, *Světová válka a naše revoluce*, Vol. III, Dokumenty, Prague, 1929

Chaloupecký, V., *Zápas o Slovensko*, Prague, 1930

Dérer, I., *The Unity of the Czechs and Slovaks*, Prague, 1938

von Glaise-Horstenau, E., *The Collapse of the Austro-Hungarian Empire*, London, 1930

Jászi, O., *The Dissolution of the Hapsburg Monarchy*, Chicago, 1929

Levée, Madeleine, *Les précurseurs de l'indépendence tchèque et slovaque à Paris*, Paris, 1936

Masaryk, T. G., *The Making of a State*, London, 1927

———, *Cesta demokracie 1918-1920 I*, Prague, 1933

Nosek, Vl., *Independent Bohemia*, London, 1918

———, *The Spirit of Bohemia*, London, 1926

Opočenský, J., *The Collapse of the Austro-Hungarian Monarchy and the Rise of the Czechoslovak State*, Prague, 1928

Papoušek, J., *Rusko a československá legie v letech 1914-1918*, 2 vols., Prague, 1936

Pekař, J., *Z české fronty*, 2 vols., Prague, 1917, 1919

Selver, Paul, *Masaryk*, London, 1940

Seton-Watson, R. W., *Slovakia Then and Now*, London, 1931

———, *Masaryk in England*, Cambridge (England), 1943

BIBLIOGRAPHY

Soukup, F., *28 říjen, 1918*, 2 vols., Prague, 1928
Šrobár, V., *Pamäti z vojny a z väzeniä*, Bratislava, 1922
Strong, D. F., *Austria October 1918-March 1919*, New York, 1939
Tobolka, Z., *Česká politika za světové války*, Prague, 1923
Werstadt, J., *Československý odboj*, Prague, 1923
Zuman, F., *Osvobozenská Legenda*, 2 vols., Prague, 1922

Chapter XIII

Borovička, J., *Ten Years of Czechoslovak Politics*, Prague, 1929
Chmelář, J., *Political Parties in Czechoslovakia*, Prague, 1926
Deset let československé republiky, Prague, 1928. 3 vols. Official.
Diplomaticus, *The Czechs and their Minorities*, London, 1938
Gruber, Joseph, ed., *Czechoslovakia: A Survey of Economic and Social Conditions*, New York, 1924
Hoetzl, J. and Joachim, V., *The Constitution of the Czechoslovak Republic*, Prague, 1920
Kerner, R. J., ed., *Czechoslovakia: Twenty Years of Independence*, Berkeley, 1940
Krofta, Kamil, *Z dob naše republiky*, Prague, 1938
Lewis, Brackett, *Facts about Democracy in Czechoslovakia*, Prague, 1938
Roucek, J. S., *National Minorities in Czechoslovakia*, Prague, 1936
Rašín, Alois, *Financial Policy of Czechoslovakia during the first years of its history*, Oxford, 1923
Schacher, Gerhard, *Central Europe and the Western World*, London, 1936
Schneefuss, Walter, *Deutsch-Böhmen*, Leipzig, 1938
Slaminka, Vladimír, *Národnostní vývoj československé republiky*, Vyškov, 1938
Sobota, Emil, *Das tschechoslowakische Nationalitätenrecht*, Prague, 1931
Seton-Watson, R. W., *Slovakia Then and Now, The New Slovakia*, Prague, 1924
Stranský, R., *The Educational and Cultural System of the Czechoslovak Republic*, Prague, n.d. (1938)
Stuerm, F. H., *Training in Democracy*, New York, 1938
Textor, Lucy E., *Land Reform in Czechoslovakia*, London, 1923

Wiehen, Joseph, *Die Bodenreform der tschechoslowakischen Republik*, Berlin, 1924

Wiskemann, Elizabeth, *Czechs and Germans*, London, 1938

Witt, Kurt, *Wirtschaftskräfte und Wirtschaftspolitik der Tschechoslowakei*, Leipzig, 1938

Young, E. P., *Czechoslovakia, Keystone of Peace and Democracy*, London, 1938

Zurcher, A. J., *The Experiment with Democracy in Central Europe*, New York, 1933

CHAPTER XIV

Anonymous, *Deset let zahraniční politiky československé*, Prague, 1928

Beneš, Edvard, *Five Years of Czechoslovak Foreign Policy*, Prague, 1924

――, *Problemy nové Evropy a zahraniční politika československá*, Prague, 1924

――, *Germany and Czechoslovakia*, I, II, Prague, 1937

Most of Beneš's important reports to Parliament have been published in English translation in the series *Czechoslovak Sources and Documents* or separately by Orbis Publishing Co., Prague, and a complete collection of his speeches in Czech, under the title: *Boj o mír a bezpečnost státu*, Prague, 1934

Codresco, F., *La Petite Entente*, Paris, 2 vols., 1931

Crane, J. O., *The Little Entente*, New York, 1931

Hitchcock, Edward, *I Built a Temple for Peace*, New York, 1940

Hoffmann, Walter, *Donau-Raum Völkerschicksal*, Leipzig, 1939

Krebs, Hans, *Kampf in Böhmen*, Berlin, 1937

Krofta, Kamil, *Československo v mezinárodní politice*, Prague, 1934

――, *Czechoslovakia and the Crisis of Collective Security*, Prague, 1936

Machray, Robert, *The Little Entente*, New York, 1930

――, *The Struggle for the Danube and the Little Entente, 1929-1938*, London, 1938

Malynski, E., *Les problèmes de l'est et la Petite Entente*, Paris, 1931

Schacher, Gerhard, *Central Europe and the Western World*, London, 1936

BIBLIOGRAPHY

Strauss, Emil, *Tschechoslowakische Aussenpolitik*, Prague, 1936

Toynbee, A. J., *Survey of International Affairs*, annual, 1920-1935, London

Vondracek, Felix, *Foreign Policy of Czechoslovakia 1918-1935*, New York, 1937

Central European Observer, published weekly in Prague until 1932, thereafter twice monthly, contained many articles and documents on foreign relations. It was a government publication.

Zahraniční Politika, an official monthly journal, containing articles by scholars as well as by active politicians.

There have been many important articles on various aspects of Czechoslovak foreign policy and Danubian affairs in the *Slavonic Review* and *Foreign Affairs*. For an adverse treatment of Czechoslovak and Little Entente policies the *Hungarian Quarterly*, the *Danubian Review* and the *Nouvelle Revue de Hongrie* may profitably be consulted.

CHAPTER XV

Much has been written about the diplomatic crisis centered around the Munich meeting. Only a small part of that literature will be cited here. It should be remarked at the outset that until further diplomatic revelations have been made generally available, the accounts of the more reliable newspaper correspondents on the spot are of cardinal importance. The reports of G. E. R. Gedye from Prague in the *New York Times* are perhaps the best of the lot. For the respective points of view of their governments the London *Times* and the Paris *Le Temps* are indispensable. I have also used the Czech dailies, *Prager Presse*, *České Slovo* and *Lidové Noviny*.

Armstrong, Hamilton Fish, *When There is No Peace*, New York, 1939, contains a valuable chronology of events leading up to Munich

Beneš, Vojta, *Ten Million Prisoners*, Chicago, 1940

Buk, Pierre, *La tragédie tchécoslovaque de septembre 1938 à mars 1939*, Paris, 1939

Gedye, G. E. R., *Betrayal in Central Europe*, New York, 1939

George, G. J., *They Betrayed Czechoslovakia*, Penguin Books, 1938

Griffin, J. and J., *Lost Liberty*, New York, 1939

Hanč, Josef, "Czechs and Slovaks Since Munich," *Foreign Affairs*, April, 1939

———, "The Last Mile of Appeasement," *Journal of Central European Affairs*, April, 1941, 5-17

Henderson, Nevile, *Failure of a Mission*, New York, 1941

Hutton, *Survey after Munich*, New York, 1939

Hindus, Maurice, *We Shall Live Again*, New York, 1939

Knapton, E. J., "Duel for Central Europe: Some Aspects of French Diplomacy, 1936-1938," *Journal of Central European Affairs*, April, 1942

Nizan, Paul, *Chronique de Septembre*, Paris, 1939

Ripka, Hubert, *Munich: Before and After*, London, 1939. This is by far the most complete story of the crisis, told by one who has had access to the Czech documents. It contains many documents not elsewhere published

Schmitt, B. E., "The Road to Munich" in *Czechoslovakia*, ed. R. J. Kerner

Schuman, Frederick L., *Europe on the Eve*, New York, 1939

Seton-Watson, R. W., *Munich and the Dictators*, London, 1939

Taborsky, Edward, " 'Munich,' the Vienna Arbitration and International Law," in *Czechoslovak Yearbook of International Law*, London, 1942

The official papers published by the respective governments are also of interest, but must all be used with some circumspection. Selection has naturally been resorted to by each.

Documents on the Events Preceding the Outbreak of the War German White Book, New York, 1940

The French Yellow Book

British Foreign Office: *Correspondence Respecting Czechoslovakia*, Command Paper 5847, London, 1938; and *Further Documents Respecting Czechoslovakia*, Command Paper 5848, London, 1938

◄ Index ►

St. Adalbert (Vojtěch), 91
Agrarian Party, 190, 238, 289, 341
  343
Agriculture, 298
Albania (Albanians), 166, 265, 324
Albert of Stade, chronicler, 30
Albrecht, Emperor, 53 ff., 61
Alexander II, Czar, 174
Alienigenae, 95 f., 115
Allied Territorial Commission, 311
American Czechs and Slovaks, 247 ff.,
  251 ff., 271 ff.
Andrássy, Count, 175
Angevin Kings of Hungary, 203
Anglo-French proposals (Sept. 1938),
  339, 342, 346
Anschluss (Austro-German), 315 f.,
  321, 327 f., 330
Anti-Semitism, *see* Nürnberg
Army, 241 ff., 256 ff., 268 f., 335, 357
Arndt, E. M., 123
Arnulf, Frankish King, 11
Árpád dynasty, 203
Arts, 108, 186
Asch-Egerland salient, 309
Asinara, 265
Asquith, Rt. Hon. Herbert, 249
Auersperg, Count K., 135
Augsburg Confession, 105 n., 161
Augsburg, Imperial Diet of (1548),
  40
Ausgleich (Compromise) of 1867,
  172 ff., 224 f., 305
Austerlitz, battle of, 123
Austria, 13, 16, 26, 38, 45, 57, 72 f.,
  114, 118; Turks, 59; under Maria
  Theresa, 80 ff.; clericalism, 138;
  Revolution of 1848, 164 f.; war
  with Prussia, 135; relations with
  Italy in World War I, 247; condi-
  tions in wartime, 275; Imperial
  Manifesto (1918), 281; post-war
  economic conditions, 298 f., 315;
  relations with Czechoslovakia,
  308 ff.; *Anschluss*, 315 f., 327 f.,
  330; relations with the Third
  Reich, 330 ff., 334 f.

Austria-Hungary (Austrian Empire),
  38, 43, 48, 55, 123 f., 164 ff.; Joseph II, 148 f.; Austrian Empire
  (1804), 87; Metternich régime,
  155 f.; centralism, 223; dualism,
  223 ff.; foreign policy after 1848,
  177, 305 ff.; annexation of Bosnia-
  Herzegovina, 234; World War I,
  236 ff., 241 ff., 249, 253 f., 259 ff.,
  277; dissolution, 268, 271, 274,
  278 ff.; post-war finance, 297; industry, 298
Austrian Chancery, 82, 285
Austrian Germans, 90, 117, 175, 235,
  303
Austrian Nazis, 330
Austro-Bohemian Chancery, 83
Austro-German Customs Union, 327
Austro-Prussian War, 171
Avars, 198

Babenberg, 25
Bach, A., 132, 134
Bachmann, A., 90, 120 n.
Bachmatch, 194
Balbín, Bohuslav, 73, 108
Balfour, A. J., 267
Baroque, 108, 186
Bartered Bride (*Prodaná nevěsta*)
  (Smetana), 186
Bartoš Písař, 59, 102
Bauer, O., 315
Bautzen, 28
Bavaria, 94, 97, 119 f., 127; Duke of,
  22, 56, 76
Bayonne, 265
Beck, M. V. von, 142
Bečko, J., 357
Belgium, 321
Beneš, Eduard, early leadership of
  Czech cause, 238; in Paris (1915-
  1916), 246, 250 ff., 259 f.; in Rome
  (1917), 263; wins recognition for
  National Council, 267 ff.; on Su-
  preme War Council, 270, 308; de-
  clares Provisional Government,
  273; Geneva and Paris (1918), 282;

INDEX

Foreign Minister, 285 ff.; Paris Peace Conference, 288; western orientation, 308; post-war settlements, 309, 311, 313 ff.; loan to Austria, 316; Little Entente, 316 f.; Soviet relations, 317, 330; League of Nations, 318 ff.; Italy, 319 ff.; Geneva Protocol, 320; Poland, 321 f.; Vatican, 323; Briand-Kellogg Pact, 325; Disarmament Conference, 325; *Anschluss*, 327; Germany, 329 f.; President, 332; Sudeten crisis, 334 ff.; resignation, 350; in London, 350, 355 ff.

Beneš, Vojta, 248, 250 f.

Beran, R., 350

Berchtesgaden, 336 ff.

Berlin, University of, 138; Henlein in, 336; visit of Sir Horace Wilson, 345; *see also* Germany

Bernolák, Antonín, 216, 218, 221

Bethlen Gabor, Duke of Transylvania, 67

Beust, Baron F., 175

Bible of Kralice (Bible Kralická), 209

Biedermeier, 127

Bienerth, Baron R. von, 142

Bilá Hora, *see* White Mountain

Billings, March of, 15

Bismarck, Prince Otto von, 4, 135, 138, 170 f.

Bissolati, L., 247

Bittner, K., 113 f.

Bohemia Under Hapsburg Misrule (Th. Čapek), 271

Bohemian Brethren, *see* Unity of Czech Brethren

Bohemian Confession of 1575, 104 f.

Bohemian Diet, 60, 65, 70, 105 n., 136, 142, 175, 224

Bohemian Estates, 27, 32 f., 35, 37, 39 ff., 44, 56, 60 ff., 86, 98, 103, 105 f., 146, 161

Bohemian Germans, 96, 118 ff., 139 ff.

Bohemian Lion, 282

Boii (Celtic tribes), 7

Bolzano, B., 126

Bonn, University of, 122

Bonnet, Georges, 337 f., 339, 341

Bosnia-Herzegovina, 142, 177, 234

Bouček, V., 238

Boundaries Commission, 311

Brandenburg, 29

Bratislava, 221, 303, 310 f.

Brauner, F. A., 174

Brenner Pass, 330

Breslau, 35

Brest-Litovsk, Treaty of, 258, 277 f.

Briand, Aristide, 253

Briand-Kellogg Peace Pact (1928), 319, 325

British *White Book*, 340

Brno (Brünn), 218

Bródy, A., 351

Bruno, Bishop of Olomouc, 94

Brusilov, General, 242

Brüx, (Most), 139

Bucharest, 317

Budapest, 214, 225, 228, 232, 302, 322

Budweis (Budějovice), 139

Bulgaria, 324, 332

Bullitt, W. C., 337

Burschenschaften, 124

Byzantium, 10, 90, 202

Calixtines, 100 n.

Calvinism, 105 n., 149, 217

Canada, 249

Čapek, Th., 271

Caporetto, battle of, 264

Carinthia, 26

Carlos II, of Spain, 75

Carniola, 26

Carpathians, 9 f., 236, 312

Čas, 238

Catholic Centre Party, 189, 289

Čechoslovak, 243

Cecil, Robert, Lord, 249, 267

Čelakovský, J., 46

Central Powers, 235, 238, 247 f., 251, 255, 258 ff., 273, 277 f., 280

Čermak, Bohumil, 252

Červinka, J., 244, 274 f.

Chaloupecký, V., 208

Chamberlain, Neville, 335 f., 339, 342, 344 ff., 352, 359

Charlemagne, 16

378

INDEX

379

INDEX

Dobner, G., 111
Dobrovský, J., 110, 158
Dollfuss, Engelbert, 330
Dostojevsky, F., 185
Drabik, *see* Mikuláš
Draft Treaty of Mutual Assistance (1923), 319
Drang nach Osten, 238
Dresden, University of, 138
Dualism, 172 f., 175, 179, 221, 223, 225, 305 f.
Dukhonin, General, 257
Dürich, J., 251 f., 255 f.
Dvořák, Anton, 186

Ebert, Karl Egon, 126
Economic depression, 301, 326
Eden, Anthony, 359
Education, ministry of, 302, 304; *see also* Schools
Egerland (Chebsko), v, 27 ff., 309
Electoral College, Imperial, 29 f., 42 f.
Emler, J., *see Regesta Imperii*
England, 66, 97, 106, 148; Czechs and Slovaks in, 240, 249, 252; recognition of Czechoslovak National Council, 267 ff., 280; Sudeten crisis, 334 ff.; recognition of Provisional Government (1940), 357 f.; *see also* London
Enlightenment, 81, 84, 121, 148
Erasmus, Desiderius, 58
Erlangen, University of, 122
Ethnographic Congress (1867), 174, 385
Execution of Czech leaders (1621), 69, 106

Faust, 127
February Patent (1861), 171
Federalization, 167
Federation of Czech Catholics in America, 272
Federation of Czechoslovak Associations in Russia (*Svaz československých spolků v Rusku*), 243 f., 254 f.
Feierabend, L., 357

Ferdinand I, Emperor, 38 ff., 55 ff., 67, 78
Ferdinand II, Emperor, 67 ff., 106
Fichte, J. G., 122
Fiedler, J., 59 n.
Finance, 287, 297, 301, 326
Fisher, J. L., 248, 252
Foreign Legion (French), 245
France, 98, 148; recognition of Czechoslovak National Council, 267 f., 280; post-war relations with Czechoslovakia, 308 f., 319, 321; Sudeten crisis, 334 ff., 340 ff.; *see also* Paris
Francis I, King of France, 39
Francis I, Emperor, 43, 155
Francis II, Emperor, 87
Francis, Duke of Lorraine, 84
Francis Ferdinand, Archduke, 143, 177
Francis Joseph, Emperor, 130, 135, 169 ff., 175 f., 179 f., 190, 226, 235, 260, 274
Franco-Czechoslovak Treaty (1924), 319, 321
Franco-Prussian War, 306
Franco-Soviet Pact (1935), 330, 343
Frank, K. H., 329
Frankfort Congress (Parliament), 44, 131 ff., 165
Frankfort-on-Main, 43
Frederick I, Barbarossa, Emperor, 22 ff., 28
Frederick II, Emperor, 24
Frederick III, Emperor, 35
Frederick of the Palatinate, 66 f., 105
Frederick II, of Prussia, 76, 78 f., 82
Freikorps, 344
French *Blue Book*, 340
French Revolution, 86, 124, 155, 194, 215
Friedland, 309
Friedrich, G., vi
Fügner, Jindřich, 187
Fundamental Articles of 1871, 137, 175 f.

Gabor, *see* Bethlen
Galicia, 236, 241 ff., 256

380

INDEX

Gamelin, General, 345
Garat, M., 245
Garrigue, Charlotte, 195
Gažik, M., 293
Geneva, Beneš in (1918), 282; see also League of Nations
Geneva Protocol (1924), 318, 320
Genoa Conference, 317
St. Germain, Treaty of, 320
German Agrarian Party, 289
German Catholic Party, 330
German Christian Socialist Party, 289
German Confederation (Bund), 43 ff., 135, 170 f.
German Farmers' Party, 330
German minority, 289, 291, 333; see also Sudeten Germans
German missionaries, 10 f.
German People's Council in Bohemia (Deutsche Volksrat in Böhmen), 141
German Propaganda Ministry, 290, 333
German Protestant Princes, 61
German University of Prague, vi, 138, 181, 304
Germanic tribes, 7, 11
Germans, 3, 14, 15, 51, 88 ff., 117 ff.; migration into Bohemia and Moravia after Thirty Years War, 147; in Slovakia, XIII century, 201 f.; see also Holy Roman Empire, Germany, Prussia, Sudeten Germans, Austrian Germans
Germany, Influx of Czechs during Thirty Years War, 106; and Sudeten nationalists, 124 f., 127; revolution of 1848, 130 f., 165; nationalism, 221; relations with Francis Joseph, 170 f., 179 f.; attitude toward Danube basin, 238; and Masaryk, 194; World War I, 260, 269, 306; economic relations with Bohemia, 299; post-war relations with Czechoslovakia, 308 f., 314 ff., 325 ff.; Third Reich, 328 ff. (see also Nazis); see also Prussia, German Confederation

Geschichte von Böhmen (Dějiny českéko národu), see Palacký
Gestapo, 355
Gibbon, Edward, 185
Glass industry, 300
Glatz (Kladsko), 76
Gmund, 310
Godesberg, 342 ff.
Golden Bull (1356), 31 ff., 36
Golden Sicilian Bull (1212), 24 f., 29 f., 46, 49
Göring, Hermann, 354
Görlitz, 28
Goethe, J. W. von, 3, 111, 126 f., 185
Gottsched, L. A., 121
Grammatica Slavica (A. Bernolák), 216
Graziani, General A., 264
Greater Germany, see Grossdeutschtum
Greater Moravia, see Moravian Empire
Greece, 315
Grégr, J., 174
Grossdeutschtum (-land), 89, 123 f., 131 f., 140, 321
Grosse Schütt, 311
Guelphs, 23

Habichtsburg, 49
Hácha, E., 350 f., 353 f.
Hajn, A., 238
Halifax, Viscount, 335 f.
Halle, University of, 122, 138, 221
Hamburg, 300
Hanover, 119 f.
Hapsburgs, 38 ff., 46, 48 ff., 65 ff., 80, 108, 114, 129, 146, 194, 210 f., 314, 317, 323 f.
Hartmann, M., 126
Havlíček, K., 169 f., 306 f.
Hegel, G. W. F., 221
Heimat Front, 329, 336
Hencke, Herr, 353
Henlein, Konrad, 329, 333 f., 336 ff., 344
Henry the Fowler, 18
Henry IV, Emperor, 22
Henry, René, 191

INDEX

Herben, J., 238, 276
Herder, J. G., 110, 121, 160, 221
Hermunduri, 7
Hiawatha, 185
Hirsch, H., vi
Historia Bohemica (Aeneas Sylvius Piccolomini), 107
History of the Bohemian Language and Literature (J. Dobrovský), 110
Hitler, Adolf, 300, 326, 329 ff., 334 ff.
Hlinka, Father Andrej, 283, 293, 350
Hodža, M., 282, 293, 334 ff., 341
Hohenstaufens, 23, 28
Hohenwart ministry, 137, 175 f.
Hohenzollerns, 191, 194, 235
Holy Roman (German) Empire, 15, 23, 30, 36, 43, 45 f., 114, 194
Hradčany, castle, 180; fire of (1541), 61; defenestration, 64; Hitler at, 354 f.
Hungarian Estates, 37, 164
Hungarismus, 214 f.
Hungary, 4, 13 ff., 26, 30, 37 f., 51, 55, 57, 59, 106; origins, 199; early history, 202 ff.; XVIII century, 213 ff.; under Joseph II, 148; Diet, 163; nobility, 73, 80, 98, 152 ff., 164, 167, 213; nationalism, 130, 154, 169; *Ausgleich*, 172 ff., 224 ff., 227, 229; Archduke Joseph, 316; frontiers, 308, 310 f.; Little Entente, 316, 323, 345; counterfeiting incident (1926), 322; Irredentism, 324; relations with Third Reich, 332; claims to Slovakia, 340 ff., 349
Huns, 198
Hurban, V., 293
Hus, John, 33, 100, 146, 162, 204, 208, 276; celebration of (1925), 323
Hussite movement, v, 33, 54, 57, 60, 62, 97, 99, 100 n., 102, 108, 116, 150, 161, 163, 204, 206 ff., 215
Hussite wars, 35, 54, 100
Hviezdoslav (Pavel Országh), 267

Idea of the Austrian State, see Palacký
Iglau (Jihlava), 101, 140

Imperial Manifesto of Emperor Charles (1918), 281 f., 274
Imperial Rescript, 176
L'Indépendance Tchèque, 245
Industry, 183 f., 298 ff.
Ingr, General S., 357
Innocent III, Pope, 24
International Commission (1938-1939), 348
Ipel, 310 f.
Italians, 130, 261, 266
Italy, relations with Czechs and Slovaks during World War I, 240, 247, 261 ff., 274, 280; post-war relations, 319 f.; smuggling incident (1928), 323 f.; and the Little Entente, 324; in the Axis, 330

Jacobism, 155
Jagellons, 37 f., 57
Jahn, L., 122
Jakubec, J., vi
James I, of England, 66
Japan, 270, 280
Jena, University of, 122; battle of, 123, 138
Jesuits, 63, 66, 68, 103, 107, 109 f., 127, 135, 146 f., 158, 210 ff.
Jews, 183
Jirásek, A., 276, 278, 280
Joachimstal, 101
John of Luxemburg, King, 27 f.
John XII, Pope, 18
Jonescu, T., 315
Joseph I, Emperor, 42
Joseph II, Emperor, 73, 82, 83 ff., 109 f., 117, 148 ff., 161, 217, 227
Joseph, Archduke, 316
Journal of Central European Affairs, vi
Jungmann, J., 158 f.

Kalousek, J., 32, 46
Kant, Emanuel, 121
Karlsbad, Henlein's speech, 334, 337
Károlyi, Count, 311
Kellogg, *see* Briand-Kellogg Pact
Kerensky, A., 256
Kiev, 236, 240 ff., 251, 254
Kitchener, R., Lord, 259

382

INDEX

INDEX

Napoleon III, 174, 190, 305 f.
Napoleonic wars, 42, 122 f., 128, 155
Národní Listy, 242
Nathan der Weise (Lessing), 128
La Nation Tchèque, 246
National Assembly, 285, 287 f., 294, 296
National Committee in Prague, 274, 277, 279 ff., 285
National Democrats, 289
National Socialists, 234, 236
National Theater (Národní Dívadlo), 154, 266
Nationalism, 54, 97, 105, 117, 120 f., 129, 133, 140, 153 ff., 176, 193, 204, 218 f., 305
Nationality, law of 1868, 227
Naumann, F., 314
Nazdar, company, 245
Nazdar, journal, 245
Nazis, 137 n., 328 ff., 333 f., 336 ff.; *see also* Germany
Nečas, J., 357
Němec, F., 357
Nepomuk, St. John of, 146
Neuilly, Treaty of, 284, 320
Neurath, Baron von, 355
New World Symphony (A. Dvořák), 186
New York, 185, 240
Newton, C. B., 344
Nicholas II, Czar, 237, 241, 255
Nikolai Nikolaievich, Grand Duke, 236
Ninčić, M., 316
Nitra, 10
North March, 15
Novotný, V., vi, 276
Nürnberg, 25; Imperial Diet of (1356), 31; Nazi Party Meeting, 338; anti-Semitic laws, 350, 355

October Diploma (1860), 171
Odessa, 240
Old Czechs (conservatives), 178 f., 188, 190
Olomouc, 140; University of, 124, 126
Orlando, V. E., 264
Ostbewegung, 96

Osterbegehrschaft, 314
Ostmark, 13
Osuský, S., 252 f., 293, 334, 340, 356 f.
Otto I, Emperor, 18
Outrata, E., 357

Palacký, František, v, 90, 125 f., 157, 161 ff., 167 ff., 174, 176, 179, 191, 193, 223 ff., 228; *Dějiny českého národu*, 52 n., 112, 125, 133 f., 162 f.; Letter to Frankfort Parliament, 44 f., 52 n., 165 ff.; *The Idea of the Austrian State*, 172 f., 178
Pan-Germanism, 121, 127, 131, 133, 194, 329
Pannonia, 13
Pan-Slavism, 89, 131, 159, 173 f., 191, 230, 243 f., 254, 306 ff.
Paradise Lost (Milton), 158
Paris, University of, 204; Revolution of 1848, 130; anti-Austrian demonstrations, 236; Czech-Slovak colony, 240, 245 f., 252; Czech-Slovak headquarters, 252 ff.; *see also* France and Czechoslovak National Council
Paris Declaration of November 1915, 246
Paris Peace Conference, 288, 309, 311, 313, 315 f., 329
Pašić, Nicholas, 315
Patent of Toleration (1781), 149, 217
Pavlů, Bohdán, 242, 259
People's Party, *see* Realists
Pergler, K., 248, 252
Petrograd, 236, 240 ff., 251, 254 ff.
Philadelphia Declaration of Independence (1918), 274, 281
Pichon, S., 261, 268, 273, 309
Pilsen, 94, 218
Pilsudski, J., 322
Pirchan, G., vi
Pittsburgh, 240; Declaration of (1918), 272 f., 292
Pius II (Aeneas Sylvius Piccolomini), 107
Pius XI, Pope, 323
Poděbrady, George of, King, 35 f., 101, 206

385

INDEX

Poincaré, R., 261

Poland, Carpathian boundary, 8; relations with Holy Roman Empire, 14 ff.; union with Bohemia and Hungary under Vladislav II, 206; under Václav II, 26; appeal of Přemysl Otakar II, 51 f.; alienated by Hussitism, 54 f.; Czech influx during Thirty Years War, 106; nobility, 98, 152, 154; catholicism, 150; nationalism, 154, 159, 163 f.; post-war relations with Czechoslovakia, 308 f., 312 f., 317 f., 321 f.; Munich crisis, 340 ff., 349, 351; Polish-Czechoslovak Declaration of 1940, 357 f.

Poles, 14, 130, 176, 181, 190, 266, 344, 349; see also Poland

Polish-Czechoslovak agreement of confederation (1941), 358 ff.

Polish Government in exile, 357

Polish National Committee, 268

Political parties, 188 ff.

Popolo d'Italia, 247

Prague, 160, 180, 187, 210, 212, 218, 235 f., 239, 266 f., 277, 280 ff., 339, 343, 346, 348 f., 354; university, 99 ff., 107, 109, 124, 138, 151, 159, 181, 192, 203 f.; bishopric, 91; coronation of Maria Theresa, 78; Jesuit college, 210 f.; Old Town Square, *see* Execution

Praguers, 100 n.

Přemysl I, Prince, 18, 24 f.

Přemysl Otakar I, Prince, 26

Přemysl Otakar II, King, 26, 30, 49 ff., 94, 96

Přemyslid dynasty, 11, 19 ff., 25 ff., 46, 52, 91, 94, 203

Press, the, 236, 250

Pribina, Prince, 10

Progressives, *see* Realists

Protectorate of Bohemia-Moravia, 355 ff.

Protestants, 60 ff., 84, 103, 106, 108, 146, 149 f., 209 f., 216 ff., 294

Provisional Government (Paris, 1918), 273 f.

Provisional Government in exile (1940), 356 f.

Prussia, Lusatian Sorbs in, 14; and Hapsburgs in XVIII century, 76 ff., 84, 148, 164; war with Austria (1866), 135, 171; and Francis Joseph, 170 f., 174, 176 f.; *see also* Germany

Pubička, F., 111

Quadi, 7

Racial Problems in Hungary (R. W. Seton-Watson), 229

Radical Progressives, 238

Rádl, E., 113

Rapallo, Treaty of, 317

Rašín, A., 244, 250, 274 f., 277, 282, 285 f.

Räuber (Schiller), 128

Readmission, The (1708), 42 f., 46

Realists, 193, 234, 238

Reformation, 114

Regesta Imperii (Emler), 52 n.

Reichenberg, 140

Reichsrat, 141, 179 ff., 193, 275 f., 280, 285

Reichstag (1848-1849), 132 f.

Relationen Venetianischer Botschafter über Deutschland und Oesterreich (Fiedler), 59 n.

Republic of 1918 (Czechoslovak), 157, 196 f., 232, 239, 272 f., 284 ff.

Revised Ordinance of the Land (*Erneuerte Landesordnung*) (1627), 70, 106

Revolution of 1848, 128 ff., 163 ff., 169, 222, 305

Rezek, A., 56

Ribbentrop, J. von, 353 f.

Ribot cabinet, 257

Richelieu, Cardinal, 66

Rieger, F. L., 174, 177, 190 f., 224, 305

Ripka, H., 340 n., 357

Robert of Cornwall, Emperor, 50

Rokycany, Jan of, 33

Roman Catholic Church, 60, 102, 114, 134 f., 146, 150, 208, 215 f., 323 f.

Romanov court, 241, 243

INDEX

Romanticism, 121 f., 124, 160, 162, 221
Rome, 239, 263
Rome Congress, *see* Congress of Peoples . . .
Romeo and Juliet, 128
Roosevelt, Franklin Delano, 346
Rostislav, Moravian Prince, 10
Rousseau, J.-J., 122, 160, 221
Rudolf of Hapsburg, 26, 49 ff., 61
Rudolf II, 64 f., 69
Rumania, 313, 316 f., 322, 332, 338, 340, 342 f.
Rumanians, 164, 173, 214 f., 219, 227 f., 261, 266, 312
Rumburk, 278
Runciman, Rt. Hon. Lord, 334 ff., 344
Ruskin, John, 185
Russia, Pan-Slavism, 174, 191, 230, 239, 254; Palacký's attitude toward, 166, 179; relations with Austria-Hungary, 177, 305 ff.; World War I, 235 ff., 242 ff.; Czech-Slovak colonies in, 240 ff., 252, 254 ff.; Revolution of 1917, 256 f., 261; Soviet-Czech relations, 290, 317 f., 330, 332; Sudeten crisis, 338, 340, 342 f., 345 f., 355; recognition of Provisional Government, 358, 360
Russian Revolution, 256 ff., 261, 275
Russians, 89, 159, 239, 252
Russophilism, 230, 241, 244, 246, 254 f.
Ruthenes, 130, 342, 344, 350 f., 353
Ruthenia (Subcarpathian) 302, 313, 349, 352
Ružemberok, 293

Sachsenspiegel, 30
Šafařík, P. J., 221
Salonika, 11
Salvemini, G., 247
Šámal, P., 238
Sansboeuf, J., 245
Saxony, 14; Duke Elector of, 76, 94, 97, 118 ff., 127, 134
Sazanov, S. (Sazonov), 240 f.
Scheiner, J., 238, 244, 250, 274, 282

Schiller, J. F. von, 128, 185
Schmalfuss, A., 133
Schmalkaldic League, War of, 61
Schober, J., 326
Schönerer, G. von, 314
Schools, 151, 182, 301 ff.
Schulvereine, 139
Schwarzenberg, Prince J. A., 132
Schwarzenberg family, 294
Second Internationale, 192
Seidler, G. von, 278
Serajevo, 143, 177, 234
Serbia, 234 f., 237, 244, 247, 265; army, 255
Serbs, 227 f.
Seton-Watson, R. W., 229, 249
Seven Years War, 83
Shakespeare, 128, 185
Shelley, Percy B., 185
Siberia, 240, 258, 269, 271, 341
Sigismund, Emperor, 33 f., 53 ff., 204, 206, 208
Silesia, v; involved in Czech-Polish relations, 14; added to lands of the Bohemian crown, 28 f.; appealed to by Přemysl Otakar II, 50 ff.; Diet, 70; German emigration under Hussites, 100; German population, 119 f., 141; lost by Maria Theresa, 76 ff., 82, 164, 235; *Ausgleich*, 225; Versailles settlement, 309, 312
Škoda works, 299
Sladek, J. V., 185
Slavata, Imperial Lieutenant, 64
Slávik, J., 356 f.
Slavnici, 18
Slavophiles, 230
Slovak Catholic Party, 350 f.
Slovak League, 248, 256, 272
Slovak National Council, 280, 282
Slovak Populist Party, 293
Slovakia, 8, 196 ff., 230 f., 282, 292 f., 310 ff., 342, 350 f., 352 f.; autonomy, 349 ff.; *see also* Slovaks
Slovaks, 3 ff., 7 ff.; early history, 119 ff.; and Magyars, 13, 205 f., 215, 279 ff., 291 f.; and Germans (XIII century), 200 f.; and Hapsburgs, 48 ff.; isolation, 89; culture,

387

INDEX

202 ff.; Hussitism, 204, 207 ff.; separation from Czechs, 211 ff.; language, 216 ff.; Palacký's plan, 176, 223 ff.; nationalism, 221 ff.; *Ausgleich*, 224 ff.; Pan-Slavism, 230; re-orientation toward Czechs, 231 ff.; Masaryk, 195, 231; colonies abroad, 240 ff., 270; union with Czechs, 252 ff., 266, 269, 278, 282 f., 290; and Prague government, 292 f.; land reform, 294; education, 301 ff.; post-war settlements, 310 ff.; Munich crisis, 342, 344; autonomists, 349 ff.

Slovaks of Hungary, The (Th. Čapek), 271

Slovaques, Les (E. Denis), 203

Slovenes, 164

Šmeral, B., 237

Smetana, Bedřich, 186

Soběslav II, Prince, 93

Sobieslavum, 92

Social Democrats (Czech), 190, 289 f.

Social Democrats (German), 330

Social Democrats (Slovak), 280

Social legislation, 296

Socialist Council (Prague, 1918), 281

Socialists (Slovak), 280

Socialists, International Conference at Stockholm (1917), 276

Sokols, 186 f., 238, 240, 282

Sonnino, S., Baron, 263

Sorbs, 13

Soukup, F., 251, 279, 282

South Slavs, 12, 89, 130

Soviet-Czechoslovak Treaty (1935), 330, 333, 350

Soviet-Polish Non-Aggression Pact, 343

Soviet Union, *see* Russia

Sozentovich, Lieut.-Col., 241

Spina, F., 289

Spravedlnost, American newspaper, 248

Spytihněv, Prince, 92

Šrámek, Mgr. J., 356 ff.

Šrobár, V., 280, 282, 293

Stašek, A., 276

Steed, Wickham, 249

Steel industry, 299

Štefánik, M., 252 f., 255 f., 259, 264, 293, 356

Štefánik Technological Institute, 303

Steiermark, 13

Steinherz, S., vi

Sternberg, K., Count, 159

Stoyadinović, Milan, 331

Stříbrný, Mgr., 282

Štúr, L., 220 f., 228

Stürmer, B., 255

Styria, 26, 309

Succession States, 317

Sudetendeutsche Partei, 329

Sudeten Germans, v, 113; and Austria, 90; cultural and political development before 1848, 120 ff.; post-war conditions, 309, 321, 326 f., 329 f.; Nazi régime, 333 ff.; Munich crisis, 338, 342, 344, 348 f., 351

Sudetenlands, v, 3, 90, 118, 122, 300, 326, 337 f., 342, 344; *see also* Sudeten Germans

Supreme War Council at Versailles, 270, 308

Šusta, J., vi

Svatopluk, Moravian Prince, 10 f.

Švehla, A., 237, 279, 282, 289, 293

Svoboda, Fr. X., 276

Switzerland, 250

Sychrava, L., 251

Sýkora, J., 252

Syrový, General J., 341, 350

Taborites, 100 n., 101

Teplice, 137

Teschen (Těšín), 76, 284, 312, 340, 349

Textile industry, 299 f.

Thirty Years War, 72, 77, 81, 106, 108, 145, 147

Thomas, A., 257, 261, 263

Thun, F., Count, 142

Thuringia, 94, 97, 119

Times, London, 249

Tiso, Mgr. J., 293, 350 f., 353

Tisza, Koloman, 229

Titta, Dr., 140 f.

Torre, A., 247

Trebnitz, 140

388

INDEX

Trianon, Treaty of, 284, 312, 320, 323
Triple Entente, 238, 246 ff., 253, 256, 259 ff., 273
Trnava, 211 f.
Trojanov, Lieut.-Col., 242
Troppau (Opava), 76, 309
Tsarkoé Sélo, 174
Tschausch (Souš), 139
Tübingen, University of, 122
Turčianský Svätý Martin, 283
Turks, 37 ff., 55, 57, 59, 105 n., 166, 211, 213
Tvrzický, J., 248
Twain, Mark, 185
Tyrš, Miroslav, 187

Ukrainians, 351
Ulrich, Prince, 95
Union of Protestant Princes in Germany, 65
Unitas Fratrum, see Unity of Czech Brethren
United Nations, 361
United Netherlands, Estates of, 67
United States, 5, 184 f., 240, 247 ff., 254, 269 ff., 280, 355, 358, 360
Unity of Czech Brethren (*Unitas fratrum bohemorum, Jednota českých bratří*), 62, 102 f., 161
Utraquists, 100 n., 103

St. Václav (Wenzel), Prince, 18, 20
Václav II, King, 26
Václav III, King, 26
Václav IV, King and Emperor, 33, 99
Vajanský, S. H., 230
Varsík, B., 208
Velehrad (Great Castle), 197
Venizelos, 315
Verein der Deutschen . . . , 132 ff.
Versailles, Treaty of, 284, 293, 300, 321
Veselý, A., 252
Vienna, Hapsburg capital, 52, 66, 77 f., 107, 125, 127, 138, 143, 148 f., 164, 171, 174, 177, 180, 188, 223 ff., 235, 277; revolution of 1848, 164,

167; University of, 192; Nazi march into, 334
Vienna Award of November 1938, 349
Vienna, Congress of, 43, 123, 129, 155
Viest, General R., 356 f.
Vitkovice, 277
Vladislav, Duke, 20
Vladislav II, King, 37, 93, 206
Voigt, G., 111
Volhynia, 242 f.
Vološín, Mgr. V., 351
Vondrák, V., 254
Voska, E., 248, 252
Vratislav, King, 22
Vrchlický, J., 185

Wagram, battle of, 123
Wallachians, 166
Wallenstein (Waldstein, Valdštejn), Albrecht, 108
War Memoirs (E. Beneš), 250, 267
Warsaw, 240; Protocol (1924), 313, 340
Waterloo, battle of, 123
Weimar, 315
Weimar Republic, 329
Wends, 13
Wenzel, *see* Václav
Wesley, John, 103 n.
White Mountain (Bilá Hora), battle of (1620), 41, 66 ff., 80, 105, 117, 145 f., 161, 209 f., 294
Whitman, Walt, 185
Wiedemann, Capt. F., 335
Wilde, Oscar, 185
Wilson, Horace, Sir, 345
Wilson, Woodrow, 144, 260 f., 271, 274, 282
Windischgrätz, Prince, 322
Wolkan, R., 113
World War I, 143, 177, 181, 232 ff.
World War II, 356
Wostry, W., vi
Writers' Manifesto (1917), 275 f., 278

Young Czechs, 188, 190, 193, 239, 306
Young Slovakia, 231

389

INDEX